the new american plate cookbook

AMERICAN INSTITUTE FOR
CANCER RESEARCH

the new american plate cookbook

Recipes for a Healthy Weight and a Healthy Life

UNIVERSITY OF CALIFORNIA PRESS

Berkeley   Los Angeles   London

The American Institute for Cancer Research (AICR) is a cancer charity that fosters research on diet and cancer and educates the public about the results. It has contributed more than $70 million for innovative research conducted at universities, hospitals, and research centers across the country. AICR also provides a wide range of educational programs to help millions of Americans learn to make dietary changes for lower cancer risk. Its award-winning New American Plate program is presented in brochures, seminars, and on its web site, www.aicr.org. AICR is a member of the World Cancer Research Fund International.

FRONTISPIECE: Asian-Style Salmon, Tricolored Peppers with Fresh Herbs, Brown Rice with Scallions and Fresh Herbs, and Snow Peas with Cashews.

© 2005 American Institute for Cancer Research

University of California Press
Berkeley and Los Angeles, California

University of California Press, Ltd.
London, England

PHOTOGRAPHER: Joyce Oudkerk Pool
FOOD STYLIST: Pouké
PROP STYLIST: Carol Hacker/Tableprop
with special thanks to the contributions of Sur La Table
PHOTOGRAPHER'S ASSISTANT: Shana Lopes
FOOD STYLIST'S ASSISTANT: Jeff Larsen
COPYEDITORS: Clancy Drake, Carolyn Miller, and Laura Meyn
INDEXER: Ken DellaPenta

DESIGNER: Nicole Hayward
TEXT: Caecilia
DISPLAY: Meta
PRINTER AND BINDER: C & C Offset Printing Co., Ltd

American Institute for Cancer Research, Washington, D.C.
PRESIDENT: Marilyn Gentry
EXECUTIVE VICE PRESIDENT: Kelly B. Browning
SENIOR VICE PRESIDENT: Kathryn L. Ward

For further information on the American Institute for Cancer Research, visit us online at www.aicr.org.

Library of Congress Cataloging-in-Publication Data

The new American plate cookbook : recipes for a healthy weight and a healthy life / American Institute for Cancer Research.
    p.   cm.
  Includes index.
  ISBN 0-520-24234-3 (cloth : alk. paper)
1. Cookery, American. 2. Cancer—Diet therapy. 3. Diet in disease.   I. American Institute for Cancer Research.
  TX715.N51157 2005
  641.5'63—dc22
                                    2004017993

Manufactured in China

13 12 11 10 09 08 07 06 05
10 9 8 7 6 5 4 3 2

The paper used in this publication meets the minimum requirements of ANSI/NISO Z39.48–1992 (R 1997) (Permanence of Paper).

contents

Acknowledgments   vi

Introduction: Proportion and Portion Size   I

part 1 the new american plate 13

Vegetables   14

Salads   47

Grains   66

Fish, Poultry, and Meat   86

Sauces, Dressings, and Marinades   107

part 2 one-pot meals on the plate 125

Casseroles   126

Stews   136

Stir-Fries   147

Pilafs   158

Entrée Salads   164

Frittatas   176

Chilis   182

part 3 around the plate 189

Appetizers   190

Soups   204

Breads and Muffins   224

Desserts   241

Cooking Basics   261

Food Storage and Handling   268

Cooking with Vegetables and Fruits   271

The Science behind the New American Plate   286

Index   293

acknowledgments

The creators of this cookbook have a passion for fusing opposites. Many people assume that taste and nutrition exist in opposition, that eating pleasure and long-term health are poles apart, and that satisfaction and weight management can never be reconciled. For the authors of this book, the culinary arts and nutritional science flow together to make a great meal.

They are cooks, nutritionists, food writers, and scientists. They come from divergent backgrounds and have diverging points of view. Yet to realize their vision of a cookbook in which taste and nutrition come together as one, they learned to draw heavily on each other's expertise. They held out for consensus. If there were differences of opinion about a recipe, they went back to the kitchen to try it another way. Through intense months of developing, testing, tasting, and writing up these 200 recipes, they came to refer to themselves as "the team."

This cookbook team included Jeff Prince, Melanie Polk, MMSc, RD, FADA, Maggie Sheen, Ritva Butrum, PhD, Natasha Kirsch, Charlotte Knoll, Kathleen Spitzer, and Glen Weldon. It was supported by Eric Aiken, Peter Budka, Anna Pruett Ellis, Mary Hollander, Roberto Quiroga, Scott Von Bergener, Katie Weigle, Beverly Westermeyer, and Cathy Wolz, whose insights, discrimination, and enthusiasm were invaluable.

Chef Stefano Frigerio, Barbara Gollman, MS, RD, Belinda Hollyer, Dana Jacobi, CCP, Tom Sams, Alana Sugar, CN, Robyn Webb, MS, and Leslie Weiner, PhD, RD, all developed recipes that were adopted or adapted for this cookbook. Karen Collins, MS, RD, CDN, Sharon Salomon, MS, RD, and Bonnie Wolf also contributed their wisdom and expertise.

AICR's Ann O'Malley managed the in-house production of the manuscript in a rewarding collaboration with the University of California Press. We feel the deepest gratitude toward the editorial staff at the press. Special thanks to Stan Holwitz, who quickly recognized the promise of the New American Plate concept, Dore Brown and Chalon Emmons, who patiently guided us through an exhaustive editorial process, and Nicole Hayward, who created the simple, elegant look of these pages.

And how do we thank Joyce Oudkerk Pool for the luscious photos of our recipes? Supported by food stylist Pouké Halpern and prop stylist Carol Hacker, she created images that are remarkably truthful and enticing at the same time. They are visual proof that healthy food can have the greatest sensuous appeal.

MARILYN GENTRY, PRESIDENT
AMERICAN INSTITUTE FOR CANCER RESEARCH

Start by looking at your plate. If you are like most Americans, it holds three items: a piece of red meat, poultry, or possibly fish; a sizeable helping of potato or white rice; and a small serving of some green vegetable—most often peas or green beans. The portion of meat is so large—usually 6 to 8 ounces—that it crowds everything else to the side. Notice that the colors are brown and white with just a touch of green.

That is the traditional American plate. It was shaped by food-industry marketers and government agencies during the mid-twentieth century, and we have grown accustomed to it. It is a comforting sight—although admittedly a little drab to the eye and bland to the taste. Unfortunately, that lack of appeal is a telltale sign. As research in nutrition has advanced, it has become apparent that there is a lot wrong with this plate. There is too much animal protein—and the saturated fat that comes with it—and too little plant food. As a result, this plate delivers too many calories, too much fat, and far too few of the nutrients and nutrient-like substances that keep us healthy in the long term.

In other words, the proportion of foods on the plate is all wrong. Consistent and convincing scientific evidence suggests that for preventing both overweight and chronic disease a predominantly plant-based diet is best. This conclusion doesn't mean you have to become a vegetarian, unless other reasons prompt you to do so. It simply means shifting the proportion of food on your plate so that vegetables, fruits, whole grains, and beans take up most of the room and the portion of meat is reduced

considerably in size and importance. A good rule of thumb—one we will come back to often—is that your plate should hold two-thirds (or more) vegetables, fruits, whole grains, and beans and one-third (or less) animal protein.

That is the New American Plate. Unlike the traditional plate, it is full of color and variety. Where the traditional plate held three items, the New American Plate often holds four: two vegetable dishes, one whole grain dish, and one 3-ounce serving of meat. You can choose a medley of several vegetables or a single vegetable enhanced by bits of other vegetables, fruits, or nuts. The whole grain may be seasoned with fresh herbs, and the meat served with a salsa or fruit sauce. The variety and combination of plant foods and plant-based condiments create the delightful flavors, aromas, and textures that mean healthy eating.

The team of cooks, nutritionists, scientists, and food writers who created this cookbook is not advocating a radical break with the past. Their concept of menu planning is certainly less radical than most popular diets, which require you to eliminate whole categories of food for long periods of time. The cookbook team merely recommends that you adjust the proportion of plant food on your plate, which may mean utilizing more plant foods and adding a fourth item where you are accustomed to seeing three.

Nor does the cookbook team urge a radical break when it comes to cooking the New American Plate. Most of the techniques the team suggests are familiar. You probably already use lowfat ingredients and vegetable oils such as olive and canola oil. You may also cook with whole grains and sweeten with fruit. For those of you who do not, this cookbook provides a gentle introduction to these practices. What may seem most novel is the emphasis on creative preparations of vegetables and whole grains. You are asked to infuse such dishes with the same excitement Americans have traditionally reserved for roasted and grilled meats. *The New American Plate Cookbook* is really all about cooking with vegetables, fruits, whole grains, and beans in novel ways that delight the palate and make for a longer healthy life.

Why Plant Foods?

During the past twenty years, scientists have done an extraordinary amount of research on the effects of diet on chronic diseases such as cancer, stroke, and heart disease. There are numerous ways to study this connection. Observational studies, for example, compare eating patterns and instances of disease among large groups, even whole populations. Laboratory studies explore how certain substances in food affect the development of disease. And clinical studies attempt to test whether these substances administered in specified dosages do have the predicted effect.

One of the major activities of the American Institute for Cancer Research is interpreting the thousands of studies regarding the relationship of diet to cancer. The scientists involved in the project review the total body of research. A unique study, no matter how widely publicized, does not in itself convince them. They look for studies that have achieved significant results, that have been duplicated, and that confirm each other. More specifically, they look for repeated confirmation of an association in all three kinds of studies discussed above. Only when this level of convincing evidence is found do they conclude that the preponderance of the research indicates a link between a nutrient, food, or dietary pattern and lower cancer risk. (See "The Science behind the New American Plate," page 286.)

For at least a decade, the evidence has indicated that a diet rich in vegetables and fruits reduces cancer risk. Based on this evidence, most scientists are willing to state that a largely plant-based diet, combined with regular physical exercise, can reduce the likelihood of developing cancer by 30 to 40 percent.

This conclusion is fortunate for two reasons. First, it coincides with findings in regard to stroke, heart disease, and many other diseases that affect us as we age. Current research strongly suggests that prevention of most chronic diseases involves regularly eating meals that are high in vegetables and fruits and low in animal fat, salt, and added sugar. Second, such a dietary pattern can help prevent overweight and obesity, and, when combined with portion control and exercise, can aid weight loss. The predominance of plant foods on the plate seems to be central to managing many of the health problems that concern us most.

Just how plant foods help reduce cancer risk is the focus of much of the research that AICR funds. Clearly, the minerals, vitamins, and fiber so abundant in vegetables and fruits are instrumental. But today there is even greater interest in the role played by phytochemicals, those fascinating compounds found only in plants. Many scientists believe that what we are learning about phytochemicals in the twenty-first century will have an even greater effect on human health than discoveries made about vitamins in the last century.

Of the thousands of phytochemicals that have been identified, approximately 150 have been studied so far. For instance, the carotenoids are antioxidants, which subdue free radicals that damage our DNA. Included in this family are lycopene, found in tomatoes, pink grapefruit, and watermelon, and lutein, prevalent in leafy vegetables such as spinach and collard greens. Another powerful family of phytochemicals is the flavonoids, which decrease inflammation and impede the growth of cancer cells. One subcategory of flavonoids, the anthocyanins, is present in strawberries, raspberries, and cranberries, and another, quercetin, is abundant in apples, pears, and green tea. Saponins, to mention one last category of phytochemical, are found in whole grains and beans. They help control cholesterol, triglycerides, and blood sugar levels and may prevent the proliferation of cancer cells.

Besides boosting the body's own defenses against disease, phytochemicals seem to be the source of the characteristic colors, textures, smells, and tastes of fruits and vegetables. Lycopene, for instance, is famous for making tomatoes red and watermelon pink. Allyl sulfide compounds give garlic its unique flavor and aroma. It is likely that these colors, tastes, and smells originally attracted our ancestors to the fruits and vegetables containing the compounds that benefit us. The sensuous properties of plant foods and their nutritional value come together in a remarkably functional way.

But there is a limit to the wonders of phytochemicals. Observational studies have identified phytochemicals that are likely to protect people against disease. Laboratory studies have explained how they might work. But clinical studies designed to show that large doses of individual phytochemicals produce miraculous effects have not been uniformly successful. These inconsistent results disturb people who are seeking one substance that will cure all. It is unlikely that science will ever find that substance for them. As research progresses, it is becoming increasingly evident that phytochemicals, vitamins, and minerals interact within the body. In fact, they enhance each other's activity. Together, they create a greater effect than the sum of their individual benefits.

This interaction among phytochemicals means the shape of your whole diet is far more important to your well-being than any one substance or food. Taking large doses of lycopene supplements or deodorized garlic tablets may not hurt you. Loading up on tomato soup seasoned with garlic may even help you. But the greatest health benefits derive from eating different vegetables and fruits at each

meal and dining each week on salads, stews, casseroles, and other dishes that bring a variety of plant foods into various combinations. The evidence indicates that to strengthen the body's own defenses against the diseases that come with age, we need to eat the greatest possible variety of vegetables and fruits.

All this focus on plant foods tends to crowd meat to the side of the plate. That is ultimately a good thing. Considerable evidence suggests that red meat increases cancer risk. Grilling any kind of meat may add to that risk. Furthermore, beef, lamb, pork, and to a lesser degree poultry bring with them saturated fat, which is linked to cancer, heart disease, and stroke. Other concerns about animal protein—questions about hormones, antibiotics, and E. coli bacteria, to name just a few—remain unresolved. Current knowledge about cancer risk prompts many scientists to recommend limiting portions of red meat to 3 ounces—a guideline that can be extended to any kind of meat, poultry, or fish. Thus, heaping your plate with plant foods will accomplish two ends: it will fill you full with health-protective substances and crowd out foods with less salutary effects.

The weight of the scientific evidence suggests that we should reverse the proportions on the traditional American plate and think of plant foods as our mainstay and meat as a side dish or a condiment that adds flavor. There is no need to count calories, weigh portions, or memorize lists of phytochemicals, minerals, or vitamins and their sources. Just look at the food on your plate. Is it two-thirds (or more) vegetables, fruits, whole grains, and beans, and one-third (or less) animal protein? Does it have this proportion more often than not? If so, the shape of your diet bodes well for a long, healthy life.

Preparing the New American Plate

Your transition to the New American Plate should be gradual. Abrupt changes in diet are usually short-lived. Make changes slowly and get used to them before making further adjustments. Remember

A traditional American plate

A transitional plate

that traditional American plate—potato, peas, and 8 ounces of steak? On the first day of your transition prepare a larger portion of a more interesting vegetable. For instance, you might try Zucchini and Yellow Squash with Herbes de Provence (page 42). The flavor of the two kinds of squash enhanced by tomatoes and enriched by cheese should provoke considerable interest. If you usually have a baked potato, switch to a sweet potato flavored with a little olive oil. Since there won't be much room left for the meat, reduce the portion size to 5 ounces.

This is a good transitional plate. In succeeding days, try some of the other vegetable recipes in this book and serve yourself larger portions. Heap them high on your plate, and continue to reduce the size of your portion of meat. Red, orange, yellow, and green should stand out on your plate, indicating an abundance of protective plant substances. You will also be taking in less animal fat and more healthful plant oils. Although you have just begun the transition, you are already gaining considerable health benefits.

You may never go any further than this transitional plate. That's fine. Your health will profit from the changes you have made. But for most people, a week or two of such fare will hone the appetite for even greater variety. The next step is preparing two vegetable dishes for each meal. Select recipes that vary in both appearance and taste. For instance, a helping of Snow Peas with Cashews (page 34) offers the fragrant scent of toasted orange zest and the crunch of peas and nuts. Tricolored Peppers with Fresh Herbs (page 37) will complement the snow peas nicely. The classic combination of oregano and thyme enlivens the peppers, and the balsamic vinegar adds a little zing. Instead of the usual potatoes, why not choose a whole grain? A simple dish like Brown Rice with Scallions and Fresh Herbs (page 72) can be put on to cook while you concentrate on the vegetables.

These three intriguing new recipes will take up as much space in the imagination as on the plate. Why fuss over the meat? Is there some leftover turkey in the refrigerator? If not, defrost a turkey cutlet. Four ounces raw will cook down to a 3-ounce serving. Sauté the meat in olive oil and add it to the colorful abundance on your plate.

You have just prepared a fine example of the New American Plate. Vegetables, whole grains, herbs, and nuts make up a delicious two-thirds or more of your plate. Some lean meat makes up the other third. The colors, aromas, and tastes are engaging, and the yield of health-protective substances is prodigious.

To prepare for days when you have less time to make a meal, consider cooking once to eat twice. That is, double one or two of these recipes and refrigerate or freeze half to enjoy another day. One way to make the New American Plate practical is to keep both a prepared vegetable dish and a fresh vegetable (like green beans, broccoli, or zucchini) in the refrigerator. Just warm the former in the microwave and steam the latter and drizzle it with lemon juice—and in no time, half your meal is ready.

Another way to facilitate preparation of the New American Plate is to cook one of the many one-pot meals included in this cookbook. Although it may take a little longer to prepare some of these dishes, many cooks find it easier to concentrate on a single dish than to prepare several simultaneously. What's more, these one-pot meals are delicious. They have the complex flavor of vegetables, whole grains, herbs, spices, often beans, and even fruits that have been simmered together. Most of them have been "seasoned" with a small amount of meat, poultry, or fish. Each dish embodies the two-thirds plant food to one-third animal protein ratio that promotes health.

For instance, try Sweet Potato and Apple Stew with Turkey and Cranberries (page 138). This multicolored stew blends different levels of sweetness (from carrots, apples, sweet potato, and rutabaga) with the tart edge of cranberries and the pungency of thyme and black pepper. It also contains a range of textures, from the softness of cooked potato and the chewi-

The New American Plate

Another version of the New American Plate

The New American Plate holds two-thirds (or more) vegetables, fruits, whole grains, and beans and one-third (or less) animal protein.

ness of turkey to the crunch of celery, onions, and almonds. A spoonful of the finished product is a rich sensory experience: the aroma, taste, and mouth-feel are complex and completely engaging. Served with Heirloom Whole Wheat Bread (page 228) and a small salad, it is a perfect meal, offering an abundance of good taste and an array of healthful substances.

Some members of the cookbook team felt strongly that one-pot meals are the ultimate New American Plate—foods in the right proportion blended to produce an enticing meal. They argued that these meals would facilitate the transition to healthier eating. People enjoying their complex flavors would not notice the reduction in animal protein.

Other team members felt just as strongly that there is lingering prejudice against casseroles, stews, and chilis in America. During the last century, one-pot meals were too often concocted with leftovers and other ingredients that the cook wanted to disguise. Many of us still think of casseroles as yesterday's chicken, noodles, and canned mushroom soup baked bone dry in the oven. In many American homes, when guests arrive, the host serves meat, potatoes, and a vegetable, certainly not a casserole, chili, or stew.

So the cookbook team decided to offer the meal with two vegetables, a whole grain, and a little meat as the prototypical New American Plate. These updated one-pot meals are offered as another option. In effect, the team decided to suggest two models for a healthy meal and let you choose whether to use one, the other, or, quite sensibly, both. Whatever you decide, you will be involved in preparing meals that get the proportions right while filling your plate with spectacular food.

Thinking about Portion Size

Once you feel comfortable with the question of proportion, it's time to think about portion size. A nutritional analysis is included with each recipe in this book. (The methodology is explained on page 292.) The most important piece of information in each analysis comes first—the number of servings the recipe yields. If you are accustomed to American fare, that number may seem high to you, which means, of course, the serving size will seem small. The yield ascribed to each recipe relates not to current consumption patterns, but to the U.S. Department of Agriculture's standard serving sizes. The cookbook team considered specifying larger, more typical serving sizes. That would have made things easier for everybody. But in light of the number of Americans who are overweight, not one person favored taking the easy way out.

Scientists and educators from Europe and Asia frequently visit AICR's offices. One of the first things they mention is the vast number of overweight people they have seen in the streets of our cities. The statistics verify their observations. Since 1980, there has been an 81 percent increase in the number of overweight adults in this country and a 174 percent increase in the number of obese adults. The latest figures indicate that two-thirds of our adult population is overweight or obese.

Another thing these foreign visitors never fail to mention is the enormous portions of food on our plates. Dining in our restaurants, fast-food outlets, and coffee shops, they marvel at the 12-inch plates heaped with food, the gigantic take-out bags bulging with 1,300-calorie lunches, the huge muffins, bagels, and cinnamon buns, and the 64-ounce sodas. During the past two decades, portions in commercial eateries in this country have doubled and tripled in size, and Americans, who eat out an average of four times a week, seem to have lost their sense of appropriate portion size.

This process began slowly in the early eighties. Fast-food chains started competing for consumer dollars by offering larger portions. Since food in comparison to labor or rent is a chain's lowest cost, they were able to offer those larger portions for just a little more money. Avid for bargains, Americans began spending just a few cents more for all that extra food. Soon "value meals" and "supersizing" became standard practice. Value marketing was adapted to table-service restaurants, coffee shops, grocery stores, and convenience stores. The statistics indicate that after eating gigantic portions in commercial eateries for years, Americans are now serving them at home.

It is significant that both the people and the food portions they eat swelled at roughly the same time. It doesn't take a genius to see the connection. There are many factors that foster overweight and obesity in our culture, but two stand out as root causes: we eat too much and we exercise too little. If we want to rectify the situation, one of the first things we have to do is learn to eat smaller portions of food.

Evading the Issue

The majority of Americans resist the idea that you have to eat less in order to lose weight. In a recent AICR survey, 60 percent of the respondents said that, when you are trying to lose weight, the kind of food you eat is more important than the amount of food you eat. This kind of thinking can be traced back to one or more of the many fad diet books that have inundated the market during the last decade. These books promise that you can eat as much as you want and still lose weight. All you have to do is eliminate some demonized category of food from your diet.

We all have acquaintances who find such promises compelling. Five years ago, these people told us, "It's a cinch to lose weight. All you have to do is cut out the fat." They talked a lot about where to find the best bagel, pasta, and fat-free cookies. Today they obsess about bacon and eggs, tender steak, and cheeseburgers without the bun. "It's no sweat losing weight," they say. "All you have to do is cut out the carbs."

Is there anything to this latest craze? In searching for the causes of our obesity epidemic, some scientists have looked beyond over-consumption. They theorize that foods high in refined carbohydrates (white bread, white rice, most ready-to-eat cereals) as well as white potatoes are too quickly digested and absorbed. That is, these foods cause a rapid and steep rise in your blood sugar level, which in turn causes a rapid and profuse secretion of insulin, the hormone that ushers the sugar into muscle and fat cells. As a result, your blood sugar level plummets as rapidly as it rose. You are left feeling weak and hungry long before your next scheduled meal. The immediate result of this rapid rise and fall of blood sugar levels is overeating. The long-term results, many scientists argue, are added fat storage and ultimately higher risk of chronic disease.

This thesis merits greater study. Eventually, research may confirm it. If so, the proper response would not be purging all "carbs" from the diet. It would make more sense to substitute foods containing unrefined carbohydrates for foods that seem to cause the problem.

In most cases this substitution is easily accomplished. The recipes in this cookbook, for instance, generally call for whole grains such as stone-ground whole wheat, brown rice, and kasha; dark-colored vegetables and fruits including sweet potatoes; and a variety of beans. These ingredients are preferred because of their vitamin, mineral, and phytochemical content, but they also supply carbohydrates that are digested more slowly and evenly. Eaten in reasonable amounts, these "carbs" can help you maintain a healthy weight.

In fact, questions about the effects of carbohydrates, fats, and proteins on weight loss are still in dispute. Since we tend to eat these foods together and each affects the digestion of the others, it might be some time before these questions are sorted out. At this point in the research, there is only one certainty about diet and weight: if you take in less energy in the form of food than you expend in the form of physical activity, you will lose weight.

There is convincing scientific evidence that a predominantly plant-based diet will reduce the risk of chronic disease. The two-thirds to one-third ratio is a practical method of integrating sufficient plant foods into your diet to prolong your health. On the other hand, there is still scant evidence that you can lose weight permanently by eliminating categories of food and disrupting the healthy proportion of food on your plate. At this juncture, the best prescription for bolstering long-term health and achieving a gradual and permanent loss of weight is to maintain the two-thirds to one-third proportion and to reduce your portion sizes.

Reducing Portion Sizes

All of us, whether we're concerned about weight loss or not, need to regain our sense of appropriate portion size. To that end we need some standard by which to measure the portions we are eating. Fortunately, the U.S. Department of Agriculture (USDA) has supplied just such a measure. It has maintained a set of standard serving sizes in connection with its food guide pyramid. This scale is based on the median serving size reported in data collected from 1982 through 1985—before value marketing succeeded in confounding the issue.

One glance at this chart makes it clear that the USDA's standard servings are considerably smaller than what most people actually eat. Although restaurants frequently serve 8- to 12-ounce steaks, the standard serving of meat is 3 ounces. We regularly consume 3 or more cups of pasta; the standard serving is 1/2 cup. We fill the breakfast bowl to the brim with dry cereal, but the standard serving is 1 ounce, which ranges between 1/4 and 1 1/4 cups in

STANDARD SERVING SIZES FOR AN AVERAGE ADULT

Source: U.S. Department of Agriculture

Food	Serving	Looks like
Chopped vegetables	½ cup	½ baseball or rounded handful
Raw leafy vegetables (such as lettuce)	1 cup	1 baseball or fist
Fresh fruit	1 medium piece ½ cup chopped	1 baseball ½ baseball or rounded handful
Dried fruit	¼ cup	1 golf ball or scant handful
Pasta, rice, cooked cereal	½ cup	½ baseball or rounded handful
Ready-to-eat cereal	1 ounce, which varies from ¼ cup to 1¼ cups (see label)	—
Meat, poultry, seafood	3 ounces (boneless cooked weight from 4 ounces raw)	Deck of cards
Dried beans	½ cup cooked	½ baseball or rounded handful
Nuts	⅓ cup	Level handful
Cheese	1½ ounces (2 ounces if processed cheese)	1 ounce looks like four dice

volume. The disparity is shocking. Some of it can be explained away. Today, for better or worse, we eat pasta as an entrée. The standard serving size relates to a side dish. But, in general, the disparity in size reflects how far we have strayed from the norm.

Try measuring your own regular portions by these standard serving sizes. At your next meal, serve yourself your customary portion of a favorite food. Examine it to see how much of the plate it covers. Next, place a standard serving of the same food on the same size plate. Look at the two plates and compare. Then ask yourself this question: how many standard servings go into the portion I regularly eat?

The next question is, of course, how many standard servings *should* go into the portion you ordi-

narily eat. Match your intake to your expenditure. If you jog three miles a day, do work requiring rigorous activity, or are pregnant, you may conclude that several servings are appropriate. If you usually sit while commuting, working, and relaxing in the evening, you might decide to reduce the number of servings.

Another way to answer this question is to consider your weight. Are you happy with what the scale says? Is your weight stable? If the answer is yes on both scores, then you are probably eating the right number of standard servings at each meal. If your weight is high and climbing, it may be time to reduce the number of standard servings that go into your regular portions.

Cut back gradually. You can afford to reduce your portion sizes by stages. Even small reductions have an effect. If you allow your body to get used to slightly smaller portions, hunger will not be a problem. You may find that avoiding that overstuffed feeling is satisfying in itself. If maintaining a healthy proportion of foods on your plate and gradually reducing portion size do not bring a slow, steady reduction in weight, don't reach for the latest fad diet book. Contact your doctor or a registered dietitian for an individualized plan.

"Makes Six Servings"

It should be obvious by now why the cookbook team decided to base serving sizes on USDA standards when describing the yield of the recipes in this book. Look at the recipe for Red Pepper, Tomato, and Chicken Pilaf (page 160). The nutritional analysis in the headnote indicates that this recipe makes 6 servings. On your plate, one serving will resemble a baseball in size. Let's say you add a standard 1-cup serving of Arugula Salad with Radicchio and Blue Cheese (page 52) and one slice of Heirloom Whole Wheat Bread (page 228). Your meal will have a healthy proportion of plant foods to animal protein, a great variety of vegetables and grains, and just fewer than 500 calories. If you aren't concerned about your weight, you might even add a dish from the soup or dessert chapters.

But some people may find these portions much smaller than they are accustomed to eating. At a luncheon during our annual research conference several years ago, AICR introduced the New American Plate concept to 500 scientists. Before lunch was served, we gave a brief presentation about proportion and portion size. Then the waiters served each guest a plate with a 3-ounce piece of salmon. They also brought each table three bowls, one containing Gingered Carrots with Golden Raisins and Lemon (page 25), a second containing Green Beans with Tomatoes and Herbs (page 34), and the last containing Orange Rice Pilaf with Dried Fruit (page 72). The guests had to serve themselves the vegetables and rice, but there were no serving spoons on the table, only measuring cups. Oh, what hilarity there was in that hall as many people confronted for the first time just how much they were used to eating.

The next year at the conference luncheon, we brought back the serving spoons. After all, the attendees were our guests, and our society equates generous portions of food and drink with good hospitality. When the disastrous medical consequences of our national weight problem become evident, however, we may change our conception of caring behavior. Pressing guests or family members to eat more than they actually need might come to be seen as a hostile rather than a hospitable act. Until that time, however, you may have to do some quiet calculating before a dinner party. When preparing a dish from this cookbook, estimate how many servings each guest is likely to eat. Then, if appropriate, double the recipe to be sure you have enough.

But in your day-to-day life, you want delicious foods that contribute to your health and at the same time allow you to manage your weight. That is why serving sizes relating to USDA standard servings are given in this book. How many standard servings you choose to include in your portions may vary during different phases of your life. Weight and health fluctuate. Whatever happens, it's empowering to know that you can prepare delicious meals that strengthen your defenses against chronic disease and serve them in portion sizes that will help you maintain a healthy weight.

Enjoying the New American Plate

The New American Plate is, first of all, a style of cooking. It is a set of assumptions about what ingredients you select, how you combine them, and what preparations you use. The members of the cookbook team kept these five rules in front of them while they developed and revised the recipes:

- Introduce or increase the amount of plant foods (vegetables, fruits, whole grains, beans, herbs, and spices) whenever you can.

- Use canola and olive oil instead of animal fats. Keep the fat content of each dish below 30 percent of calories.

- Avoid refined sugar and refined grains whenever you can. Use whole grains and whole wheat flour.

- Avoid added salt.

- Mentally divide finished dishes into serving sizes consistent with USDA standards. Then adjust portion size to your needs.

These guidelines derive from science-based recommendations for reducing the risk of chronic disease. But you don't have to worry about their origin or even try to remember them. After cooking several of the recipes in this book, they will become part of your own cooking style.

After a while, you may begin to create your own recipes in this style or revamp old favorites. For instance, how about meat loaf made with ground turkey breast mixed with whole wheat bread crumbs, shredded carrots, chopped red peppers, and onion bits? You could update macaroni and cheese by using nonfat milk, a smaller amount of extra-sharp cheddar cheese, and diced peppers and onions. Or think about making apple pie using sweet apples, a lot less sugar, and the New American Plate Pie Crust (page 243). Variations on traditional recipes are endless once you get into the swing of things.

If you cook this way regularly, the New American Plate will soon become your style of eating. Your table will never look the same. You'll be dining on a larger number of smaller dishes with stronger flavors. And you'll enjoy combinations of fruits and vegetables you never encountered before. Imagine Orange and Sesame Stir-Fry with Bow Tie Pasta (page 152), Spinach, Romaine, and Strawberries with Balsamic Vinaigrette (page 52), Whole Wheat Bread with Herbs (page 226), and a plate of fresh figs for dessert. Such a meal may sound exotic now, but it will make your mouth water once you start cooking the New American Plate.

That doesn't mean you'll never again eat the foods that used to excite you. In a memorable scene from Shakespeare's *Twelfth Night,* some servants are feasting and drinking in the courtyard of a manor house. When the chief servant scolds them for their noisy carousing, one of the characters replies, "Dost thou think because thou art virtuous there shall be no more cakes and ale?" Shakespeare recognized the strengths and weaknesses of the human will. What we try to do always, we soon stop doing altogether. What we learn to do usually, we persist in doing, and that's what has an impact on our long-term health. Your goal should be to move gradually toward cooking and eating the proportions and portion sizes suggested in this book. When this style of cooking and eating becomes your general tendency, by all means treat yourself to some cakes and ale from time to time.

JEFFREY R. PRINCE
AMERICAN INSTITUTE FOR CANCER RESEARCH

the new american plate

The New American Plate reflects a novel approach to menu planning. On the old American plate, meat played a leading role. But for health reasons, we've relegated it to a more appropriate supporting role on the New American Plate. Scaling back the proportion of meat to a more healthful amount—one-third of the plate or less—creates more room for additional choices that provide the variety and appeal we look for in a satisfying meal. Taking center stage are foods that offer greater health protection: vegetables, whole grains, beans, and fruit. These diverse players are the stars of our meals. With their broad range of talents, they present an array of colors, flavors, and textures that is the culinary equivalent of great theater.

Adding extra portions of vegetables, whole grains, and other important plant foods to your plate need not mean more cooking for each meal. "Cook once, serve twice" has long been the maxim of the busy cook who has found it is easier and faster to cook two meals' worth of vegetables or whole grains and reserve the second meal's portion in the refrigerator or freezer. Today a wide selection of frozen vegetables, often packaged in appealing combinations, can be prepared in a few minutes on top of the stove or in a microwave oven.

The recipes in this section treat vegetables, grains, and salads as separate dishes but, as the section on one-pot meals suggests, there are unlimited ways to combine these elements. Cooks with a little freewheeling spirit can devise creative combinations of their own.

Remember: the number of servings in each recipe relates to USDA standard serving sizes. Depending on individual needs, you may choose to serve larger portions. (See Introduction, pages 7–10.) ■

vegetables

We all know that we should be eating many more vegetables than we do. And we know many of the reasons we should be eating those vegetables. They are packed with vitamins, minerals, and other nutrients our bodies need. Vegetables are low in calories, an important consideration since most of us are overweight by at least a few pounds. Vegetables are superior to higher-calorie processed foods, which do a poor job of keeping us going strong until it is time for the next meal. Perhaps most important, though, their rich array of phytochemicals—substances found only in plant foods—helps protect us from serious chronic health problems: diabetes, heart disease, stroke, and cancer. The best way to maximize the range of phytochemicals in your diet is to eat a wide variety of fruits and vegetables. This is why the New American Plate calls for two vegetables on the plate.

This may create a challenge for those of us who are used to eating only one or two kinds of vegetables and preparing them the same way each time. Adapting our diet to the New American Plate proportions of two-thirds vegetable dishes to one-third meat will mean using a lot of different vegetables, finding imaginative recipes that create full-flavored dishes, and learning new techniques of preparation. That is what this chapter is all about.

Some of the recipes in this section will put excitement back into the vegetables you always rely on and may take for granted. Other recipes might entice you to try vegetables you had never imagined enjoying. You may be surprised to discover that these recipes often call for fewer ingredients or for less time or effort than you had thought.

Choosing and Preparing Vegetables

The universal secret to success in preparing vegetables—whether familiar or strange—is to first choose them carefully in the produce department and then cook them in the way that best suits them.

Pick only the freshest vegetables, avoiding those that have brown spots or edges or look dried out or old. It is best to buy only as much as you can use within a few days, since many vegetables tend to lose their flavor as well as their nutrients after a few days of storage, while others, especially the cruciferous ones (like cabbage, broccoli, and Brussels sprouts), develop more bitterness.

When buying Brussels sprouts, for example, try to avoid packaged containers and instead handpick them from a loose assortment, selecting those that are roughly the same size, for uniform cooking. As a general rule, the smaller ones are more tender and have a milder taste, while the larger ones have a more assertive flavor.

Choosing the right cooking technique is crucial, too. For example, many of our unpleasant associations with certain vegetables result from their having been boiled until overdone, limp, and waterlogged. Not only is the result unappetizing, but a long boiling period is guaranteed to fill your kitchen—if not the entire house—with a strong smell, especially for cruciferous vegetables like cabbage and cauliflower, because of certain compounds they contain. (These compounds also make the vegetables taste bitter if they are cooked too long.) And all vegetables lose vitamin C and other water-soluble nutrients when they are overcooked in water.

The cookbook team found that most vegetables do best when cooked either gently or quickly. Simmering, braising, and steaming are gentle methods; quick methods include using a microwave oven, sautéing, grilling, and stir-frying. But however they are prepared, most vegetables should be cooked only until crisp but tender, to maximize both flavor and nutrients.

Root vegetables, like potatoes, carrots, and onions, are some of the exceptions to the cook-quickly-or-gently rule, unless they are very thinly sliced.

All root vegetables contain some natural sugars, although they are not always discernible to our taste buds. But certain cooking techniques can bring out their natural sweetness. Vegetables like parsnips, rutabagas, turnips, and beets benefit greatly from high-temperature cooking methods. (Winter squashes are also lovely when baked slowly until they are soft.) Oven roasting or grilling these vegetables caramelizes their sugars, producing a sweeter, richer flavor. And since most root vegetables are at their best in the winter months, oven roasting them makes great sense. A medley of roasted carrots, turnips, parsnips, rutabagas, and potatoes creates a rich, complex sensory experience that requires little of the cook's attention to produce; add chunks of peeled winter squash to the root vegetables for extra color and flavor. After the vegetables are peeled, chopped, placed in a roasting pan, and drizzled with oil, an occasional stirring later in the roasting period is all that is needed while the vegetables achieve tenderness.

Cauliflower is another vegetable that benefits from extra attention. When cooked in water, it has a tendency to discolor. To prevent this, add a tablespoon of lemon juice to the cooking water. Or, use a method in which cauliflower is not cooked in water, like steaming or stir-frying. As with cabbage, the briefer the cooking period, the less chance of developing a strong aroma and unpleasant taste.

One simple way to introduce a new vegetable to your diet is to pair it with a vegetable you already like—one that will complement its new partner. For example, dark leafy greens that are usually cooked—chard, mustard greens, kale, and collard greens—pair well with sweeter, perhaps more familiar vegetables like carrots, corn, onions, or tomatoes. (Another alternative for cooking these greens—rather than steaming or braising them—is to sauté them in canola or olive oil with minced garlic and chopped onion.) Less familiar root vegetables like parsnips and turnips also pair well with carrots and sweet potatoes.

The Vegetables section in Cooking with Vegetables and Fruits (page 271) contains additional shopping, storing, and preparation advice for a wide variety of vegetables, and the Cooking Methods section (page 261) in the Cooking Basics chapter gives more helpful details about how to use methods such as roasting, microwaving, and steaming to bring out the best in vegetables. Once you have some confidence in the basic techniques of choosing and preparing vegetables to optimize their flavor and nutritional potential, you may feel inspired to branch out even more.

Simple Techniques to Enhance Vegetables

Many of us have a standby method of cooking and seasoning our favorite vegetables: we cook them as we like, then add some salt and pepper, and perhaps top them with a pat of butter or margarine. Simple and easy? Yes. Still interesting after months, or years, of preparing them this way? Probably not.

Some simple techniques retain the quick and easy virtues of "old standby" treatments while adding dazzle to the vegetables' taste. Try adding a few squeezes of fresh lemon juice (orange juice complements the natural sweetness of carrots). Or season with chopped fresh herbs like mint, basil, marjoram, or cilantro, or a few quick grates of a garlic clove or fresh ginger. A small handful of chopped nuts adds interesting texture and taste, as do raisins or dried chopped fruits like cranberries or apricots. Instead of butter or margarine, try a drizzle of extra-virgin olive oil, which now also comes infused with a variety of flavors. Many simple additions can enliven the vegetables' taste.

Vegetables that have assertive tastes, like broccoli, Brussels sprouts, and dark leafy greens, need special attention. One strategy that softens or smoothes out the flavor of broccoli, for example, is to drizzle a little extra-virgin olive oil or sesame oil over the cooked vegetable. A second technique is to match a strong-tasting vegetable with an equally assertive seasoning: a sprinkling of balsamic vinegar, soy sauce, citrus juice, garlic, cumin, coriander, ginger, or anise seed. (One member of the cookbook team eats his Brussels sprouts with dabs of honey mustard.) Experiment with other taste enhancers, like flavored olive oil, hot sauce, or a dollop of mayonnaise.

Vinaigrettes, glazes, and sauces can also be used as flavorful toppings for vegetables. Balsamic Glaze (page 21), Hoisin Vinaigrette (page 121), and Asian-Style Peanut Sauce (page 110) all work well with assertive vegetables. You will find other toppings that complement vegetables in Sauces, Dressings, and Marinades (page 107).

One technique for serving vegetables that has become very popular with chefs in upscale restaurants is puréeing. Once cooked until tender, vegetables can be easily puréed in a blender. Starchy vegetables like sweet potatoes and carrots make a rather thick purée that needs to be thinned a little, usually with a small amount of broth. (Sweet potatoes and carrots also taste good puréed together.) Once puréed, assertive-tasting vegetables like broccoli, spinach, and turnips profit from the addition of just a little extra-virgin olive oil, milk, or evaporated nonfat milk to round out their flavors. Puréed vegetables can be served as side dishes or as beds for pieces of chicken or fish, for example, or as dips, sandwich spreads (especially in wraps), or sauces. Because they're so versatile and delicious, purées are a marvelous way to introduce more vegetables into your daily diet.

asian-style stir-fried vegetables

On-the-go Americans claim to like stir-fries because they're so quick to prepare. Yet many of these same time-conscious individuals routinely overcook stir-fries. In a stir-fry, you're trying to seal the various flavors and textures in, not cook them out. That means high heat and brief cooking. You can chop the ingredients ahead of time so you have them handy. And look for cues—the vegetables in this recipe are vividly colored and crunchy before they hit the heat, and quick cooking will ensure that they stay that way when you serve them. **MAKES 6 SERVINGS | PER SERVING: 68 CALORIES, 2 G. TOTAL FAT (LESS THAN 1 G. SATURATED FAT), 11 G. CARBOHYDRATES, 2 G. PROTEIN, 2 G. DIETARY FIBER, 223 MG. SODIUM.**

1 teaspoon canola oil

2 garlic cloves, minced

½ teaspoon minced peeled fresh ginger

3 scallions, trimmed and minced

2 carrots, peeled and sliced diagonally into ½-inch pieces

½ large red bell pepper, seeded and sliced into ¼-inch strips

1 celery rib, sliced diagonally into ¼-inch pieces

1 cup trimmed fresh snow peas

½ cup drained canned sliced water chestnuts

½ cup fat-free, reduced sodium chicken or vegetable broth, divided

1½ tablespoons reduced sodium soy sauce

2 teaspoons honey or sugar

2 teaspoons cornstarch

2 tablespoons sliced almonds, toasted*

*Note: To toast the almonds, put them in a small skillet over medium-high heat and stir frequently for 2 to 3 minutes, until lightly browned. Immediately transfer the nuts to a small dish and cool.

■ In a large nonstick skillet or wok with a tightly fitting lid, heat the canola oil over medium-high heat. Add the garlic, ginger, and scallions and stir-fry for 1 minute. Add the carrots and bell pepper and stir-fry for 2 minutes. Add the celery and stir-fry for 2 minutes. Add the snow peas, water chestnuts, and ¼ cup of the broth. Cover and cook for 2 to 3 minutes more, until the snow peas are bright green and crisp.

■ Meanwhile, in a measuring cup or small bowl, combine the remaining broth, soy sauce, honey, and cornstarch. Add this sauce to the vegetables and cook for 1 to 2 minutes, until the sauce thickens. Top the vegetables with the sliced almonds and serve.

roasted beets with dill dressing

roasted beets with dill dressing

It's a cinch to roast beets, and the reward is a deeper, more satisfying taste. Beets are easier to peel after they are roasted and cooled. But take care: beet juice can stain hands and clothing. Hold the roasted beets in the palm of your gloved hand, and simply slip the outer skin off. For an elegant look, introduce golden beets along with the sweeter red beets. MAKES 4 SERVINGS | PER SERVING: 83 CALORIES, 4 G. TOTAL FAT (LESS THAN 1 G. SATURATED FAT), 12 G. CARBOHYDRATES, 2 G. PROTEIN, 3 G. DIETARY FIBER, 96 MG. SODIUM.

- 3 teaspoons extra-virgin olive oil, divided
- 4 medium beets, stems, tops, and roots removed
- 2 tablespoons white wine vinegar
- 2 teaspoons minced fresh dill
- ¼ teaspoon honey

  Salt and freshly ground black pepper

■ Preheat the oven to 400 degrees.

■ Drizzle 1 teaspoon of the olive oil over the beets in a 9-inch square baking pan and turn the beets to coat them in oil. Roast, uncovered, for about 1 hour, until tender when pricked with a fork. Remove the beets from the oven and cool slightly. Peel the beets and cut them into quarters. In a serving bowl, combine the remaining 2 teaspoons of oil, vinegar, dill, honey, and salt and pepper to taste. Add the roasted beets, toss well, and serve warm.

roasted asparagus with garlic

Although it's now available year-round, there's something special about asparagus in early spring, the height of asparagus season. Roasted asparagus is quick to make and more intensely flavored than steamed or boiled asparagus, but make sure to buy your bunches carefully. For this recipe, select stalks that have about the same thickness. MAKES 4 SERVINGS | PER SERVING: 48 CALORIES, 2 G. TOTAL FAT (LESS THAN 1 G. SATURATED FAT), 6 G. CARBOHYDRATES, 3 G. PROTEIN, 2 G. DIETARY FIBER, 3 MG. SODIUM.

- 1 pound fresh asparagus, trimmed
- 2 teaspoons olive oil
- 2 garlic cloves, minced

  Salt and freshly ground black pepper

  Lemon wedges, for garnish

■ Preheat the oven to 500 degrees.

■ In a shallow roasting pan, toss the asparagus with the olive oil to coat. Sprinkle the asparagus with the garlic and season with salt and pepper. Roast, uncovered, for 6 to 8 minutes (depending on the thickness of the spears), until crisp but tender, shaking the pan occasionally. Serve immediately with lemon wedges.

broccoli, white bean, and roasted garlic purée

Purées are simple and versatile, yet they have a certain upscale flair. In this recipe, olive oil and white beans enrich the broccoli's flavor, and cayenne and hot pepper sauce add as much bite as you like. Use this purée as a dip with spears of bell pepper, celery, zucchini, and other raw vegetables, or simply spread it on crackers. As part of a light meal, spread it on pita bread or tortillas to make roll-ups. (Add a bit more olive oil to make the purée spreadable.) You can also use this purée as an elegant, flavorful bed for roasted poultry or fish. **MAKES 6 SERVINGS | PER SERVING: 63 CALORIES, 3 G. TOTAL FAT (LESS THAN 1 G. SATURATED FAT), 8 G. CARBOHYDRATES, 3 G. PROTEIN, 3 G. DIETARY FIBER, 98 MG. SODIUM.**

4 garlic cloves, peeled, or to taste

3 teaspoons extra-virgin olive oil, divided

⅛ teaspoon cayenne, or to taste (optional)

2½ cups small broccoli florets

1 tablespoon water

1 cup canned cannellini (white kidney) beans, drained and rinsed

1 tablespoon freshly squeezed lemon juice, or to taste

1 tablespoon finely minced fresh chives or 1 teaspoon crushed dried chives

Salt and freshly ground white pepper

Hot pepper sauce (optional)

- Preheat the oven to 350 degrees.
- Put the garlic, 1 teaspoon of the olive oil, and the cayenne on a square of foil and seal well into a packet. Bake until the garlic is tender, about 35 minutes. Set aside to cool slightly. Meanwhile, put the broccoli florets and water in a microwave-safe bowl and cover. In a microwave oven, cook the broccoli on high (100% power) for 2 minutes, until tender. Drain the broccoli and rinse it quickly with cold water to stop the cooking process.
- Transfer the broccoli to a blender or food processor. Add the beans, lemon juice, chives, roasted garlic mixture, and the remaining olive oil and purée until smooth. Season to taste with salt, white pepper, and hot sauce. The purée can be stored in a covered container for up to 3 days in the refrigerator. Bring the chilled purée to room temperature before serving.

broccoli with scallion dressing and hazelnuts

With this recipe you can transform broccoli by flavoring it with scallions, toasted sesame oil, and hazelnuts and allowing it to cool before serving. Hazelnuts lend the dish a satisfying crunch and can be bought at most health food stores and many supermarkets. If you can't find them, pecans will do the job nicely. **MAKES 6 SERVINGS | PER SERVING: 54 CALORIES, 3 G. TOTAL FAT (LESS THAN 1 G. SATURATED FAT), 5 G. CARBOHYDRATES, 3 G. PROTEIN, 3 G. DIETARY FIBER, 88 MG. SODIUM.**

3 cups small broccoli florets

2 teaspoons toasted sesame oil

2 scallions, trimmed and thinly sliced

2 garlic cloves, finely minced

2 teaspoons reduced sodium soy sauce

2 tablespoons coarsely chopped toasted hazelnuts*

*Note: To toast the hazelnuts, put them in a small skillet over medium-high heat and stir frequently for 3 to 4 minutes, until lightly browned. Immediately transfer the nuts to a small dish and cool.

- Bring a large pot of water to a boil. Add the broccoli and cook for 4 minutes. Drain the broccoli and rinse it with cold water to stop the cooking process. In a medium bowl, combine the sesame oil, scallions, garlic, and soy sauce. Add the broccoli, toss well, and top with the hazelnuts. Serve at room temperature.

brussels sprouts with balsamic glaze

The cruciferous family of vegetables—including Brussels sprouts, kale, broccoli, and cauliflower—is perhaps the most extensively researched group of plants in history. Nutrition scientists who study the health-protective effects of foods believe these vegetables contain a range of different substances that work in complex ways to reinforce the body's natural defenses. Unfortunately, cruciferous vegetables—and Brussels sprouts in particular—are commonly overcooked, which has given them an undeserved reputation for bitterness. But by keeping a few simple things in mind, you can ease them into your diet without sacrificing taste. When buying Brussels sprouts, make sure to select the smallest you can find, and steam them only until they're tender. They should stay a bright, fresh-looking green. In this recipe, we've paired Brussels sprouts with a sweet balsamic glaze. This glaze can also be used to take the edge off of a wide variety of vegetables that have a reputation for bitterness, such as cauliflower, kale, broccoli, cabbage, chard, rutabagas, and turnips.

MAKES 6 SERVINGS | PER SERVING: 49 CALORIES, 1 G. TOTAL FAT (LESS THAN 1 G. SATURATED FAT), 10 G. CARBOHYDRATES, 2 G. PROTEIN, 2 G. DIETARY FIBER, 15 MG. SODIUM.

3 cups fresh Brussels sprouts (about 12 ounces)

BALSAMIC GLAZE

¼ cup balsamic vinegar

1 tablespoon honey, or to taste

1 teaspoon minced garlic

1 teaspoon minced peeled fresh ginger

1 teaspoon extra-virgin olive oil

1 small tomato, seeded and chopped

Salt and freshly ground black pepper

■ Remove any yellow leaves from the Brussels sprouts and rinse them thoroughly. Trim the bottoms and, with the tip of a knife, make an X in each stem end to help the sprouts cook evenly. Place a steamer basket inside a pot and add about 2 inches of water. Bring the water to a boil and put the sprouts in the steamer. Cover and steam over high heat for about 10 minutes, until sprouts are a bright, fresh green and just tender but still crisp. Don't let them cook until they turn a deep olive color; by that point, they are more likely to turn bitter. (Sprouts can also be steamed in a microwave-safe container in the microwave.) Drain the sprouts, return them to the pot, cover to keep warm, and set aside.

■ Meanwhile, combine the vinegar, 1 tablespoon honey, garlic, ginger, oil, tomato, and salt and pepper to taste in a blender and blend just until puréed. Transfer the mixture to a nonstick saucepan. Bring it to a boil, then immediately reduce the heat to medium. Cook, stirring frequently, until the sauce is slightly syrupy, about 5 minutes. Taste the sauce. If it tastes too acidic, stir in a little more honey. Adjust salt and pepper to taste. Drizzle the sauce over the hot Brussels sprouts and serve immediately.

brussels sprouts with shallots and nutmeg

Brussels sprouts aren't supposed to be bitter. Believe it or not, noted chef Alice Waters describes the flavor of perfectly cooked Brussels sprouts as "sweet and nutty." Many people make them bitter by overcooking them or storing them too long. That's why it's important to do it right from the beginning: buy them fresh, in small amounts, and cook them right away. You'll find that smaller sprouts have the mildest flavor. When cooking, use the gentlest touch possible—steam them just until the moment they reach tenderness. Their color should stay a fresh, vivid green. The shallots and nutmeg in this recipe bring out the true character of the sprouts. Add some parsley and toasted almonds to round out the flavors even more.

MAKES 4 SERVINGS | PER SERVING: 51 CALORIES, 2 G. TOTAL FAT (LESS THAN 1 G. SATURATED FAT), 6 G. CARBOHYDRATES, 3 G. PROTEIN, 3 G. DIETARY FIBER, 90 MG. SODIUM.

10 ounces fresh Brussels sprouts (about 3 cups)

2 teaspoons olive oil

2 small shallots, thinly sliced

½ cup fat-free, reduced sodium chicken or vegetable broth

⅛ teaspoon ground nutmeg

Salt

3 tablespoons chopped toasted almonds (optional)*

2 tablespoons chopped flat leaf parsley (optional)

*Note: To toast the almonds, put them in a small skillet over medium-high heat and stir frequently for 3 to 4 minutes, until lightly browned. Immediately transfer the nuts to a small dish and cool.

■ Remove any yellow leaves from the Brussels sprouts and rinse them thoroughly. Trim the bottoms and, with the tip of a knife, make an X in each stem end to help the sprouts cook evenly. Place a steamer basket inside a pot and add about 2 inches of water. Bring the water to a boil and put the sprouts in the steamer. Cover and steam over high heat for about 8 minutes, until sprouts are a bright, fresh green, and just tender but still crisp. (Sprouts can also be steamed in a microwave-safe container in the microwave.) Drain the sprouts and set them aside.

■ In a medium skillet over medium-high heat, heat the olive oil. Add the shallots and sauté for about 2 minutes, until translucent. Add the sprouts and the broth, cover, and cook over medium heat for 2 minutes. Remove the cover and cook for 1 to 2 minutes more, until the broth is absorbed. Stir in the nutmeg and season with salt to taste. Transfer to a serving dish, sprinkle the almonds and parsley over the top, and serve immediately.

red cabbage with apples

Here's a classic marriage: the invigorating color and crunch of red cabbage with the sweetness of grated apples. A touch of allspice complements the familiar flavors. There's an ample dose of fiber and a panoply of phytochemicals. But mostly there is rich, layered flavor. MAKES 4 SERVINGS | PER SERVING: 96 CALORIES, LESS THAN 1 G. TOTAL FAT (0 G. SATURATED FAT), 24 G. CARBOHYDRATES, 1 G. PROTEIN, 3 G. DIETARY FIBER, 85 MG. SODIUM.

2 cups apple juice or cider

2 tablespoons apple cider vinegar

½ teaspoon ground allspice

3 cups shredded red cabbage (about ⅔ pound)

2 medium sweet apples (such as Red Delicious), peeled, cored, and grated

Pinch of salt

■ In a medium saucepan over high heat, bring the apple juice, vinegar, and allspice to a boil. Add the cabbage, apples, and salt. Lower heat and simmer, uncovered, for 30 minutes, stirring occasionally, until cabbage is tender. Serve at room temperature or chilled.

mushrooms with apple-herb stuffing

Here is the taste of the forest on a cool autumn afternoon. Mushrooms are a nutrient-dense food. Low in calories, they are high in phytochemicals, including terpenes, which are being studied for their cancer-fighting capacity. Stuffing the mushrooms may take a little patience, but the blend of tastes—apples, leeks, basil, and oregano as well as mushrooms—is well worth the effort.

MAKES 10 SERVINGS | PER SERVING: 71 CALORIES, 3 G. TOTAL FAT (LESS THAN 1 G. SATURATED FAT), 10 G. CARBOHYDRATES, 3 G. PROTEIN, 2 G. DIETARY FIBER, 133 MG. SODIUM.

Canola oil spray

20 large button mushrooms, wiped with a damp cloth

1 tablespoon reduced sodium soy sauce

4 teaspoons canola oil, divided

3 teaspoons balsamic vinegar, divided

1 small leek, white part only, rinsed well and finely diced (about ¾ cup)

1 celery rib, minced

1 medium red apple, peeled, cored, and finely diced

2 tablespoons minced flat leaf parsley

¼ teaspoon minced fresh oregano or a pinch of dried

¼ teaspoon minced fresh basil or a pinch of dried

Salt and freshly ground black pepper

½ cup whole wheat bread crumbs

2 tablespoons freshly grated Parmesan cheese

2 teaspoons vegetable broth or water

■ Preheat the oven to 450 degrees. Lightly coat a baking sheet with canola oil spray.

■ Scoop the stems out of the mushroom caps with a small spoon. Trim and discard the bottoms of the stems, finely chop the stems, and set them aside.

■ In a large bowl, mix the soy sauce, 1 teaspoon of the canola oil, and 1 teaspoon of the balsamic vinegar. Add the mushroom caps. Using your hands or a large spoon, toss to coat each mushroom with the soy sauce mixture and place, cavity side up, on the prepared baking sheet. Set aside.

■ In a medium skillet over medium heat, heat 1 teaspoon of the canola oil and sauté the mushroom stems, leek, celery, apple, parsley, oregano, and basil for 7 minutes, until celery and apple are tender. Remove from heat and season the mixture with salt and pepper. Add the bread crumbs and the remaining 2 teaspoons of canola oil and stir to combine. Transfer the mixture to a bowl and stir in the Parmesan cheese and broth. Stuff each mushroom with a slightly rounded table-spoon of filling. Brush the remaining balsamic vinegar over the tops of the mushrooms. Bake uncovered for 25 minutes or until the mush-rooms are tender when pierced with a fork. Serve immediately.

gingered carrots with golden raisins and lemon

gingered carrots with golden raisins and lemon

You'd be surprised what one minute in a hot skillet can do. As the heat hits the carrots and raisins in this dish, their natural sugars begin to caramelize and a more complex flavor emerges. Minced ginger and lemon zest—both of which boast impressive profiles of protective phytochemicals—serve to balance the dish's sweetness and harmonize its flavors. MAKES 4 SERVINGS | PER SERVING: 119 CALORIES, 3 G. TOTAL FAT (LESS THAN 1 G. SATURATED FAT), 25 G. CARBOHYDRATES, 1 G. PROTEIN, 3 G. DIETARY FIBER, 28 MG. SODIUM.

½ cup golden raisins

1 cup hot tap water

6 medium carrots (12 ounces), peeled and cut diagonally into ½-inch slices

1 teaspoon finely minced peeled fresh ginger

1 teaspoon freshly squeezed lemon juice

2 teaspoons canola oil

2 teaspoons packed light brown sugar

2 teaspoons cornstarch

1 teaspoon grated lemon zest

Pinch of salt (optional)

■ In a medium bowl, combine the raisins and hot water and let stand for about 15 minutes. Meanwhile, bring a medium pot of water to a boil and add the carrots, ginger, and lemon juice. Boil for 6 to 7 minutes, then drain the carrots and set them aside. Drain the raisins, reserving ¾ cup of the liquid, and set them aside.

■ In a medium skillet, heat the canola oil over medium heat. Add the brown sugar and cook, stirring constantly, for 30 seconds. Mix the cornstarch into the reserved raisin water and add it to the oil and brown sugar mixture. Cook, stirring constantly, for about 1 minute, until the mixture thickens. Add the raisins and carrots and cook for 1 minute more. Remove from the heat and stir in the lemon zest and salt. Serve immediately.

grilled portobello mushrooms with garlic and herbs

The standard line on portobello mushrooms is that their taste and texture make them an ideal substitute for meat. A well-prepared portobello mushroom can be both more subtle and more satisfying than a hamburger patty, especially when some fresh herbs are added. Try the following recipe on a whole wheat bun with lettuce and tomato. It also works well as one of two vegetables on the New American Plate. MAKES 4 SERVINGS | PER SERVING: 94 CALORIES, 7 G. TOTAL FAT (1 G. SATURATED FAT), 6 G. CARBOHYDRATES, 2 G. PROTEIN, 1 G. DIETARY FIBER, 8 MG. SODIUM.

4 large portobello mushrooms, cleaned

2 garlic cloves, very thinly sliced

1 teaspoon finely chopped fresh rosemary or ½ teaspoon dried (optional)

1 teaspoon finely chopped fresh thyme or ½ teaspoon dried (optional)

3 tablespoons olive oil

3 tablespoons balsamic or red wine vinegar

Salt and freshly ground black pepper

■ Preheat the broiler or prepare a barbecue grill to medium-high heat.

■ Remove the stems from the mushrooms and, with a paring knife, make slits about ¼ inch deep in the top of the caps. Stuff slivers of the garlic and herbs into the slits.

■ In a small bowl, whisk together the olive oil and vinegar with salt and pepper to taste. Brush the mushrooms with the olive oil mixture. Place the mushrooms, cap down, on a pan or hot grill and broil or grill for about 3 to 5 minutes per side, until soft and brown. Serve immediately.

curried cauliflower with chickpeas and green peas
Cauliflower is often unpopular with Americans who grew up eating cauliflower that was overcooked and therefore bitter and mushy. But this modest vegetable has been a beloved dietary staple in India for thousands of years. What do Indian cooks know that we don't? For one thing, they understand that certain flavors, like those of mild curry, coconut milk, and chickpeas, provide a gentle contrast that makes the most of cauliflower's unique taste and texture. **MAKES 8 SERVINGS | PER SERVING: 91 CALORIES, 1 G. TOTAL FAT (LESS THAN 1 G. SATURATED FAT), 16 G. CARBOHYDRATES, 5 G. PROTEIN, 5 G. DIETARY FIBER, 200 MG. SODIUM.**

¼ cup canned light coconut milk, divided

1 small red onion, finely chopped

1 garlic clove, minced

2 teaspoons curry powder

¾ cup lowfat milk

4 cups small cauliflower florets (about 1½ pounds)

1 can (15 ounces) chickpeas, rinsed and drained

1 cup frozen green peas

2 teaspoons freshly squeezed lime juice

Salt and freshly ground black pepper

¼ cup fresh cilantro leaves, loosely packed, for garnish

■ In a large nonstick skillet, heat 1 tablespoon of the coconut milk over medium-high heat. When the liquid starts to bubble, stir in the onion and garlic. Cook for about 4 minutes, stirring, until the onion is translucent. Stir in the curry powder and cook for about 30 seconds, until the mixture becomes fragrant.

■ Add the remaining coconut milk and the lowfat milk, cauliflower, and chickpeas. Bring to a simmer, cover, reduce the heat, and cook for 6 to 8 minutes, until the vegetables are almost tender. Add the green peas, cover, and cook for 4 minutes. Mix in the lime juice and season to taste with salt and pepper. Transfer to serving bowl. Garnish with cilantro leaves and serve.

braised kohlrabi
Kohlrabi is an eccentric-looking vegetable: think of an overgrown turnip with several large, leafy stems. Its looks might be one reason it has never really caught on in America. Another reason might be that Americans have just never figured out what to do with it. Kohlrabi needs to be cooked thoroughly to bring out its flavor, which reminds many people of a sweet turnip. In this recipe, the vegetable is braised in broth to bring out its natural character. You can find out more about braising in Cooking Methods (see page 262). **MAKES 4 SERVINGS | PER SERVING: 31 CALORIES, 1 G. TOTAL FAT (LESS THAN 1 G. SATURATED FAT), 5 G. CARBOHYDRATES, 2 G. PROTEIN, 3 G. DIETARY FIBER, 232 MG. SODIUM.**

1 teaspoon olive oil

1½ pounds kohlrabi, peeled and cut into ¼-inch strips

1½ cups fat-free, reduced sodium chicken or vegetable broth

Freshly ground black pepper

Freshly squeezed lemon juice (optional)

■ In a medium nonstick skillet, heat the olive oil over medium heat. Add the kohlrabi and sauté for 5 minutes to coat with oil and begin the cooking process. Add the broth, bring to a boil, cover, and reduce heat to low. Cook for 15 to 20 minutes, until the kohlrabi is tender. The cover may be removed during the last 5 minutes. Season to taste with pepper. Sprinkle with a few drops of fresh lemon juice, if desired. Drain off the broth and serve.

curried cauliflower with chickpeas and green peas

braised escarole with garlic

braised escarole with garlic

braised escarole with garlic Escarole is a member of the chicory family, which also includes such upscale salad stars as endive and radicchio. Known for its large green leaves and pale yellow stems, escarole has a peppery kick that finds a home in salads, sautés, and soups. In this pleasantly garlicky dish, the mild bitterness of escarole is significantly softened. Be sure to wash escarole thoroughly to remove any sand or grit. MAKES 4 SERVINGS | PER SERVING: 109 CALORIES, 7 G. TOTAL FAT (1 G. SATURATED FAT), 10 G. CARBOHYDRATES, 4 G. PROTEIN, 8 G. DIETARY FIBER, 273 MG. SODIUM.

- 2 heads (about 2½ pounds total) escarole, bases removed, leaves rinsed
- 2 tablespoons olive oil
- 4 large garlic cloves, cut lengthwise into thick slices
- 1½ cups fat-free, reduced sodium chicken broth
- ⅛ teaspoon dried red pepper flakes (optional)
- Salt and freshly ground black pepper

■ Bring a large pot of water to a boil, add the escarole, and cook for 2 minutes. Transfer to a strainer and run cold water over the greens to stop the cooking process. Drain them well, pressing to extract any excess water, then using your hands to squeeze the greens, in several batches, removing as much water as possible. Slice each batch of greens into ½- to 1-inch strips.

■ Heat the oil in a large skillet over medium heat. Sauté the garlic for about 3 minutes, stirring often, until golden. Remove the garlic and set it aside in a small bowl. Add the escarole to the skillet, stirring to coat the leaves with the olive oil. Pour in the broth and add the red pepper flakes. Bring the liquid to a boil, then immediately reduce the heat to a simmer. Cook for 15 minutes, uncovered, until the escarole is tender.

■ Remove the greens from the heat and season to taste with salt and pepper. Serve hot, warm, or at room temperature, garnished with the reserved garlic slices.

kale with sweet corn

kale with sweet corn Kale is a cruciferous vegetable (a member of the cabbage family) and a nutritional powerhouse with a wide range of nutrients and phytochemicals. Some of those very same healthy substances, however, lend kale a distinctive flavor—what some call a bite. This flavor can be easily tamed by pairing kale with vegetables high in natural sugars, like corn and sweet onions. This recipe makes for a wonderful introduction to the flavorful, nutrient-rich world of greens. MAKES 5 SERVINGS | PER SERVING: 68 CALORIES, 2 G. TOTAL FAT (LESS THAN 1 G. SATURATED FAT), 11 G. CARBOHYDRATES, 2 G. PROTEIN, 2 G. DIETARY FIBER, 121 MG. SODIUM.

- ¾ pound kale, tough stems removed
- 2 teaspoons olive oil
- ½ cup finely chopped sweet onion (such as Vidalia)
- 2 scallions, trimmed and chopped
- ¾ cup frozen (thawed) or drained canned corn
- ¼ cup vegetable broth
- Salt and freshly ground black pepper

■ In a large pot, bring 3 inches of water to a boil. Add the kale, cover, and reduce the heat to medium. Cook the kale for about 12 minutes, until tender. Drain. When the kale is cool enough to handle, press the leaves between paper towels to remove the remaining water. Cut the kale into strips, then slice the strips into squares and set aside, or refrigerate in a closed container for up to 24 hours.

■ When ready to serve, heat the olive oil in a medium skillet over medium-high heat. Sauté the onion and scallions for 3 minutes, until the onion is soft. Add the kale, corn, and broth. Reduce the heat to low and cook for about 3 minutes, stirring often, until the corn and greens are heated through. Season to taste with salt and pepper, and serve.

steamed greens with ginger and water chestnuts

Adapted from an Asian dish, this recipe calls for water chestnuts, which add a crunchy texture that complements the greens. If you have access to Asian greens, try bok choy (Chinese cabbage or chard), choy sum (Chinese flowering cabbage), or amaranth leaves (Chinese spinach). Leafy greens are rich in lutein and other phytochemicals that protect against many chronic diseases from cataracts to cancer. MAKES 4 SERVINGS | PER SERVING: 31 CALORIES, 2 G. TOTAL FAT (LESS THAN 1 G. SATURATED FAT), 3 G. CARBOHYDRATES, 1 G. PROTEIN, 1 G. DIETARY FIBER, 47 MG. SODIUM.

3 cups mixed leafy greens (such as spinach, Swiss chard, or Chinese greens), thoroughly washed, stems removed

1 teaspoon finely minced peeled fresh ginger

1 teaspoon finely minced fresh garlic

½ cup canned water chestnuts, drained and diced

½ tablespoon toasted sesame oil

Salt and freshly ground black pepper

■ Pour 2 inches of water into a pot and insert a steamer basket. Bring the water to a boil and put the greens in the basket. Sprinkle the ginger and garlic over the top of the greens, and then scatter the water chestnuts on top. Sprinkle the sesame oil evenly over the greens. Cover and steam the greens until they are tender, about 30 seconds. Remove from heat, season to taste with salt and pepper, and serve immediately.

braised collard greens with garlic and shallots

Like other members of the cabbage family, collard greens are at their best if you buy them at their freshest and cook them right away. After a few days in the refrigerator, their natural flavor becomes increasingly bitter, and their health-protective substances begin to fade away. It's easy to undercut the bite of these greens by cooking them gently with sautéed garlic. This recipe also calls for shallots, a smaller and pleasantly mild relative of the everyday onion. MAKES 4 SERVINGS | PER SERVING: 110 CALORIES, 6 G. TOTAL FAT (1 G. SATURATED FAT), 13 G. CARBOHYDRATES, 5 G. PROTEIN, 3 G. DIETARY FIBER, 129 MG. SODIUM.

1 tablespoon plus 1 teaspoon olive oil, divided

3 medium shallots, minced (about ⅓ cup)

3 large garlic cloves, minced

1 bunch (about 1 pound) collard greens, stems removed, leaves washed and coarsely chopped

¼ cup fat-free, reduced sodium chicken broth

Salt and freshly ground black pepper

1 strip lean turkey bacon, cut in half lengthwise, then across into ¼-inch strips

■ In a medium skillet, heat 1 tablespoon of the olive oil over medium-high heat. Add the shallots and sauté for 1 minute. Add the garlic and sauté for 30 seconds. Stir in the greens, add the broth, and sprinkle with salt and pepper. Cover and reduce the heat to low. Cook for 10 minutes, until the greens are bright in color and tender.

■ Meanwhile, in a small nonstick skillet over medium heat, cook the turkey bacon in the remaining 1 teaspoon of olive oil until crispy and golden, about 3 minutes, stirring frequently. When the greens are done, stir in the turkey bacon and its pan drippings. Adjust the seasonings to taste and serve the greens immediately.

steamed greens with ginger and water chestnuts

honey-roasted parsnips with sweet potatoes and apples

honey-roasted parsnips with sweet potatoes and apples

Many Americans are unfamiliar with parsnips, which is a shame, because they are so tremendously versatile. When roasted, their flavor, like that of other root vegetables, mellows and deepens in unexpected ways. This recipe, which contains the familiar flavors of apple and honey, is a great way to introduce even the most skeptical eater to the rich roasted delights of caramelized root vegetables. **MAKES 6 SERVINGS | PER SERVING: 112 CALORIES, 2 G. TOTAL FAT (LESS THAN 1 G. SATURATED FAT), 23 G. CARBOHYDRATES, 1 G. PROTEIN, 4 G. DIETARY FIBER, 208 MG. SODIUM.**

Canola oil spray

½ pound parsnips, peeled and cut into bite-sized chunks

1 large orange-flesh sweet potato, peeled and cut into bite-sized chunks (about 1½ to 2 cups)

2 firm, sweet apples (such as Red Delicious), peeled, cored, and cut into bite-sized chunks (about 2 cups)

1 tablespoon canola oil

1 tablespoon honey

2 tablespoons reduced sodium soy sauce

Salt and freshly ground black pepper

■ Preheat the oven to 375 degrees. Lightly coat a medium casserole dish with canola oil spray and set it aside.

■ Put the parsnips, sweet potato, and apples in a large mixing bowl and set aside. Combine the canola oil and honey in a microwave-safe bowl and heat in a microwave oven on medium (50% power) for 10 seconds, until warm. Mix the soy sauce into the honey mixture. Pour the sauce over the vegetables and apples. Toss to coat well. Transfer the mixture to the prepared casserole dish, cover, and bake for 1 hour, until tender. Season to taste with salt and pepper. Serve warm.

petite peas with garlic and pimientos

Petite peas are more tender and generally more flavorful than standard green peas. Here they are cooked simply with minced garlic for added flavor and some colorful pimientos for eye-catching contrast. **MAKES 4 SERVINGS | PER SERVING: 90 CALORIES, 4 G. TOTAL FAT (LESS THAN 1 G. SATURATED FAT), 11 G. CARBOHYDRATES, 4 G. PROTEIN, 4 G. DIETARY FIBER, 82 MG. SODIUM.**

1 package (10 ounces) frozen petite peas

1 tablespoon olive oil

2 garlic cloves, minced

1 jar (2 ounces) pimientos, well drained, minced

1 teaspoon freshly squeezed lemon juice

Salt and freshly ground black pepper

■ Cook the peas according to the package directions, either in the microwave or on the stovetop. Drain and set the peas aside. In a small skillet, heat the olive oil over medium-high heat. Add the garlic and sauté for 30 seconds, stirring constantly, until fragrant. Add the pimientos and sauté for 2 minutes, stirring constantly. Pour the pimiento mixture over the peas and stir well. Stir in the lemon juice. Season to taste with salt and pepper and serve immediately.

snow peas with cashews

In this recipe, an interesting blend of textures—the crispness of snow peas, the crunchy creaminess of cashews—is enlivened by bits of citrus peel. Cashews are a good source of heart-healthy monounsaturated fat. And even the tiny bit of orange zest in this dish helps augment its overall phytochemical punch. **MAKES 4 SERVINGS | PER SERVING: 66 CALORIES, 2 G. TOTAL FAT (LESS THAN 1 G. SATURATED FAT), 8 G. CARBOHYDRATES, 4 G. PROTEIN, 3 G. DIETARY FIBER, 5 MG. SODIUM.**

1 teaspoon canola oil

1 teaspoon grated orange zest

3 cups trimmed fresh snow peas (about ¾ pound)

Salt and freshly ground black pepper

1 tablespoon finely chopped toasted cashews*

*Note: To toast the cashews, put them in a small skillet over medium-high heat and stir frequently for 2 to 3 minutes, until lightly browned. Immediately transfer the nuts to a small dish and cool.

■ In a medium nonstick skillet, heat the canola oil over medium-low heat. Add the orange zest and cook, stirring frequently, for 2 minutes until zest begins to shrivel. Add the snow peas, season to taste with salt and pepper, and increase heat to medium. Stirring constantly, cook for 3 to 4 minutes, until the snow peas are bright green and crunchy. Sprinkle with the cashews and serve.

green beans with tomatoes and herbs

Americans eat a lot of green beans, but we usually serve them plain. As delicious as they are with salt and pepper or a squeeze of lemon juice, these vegetables benefit from a little extra attention. In this dish, tomatoes enhance the flavor of the string beans. The distinctive tastes and aromas of basil and oregano meld with other classic flavors of Sicily. Fresh herbs, when available, are best. **MAKES 4 SERVINGS | PER SERVING: 54 CALORIES, 2 G. TOTAL FAT (LESS THAN 1 G. SATURATED FAT), 10 G. CARBOHYDRATES, 2 G. PROTEIN, 3 G. DIETARY FIBER, 7 MG. SODIUM.**

1 teaspoon olive oil

1 small onion, minced

1 large ripe tomato, diced, or ½ can diced tomatoes (about 7 ounces), drained

2 garlic cloves, finely minced

1 teaspoon minced fresh basil or ½ teaspoon dried basil

1 teaspoon minced fresh oregano or ½ teaspoon dried oregano

¾ pound fresh green beans, trimmed, or 1 package (10 ounces) frozen green beans, thawed

Salt and freshly ground black pepper

■ In a medium nonstick skillet, heat the olive oil over medium heat. Add the onion and sauté for 5 minutes, until onion is translucent and tender. Add the tomato, garlic, basil, and oregano and cook for 2 minutes. Add the green beans, cover, and cook for 6 minutes, until beans are crisp but tender. Season to taste with salt and pepper.

snow peas with cashews

tricolored peppers with fresh herbs

tricolored peppers with fresh herbs

Even the most vividly colored red, yellow, and orange sweet peppers start their lives as humble green peppers. The colors we find so attractive are actually the result of extra time ripening on the vine. That extra time also provides a boost in vitamins A and C. In this recipe, the vibrant colors of three peppers mix with a distinctly Mediterranean assortment of herbs to produce a quick, flavorful, and attractive dish. MAKES 4 SERVINGS | PER SERVING: 59 CALORIES, 3 G. TOTAL FAT (LESS THAN 1 G. SATURATED FAT), 10 G. CARBOHYDRATES, 1 G. PROTEIN, 2 G. DIETARY FIBER, 3 MG. SODIUM.

2 teaspoons olive oil

1 large red bell pepper, seeded and julienned

1 large yellow bell pepper, seeded and julienned

1 large orange bell pepper, seeded and julienned

2 garlic cloves, minced

1 teaspoon balsamic vinegar

1 tablespoon minced fresh basil

1 teaspoon minced fresh oregano

1 teaspoon minced fresh thyme

Salt and freshly ground black pepper

■ In a large skillet or wok, heat the olive oil over medium-high heat. Add the peppers and sauté, stirring often, for 3 to 5 minutes, until crisp but tender. Add the garlic and sauté for 2 more minutes, stirring often. Add the vinegar, basil, oregano, and thyme. Season to taste with salt and pepper, cover, and cook for 1 minute. Serve immediately.

sesame and garlic spinach

Spinach contains iron, folic acid, and the phytochemical called lutein—an antioxidant now receiving a great deal of scientific attention for its potential to protect against a host of different diseases. You'll notice that this recipe calls for a very small amount of toasted sesame oil. That's because this oil is so intensely flavored that only a teaspoon is needed to imbue the dish with its distinctively rich, smoky taste. MAKES 4 SERVINGS | PER SERVING: 102 CALORIES, 2 G. TOTAL FAT (LESS THAN 1 G. SATURATED FAT), 12 G. CARBOHYDRATES, 10 G. PROTEIN, 3 G. DIETARY FIBER, 269 MG. SODIUM.

3 pounds fresh spinach, preferably baby spinach leaves, washed and stemmed

1 teaspoon toasted sesame oil

2 garlic cloves, minced

1 tablespoon sesame seeds, toasted*

Salt and freshly ground black pepper

*Note: To toast the sesame seeds, put them in a small skillet over medium heat for 1 to 2 minutes, stirring constantly, until the seeds are light brown. Watch carefully: sesame seeds can burn quickly. Immediately transfer seeds to a small dish and cool.

■ Heat a medium skillet over medium-high heat and add the spinach with water still clinging to the leaves. Cover and cook for 2 minutes. Uncover and cook for 2 more minutes, stirring often, until wilted. Drain the spinach in a colander, let it cool enough to handle, and squeeze out any excess water.

■ In a medium skillet, heat the sesame oil briefly over medium-low heat. Add the garlic and sauté for 30 seconds, stirring constantly. Add the spinach and sesame seeds and season with salt and pepper to taste. Sauté for 1 minute and serve.

spaghetti squash with marinara sauce

spaghetti squash with marinara sauce When cooked, the flesh of the spaghetti squash separates easily into long, golden yellow spaghetti-like strands. These strands have a nice, tender texture and a very mild flavor, so when you're cooking with spaghetti squash, it's really about the sauce. This recipe pairs the squash with marinara sauce, a familiar tomato-based favorite redolent with garlic, fresh basil, and other herbs. MAKES 8 SERVINGS | PER SERVING: 109 CALORIES, 3 G. TOTAL FAT (1 G. SATURATED FAT), 19 G. CARBOHYDRATES, 4 G. PROTEIN, 4 G. DIETARY FIBER, 223 MG. SODIUM.

1 small spaghetti squash (about 3 pounds)

2 teaspoons olive oil

2 shallots, minced

2 garlic cloves, minced

1 can (28 ounces) crushed tomatoes

1 teaspoon dried thyme

½ teaspoon dried rosemary

Salt and freshly ground black pepper

3 tablespoons chopped fresh basil, divided

¼ cup freshly grated Parmesan cheese

■ With the tip of a knife, pierce the squash in several places. In a microwave oven, heat the squash on high (100% power) for 15 to 18 minutes, or until tender when pierced with a fork, then let cool for 10 minutes.

■ Meanwhile, in a medium saucepan, heat the olive oil over medium-high heat. Add the shallots and garlic and sauté, stirring frequently, for 2 minutes, until shallots are translucent. Add the tomatoes, thyme, and rosemary and season to taste with salt and pepper. Bring to a boil, stirring frequently. Reduce the heat and simmer for 10 minutes, stirring frequently. Remove the pan from the heat and stir in 2 tablespoons of the basil.

■ Carefully halve the squash crosswise and scoop out the seeds. Scrape the inside of the squash with a fork to remove the spaghetti-like strands. Divide the spaghetti squash among 8 plates and top each serving with sauce, remaining basil, and Parmesan cheese. Serve immediately.

acorn squash stuffed with apricots and cornbread

This very American dish was a big hit with AICR's cookbook team. They loved the blend of colors, textures, and flavors and marveled at the sweet mix of acorn squash and apricots. The many golden ingredients abound in carotenoids, folate, and even vitamin C, all of which are important in the fight against cancer and other chronic diseases. **MAKES 12 SERVINGS | PER SERVING: 212 CALORIES, 8 G. TOTAL FAT (2 G. SATURATED FAT), 33 G. CARBOHYDRATES, 3 G. PROTEIN, 4 G. DIETARY FIBER, 312 MG. SODIUM.**

4 cups cornbread, cut into ½-inch cubes

2 tablespoons extra-virgin olive oil, plus more for brushing squash

2 large Spanish onions, thinly sliced

½ cup finely diced celery, including 3 to 4 leaves

2 tablespoons finely chopped fresh sage or 1½ teaspoons dried

2 teaspoons finely chopped garlic

1½ cups hot water or hot vegetable broth

½ cup chopped dried apricots

½ cup lightly toasted chopped pecans (optional)*

2 tablespoons finely chopped flat leaf parsley

Salt and freshly ground black pepper

3 large acorn squash, halved lengthwise and seeded

*Note: To toast the pecans, put them in a small skillet over medium-high heat and stir frequently for 2 to 3 minutes, until lightly browned. Immediately transfer the nuts to a small dish and cool.

■ Preheat the oven to 400 degrees.

■ Spread the cornbread cubes on a baking sheet and toast them in the oven for about 10 minutes, turning occasionally, until lightly browned. Transfer them to a bowl and set it aside.

■ In a large, heavy saucepan, heat the 2 tablespoons of olive oil over medium-low heat. Add the onions, celery, sage, and garlic and sauté for 20 minutes, stirring frequently, until onions are caramelized. Add the water, apricots, and pecans. Raise heat to high, bring mixture to a boil, then reduce heat to low to simmer for about 10 minutes, until the liquid is reduced by about ⅓. Remove from the heat and stir in the parsley. Gently mix the cornbread into the onion mixture and add salt and pepper to taste. Set this mixture aside while you prepare the squash.†

■ Reduce the oven temperature to 350 degrees.

■ Place the squash halves cut side down in a baking pan or pans large enough to hold the squash in a single layer. Brush the skin lightly with olive oil. Pour ½ inch of boiling water into the pans and bake for 20 minutes, until the squash is halfway cooked. Squash should be barely tender when pierced with a fork. Transfer the squash to a plate and set it aside until it is cool enough to handle. Fill the squash halves with the cornbread mixture, set them in the baking pans stuffing side up, and return to the 350-degree oven. Bake for about 1 hour, until the tip of a knife pierces the squash easily. Before serving, cut each squash in half lengthwise again.

†Note: Filling can be prepared up to 1 day in advance; refrigerate in a tightly covered container. Half-cooked squash can be refrigerated up to 8 hours, tightly wrapped in plastic wrap. Filled squash halves can likewise be wrapped in plastic wrap and refrigerated for up to 4 hours before being baked.

zucchini and yellow squash with herbes de provence

This mixture of squash and tomatoes is enhanced with herbes de Provence, an aromatic blend of dried basil, fennel seed, marjoram, rosemary, sage, summer savory, and thyme. You can find it in the spice section of most supermarkets. If you can't, try substituting one or two of the herbs it contains. Everything about this dish is classically French—except the feta cheese, which provides a pleasant, tangy zip. MAKES 4 SERVINGS | PER SERVING: 62 CALORIES, 3 G. TOTAL FAT (LESS THAN 1 G. SATURATED FAT), 7 G. CARBOHYDRATES, 3 G. PROTEIN, 2 G. DIETARY FIBER, 98 MG. SODIUM.

2 teaspoons olive oil

½ cup chopped onion

1 large zucchini, cut into 1-inch cubes (about 2 cups)

1 large yellow squash, cut into 1-inch cubes (about 2 cups)

2 garlic cloves, finely minced

1 teaspoon dried herbes de Provence

½ cup halved cherry tomatoes

Salt and freshly ground black pepper

¼ cup crumbled reduced fat feta cheese

■ Preheat the broiler.

■ In a large skillet, heat the olive oil over medium-high heat. Add the onion and sauté for 3 minutes, until translucent. Add the zucchini and yellow squash and sauté for 5 to 6 minutes. Add the garlic and sauté, stirring frequently, for 2 more minutes until garlic is soft. Add the herbes de Provence and cherry tomatoes and season to taste with salt and pepper. Transfer the vegetable mixture to a casserole dish. Sprinkle with the cheese. Place the casserole under the broiler for 3 to 5 minutes, watching carefully, until the cheese melts. Serve immediately.

cider-glazed sweet potatoes with cranberries

Sweet potatoes are a healthier choice than white potatoes. The orange and gold colors indicate the presence of carotenoids. Sweet potatoes are also rich in vitamins B6, C, and E as well as fiber. The colors and flavors of this dish will remind you of autumn harvest. MAKES 6 SERVINGS | PER SERVING: 143 CALORIES, 2 G. TOTAL FAT (LESS THAN 1 G. SATURATED FAT), 30 G. CARBOHYDRATES, 1 G. PROTEIN, 2 G. DIETARY FIBER, 12 MG. SODIUM.

Salt

2 large orange-flesh sweet potatoes (about 1½ pounds total), peeled and cut into 1-inch chunks

1½ cups apple cider or apple juice, plus more to thin glaze

1 tablespoon canola oil

½ teaspoon ground nutmeg

½ teaspoon ground allspice

Freshly ground black pepper

½ cup dried cranberries

■ In a large pot of boiling salted water, cook the sweet potatoes for about 5 minutes, until a knife inserted into the center of the sweet potatoes encounters resistance. Drain the sweet potatoes.

■ In a large saucepan over medium-high heat, combine the 1½ cups of apple cider, canola oil, nutmeg, and allspice. Bring to a boil, stirring often. Add the sweet potatoes and reduce the heat so the liquid simmers. Cook until sweet potatoes are tender, about 3 to 5 minutes, stirring occasionally. Turn off heat and transfer sweet potatoes with a slotted spoon to a bowl. Season to taste with salt and pepper.

■ Add the cranberries to the pan and bring to a boil. Reduce heat and simmer for about 10 minutes, or until the cranberries have cooked through and the liquid is reduced to a syrupy glaze. (If the glaze becomes too thick before the cranberries are completely cooked, thin with a small amount of cider.) Return the sweet potatoes to the pan and stir over low heat until they have completely heated through. Transfer to a serving bowl. Season to taste with salt and pepper and serve.

sweet potato and pumpkin purée

Purées are an intriguing way to slip more vegetables onto the plate of a meat-and-potatoes person. In many fine restaurants, meat is served on a bed of puréed vegetables. But purées are also delightful served on their own, garnished with sour cream or parsley, as your second vegetable. This purée has such a lovely color and such an intriguing touch of sweetness and spice that it might well steal the spotlight from the meat. **MAKES 4 SERVINGS | PER SERVING: 224 CALORIES, 8 G. TOTAL FAT (4 G. SATURATED FAT), 33 G. CARBOHYDRATES, 7 G. PROTEIN, 6 G. DIETARY FIBER, 234 MG. SODIUM.**

1 tablespoon olive oil

1 medium yellow onion, chopped

2 celery ribs, chopped

2 medium orange-flesh sweet potatoes (about 1 pound total), peeled and chopped

1 can (15 ounces) pumpkin

1½ cups fat-free, reduced sodium chicken or vegetable broth, plus more to thin purée

⅛ teaspoon ground cinnamon

⅛ teaspoon curry powder

⅛ teaspoon ground white pepper

Salt

¾ cup lowfat sour cream, divided

¼ cup minced flat leaf parsley, loosely packed

■ In a large saucepan, heat the olive oil over low heat. Add the onion and celery and sauté for 5 minutes, until soft and translucent. Add the sweet potatoes, pumpkin, broth, cinnamon, curry powder, and pepper. Season to taste with salt. Bring to a boil, reduce heat to low, and simmer, covered, until the sweet potatoes are very tender, about 15 minutes. Let cool slightly. In a blender or food processor, carefully purée the mixture in two batches, adding more hot broth to thin the purée if needed, and return it to the saucepan. Heat through. Stir in 1/4 cup of the sour cream and adjust the seasonings. Serve hot, with a dollop of the remaining sour cream and a sprinkling of the parsley atop each serving.

grilled fresh vegetables with dijon-herb sauce

This recipe requires a bit of prep time, but when you see how the many different colors, textures, and flavors come together in this hearty, healthy dish—packed with nutrients and phytochemicals—you'll be glad you made the effort. You can make the savory Dijon-Herb Sauce a few hours ahead and store it in the refrigerator. Simply warm the sauce over low heat before using. **MAKES 8 SERVINGS | PER SERVING: 115 CALORIES, 7 G. TOTAL FAT (1 G. SATURATED FAT), 13 G. CARBOHYDRATES, 2 G. PROTEIN, 3 G. DIETARY FIBER, 60 MG. SODIUM.**

SAUCE

- ¼ cup extra-virgin olive oil
- 2 tablespoons finely chopped shallots
- 2 garlic cloves, peeled and finely minced
- 1 tablespoon Dijon mustard
- 2 teaspoons freshly squeezed lemon juice
- 1 teaspoon grated lemon zest
- 2 teaspoons finely minced fresh tarragon or ¼ teaspoon crushed dried tarragon
- 1 tablespoon finely minced fresh thyme or ¾ teaspoon crushed dried thyme
- Salt and freshly ground black pepper

VEGETABLES

- 1 small orange-flesh sweet potato, peeled, halved lengthwise, and cut into ½-inch slices
- 1 large carrot, peeled and cut diagonally into ½-inch slices
- 1 medium parsnip, peeled and cut diagonally into ½-inch slices
- 1 large zucchini, trimmed, cut lengthwise into quarters and halved
- 1 large red onion, cut into ¾-inch slices
- 1 large red bell pepper, seeded and cut lengthwise into 6 pieces
- 1 portobello mushroom, cleaned, stem removed, and cut into quarters
- Olive oil spray, to oil the grilling tray (optional)
- Salt and freshly ground black pepper
- Finely chopped flat leaf parsley for garnish

■ Prepare a grill for medium-high heat or preheat the broiler.

■ In a medium saucepan, stir together the first 8 sauce ingredients until well blended. Heat over medium-low heat until warm. Season to taste with salt and pepper. Arrange the vegetables in a single layer in a large, shallow nonstick baking pan. With a pastry brush, lightly coat all sides of the vegetables with the sauce. If using a grill, transfer the vegetables to a lightly oiled grilling tray; if using a broiler, place the baking pan under the broiler.

■ Grill or broil the vegetables until tender and lightly browned, brushing occasionally with sauce if the vegetables seem to be drying out and turning them with a slotted spoon or tongs so they cook evenly on all sides. The sweet potato, carrot, and parsnip will take about 8 to 10 minutes on each side to cook, the zucchini, onion, and bell pepper about 4 to 5 minutes on each side, and the mushroom about 3 to 4 minutes on each side. As the vegetables are cooked, transfer them to a serving platter and cover to keep them warm. Before serving, season the vegetables to taste with salt and pepper and sprinkle with chopped parsley.

classic ratatouille

A popular all-vegetable stew, ratatouille comes from Nice, France. Its name derives from a verb meaning "to stir up." In late summer when fresh tomatoes, zucchini, eggplant, and peppers are available in abundance, this recipe will put them to delicious use. This dish is so appetizing it could be the focus of a meal, especially served over brown rice or whole wheat couscous. **MAKES 10 SERVINGS | PER SERVING: 86 CALORIES, 6 G. TOTAL FAT (1 G. SATURATED FAT), 9 G. CARBOHYDRATES, 2 G. PROTEIN, 3 G. DIETARY FIBER, 8 MG. SODIUM.**

¼ cup olive oil

1 large onion, coarsely chopped

1 large green bell pepper, seeded and chopped into bite-sized pieces

1 large eggplant, diced into 1-inch cubes

2 medium zucchini, sliced into ½-inch rounds

3 large tomatoes, seeded and chopped

¼ cup chopped flat leaf parsley, loosely packed

1 tablespoon minced garlic

1 teaspoon dried oregano

1 teaspoon dried basil

Pinch of cayenne, or to taste

Salt and freshly ground black pepper

■ In a large saucepan, heat olive oil over medium heat. Add the onion and bell pepper and sauté for 5 minutes, stirring frequently. Add the eggplant and zucchini and continue to sauté for an additional 3 minutes. Stir in the tomatoes, parsley, garlic, oregano, basil, and cayenne, and season to taste with salt and pepper. Bring to a boil, reduce heat to low, cover, and simmer for 30 minutes, until mixture is thick and vegetables are tender. Adjust the seasonings to taste and serve.

salads

Many people think that making a side salad is a no-brainer: they just slice a wedge of iceberg lettuce onto a plate, toss on some slices of tomato and cucumber, and set out a bottle of salad dressing. But although this combination qualifies as a side salad, few of us would want to eat it every day. When it comes to food, we thrive on variety. Luckily, today's food markets make it easy for cooks to vary the composition of salads so that their colors, textures, and flavors keep changing, making us look forward to the next one.

A side salad is so simple and fast to make, and performs so many valuable functions, that it should play a role in almost every meal. A simple leafy green salad is an easy way to spark the appetite at the beginning of a meal or refresh the palate during or after the main course. Those who are watching their weight appreciate a salad's ability to create the maximum "full" feeling with the minimum calories. The side salad is also a savvy way to ensure we get enough of the vitamins, minerals, dietary fiber, and phytochemicals that our bodies need for optimum performance and health protection.

This chapter contains a range of side salads, from familiar leafy greens to bean- and grain-based salads to those containing cooked vegetables like carrots, potatoes, and Brussels sprouts, and even a fruity Jicama and Orange Salad with Mint (page 62). Looking through the recipes in this chapter, you will notice that they include a variety of textures, colors, and tastes. Not only does this variety maximize the flavors and eye appeal of each salad, it also ensures that the salads contain more nutrients and phyto-

chemicals than, for example, a green salad with a few slices of tomato and onion.

You'll find more substantial entrée salads in Part II of this book (starting on page 125), and a variety of salad dressing recipes in Sauces, Dressings, and Marinades (page 107). Cooking with Vegetables and Fruits (page 271) has a wealth of information on choosing and using these foods.

Lettuce and Other Leafy Greens

A look around your supermarket's produce section or farmers' market will demonstrate how easy it is to create interesting and varied green salads. With the improved transportation of perishable food and the blossoming of farmers' markets across the country, there are probably more salad greens available than you might be able to name, from standards like romaine, butter lettuce, and spinach to increasingly familiar exotics like radicchio, escarole, chicory, arugula, frisée, and mâche. You can buy all these greens separately, of course, but they are often combined into assortments of "mixed greens" and sold loose or packaged in cellophane bags.

The availability of all these different greens (some of which are actually purple, white, or red) will remind you that the salad base of a green salad doesn't have to be the ubiquitous but virtually tasteless iceberg lettuce. In fact, iceberg lettuce should be your last choice when selecting a salad green. Its nutritional value is so low that one food scientist told our staff it should be called "crunchy water." The main selling point of iceberg lettuce is its crispness, which adds a nice contrast to the soft ingredients in a sandwich or hamburger. But its near tasteless-ness makes it a poor candidate for a nutritious side salad. When buying greens, select only the freshest leaves and bunches, free of brown stems, edges, or spots, and with firm, not limp, leaves. Leafy greens are highly perishable and quickly lose their flavor, so buy only as much as you can use within a few days. Most unwashed greens will keep three to four days in plastic bags with holes poked through them, stored in the vegetable drawer of your refrigerator.

When ready to make a salad, wash the greens in cold water to eliminate fine grit and sand. (Even pre-washed greens packaged in cellophane bags should get a quick rinse, for safety's sake.) Handle them gently under running water, a leaf at a time, to avoid bruising. Or fill the sink or a large bowl or pot with water, gently swish the leaves in the water to loosen grit, then rinse them off. Drain the leaves thoroughly, either in a colander or on paper towels, gently pressing to absorb excess moisture, or in a salad spinner filled no more than half full. Overcrowding the spinner will bruise the greens and slow the drying process.

Sort through the washed greens to discard any tough stems and leaves with brown or wilted spots. Gently tear the larger leaves by hand (never with a knife or scissors, which will result in brown edges). The pieces should be bite-sized for easy eating. Greens can be used as a bed for the salad's other ingredients, as with a composed salad, or tossed lightly with the other ingredients in a large bowl.

Garnishing Green Salads

In addition to some form of leafy greens, the most popular ingredients for a side salad are cucumbers, tomatoes, green peppers, onions, and scallions. These help vary the salad's colors, flavors, and textures. Since the lettuce is usually green, select a red, orange, or yellow bell pepper instead of a green one, and use red onion instead of yellow. Fruit can add an extra tang, crunch, or juiciness to a salad. The sweetness of halved seedless grapes, slices of apple

or nectarine, or tangerine segments will nicely complement the slightly bitter quality of some greens. A light sprinkling of chopped toasted nuts also adds texture and flavor.

Salad Dressings

Next to selecting the vegetables, fruits, and other ingredients to be included, the most critical step in creating a salad is making the dressing. Many prepared dressings are available, and while bottled dressings seem like a convenient blessing, they have many downsides, including excess fat (or additives to give lowfat or nonfat dressings some body), sugar, and processed flavorings that offer far less taste and fewer phytochemicals than made-from-scratch dressings. Each recipe in this chapter includes a dressing component for the salad; you can find more dressing recipes in the chapter Sauces, Dressings, and Marinades (page 107).

Homemade salad dressing is also quick and easy to make without a specific recipe, using ingredients you probably already have on hand. A salad dressing "pantry" is easy to stock and will guarantee an interesting variety of flavors for future salads. There are a variety of vinegars and oils available today, including those that contain herbs and other flavorings. A basic selection would include white and red wine vinegars, and perhaps a bold balsamic vinegar, a delicate rice wine vinegar, and a cider vinegar. Citrus juices—lemon, orange, and lime—are refreshing alternatives to vinegar. Extra-virgin olive oil represents the "gold standard" in salad oils, but a less-expensive grade of olive oil or canola oil will do in a pinch (though the latter won't add any flavor). Many herb-flavored oils and specialty oils—apricot, avocado, walnut, and pumpkin seed, for example—are also popular. These oils, however, are not inexpensive, and you might want to reserve them for special occasions. But again, that standard workhorse, canola oil, can be used.

If you have them on hand, fresh herbs can elevate a simple homemade dressing to a whole new level. Dried herbs, although less flavorful than fresh, are still far more satisfactory than the seasonings in commercial dressings. Basil, mint, dill, thyme, chives, and chervil are just a few of the many fresh herbs now available in food stores and farmers' markets. A little dried or prepared mustard can add a pleasant sharpness to a dressing; a small amount of honey is usually added as well, to balance the pungency of mustard. Minced garlic, onion, or shallots are frequently used in dressings.

The standard proportion of oil to vinegar in a salad dressing is usually three to four parts oil to one part vinegar. (In other words, three to four tablespoons of oil to one tablespoon vinegar.) When the cookbook team tested dressings, we found there was a lot of individuality involved in judging them. Some members of the cookbook team preferred a tangier dressing, with a smaller proportion of oil, while others preferred smoother dressings, with a larger proportion of oil. Also, leafy greens with a sharp "bite," like arugula and mustard greens, may need a bit more oil to smooth out their slightly bitter flavor.

To make enough dressing to serve three to four people, whisk the ingredients together in a small bowl or combine the ingredients in a small, leak-proof container, blending the ingredients with a few shakes of the arm. A blender is more convenient for mixing larger quantities of dressing. A small bottle, such as those used for bottled water, is useful, especially when it's time to drizzle the dressing over the salad. To pour, use a thumb or finger to partially close off the narrow opening as you drizzle the dressing lightly and evenly, then toss the salad gently to distribute the dressing.

The amount of dressing a salad needs is each individual's judgment call, but less is usually more—too much dressing will mask the flavors and fresh quality of the greens. The salad ingredients should just lightly glisten with dressing. When in doubt, it is always better to start with too little dressing and add a little more later, if necessary. Salad greens should always be dressed at the very last minute, as they will go limp and soggy after sitting too long in their dressing.

mixed greens with blueberries and feta

With good taste and high amounts of disease-fighting antioxidants, blueberries are all-around winners. They add sweetness and deep blue color, and the berry-flavored vinegar spreads the fruit flavor throughout the salad. A simply prepared entrée of chicken or fish will best accompany this complex, flavorful salad. **MAKES 8 SERVINGS | PER SERVING: 64 CALORIES, 4 G. TOTAL FAT (1 G. SATURATED FAT), 5 G. CARBOHYDRATES, 3 G. PROTEIN, 2 G. DIETARY FIBER, 126 MG. SODIUM.**

2 tablespoons raspberry-flavored or blueberry-flavored vinegar

¼ cup fat-free, reduced sodium chicken broth

2 tablespoons extra-virgin olive oil

1 teaspoon honey

2 small fresh mint leaves

1 cup plus 10 fresh blueberries

8 cups mixed salad greens, torn into bite-sized pieces

2 ounces crumbled reduced fat feta cheese

■ In a blender, combine the vinegar, broth, olive oil, honey, mint leaves, and 10 blueberries. Blend the mixture at low speed just until smooth and well combined. Transfer the vinaigrette to a jar with a tight-fitting lid and refrigerate until needed; it will keep for up to 3 days.

■ In a large bowl, toss the mixed greens with the remaining cup of blueberries. Shake the vinaigrette until thoroughly blended, drizzle over the salad, and toss lightly. Sprinkle the cheese over the top and serve.

brussels sprouts salad with garlic-lemon dressing

Brussels sprouts, like all cruciferous vegetables, contain compounds that help ward off cancer. With this quick recipe, you have the option of serving them cold. The secret to the good taste here comes from pairing the bold flavor of Brussels sprouts with the equally assertive flavors of garlic and lemon juice. **MAKES 4 SERVINGS | PER SERVING: 65 CALORIES, 4 G. TOTAL FAT (LESS THAN 1 G. SATURATED FAT), 7 G. CARBOHYDRATES, 3 G. PROTEIN, 3 G. DIETARY FIBER, 18 MG. SODIUM.**

¾ pound fresh Brussels sprouts

1 tablespoon extra-virgin olive oil

1 garlic clove, finely minced

1 teaspoon freshly squeezed lemon juice, or to taste

¼ cup minced red bell pepper

2 tablespoons chopped flat leaf parsley

Salt and freshly ground black pepper

4 large lettuce leaves

■ Remove any yellow leaves from the sprouts and rinse them thoroughly. Trim the bottoms and, with the tip of a knife, make an X in each stem end to help the sprouts cook evenly. Place a steamer basket inside a pot and add about 2 inches of water. Steam the Brussels sprouts just until cooked through, about 10 minutes. Meanwhile, in a small bowl, whisk olive oil, garlic, and lemon juice to blend. Set the dressing aside.

■ When the Brussels sprouts are done, drain them and pat them dry with a paper towel. Cut each sprout in half. In a salad bowl, toss the sprouts with the dressing. Add the red pepper and parsley, season to taste with salt and pepper, and toss again. Serve the salad at room temperature or refrigerate until chilled. To serve, place a lettuce leaf on each of 4 salad plates and spoon the salad over the leaf.

mixed greens with blueberries and feta

arugula salad with radicchio and blue cheese

This salad will excite your taste buds with a variety of nutritious greens. The critical ingredient is arugula, a dark green member of the cruciferous vegetable family with a pungent, peppery bite. The more mature the leaves, the stronger the taste. Radicchio is slightly less aggressive. Mixing radicchio with milder greens, such as baby romaine, creates a nicely balanced salad.

MAKES 4 SERVINGS | PER SERVING: 92 CALORIES, 8 G. TOTAL FAT (2 G. SATURATED FAT), 3 G. CARBOHYDRATES, 2 G. PROTEIN, 1 G. DIETARY FIBER, 67 MG. SODIUM.

- 2 cups loosely packed regular or baby arugula leaves
- 2 cups loosely packed baby romaine or field greens
- ½ cup thinly sliced radicchio
- 2 tablespoons balsamic vinegar
- 2 tablespoons extra-virgin olive oil
- 1 tablespoon minced shallot
- 1 tablespoon minced fresh chives
- Salt and freshly ground black pepper
- 2 tablespoons crumbled blue cheese

■ In a salad bowl, gently toss the arugula with the romaine and radicchio. Set the bowl aside.

■ Whisk together the vinegar and oil in a small bowl. Add the shallot and chives, blend, and season to taste with salt and pepper. Drizzle the dressing over the salad and toss lightly to distribute the dressing evenly. Sprinkle the blue cheese over the top and serve.

spinach, romaine, and strawberries with balsamic vinaigrette

If you're skeptical about adding fruit to salads, try this recipe. The juicy sweetness of strawberries is a wonderful contrast to the crisp greens. You'll also find out why the aromatic, slightly sweet taste of balsamic vinegar makes it a classic dressing for strawberries. This salad is elegant enough for formal occasions. MAKES 6 SERVINGS | PER SERVING: 75 CALORIES, 5 G. TOTAL FAT (LESS THAN 1 G. SATURATED FAT), 7 G. CARBOHYDRATES, 2 G. PROTEIN, 2 G. DIETARY FIBER, 30 MG. SODIUM.

- 1 head romaine lettuce, leaves washed and torn into bite-sized pieces
- 6 ounces fresh spinach, leaves washed and torn into bite-sized pieces
- 2 cups fresh strawberries, hulled and quartered
- ¼ cup loosely packed, coarsely chopped flat leaf parsley
- 1 tablespoon balsamic vinegar, or to taste
- 2 tablespoons extra-virgin olive oil
- Salt and freshly ground black pepper

■ In a large bowl, toss together the lettuce, spinach, and strawberries, or arrange them on 6 individual plates. Sprinkle the parsley on top.

■ Whisk vinegar and olive oil in a small bowl to blend. Drizzle the dressing over the salad. Season salad to taste with salt and pepper and serve immediately.

shrimp with grapefruit and black bean salsa

Here shrimp are served with a bold salsa that combines the crisp acidity of tomatoes and citrus with the satisfying earthiness of black beans. Served with Heirloom Whole Wheat Bread (page 228), this salad would make a refreshing, low-cal lunch or supper.

MAKES 4 SERVINGS | PER SERVING: 103 CALORIES, LESS THAN 1 G. TOTAL FAT (LESS THAN 1 G. SATURATED FAT), 19 G. CARBOHYDRATES, 7 G. PROTEIN, 3 G. DIETARY FIBER, 147 MG. SODIUM.

12 uncooked jumbo shrimp

1 cup medium grapefruit segments, seeded (about ½ grapefruit)

½ medium tomato, seeded and diced small

1 small cucumber, peeled and diced small

¼ cup red onion, diced small

½ cup cooked or canned black beans, drained and rinsed

½ serrano or jalapeño chile, seeded and minced*

Juice of ½ orange

Juice of ½ lime

Salt and freshly ground black pepper

2 tablespoons chopped fresh cilantro, for garnish

1 tablespoon chopped fresh mint, for garnish

*Note: Wear rubber gloves to handle fresh chiles, and keep your hands away from your eyes.

■ Bring a large saucepan filled with cold water to a boil over medium-high heat. Add the shrimp and cook 5 to 6 minutes, until they are pink and curled. Drain them promptly. As soon as the shrimp are cool enough to handle, peel and devein them. Set them aside.

■ In a medium bowl, combine the grapefruit, tomato, cucumber, onion, beans, chile, orange juice, and lime juice. Toss together, and season to taste with salt and pepper.

■ Arrange three shrimp in a pinwheel, tails inside, on each of four dinner plates. Spoon ¼ of the salsa onto the center of each plate. Sprinkle ¼ of the cilantro and mint over each plate and serve.

broccoli, cherry tomato, and watercress salad

Despite its leafy green appearance, watercress belongs to the same family of vegetables as broccoli. Both contain the anticancer phytochemical sulforaphane. Watercress is easy to use—just snap off the stems and wash the leaves. It brings a strong, almost peppery taste to this quick salad, which is rich in vitamins A and C. MAKES 4 SERVINGS | PER SERVING: 56 CALORIES, 4 G. TOTAL FAT (LESS THAN 1 G. SATURATED FAT), 6 G. CARBOHYDRATES, 2 G. PROTEIN, 2 G. DIETARY FIBER, 18 MG. SODIUM.

- 2 cups small broccoli florets
- ½ tablespoon red wine vinegar, or to taste
- 1 tablespoon extra-virgin olive oil
- ½ teaspoon minced garlic

    Salt and freshly ground black pepper
- 2 cups halved cherry tomatoes
- 1 bunch watercress, stems removed and leaves washed

■ In a vegetable steamer set over boiling water, steam the broccoli, covered, for about 4 minutes, until tender. Rinse the broccoli with cold water and drain well.

■ In a large bowl, whisk together the vinegar, olive oil, garlic, and salt and pepper to taste. Add the broccoli, tomatoes, and watercress. Toss to blend and serve.

sweet and spicy carrot salad with pine nuts

Carrots are a great source of alpha carotene, beta carotene, flavonoids, and terpenes. They are low in calories yet delightfully sweet—especially when prepared in the Moroccan style with its complex spices to heat up that sweetness. MAKES 6 SERVINGS | PER SERVING: 116 CALORIES, 2 G. TOTAL FAT (LESS THAN 1 G. SATURATED FAT), 24 G. CARBOHYDRATES, 2 G. PROTEIN, 4 G. DIETARY FIBER, 90 MG. SODIUM.

- 1½ pounds carrots, peeled and chopped into bite-sized pieces
- 3 tablespoons freshly squeezed lemon juice
- ½ tablespoon honey
- 1 teaspoon extra-virgin olive oil
- 1 garlic clove, minced
- ¼ teaspoon ground cumin
- ¼ teaspoon ground cinnamon
- ¼ teaspoon ground ginger
- ⅛ teaspoon salt

    Generous dash of cayenne
- ½ cup golden raisins
- 2 tablespoons pine nuts, toasted*

*Note: To toast the pine nuts, put them in a small skillet over medium heat, shaking or stirring frequently until golden brown, about 2 minutes. Immediately transfer the nuts to a small dish and cool.

■ In a large saucepan, bring 2 quarts of water to a boil. Add the carrots and return the water to a boil. Cook the carrots for 2 minutes, until they are crisp but tender. Drain well and let them cool slightly.

■ In a large bowl, whisk together the lemon juice, honey, olive oil, garlic, cumin, cinnamon, ginger, salt, and cayenne. Add the carrots and raisins to the bowl and toss. Refrigerate the salad for about 3 hours, until chilled. Top with the pine nuts and serve.

broccoli, cherry tomato, and watercress salad

two-potato salad with spinach and fresh herb dressing

two-potato salad with spinach and fresh herb dressing

This potato salad, with its unusual combination of yellow and sweet potatoes, is a great alternative to standard deli-style potato salads. It's also significantly lower in fat. For the best flavor, use fresh rosemary and thyme. The sweet potatoes are nicely balanced by the Dijon mustard in the dressing. MAKES 12 SERVINGS | PER SERVING: 128 CALORIES, 5 G. TOTAL FAT (LESS THAN 1 G. SATURATED FAT), 19 G. CARBOHYDRATES, 2 G. PROTEIN, 2 G. DIETARY FIBER, 148 MG. SODIUM.

- 1 pound boiling potatoes, preferably yellow-fleshed (such as Yukon Gold), peeled and cut into ¾-inch pieces
- 1 pound orange-flesh sweet potatoes, peeled and cut into ¾-inch pieces
- ¼ cup Dijon mustard
- 3 tablespoons white wine vinegar
- ¼ cup extra-virgin olive oil
- ⅔ cup minced shallots
- 1 tablespoon minced fresh rosemary
- 1 tablespoon minced fresh thyme
  Salt and freshly ground black pepper
- 4 cups spinach leaves, washed and torn into bite-sized pieces, tightly packed

■ Put the boiling potatoes and sweet potatoes in two separate pots with enough cold water to cover them. Cover both pots with tight-fitting lids and bring the water to a boil. Reduce the heat to a simmer and cook until just barely tender when pierced with a fork, about 4 to 5 minutes. (The potatoes will continue cooking after they are removed from the pot.)

■ Meanwhile, in a medium bowl, whisk together the mustard and vinegar. Gradually whisk in the olive oil until the mixture is smooth and well combined. Mix in the shallots, rosemary, and thyme, and season to taste with salt and pepper.

■ Drain the potatoes and transfer them to a large bowl. Drizzle in half of the dressing (about ¼ cup), toss gently, and set the salad aside to allow the potatoes to absorb the flavors while cooling. When the potatoes are at room temperature, gently mix in the spinach and the remaining dressing. Adjust the seasoning and serve at room temperature.

cabbage and carrot slaw with roasted peanuts

Slaws made with mayonnaise are heavy with fat and often dull to the taste. This slaw stands out because of its lively, tart vinaigrette dressing. Eat it with a sandwich or pack it for a picnic. The peanuts, which contain healthy fat and protein, add more pizzazz.
MAKES 8 SERVINGS | PER SERVING: 70 CALORIES, 5 G. TOTAL FAT (LESS THAN 1 G. SATURATED FAT), 6 G. CARBOHYDRATES, 2 G. PROTEIN, 2 G. DIETARY FIBER, 38 MG. SODIUM.

- 1 tablespoon rice wine vinegar, or to taste
- 1 tablespoon sesame oil
- 1 teaspoon honey
- 1 teaspoon reduced sodium soy sauce
- 2 cups coarsely shredded carrots
- 2 cups coarsely shredded cabbage
- ⅓ cup chopped unsalted dry-roasted peanuts

■ In a large bowl, whisk together the vinegar, sesame oil, honey, and soy sauce. Add the carrots and cabbage and toss to blend. Sprinkle the peanuts on top and serve at room temperature.

southwestern black bean salad with barley

Black beans are a good source of phytoestrogens as well as folate. Barley contains tocotrienols and lignans. All of these substances are believed to fight cancer in different ways. Furthermore, barley is the only grain other than oats that supplies significant amounts of the soluble fiber that can help lower blood cholesterol. Here, the moist chewiness of barley contrasts well with the drier texture of beans. **MAKES 8 SERVINGS | PER SERVING: 104 CALORIES, LESS THAN 1 G. TOTAL FAT (0 G. SATURATED FAT), 20 G. CARBOHYDRATES, 5 G. PROTEIN, 5 G. DIETARY FIBER, 168 MG. SODIUM.**

1¼ cups water

⅓ cup pearl barley, rinsed and drained

½ teaspoon salt (optional)

1 can (15 ounces) black beans, rinsed and drained

1 small yellow bell pepper, seeded and chopped

1 small tomato, seeded and chopped

1 cup frozen corn, thawed

1 medium scallion, chopped, trimmed, white part only

1 teaspoon dried oregano

1 teaspoon dried basil

Juice of ½ a lime

Salt and freshly ground black pepper

2 ounces shredded pepper or plain Monterey Jack cheese, for garnish

■ In a medium saucepan, bring the water to a boil. Add the barley and ½ teaspoon of salt, if desired. Reduce the heat, cover, and simmer for about 30 minutes, until the barley is tender. Drain well.

■ In a large bowl, combine the barley, beans, bell pepper, tomato, corn, scallion, oregano, basil, and lime juice. Stir the mixture with a fork. Season to taste with salt and pepper, top with the shredded cheese, and serve.

white bean and tomato salad with parsley

There are several popular varieties of white beans: Great Northern, flageolet, and cannellini (white kidney). Each could be used for this recipe, but the creamy cannellini best suits the Italian seasonings. Don't skimp on the amount of parsley called for: like other herbs, it is a storehouse of phytochemicals that promote good health. **MAKES 5 SERVINGS | PER SERVING: 130 CALORIES, 3 G. TOTAL FAT (LESS THAN 1 G. SATURATED FAT), 20 G. CARBOHYDRATES, 6 G. PROTEIN, 5 G. DIETARY FIBER, 246 MG. SODIUM.**

1 can (15 ounces) white beans, rinsed and drained

1 medium tomato, seeded and chopped

½ small red onion, finely chopped

1 cup loosely packed, chopped flat leaf parsley

4 fresh basil leaves, chopped, or ½ teaspoon dried basil

1 teaspoon lemon zest

1 tablespoon white wine vinegar, or to taste

1 tablespoon extra-virgin olive oil

½ teaspoon salt

Freshly ground black pepper

■ In a large bowl, combine the beans, tomato, onion, parsley, basil, and lemon zest and mix with a fork.

■ In a small bowl, whisk together the vinegar, oil, salt, and pepper to taste. Pour the dressing over the bean mixture and toss with a fork to distribute the dressing evenly. This salad will keep in the refrigerator in a tightly covered container for up to 2 days. Serve chilled or at room temperature.

black-eyed pea, corn, and spinach salad

The earthy taste of the Southern favorite, black-eyed peas, makes for a good salad that is high in fiber and protein. It has a comforting medley of colors, textures, and tastes and plenty of health-protective phytochemicals. You could increase the serving to a cup or a cup and a half, and serve this salad as a main dish. **MAKES 8 SERVINGS | PER SERVING: 123 CALORIES, 4 G. TOTAL FAT (LESS THAN 1 G. SATURATED FAT), 21 G. CARBOHYDRATES, 6 G. PROTEIN, 5 G. DIETARY FIBER, 395 MG. SODIUM.**

1 celery rib, diced

1 cup grated carrots

1 cup finely chopped fresh spinach, tightly packed

1 cup frozen corn, thawed

½ cup diced red onion

2 cans (15 ounces each) black-eyed peas, rinsed and drained

2 tablespoons extra-virgin olive oil

1 tablespoon balsamic vinegar, or to taste

2 tablespoons freshly squeezed lemon juice

Salt and freshly ground black pepper

■ In a large bowl, combine the celery, carrots, spinach, corn, onion, and black-eyed peas. In a separate bowl, whisk together the oil, vinegar, and lemon juice. Pour the dressing over the salad and toss well. Season to taste with salt and pepper. The salad can be served chilled or at room temperature.

three-bean salad with cilantro-chile dressing

You can assemble this hearty salad quickly with common canned foods. The high-quality protein of this bean salad makes it a perfect picnic or patio entrée when it's too hot to cook. Canned corn can be substituted for one of the cans of beans. **MAKES 8 SERVINGS | PER SERVING: 170 CALORIES, 5 G. TOTAL FAT (LESS THAN 1 G. SATURATED FAT), 34 G. CARBOHYDRATES, 8 G. PROTEIN, 8 G. DIETARY FIBER, 438 MG. SODIUM.**

1 can (15 ounces) kidney beans, rinsed and drained

1 can (15 ounces) chickpeas, rinsed and drained

1 can (15 ounces) black or pinto beans, rinsed and drained

1 can (15 ounces) corn, rinsed and drained (optional, in place of 1 can of beans)

¼ cup freshly squeezed lemon juice, or to taste

2 tablespoons extra-virgin olive oil

4 garlic cloves, finely minced

½ tablespoon chile pepper flakes, or to taste

3 tablespoons dried cilantro, crushed, or ½ cup chopped fresh cilantro, loosely packed

Salt and freshly ground black pepper

■ In a large bowl, mix the first 4 ingredients and set aside. In a blender, combine the lemon juice, olive oil, garlic, chile flakes, and cilantro. Purée until the mixture is smooth and well blended. Adjust the seasonings, adding salt and pepper to taste.

■ Toss the beans with the dressing. Cover and refrigerate the bean mixture for 3 to 12 hours, stirring occasionally. Serve cold.

jicama and orange salad with mint

The cool, refreshing taste of this salad comes from oranges and jicama, a root vegetable now widely available. Famous as a source of vitamin C, oranges also contain too many phytochemicals to name. Jicama adds additional vitamin C and lots of fiber. Furthermore, the white flesh of this crunchy, mild-flavored vegetable tempers the acidity of the oranges, provides a nice color contrast, and adds texture. On a hot day, this salad is especially appealing. **MAKES 8 SERVINGS | PER SERVING: 76 CALORIES, 1 G. TOTAL FAT (LESS THAN 1 G. SATURATED FAT), 17 G. CARBOHYDRATES, 1 G. PROTEIN, 5 G. DIETARY FIBER, 10 MG. SODIUM.**

1 medium jicama (about ¾ pound), peeled and cut into 1½-inch matchsticks

2 medium carrots, peeled and coarsely grated or julienned

2 small seedless navel oranges, peeled and sliced

½ tablespoon extra-virgin olive oil

2 tablespoons orange juice

2 tablespoons honey

1 tablespoon freshly squeezed lime juice, or to taste

Salt

8 fresh mint leaves, thinly slivered

■ In a medium bowl, combine the jicama, carrots, and oranges. In a small bowl, combine the olive oil, orange juice, honey, and lime juice and add salt to taste. Whisk the dressing and pour it over the jicama mixture. Toss to coat. Refrigerate the salad for 2 to 3 hours. Top with the mint leaves before serving.

pear salad with ricotta cheese and toasted pistachios
The mellow pear slices in this salad complement the soft, rich taste of the butter lettuce. The ricotta cheese adds creaminess and the pistachios a crunch. This salad proves that elegant foods can be easy to prepare. **MAKES 4 SERVINGS | PER SERVING: 134 CALORIES, 6 G. TOTAL FAT (1 G. SATURATED FAT), 19 G. CARBOHYDRATES, 4 G. PROTEIN, 3 G. DIETARY FIBER, 23 MG. SODIUM.**

SALAD

- 1 medium head butter lettuce, leaves separated and washed
- 2 large ripe pears, cored, halved, and thinly sliced
- 2 tablespoons chopped pistachio nuts, toasted*
- 4 tablespoons skim ricotta cheese

DRESSING

- ¼ cup orange juice
- 1 tablespoon balsamic vinegar
- 1 teaspoon honey
- 2 teaspoons walnut or canola oil

*Note: To toast the pistachios, put them in a small skillet over medium-high heat and stir frequently for 2 to 3 minutes, until lightly browned. Immediately transfer the nuts to a small dish and cool.

■ Arrange the lettuce equally on 4 plates. Top each plate with an equal amount of sliced pears. Sprinkle ½ tablespoon of the nuts over each salad. Place 1 tablespoon of the ricotta cheese in the center of each salad. In a small bowl, whisk together the dressing ingredients, drizzle dressing over each salad, and serve.

grains

Grains have been central to human civilization—entire societies formed around their cultivation. Their rich, reliable supply of protein and carbohydrates made grains vital as people turned from hunting and gathering to cultivated agriculture. The nutritious and health-protective benefits of grains as well as their inexpensive availability make them an important staple throughout the world.

There are still many reasons for us to revere this important food source. Unrefined (or "whole") grains are an excellent source of dietary fiber, which is important for the proper functioning of the digestive tract. The vitamins, minerals, and especially the phytochemicals in grains also help protect us against serious and chronic health problems. We already know that phytochemicals can help reduce the risk or severity of a range of problems, including diabetes, stroke, heart disease, and several types of cancer. But scientists are only now beginning to understand that whole grains contain far more phytochemicals than we previously thought. New types of phytochemicals in grains are continually being discovered.

The textures and flavors of whole grains are almost as varied as the ways in which they can be used. In America, "grains" usually brings bread and breakfast cereal to mind. But as many cuisines illustrate, there is an almost mind-boggling variety of grains and ways to prepare them, and they can play major roles in one-pot meals like pilafs and stir-fries, or co-star with vegetables and beans in side dishes. Grains appear as side dishes in this chapter, but they're also featured in recipes in other chapters, from Appetizers (page 190) to Desserts (page 241). The chapter Cooking with Vegetables and Fruits contains a section on using whole grains (page 279).

Whole-Grain Pasta and Rice

Aside from bread and breakfast cereal, pasta and rice are probably the two most popular forms of grains in America. And the increasing availability of new varieties of whole-grain rice and pasta is a big help to cooks who want to add more whole grains to their diets while still relying on familiar ingredients and techniques.

All the pasta recipes in this chapter call for whole wheat pastas. Because Americans in general are more familiar with refined forms of pasta, some members of the cookbook team were resistant to whole-grain pastas, saying they were too chewy compared with the more familiar refined versions. But much to their surprise, they discovered at the tastings that they truly enjoyed, for example, Fettuccine with Figs and Chiles (page 80), Angel Hair Pasta with Sesame-Peanut Sauce (page 79), and Whole Wheat Pasta with Zucchini, Mushrooms, and Basil (page 83). As with the converted "pasta doubters" on our cookbook team, those who had spent a long time in Asia, or had been long-term devotees of Asian cuisines, were resistant to whole-grain rice, especially if it was an accompaniment to an Asian-style dish. But they too found that they thoroughly enjoyed Brown Rice with Scallions and Fresh Herbs (page 72) and the pilafs, like Orange Rice Pilaf with Dried Fruit (page 72).

At one time, American supermarkets offered only

one brown, or whole-grain, rice. But there are now many varieties of cultivated whole-grain rice that are beginning to be more widely available in American markets. The cookbook team found twelve different varieties of whole-grain rice at a local food store—some grown in the United States, others imported, including brown basmati, Black Japonica (a mix of black and "mahogany" domestic varieties), Bhutanese red rice, and "Forbidden Rice," a Chinese black rice. With their different textures, flavors, and colors, we can no longer make generalizations about whole-grain rice.

There's More to Grains Than Pasta: The Wider World of Grains

Whole-grain pasta and rice are great additions to any cook's repertoire, but there are many other whole grains to enjoy, each with its own texture and flavor, from mild quinoa to crunchy millet. Some grains are hard to find without a search through natural foods stores, but others—like bulgur, barley, quinoa, and kasha—are probably available in your neighborhood market.

Bulgur, a form of wheat that is a staple in the Middle East, has a somewhat nutty flavor and a tender, chewy texture. It should rate highly with any frazzled cook working against the clock as mealtime approaches, as it needs only a few minutes of steeping in boiling hot water to "cook" itself before it is served. It is used in many types of dishes, most popularly in salads but also in hot dishes. It makes an easy, great-tasting pilaf, as in Bulgur Pilaf with Red Peppers and Herbs (page 74).

Barley is sometimes used in vegetable and chicken soups, much as rice is. It has a mild, slightly nutty taste. Because of its similar texture, barley can be substituted for rice in salads, pilafs, and casseroles. You may want to try experimenting with your favorite rice-based recipes, using barley instead. Hulled, or whole-grain, barley is the most nutritious

form of this grain. It is generally found in health-food stores. More commonly found is pearl barley, which has had the bran removed. You can also cook it on its own following the package instructions and add sautéed mushrooms, onion, or bell pepper, plain or toasted pumpkin seeds, or chopped toasted almonds, peanuts, pecans, cashews, or macadamia nuts. Or try Lemon Barley (page 73).

Quinoa (pronounced "keen-wah") deserves to be much better known than it currently is. An ivory-colored grain with a delicate, mild taste similar to that of couscous, it contains more protein than any other grain. It is also higher in unsaturated fats and lower in carbohydrates than most grains. Its small, bead-shaped grains take only half the cooking time of regular (white) rice, and it expands during cooking to four times its original volume. If you haven't cooked with quinoa yet, try Quinoa with Dried Cranberries, Apricots, and Pecans (page 77) or Quinoa Pilaf with Peas and Sage (page 77). These recipes are good models for creating your own quinoa side dishes, whether savory with herbs and vegetables, or crunchy and slightly sweet with fruit and nuts.

Millet is another protein-rich grain with a mild flavor. It looks like a small seed, has a delicate flavor, and is prepared very much like rice. Once you try Millet with Sautéed Mushrooms and Pumpkin Seeds (page 78), you will be inspired to create your own dishes with this flexible grain.

Kasha is a Russian word that refers to buckwheat groats. Although technically buckwheat is in the same plant family as rhubarb, it cooks and tastes like a grain. Kasha's popularity originated in Russia and Eastern Europe, but it is also well known to many Americans. Its toasted, nutty flavor marries well with mushrooms and nuts and hearty autumnal ingredients like root vegetables, and it is perfectly suited to a mixed side dish like Quick Kasha Pilaf (page 74).

snow pea and carrot pilaf

For a new kind of pilaf, or a lowfat alternative to fried rice, you can't beat this recipe. It combines sweet red bell peppers, snow peas, carrots, and scallions with brown rice and the Asian flavors of fresh ginger and cilantro. Garlic and a few hot red pepper flakes add zip. The pilaf is a healthful meal in itself when accompanied by a 3-ounce serving of fish, poultry, meat, or some tofu. **MAKES 8 SERVINGS | PER SERVING: 107 CALORIES, LESS THAN 1 G. TOTAL FAT (LESS THAN 1 G. SATURATED FAT), 22 G. CARBOHYDRATES, 3 G. PROTEIN, 2 G. DIETARY FIBER, 228 MG. SODIUM.**

Canola oil spray

1 medium red bell pepper, seeded and coarsely chopped

1 garlic clove, minced

1 teaspoon chopped peeled fresh ginger

1 cup brown rice

2 cups fat-free, reduced sodium chicken or vegetable broth

1 cup trimmed snow peas

1 cup thinly sliced carrots

¼ cup scallions, trimmed and chopped

¼ cup chopped fresh cilantro, loosely packed

1 tablespoon reduced sodium soy sauce

⅛ teaspoon crushed red pepper flakes

■ Coat a large saucepan with canola oil spray and heat it over medium heat. Add the bell pepper, garlic, and ginger and sauté for 5 minutes. Stir in the rice and sauté for 3 more minutes. Add the broth and bring to a boil. Lower heat to medium-low, cover, and simmer for about 35 minutes, until the rice is nearly tender and almost all the liquid is absorbed. Stir in the snow peas, carrots, scallions, cilantro, soy sauce, and red pepper flakes, and cook for 5 more minutes. Serve immediately.

curried sweet potato and apple pilaf

Autumn's great variety of vegetables and fruits provides a bounty of cancer-fighting phytochemicals and dietary fiber. The following dish layers textures and flavors ranging from apple and sweet potato to kale and curry in a nutrition-packed pilaf. **MAKES 10 SERVINGS | PER SERVING: 99 CALORIES, 2 G. TOTAL FAT (LESS THAN 1 G. SATURATED FAT), 19 G. CARBOHYDRATES, 2 G. PROTEIN, 2 G. DIETARY FIBER, 96 MG. SODIUM.**

1 tablespoon canola oil

1 small onion, coarsely chopped (about ½ cup)

1 cup quick-cooking brown rice

1 tablespoon curry powder

1 medium orange-flesh sweet potato, peeled and coarsely chopped (about 1½ cups)

1 cup coarsely chopped fresh kale, loosely packed

2 cups fat-free, reduced sodium chicken broth

3 small tart apples (such as Granny Smith), cored and coarsely chopped (about 2½ cups)

¼ cup currants or raisins

Salt and freshly ground black pepper

■ In a large skillet, heat the canola oil over medium-high heat. Add the onion and sauté for about 5 minutes, until golden. Add the rice and curry powder and sauté for 3 minutes. Stir in the sweet potato and kale and sauté for 2 minutes.

■ Add the broth and bring the mixture to a boil, stirring occasionally. Reduce the heat to low, cover, and simmer for about 15 minutes, until the rice and sweet potato are nearly tender and the liquid is almost all absorbed. If the mixture becomes too dry, additional broth can be added.

■ Stir in the apples and currants. Simmer about 5 minutes, stirring frequently, until the apples are tender and all of the liquid is absorbed. Season to taste with salt and pepper and serve.

orange rice pilaf with dried fruit

Adding the sweetness of dried fruits to savory grains is a tradition in the Middle East. The nutty taste and chewy texture of brown rice blend well with dried fruits that have a bit of tartness, such as those suggested here. Choose one or use a combination of all three fruits. This dish goes especially well with poultry. MAKES 6 SERVINGS | PER SERVING: 152 CALORIES, 1 G. TOTAL FAT (LESS THAN 1 G. SATURATED FAT), 34 G. CARBOHYDRATES, 4 G. PROTEIN, 3 G. DIETARY FIBER, 158 MG. SODIUM.

¾ cup chopped dried apricots, cherries, or cranberries, or a combination

⅓ cup raisins

1½ cups quick-cooking brown rice

3 tablespoons chopped fresh flat leaf parsley or 1 tablespoon dried parsley

2 teaspoons orange zest

Fat-free, reduced sodium chicken broth

■ Put the dried fruits and raisins in a small bowl. Add hot water to cover, let them soak for 5 to 10 minutes, and then drain. In a large saucepan, cook the rice with the fruits, parsley, and orange zest in chicken broth according to package instructions. Remove the pilaf from the heat and fluff gently with a fork before serving.

brown rice with scallions and fresh herbs

Whole grains are digested more slowly and steadily than refined grains. They won't leave you hungry for more "carbs" in just a few hours. The rich flavor of this rice comes from cooking it in chicken broth, adding nutritious carrots, scallions, garlic, and chives, and seasoning it with fresh herbs. It's easy to make and can accompany many other New American Plate dishes. You'll get considerably more dietary fiber, magnesium, and vitamin E than is provided by white rice, along with phytochemicals like oryzanol. MAKES 6 SERVINGS | PER SERVING: 138 CALORIES, 5 G. TOTAL FAT (LESS THAN 1 G. SATURATED FAT), 19 G. CARBOHYDRATES, 3 G. PROTEIN, 2 G. DIETARY FIBER, 160 MG. SODIUM.

1½ cups quick-cooking brown rice

¼ teaspoon ground cumin

Fat-free, reduced sodium chicken broth

2 tablespoons olive oil

1 cup scallions, trimmed and chopped

¼ cup shredded carrots

1 tablespoon minced garlic

2 tablespoons minced chives

½ tablespoon minced fresh thyme

½ tablespoon minced fresh sage

½ tablespoon minced fresh rosemary

Salt and ground black pepper

■ Cook the rice with the cumin in the chicken broth according to the package instructions. A few minutes before the rice is done, heat the olive oil in a medium nonstick skillet over medium-high heat. Add the scallions and carrots and sauté for 3 to 4 minutes. Add the garlic and herbs and sauté for an additional minute. Pour this mixture over the rice. Mix well, season to taste with salt and pepper, and serve.

mixed grains with garlic and scallions

Here, a variety of whole grains—quinoa, millet, and brown rice—combine to create a harmonious dish. Because they are unrefined, these grains are a rich source of antioxidants and fiber. Brown rice and especially quinoa supply protein as well. You can use this mixture to stuff vegetables like bell peppers, mushrooms, or zucchini and then bake them, or serve it as a unique and tasty side dish. MAKES 12 SERVINGS | PER SERVING: 145 CALORIES, 2 G. TOTAL FAT (LESS THAN 1 G. SATURATED FAT), 26 G. CARBOHYDRATES, 4 G. PROTEIN, 2 G. DIETARY FIBER, 118 MG. SODIUM.

1 tablespoon olive oil

½ cup scallions, trimmed and chopped, plus ½ cup sliced scallions, for garnish

2 large garlic cloves, minced

½ cup quinoa, thoroughly rinsed and drained

½ cup millet

1 cup quick-cooking brown rice

3 to 4 cups fat-free, reduced sodium chicken or vegetable broth, divided

Salt and freshly ground black pepper

■ In a large nonstick skillet with a tightly fitting lid, heat the olive oil over medium-high heat. Add the ½ cup of chopped scallions and the garlic and sauté for 2 minutes. Add the quinoa, millet, and rice and stir to coat the grains with the olive oil. Add 3 cups of broth and bring the mixture to a boil. Reduce the heat to low, cover, and simmer for 25 to 30 minutes, until all of the liquid is absorbed. If the millet is not yet tender, add additional broth, ¼ cup at a time (up to 1 cup), and continue to simmer until the broth is absorbed and the millet is tender. Season to taste with salt and pepper. Serve hot, garnished with the ½ cup sliced scallions.

lemon barley

Barley, one of the first grains our ancestors grew, is usually confined to use in vegetable soup. But its slightly chewy and pasta-like texture makes it a versatile ingredient in all kinds of dishes. It contains some protein and a high amount of soluble fiber. Give barley a try by serving this lemony side dish with fish, poultry, white beans, or vegetables. MAKES 8 SERVINGS | PER SERVING: 123 CALORIES, 4 G. TOTAL FAT (LESS THAN 1 G. SATURATED FAT), 20 G. CARBOHYDRATES, 3 G. PROTEIN, 4 G. DIETARY FIBER, 172 MG. SODIUM.

1 cup pearl barley, rinsed and drained

3 cups fat-free, reduced sodium chicken or vegetable broth

1 large garlic clove, minced

¼ cup chopped loosely packed flat leaf parsley

2 tablespoons extra-virgin olive oil

½ tablespoon lemon zest

1 tablespoon freshly squeezed lemon juice

⅛ teaspoon fennel seed, whole

Salt and freshly ground black pepper

■ In a medium saucepan over high heat, bring the barley and broth to a boil. Reduce heat to medium-low, cover, and simmer for about 45 minutes, stirring occasionally, until the barley is tender. Add the garlic and cook for 5 more minutes. Transfer the barley to a fine strainer, drain well, and transfer to a bowl. Cover the barley and refrigerate until chilled completely, about 4 hours. The barley can be refrigerated for up to 3 days before adding the remaining ingredients. Just before serving, add the parsley, olive oil, lemon zest, lemon juice, fennel seed, and salt and pepper to taste, and toss well to combine.

bulgur pilaf with red peppers and herbs

Bulgur, a type of cracked wheat, has a great capacity for absorbing different flavors. You might have had it in tabbouleh, a Mediterranean salad with chopped parsley and tomato. It can also be eaten as a hot cereal with fresh or dried fruit. This recipe features bulgur as a savory accompaniment to vegetables. The fresh herbs add a depth of flavor that dried herbs do not. MAKES 6 SERVINGS | PER SERVING: 137 CALORIES, 5 G. TOTAL FAT (LESS THAN 1 G. SATURATED FAT), 21 G. CARBOHYDRATES, 4 G. PROTEIN, 5 G. DIETARY FIBER, 150 MG. SODIUM.

1	cup bulgur
1½	cups fat-free, reduced sodium chicken broth
2	tablespoons olive oil
1	cup diced red bell pepper
¼	cup minced shallots
1	tablespoon minced garlic
2	tablespoons minced chives
½	tablespoon minced fresh basil leaves
½	tablespoon minced fresh oregano leaves
	Salt and freshly ground black pepper

■ Put the bulgur in a medium bowl. Bring the chicken broth to a boil, pour it over the bulgur, and let it stand for 30 minutes, until broth is absorbed. A few minutes before the bulgur is done, heat the olive oil over medium-high heat in a medium nonstick skillet and sauté the bell pepper and shallots for 4 minutes. Add the garlic and herbs and sauté for 1 more minute. Pour the mixture over the bulgur. Mix well, season to taste with salt and pepper, and serve.

quick kasha pilaf

Kasha is the Russian term for whole roasted buckwheat kernels, or "groats," which have a toasted, nutty flavor. A longtime staple in the diets of Poles and other Eastern Europeans, kasha is often prepared as a holiday dish with bow tie pasta. Although it is usually made with an egg, this step can be eliminated, as it is here. In this recipe, the wonderful taste of kasha is enhanced by vegetables and chicken broth. Once considered exotic, kasha is now readily available in supermarkets. MAKES 4 SERVINGS | PER SERVING: 107 CALORIES, 3 G. TOTAL FAT (LESS THAN 1 G. SATURATED FAT), 19 G. CARBOHYDRATES, 4 G. PROTEIN, 2 G. DIETARY FIBER, 305 MG. SODIUM.

2	teaspoons olive oil
1	small carrot, finely chopped
1	small onion, finely chopped
½	celery rib, finely chopped
½	cup kasha
2	cups fat-free, reduced sodium chicken or vegetable broth
	Salt and freshly ground black pepper
2	tablespoons chopped flat leaf parsley, for garnish

■ In a large, heavy pan or Dutch oven, heat the olive oil over medium-high heat. Add the carrot, onion, and celery and sauté for about 4 minutes, stirring occasionally, until the vegetables are soft. Add the kasha to the sautéed vegetables and stir for 1 to 2 minutes, until the kasha is fragrant and looks slightly darker in color. Pour the broth into the kasha, cover the pot tightly, and bring to a boil. Reduce the heat and simmer, covered, for about 10 minutes, until all of the liquid is absorbed. Turn the heat off and let the pilaf sit for 5 minutes. Fluff the pilaf with a fork, season to taste with salt and pepper, and sprinkle with chopped parsley. Serve immediately.

bulgur pilaf with red peppers and herbs

quinoa with dried cranberries, apricots, and pecans

quinoa with dried cranberries, apricots, and pecans

Quinoa (pronounced "*keen*-wah") may be a delicate grain, but it is one of the best sources of plant protein. It also provides iron, potassium, folate, and several minerals. It is important to rinse quinoa very thoroughly before cooking it to avoid a bitter flavor. Sweetened with dried fruits, thyme, and pecans, as in this recipe, quinoa can add a unique twist to your New American Plate. **MAKES 6 SERVINGS | PER SERVING: 177 CALORIES, 5 G. TOTAL FAT (LESS THAN 1 G. SATURATED FAT), 28 G. CARBOHYDRATES, 5 G. PROTEIN, 3 G. DIETARY FIBER, 156 MG. SODIUM.**

2 cups fat-free, reduced sodium chicken or vegetable broth or water

1 cup quinoa, thoroughly rinsed and drained

Pinch of salt (optional)

¼ cup dried cranberries

¼ cup diced dried apricots

2 tablespoons minced fresh thyme leaves

¼ cup finely chopped toasted pecans*

*Note: To toast the pecans, put them in a small skillet over medium-high heat and stir frequently for 2 to 3 minutes, until lightly browned. Immediately transfer the nuts to a small dish and cool.

■ In a medium saucepan, bring the broth to a boil. Add the quinoa and salt. Reduce heat to low, cover, and simmer for 12 to 15 minutes, until all the liquid is absorbed. Stir the cranberries, apricots, and thyme into the hot quinoa. Top with pecans and serve hot or cold.

quinoa pilaf with peas and sage

Quinoa is a delightful grain to use in a vegetable pilaf for a spring or summertime meal. You'll find that the volume of cooked quinoa increases about four times beyond its raw amount. Peas, bell peppers, and pine nuts add both substance and nutrients to this fluffy pilaf, which is laced with sage. **MAKES 8 SERVINGS | PER SERVING: 133 CALORIES, 4 G. TOTAL FAT (LESS THAN 1 G. SATURATED FAT), 20 G. CARBOHYDRATES, 5 G. PROTEIN, 3 G. DIETARY FIBER, 144 MG. SODIUM.**

1 cup quinoa, thoroughly rinsed and drained

2 cups fat-free, reduced sodium chicken or vegetable broth

1 tablespoon olive oil

½ cup diced onion

½ cup diced celery

½ cup diced green bell pepper

½ cup diced red bell pepper

1 cup frozen peas, thawed

½ teaspoon dried sage, or to taste

2 tablespoons pine nuts, toasted*

Salt and freshly ground black pepper

*Note: To toast the pine nuts, put them in a small skillet over medium heat, shaking or stirring frequently until lightly browned, about 2 to 3 minutes. Immediately transfer the nuts to a small dish and cool.

■ In a medium saucepan, combine the quinoa and broth and bring to a boil. Reduce the heat to low, cover, and simmer for about 12 to 15 minutes, until the broth is absorbed.

■ A few minutes before the quinoa is done, heat the olive oil over medium-high heat in a large nonstick skillet. Add the onion, celery, and bell peppers and sauté for 4 minutes. Stir in the peas and cook for 1 more minute. Stir in the cooked quinoa and mix well. Stir in the sage and pine nuts, season to taste with salt and pepper, and serve immediately.

millet with sautéed mushrooms and pumpkin seeds

In this dish, earthy mushrooms impart their rich taste to millet, a whole grain that is well suited for casseroles because of its soft texture. Pumpkin seeds add a delightful crunch. Be sure you eat millet soon after it is cooked, because the texture can solidify when it cools. Millet is a good alternative to wheat grains like bulgur and couscous. **MAKES 8 SERVINGS | PER SERVING: 147 CALORIES, 5 G. TOTAL FAT (LESS THAN 1 G. SATURATED FAT), 22 G. CARBOHYDRATES, 5 G. PROTEIN, 3 G. DIETARY FIBER, 234 MG. SODIUM.**

1 cup millet

Fat-free, reduced sodium chicken or vegetable broth

2 tablespoons olive or canola oil

8 ounces mushrooms, cleaned and sliced

½ cup diced onion

½ cup diced celery

1 tablespoon reduced sodium soy sauce

1 teaspoon Worcestershire sauce

Salt and freshly ground black pepper

¼ cup toasted pumpkin seeds*

2 tablespoons finely minced flat leaf parsley

*Note: To toast the pumpkin seeds, put them in a small skillet over medium-high heat and stir constantly for 2 to 3 minutes until lightly browned. Immediately transfer the pumpkin seeds to a small dish and cool.

■ Cook the millet according to the package instructions, using chicken broth instead of water. A few minutes before the millet is done, heat the olive oil over medium-high heat in a large nonstick skillet. Add the mushrooms, onion, celery, soy sauce, and Worcestershire sauce and cook for about 7 minutes, stirring constantly, until the mushrooms have released their liquid. Add the cooked millet to the vegetables in the skillet. Season to taste with salt and pepper. If the millet seems too dry or too thick, use a little extra broth to thin the mixture. Sprinkle with the pumpkin seeds and parsley and serve immediately.

angel hair pasta with sesame-peanut sauce

Most regular pasta is made from semolina, which has the nutritious germ and bran removed during milling. Whole wheat pasta retains these elements. Adapting your taste to whole wheat pasta instead of regular pasta can be easy with this tasty peanut sauce. It's simple to make, yet so flavorful that it's likely to become a favorite dish in your household. Seasoned rice vinegar can be found in an Asian grocery store or in large supermarkets. If it is unavailable, you can substitute white wine vinegar. You can make this dish spicier by adding more cayenne. **MAKES 4 SERVINGS | PER SERVING: 311 CALORIES, 10 G. TOTAL FAT (1 G. SATURATED FAT), 48 G. CARBOHYDRATES, 13 G. PROTEIN, 8 G. DIETARY FIBER, 204 MG. SODIUM.**

8 ounces whole wheat angel hair pasta

4 tablespoons smooth peanut butter

¼ cup fat-free, reduced sodium chicken broth

1 tablespoon reduced sodium soy sauce

2 large garlic cloves, peeled

1 tablespoon minced peeled fresh ginger

1 tablespoon seasoned rice vinegar

1 teaspoon toasted sesame oil

1 tablespoon evaporated fat-free milk, plus more as needed to thin sauce

Dash of cayenne or pinch of dried red pepper flakes (optional)

1 cup shredded or grated carrots, for garnish

½ cup thinly sliced scallions, trimmed, for garnish

2 tablespoons chopped peanuts, for garnish

■ Cook the pasta according to the package instructions. Meanwhile, in a blender or food processor, blend the peanut butter, broth, soy sauce, garlic, ginger, vinegar, sesame oil, milk, and cayenne until completely emulsified. When the pasta is done, drain it in a colander and return it to the hot pan. Add the peanut sauce and toss to coat. Garnish with carrots, scallions, and peanuts. Serve immediately.

fettuccine with figs and chiles

Impress your dinner guests with this unusual and sophisticated entrée. A rich, mellow sauce brings together fresh figs with whole wheat fettuccine. The figs add an earthy sweetness. Lemon and chiles give this sweetness an exciting edge. It takes strong flavor to bring out the best in whole wheat pasta, and this exquisite sauce does the job. **MAKES 6 SERVINGS | PER SERVING: 318 CALORIES, 7 G. TOTAL FAT (2 G. SATURATED FAT), 58 G. CARBOHYDRATES, 12 G. PROTEIN, 10 G. DIETARY FIBER, 98 MG. SODIUM.**

8 fresh black mission figs, rinsed, dried, and stems removed

2 dried chiles (use any medium-heat chile, such as ancho)

2 lemons

½ cup plain fat-free yogurt

12 ounces whole wheat fettuccine

2 tablespoons olive oil

Salt and freshly ground black pepper

¼ cup freshly grated Parmesan cheese

A few sprigs of fresh mint or flat leaf parsley, for garnish

■ Cut figs in quarters or eighths, depending on size. (About 1 to 2 cups, depending on size of figs.) Place figs cut-side up on a plate. Tear the chiles into small pieces, discarding the seeds and stems; measure about 1 tablespoon torn chiles to use in this recipe.* Sprinkle the chile pieces over the figs and set aside.

■ Grate the zest of both lemons and squeeze the juice of one lemon. Stir the lemon zest and juice into the yogurt and set it aside.

■ Cook the fettuccine in a large pot of boiling water until just tender, or al dente.

■ Meanwhile, in a large nonstick skillet over medium heat, heat the olive oil. Add the figs and sauté for about 3 minutes, stirring constantly. Add the chile and season to taste with salt and pepper. Continue to sauté for 1 minute. Remove the skillet from the heat.

■ Drain the fettuccine. Return to pot. Stir in the lemon and yogurt mixture and the Parmesan cheese. Transfer pasta to a serving platter and spoon the fig and chile mixture over the top. Garnish with the sprigs of mint or parsley and serve immediately.

*Note: Wear rubber gloves to handle chiles, and keep your hands away from your eyes.

whole wheat fettuccine with citrus sauce
Fruit can be used in more ways than most of us imagine. In this instance, it endows a sauce with flavor strong enough to stand up to whole wheat pasta. Butter and oil buffer the tartness, and vanilla adds another level of taste. Canola or olive oil is used to reduce the amount of saturated fat, and a small amount of cornstarch ensures that this healthier version of the sauce retains its appealing mouthfeel and appearance. Leftover sauce can be used on a 3-ounce serving of fish or poultry.

MAKES 8 SERVINGS | PER SERVING: 165 CALORIES, 6 G. FAT (2 G. SATURATED FAT), 25 G. CARBOHYDRATES, 5 G. PROTEIN, 4 G. DIETARY FIBER, 100 MG. SODIUM.

1 tablespoon canola oil

Pinch of salt

8 ounces whole wheat fettuccine

1 cup rich fish stock

½ tablespoon vanilla extract

2 tablespoons fresh lime juice, strained

¾ cup plus 1 tablespoon fresh orange juice, strained and separated

2 tablespoons grated orange zest

1 teaspoon grated lime zest

1 sprig fresh thyme, or 1 teaspoon dried

1½ teaspoons cornstarch

1½ tablespoons canola oil or extra-virgin olive oil

2 tablespoons cold butter

White pepper

4 sprigs fresh thyme, for garnish (optional)

■ Preheat oven to its lowest temperature and place a large, heat-proof bowl on an oven rack set in the middle of the oven. Heat a large pot of water over high heat with 1 tablespoon canola oil and a generous pinch of salt. Prepare the fettuccine according to the package directions until just tender, or al dente. Drain the fettuccine thoroughly. Transfer fettuccine to the warmed bowl and place in the oven until ready to combine with the sauce.

■ To prepare the sauce, place the stock in a medium saucepan. Add the vanilla. Bring to a boil, then immediately reduce heat to medium. Cook until reduced by half, about 7 to 8 minutes.

■ Stir in the lime juice and ¾ cup of orange juice, the zest, and the thyme. (If using dried thyme, first crumble it between your fingers until it is almost powdery.) Reheat the sauce until it comes to a boil, then immediately reduce heat to a simmer. Gently simmer 3 minutes. Meanwhile, in a small cup, mix the cornstarch into the remaining tablespoon of orange juice until well combined.

■ Reduce heat to low. Add the cornstarch mixture to the sauce and continue stirring until the sauce thickens slightly and becomes translucent. Remove the thyme sprig, if using, and whisk in the canola or olive oil. Whisk in the butter until it dissolves, about 1 to 2 minutes. Season to taste with pepper. The sauce should take on a satiny finish.

■ Return the sauce to medium-high heat. Add the hot fettuccine, shaking the pan to coat the noodles with the sauce. Serve immediately. Garnish each serving with a sprig of fresh thyme, if desired.

whole wheat pasta with zucchini, mushrooms, and basil

You may have heard of pasta primavera, which means "springtime pasta" in Italian. This is the pasta for summertime, with a colorful mélange of cancer-fighting garden vegetables. Fortified with portobello mushrooms and whole wheat pasta to satisfy your appetite, this entrée is topped off with a touch of balsamic vinegar, fresh basil, and parsley. Like brown rice, whole wheat pasta provides more fiber and nutrients than regular refined pasta. **MAKES 6 SERVINGS | PER SERVING: 255 CALORIES, 4 G. TOTAL FAT (LESS THAN 1 G. SATURATED FAT), 48 G. CARBOHYDRATES, 10 G. PROTEIN, 9 G. DIETARY FIBER, 208 MG. SODIUM.**

1 small yellow bell pepper, seeded and julienned

½ medium orange bell pepper, seeded and julienned

1 medium zucchini, julienned

1 medium carrot, peeled and julienned

½ cup finely chopped fresh basil, loosely packed

1 garlic clove, minced

1 teaspoon orange zest

1 tablespoon balsamic vinegar

1½ tablespoons canola oil

½ teaspoon salt, or to taste

Pinch of cayenne

12 ounces whole wheat linguine

2 large portobello mushrooms, cleaned

½ cup chopped flat leaf parsley, loosely packed, for garnish

■ Put the bell peppers, zucchini, and carrot in a medium bowl. Add the basil, garlic, orange zest, vinegar, oil, salt, and cayenne. Toss the ingredients well to combine. Set aside the mixture to marinate.

■ Cook the pasta according to the package instructions. Meanwhile, prepare the mushrooms. Remove stems and discard or save for later use. Cut the edges off each mushroom to make squares. Discard edges or save for later use. Halve each square. Slice away the brown undersides, including the gills, and discard. Then slice the mushrooms into long, thin strips and add them to the bowl with the marinated vegetables. Toss well, until the mushrooms are moist and start to soften.

■ Drain the pasta and divide it among 6 shallow bowls or plates. Top each serving with a quarter of the vegetables. Spoon the marinating liquid over the vegetables. Garnish with the parsley and serve.

whole wheat stuffing with cranberries and walnuts

This easy-to-prepare recipe adds health-boosting cranberries, walnuts, onion, and scallions to whole wheat stuffing. (Walnuts are one of the few plant sources of omega-3 fats.) Broth is used as an alternative to butter or margarine, and this stuffing tastes so good you won't miss the unhealthy fat. For food safety reasons, the stuffing should be cooked in the oven separately from the bird. This enables you to serve this stuffing with any kind of poultry, meat, or cold-weather vegetables, which means you don't have to save this recipe just for the holidays. MAKES 18 SERVINGS | PER SERVING: 175 CALORIES, 4 G. TOTAL FAT (LESS THAN 1 G. SATURATED FAT), 28 G. CARBOHYDRATES, 6 G. PROTEIN, 4 G. DIETARY FIBER, 293 MG. SODIUM.

1 loaf (24 ounces) day-old whole wheat bread, sliced

2 cups dried cranberries or mix of dried cranberries, cherries, and golden raisins

2 teaspoons canola oil

1 medium onion, finely chopped

1 bunch scallions, trimmed and finely chopped

2 teaspoons dried thyme, or to taste

½ cup chopped walnuts

¼ cup finely chopped flat leaf parsley, loosely packed

¼ cup chopped fresh chives

Salt and freshly ground black pepper

About 3 ½ cups hot fat-free, reduced sodium chicken broth

Canola oil spray

- Preheat the oven to 250 degrees.
- Arrange the bread slices on the oven rack and bake for about 30 minutes, until very dry but not brown. Shut the oven off and allow the bread to cool in the oven until it is easy to handle.
- Put the dried fruit in a large heat-proof bowl and cover with very hot tap water. Let it stand until the water is lukewarm. Drain and set the fruit aside.
- Remove the bread and preheat the oven to 325 degrees.
- In a medium nonstick skillet over medium-high heat, heat the canola oil until very hot. Add the onion and sauté for 7 to 8 minutes, until the onion is translucent and golden. Stir in the scallions and thyme. Transfer the mixture to the bowl containing the drained fruit.
- By hand, break the bread into coarse crumbs. Mix the crumbs with the dried fruit and sautéed onions. Mix in the walnuts, parsley, and chives. Season to taste with salt and pepper.
- Add enough hot broth, starting with 1 cup and adding ½ cup at a time as needed to make the mixture moist but not too wet. Gently toss the mixture to distribute the broth evenly. Taste and adjust the seasoning if necessary by adding salt, pepper, and thyme. If the mixture seems dry, add additional hot broth.
- Lightly coat a 13 × 9-inch baking pan with canola oil spray and transfer the stuffing to the pan. Lightly coat the dull side of a sheet of foil, large enough to seal the pan, with canola oil spray. Cover and seal the baking pan with the foil (shiny side out). Bake for about 1 hour. For a less moist stuffing with a slightly crisp top, remove the foil halfway through the baking time. Serve immediately or store, tightly covered, in the refrigerator for up to 2 days. Reheat the chilled stuffing before serving.

chestnut and dried fruit stuffing

In place of raw chestnuts, which take time to shell and cook, this recipe calls for commercially prepared and cooked chestnuts. They are sold vacuum-packed in jars and plastic pouches, as well as canned. Choose your favorite dried fruits to dress up this light side dish. **MAKES 9 SERVINGS | PER SERVING: 163 CALORIES, 4 G. TOTAL FAT (LESS THAN 1 G. SATURATED FAT), 29 G. CARBOHYDRATES, 3 G. PROTEIN, 2 G. DIETARY FIBER, 200 MG. SODIUM.**

Canola oil spray

4 cups cubed day-old whole wheat bread

2 tablespoons olive oil

1 celery rib, chopped

1 medium leek, white part only, rinsed well and chopped

1 medium onion, chopped

2 tablespoons chopped shallots

1 cup packaged cooked whole chestnuts, chopped coarsely

1 cup diced dried fruits (apples, pears, peaches, apricots, or a combination)

¼ teaspoon poultry seasoning, or to taste

1½ cups fat-free, reduced sodium chicken broth

Salt and freshly ground black pepper

■ Preheat oven to 350 degrees. Spray an 8-inch square baking dish with canola oil spray and set aside.

■ Put the bread cubes in a large bowl and set it aside. In a medium skillet, heat the olive oil over medium-high heat. Sauté the celery, leek, onion, and shallots for about 5 minutes, until soft.

■ Add the sautéed vegetables, chestnuts, dried fruits, and poultry seasoning to the bread crumbs. Pour in the broth and mix to combine all of the ingredients. Season to taste with salt and pepper.

■ Press the stuffing lightly into the prepared baking dish, cover, and bake for 15 minutes. Uncover and bake for 15 more minutes for a fluffy, crusty stuffing. Serve immediately or store, tightly covered, in the refrigerator for up to 2 days. Reheat the chilled stuffing before serving.

fish, poultry, and meat

Americans have had a long love affair with meat. Perhaps at this point it should be called a marriage, for meat—especially red meat—has never gone out of style, despite our ever-changing tastes. Barbecuing, or grilling, has grown far more popular since the old-fashioned cookout first took hold in American suburbs. Whether we're at home or in restaurants, meat seems to take the major share of the traditional American plate. Yet nutrition experts tell us that we eat far more meat than we need for the proper functioning of our brains and bodies.

By eating more meat, poultry, and fish than we need, we're eating less of the foods that protect us against chronic health problems. Although animal foods provide us with important nutrients, only plant-based foods offer the literally thousands of different phytochemicals that help us control our cholesterol, manage diabetes, and reduce our risk of stroke, cancer, and heart disease.

Because Americans need to eat proportionately less meat and more plant-based foods than we do (the healthful proportion is one-third meat to two-thirds plant foods), the New American Plate holds just 3 ounces of meat. A piece of cooked meat, poultry, or fish weighing 3 ounces looks roughly the size of a deck of playing cards.

That portion size may sound skimpy to you. It did, at first, to many of the members of the cookbook team. The fact that they most looked forward to the meat and dessert tastings was a signal to our recipe developers that creating satisfying meat dishes with only 3 ounces of meat per serving would

be a challenging exercise. Their success was clearly apparent at the tastings for the dishes they developed. The meat lovers on our cookbook team discovered that less can be more and that by focusing on taste rather than quantity, and using the enormous array of seasonings and herbs now available, it is possible to be satisfied with more healthful portions of meat.

As you look through the recipes in this chapter, keep in mind that all meats are not nutritionally equal. Among the three main types of animal protein—red meat, poultry, and fish—fish is the healthiest choice because it is the richest in important omega-3 fats. Because it has less saturated fat than red meat, poultry is the next best choice.

Whatever type of meat you choose, buy 4 ounces for each 3-ounce serving. The cooking process will eliminate the extra ounce. When preparing red meat or poultry for cooking, trim off as much visible fat as possible to eliminate unwanted saturated fat.

If you're grilling or using another high-heat cooking method, consider using a marinade first. Researchers have found that marinating meats for at least thirty minutes significantly reduces the amount of carcinogens that are produced when meat is cooked at high temperatures. Although scientists still don't understand how large a health consideration this risk is, erring on the side of caution is a good practice. You may want to consider marinades in any case, because of their culinary benefits. Marinades can help tenderize tougher cuts of meat, and they also provide extra flavor. The chapter Sauces, Dressings, and Marinades (page 107) contains several recipes for simple and delicious marinades.

A major advantage of using medium or low levels of heat during cooking is that doing so generally prevents red meat, poultry, and fish from drying out or toughening. Baking, braising, and steaming—either on the stove or in a microwave—are some of the techniques used to prepare the dishes in this chapter. You may want to consider adapting your current collection of meat recipes to these methods.

In this chapter you will find a wide range of techniques, styles, and seasonings for preparing red meat, poultry, and fish, representing influences from many ethnic cuisines. We hope they will inspire you to see how the meat dishes you currently enjoy can be adapted to a place on the New American Plate. For a taste of Morocco, try Chicken with Tomatoes, Honey, and Cinnamon (page 100). For seafood with a Mediterranean twist, try Baked Fish with Tomatoes, Spinach, and Olives (page 88) or Greek-Style Scallops (page 97). Among the dishes with Asian influences you will find Steamed Fish with Black Bean and Garlic Sauce (page 89) and Asian-Style Salmon with Sautéed Carrots and Leeks (page 90). American-style dishes include Cranberry Chicken (page 98), classic Cornish Hens with Orange Sauce (page 100), and a Cajun-style Spicy Tomato-Pepper Pot Roast (page 106). Regardless of their ethnicity or style, all the meat dishes offer a rich panoply of flavors and textures.

baked fish with tomatoes, spinach, and olives

Technically, these fish fillets are not baked, but steamed. It'll seem like you're baking them, though, because you don't use a steamer—just an oven rack. The fish is wrapped in foil and parchment and popped in the oven, where its natural moisture turns to steam and cooks the flesh until it's tender and juicy. Chefs call this method *en papillote,* but you'll call it easy, fast, and delicious. **MAKES 4 SERVINGS | PER SERVING: 136 CALORIES, 2 G. TOTAL FAT (LESS THAN 1 G. SATURATED FAT), 10 G. CARBOHYDRATES, 20 G. PROTEIN, 4 G. DIETARY FIBER, 176 MG. SODIUM.**

- 1 package (10 ounces) frozen chopped spinach, thawed
- 4 four-ounce white fish fillets (such as catfish or tilapia)
- 2 small tomatoes (plum tomatoes, if available), each cut into 8 slices
- 2 scallions, trimmed and thinly sliced
- 2 tablespoons sliced black olives
- 2 tablespoons orange juice concentrate, thawed

  Salt and freshly ground black pepper
- 8 thin slices of lemon

■ Preheat the oven to 400 degrees. Drain the spinach in a sieve, pressing out as much liquid as possible. Cut 4 pieces of aluminum foil and 4 pieces of parchment paper large enough to wrap the fillets in. Place the paper on top of the foil. Lay 1 fillet on each piece of paper. Top each fillet with 2 tablespoons of spinach, 4 slices of tomato, 1/4 of the scallions, and 1/2 tablespoon of olives. Drizzle 1/2 tablespoon of the orange juice concentrate over each fillet and season with salt and pepper. Top each fillet with 2 slices of lemon. Completely wrap the fish, sealing the edges of the foil. Place on a baking sheet and bake until the fish is opaque and flakes easily when tested with a fork, about 10 to 15 minutes. Cooking time will vary depending on the thickness of the fish. Cook fish about 10 minutes per inch of thickness. Serve immediately.

steamed fish with black bean and garlic sauce

Steaming is the gentlest way to cook. The moist vapor seals in flavor, juices, and nutrients. This recipe borrows heavily from Chinese cuisine, in which steaming figures prominently. An aromatic paste of spices and black bean and garlic sauce enlivens the delicate, flaky fish. You can find this sauce in some supermarkets and in Asian markets. Try this recipe alongside steamed brown rice, steamed broccoli, and the Asian-Style Stir-Fried Vegetables on page 17. **MAKES 4 SERVINGS | PER SERVING: 117 CALORIES, 5 G. TOTAL FAT (LESS THAN 1 G. SATURATED FAT), 2 G. CARBOHYDRATES, 16 G. PROTEIN, LESS THAN 1 G. DIETARY FIBER, 100 MG. SODIUM.**

2 teaspoons black bean and garlic sauce

¼ teaspoon Chinese five-spice powder (optional)

½ teaspoon grated peeled fresh ginger

1 tablespoon sesame oil, divided

¾ pound white fish fillet (such as halibut or cod), scallops, or peeled and deveined medium shrimp

2 scallions, trimmed, finely chopped, divided

¼ cup thinly shredded carrots, for garnish

■ In a cup, mash the bean sauce with the five-spice powder, ginger, and ½ tablespoon of the sesame oil. Rub into the surface of the fish and set aside on a heat-proof plate or baking dish just large enough to comfortably hold the fish. Set the fish aside to marinate for 10 to 20 minutes.

■ To steam the fish, place the plate with the fish in a steamer or on a steaming rack in a wok over about 2 inches of water.* (There must be enough space for the steam to circulate around the plate.) Sprinkle the fish with ½ of the scallions. Bring the water to a boil over high heat. Reduce the heat to a simmer, cover, and steam the fish for 5 to 10 minutes, until it flakes easily when tested with a fork. (Add water to the wok if needed.) Fish fillets are done when opaque throughout, but they continue to cook after they are removed from the heat source, so remove them just before they reach this stage. Scallops are done when they are opaque throughout; check with a fork to make sure they are very tender in the center, after about 4 to 5 minutes. Shrimp are done when they turn pink, in about 3 to 4 minutes.

■ Using two spatulas or large serving forks, carefully transfer the fish to a serving plate. Drizzle with the remaining sesame oil. Sprinkle with the remaining scallions and shredded carrots, and serve.

*Note: If you don't have a steamer, a steaming rack, or a wok, you can improvise a steamer using any large pot with a tight-fitting lid. The pot must be larger than the heat-proof plate, so that you can carefully lower the plate into the pot and so that steam can circulate. Set a wide empty food can, with labels and ends removed, in the pot to make a stable rack for the plate. Put about 2 inches of water into the pot. The plate should be 2 to 4 inches above the water when it boils. The fish can also be cooked on parchment paper placed in a bamboo steamer in a wok.

asian-style salmon with sautéed carrots and leeks

Chinese five-spice powder is a commercially available blend of cinnamon, cloves, fennel, star anise, and Szechuan pepper. (Sometimes ginger and cardamom are added.) The mix is aromatic and surprisingly mild. It is worth noting that when any kind of meat—even fish—is cooked using a high-heat method like broiling, potentially hazardous carcinogens are produced. The good news is that a piquant marinade like the one used in this recipe seems to dramatically reduce the production of these substances. Topped off with a carrot-leek mixture infused with the flavor of sesame, this dish pairs well with steamed cauliflower, Snow Peas with Cashews (page 34), or Quick Kasha Pilaf (page 74). This recipe calls for prepared Chinese-style mustard, which is available in Asian markets and the ethnic food section of many grocery stores. If you cannot find it, substitute any sharp mustard. **MAKES 4 SERVINGS | PER SERVING: 329 CALORIES, 17 G. TOTAL FAT (4 G. SATURATED FAT), 9 G. CARBOHYDRATES, 30 G. PROTEIN, 1 G. DIETARY FIBER, 738 MG. SODIUM.**

½ cup reduced sodium soy sauce, divided

¼ cup freshly squeezed lemon juice

1 tablespoon Chinese-style mustard

½ teaspoon Chinese five-spice powder

4 salmon fillets (4 ounces each), skinned
   Canola oil spray

1 tablespoon sesame seeds

2 small carrots, peeled and julienned

1 leek (white part only), rinsed well and julienned

1 cup fat-free, reduced sodium chicken or vegetable broth or water

1 teaspoon toasted sesame oil

■ In a small bowl, combine 1/4 cup of the soy sauce, the lemon juice, mustard, and five-spice powder. Put the salmon fillets in a shallow dish and brush the soy sauce mixture over both sides of the fish. Cover with plastic wrap and refrigerate for 30 minutes. Turn fillets, re-cover, and refrigerate for another 30 minutes.

■ Coat a medium skillet with canola oil spray and place over medium heat. Add the sesame seeds and sauté, stirring constantly, until golden, about 1 to 2 minutes. Transfer the sesame seeds to a small dish. In the same skillet, sauté the carrots and leeks until tender, about 5 minutes. Add the broth, the remaining 1/4 cup soy sauce, and the sesame oil. Bring to a boil, reduce heat, and simmer until no liquid remains, about 10 to 15 minutes.

■ Meanwhile, preheat the broiler.

■ Place the salmon on a heated broiler pan and broil, 4 inches from the heat, until the fish is just cooked through, about 10 minutes per inch thickness of fish. Salmon continues to cook once removed from heat. Spoon 1/4 of the leek mixture onto each of 4 plates. Arrange the salmon on top of the leek mixture and sprinkle with the sesame seeds. Serve immediately.

grilled ginger tuna Recent research has shown that marinating animal proteins—even briefly—before grilling can significantly cut down on the formation of carcinogens that results from exposing meat to smoke, direct flame, and intense heat. In this recipe the fresh tuna is dipped briefly in a spicy ginger-lime marinade before grilling, which pays off in both health protection and extra flavor. Interestingly, plant-based foods do not seem to form the potentially dangerous substances that concern health experts. So while the coals are hot, grill some of your favorite vegetables like zucchini, red bell peppers, and red onion. MAKES 4 SERVINGS | PER SERVING (DOES NOT INCLUDE SALSA): 180 CALORIES, 7 G. TOTAL FAT (2 G. SATURATED FAT), LESS THAN 1 G. CARBOHYDRATES, 26 G. PROTEIN, LESS THAN 1 G. DIETARY FIBER, 190 MG. SODIUM.

1 pound fresh tuna, boneless and skinless

1 teaspoon canola oil

1 teaspoon grated peeled fresh ginger

1 small jalapeño chile, seeded and minced,* or to taste

¼ teaspoon salt

Freshly ground black pepper

1 tablespoon freshly squeezed lime juice

Pineapple, Corn, and Mango Salsa (page 114) (optional)

*Note: Wear rubber gloves to handle fresh chiles, and keep your hands away from your eyes.

■ Prepare a barbecue grill to medium-high or preheat the broiler to high. Cut the tuna into 16 equal cubes and put in a bowl. Add the canola oil and toss fish to coat. Add the ginger, jalapeño, salt, a few grinds of pepper, and lime juice. Toss all of the ingredients to combine. Cover and refrigerate 20 to 30 minutes.

■ To grill, divide the tuna cubes evenly among 4 skewers. Grill for 4 to 5 minutes, turning the fish frequently, using tongs. The fish is done when it is just cooked through and no longer pink on the inside.

■ To broil, arrange the marinated fish in a shallow pan so the pieces do not touch. Place the fish 4 inches below the broiler for 3 minutes. Using tongs, turn each cube. Broil for 1 to 2 more minutes, until the fish is just cooked through and no longer pink on the inside. Serve immediately, with Pineapple, Corn, and Mango Salsa, if desired.

tilapia with sweet peppers

Delicate slivers of bright yellow, red, and green peppers bring an air of sophistication to this simple-to-prepare dish. If you don't like or can't find tilapia, this recipe works well with any kind of white fish. To fill the remaining two-thirds of your New American Plate, try Brussels Sprouts with Shallots and Nutmeg (page 22), Arugula Salad with Radicchio and Blue Cheese (page 52), or Curried Sweet Potato and Apple Pilaf (page 71). **MAKES 4 SERVINGS | PER SERVING: 161 CALORIES, 5 G. TOTAL FAT (LESS THAN 1 G. SATURATED FAT), 12 G. CARBOHYDRATES, 19 G. PROTEIN, 3 G. DIETARY FIBER, 271 MG. SODIUM.**

1 tablespoon olive oil

¼ cup chopped red onion

1 red bell pepper, seeded and julienned

1 yellow bell pepper, seeded and julienned

1 green bell pepper, seeded and julienned

2 garlic cloves, minced

1 can (14.5 ounces) "no salt added" whole tomatoes in juice, chopped and juice reserved

1 tablespoon Worcestershire sauce

1 tablespoon balsamic or red wine vinegar

¾ teaspoon dried basil

¼ teaspoon salt

Pinch of cayenne

4 four-ounce tilapia fillets or other white fish fillets, such as haddock or cod

■ In a large nonstick skillet or wok, heat the olive oil over medium heat until hot. Add the onion, peppers, and garlic. Sauté for about 5 minutes, stirring frequently, until the onions are translucent.

■ Add the chopped tomatoes, reserved tomato juice, Worcestershire sauce, vinegar, basil, salt, and cayenne and bring to a boil.

■ Add the fillets, spooning the tomato mixture over the fish. Reduce the heat to low, cover, and simmer for 5 to 8 minutes, until the fish is opaque and flakes easily when tested with a fork. Serve immediately.

shrimp curry with asparagus and snap peas

Brilliant colors and bold flavors combine in this simple shrimp dish. Here, as with all dishes on the New American Plate, the accent is on the fresh vegetables and seasonings, while the shrimp adds flavor and substance. Try this atop steamed brown rice and alongside Steamed Greens with Ginger and Water Chestnuts (page 30). **MAKES 4 SERVINGS | PER SERVING: 167 CALORIES, 5 G. TOTAL FAT (LESS THAN 1 G. SATURATED FAT), 10 G. CARBOHYDRATES, 20 G. PROTEIN, 2 G. DIETARY FIBER, 277 MG. SODIUM.**

- 1 tablespoon cornstarch
- 2 teaspoons curry powder
- ½ teaspoon sugar
- 1 tablespoon reduced sodium soy sauce
- ¾ cup fat-free, reduced sodium chicken broth
- 3 teaspoons canola or peanut oil, divided
- 8 asparagus stalks, tough ends trimmed, and cut into 1-inch pieces
- 1 red bell pepper, seeded and diced
- ¼ pound sugar snap peas, strings on both edges removed
- 2 teaspoons grated or minced peeled fresh ginger
- 1 large garlic clove, minced
- ¾ pound medium shrimp, peeled and deveined

■ In a small bowl, combine the cornstarch, curry powder, and sugar. Mix in the soy sauce and then the chicken broth. Set the mixture aside.

■ In a heavy skillet or wok, heat 1 teaspoon of the oil over high heat. Add the asparagus, red pepper, peas, ginger, and garlic. Stir-fry until the vegetables are bright in color, about 1 minute. Transfer them to a plate with a slotted spoon.

■ Heat the remaining 2 teaspoons of oil. Add the shrimp and stir-fry until they turn pink, about 1 minute. Return the vegetables to the skillet. Stir the sauce and then pour it into the skillet. Bring to a boil, reduce the heat, and simmer gently until the shrimp are white in the center, about 2 to 3 minutes. Serve immediately.

greek-style scallops

Olive oil, lemon juice, garlic, feta, and pine nuts are staples of classic Mediterranean cuisine that have now found their way into meals across the globe. Here, these pungent ingredients complement the slightly sweet meat of sea scallops. If desired, trim the large muscle from the sides of the scallops before cooking. Try serving this dish with brown rice, steamed carrots, and Broccoli with Scallion Dressing and Hazelnuts (page 20). MAKES 4 SERVINGS | PER SERVING: 196 CALORIES, 10 G. TOTAL FAT (2 G. SATURATED FAT), 13 G. CARBOHYDRATES, 14 G. PROTEIN, 2 G. DIETARY FIBER, 475 MG. SODIUM.

4 teaspoons olive oil, divided

1 pound sea scallops

1 cup chopped onion

1 cup sliced mushrooms (3 ounces)

2 large garlic cloves, minced

2 large tomatoes, seeded and chopped

2 teaspoons freshly squeezed lemon juice

¼ cup chopped flat leaf parsley, loosely packed

1 teaspoon chopped fresh oregano
   or ¼ teaspoon dried oregano

Salt and freshly ground black pepper

⅓ cup crumbled reduced fat feta cheese

2 tablespoons pine nuts, toasted*

*Note: To toast the pine nuts, put them in a small skillet over medium heat, shaking or stirring frequently until lightly browned, about 2 to 3 minutes. Immediately transfer the nuts to a small dish and cool.

■ In a large nonstick skillet, heat 2 teaspoons of the olive oil over medium-high heat. Add the scallops and cook, stirring often, for 5 to 6 minutes, until opaque throughout and tender in the center. Transfer the scallops and liquid from the skillet to a bowl; set aside. Cool the skillet slightly and then rinse under hot water and dry.

■ In the same skillet, heat the remaining 2 teaspoons of olive oil over medium-high heat. Add the onion and sauté, stirring often, for 2 minutes. Add the mushrooms and sauté, stirring often, for 3 to 5 minutes, until the onion is soft. Add the garlic and sauté, stirring, for 1 minute. Add the tomatoes, lemon juice, parsley, oregano, and salt and pepper to taste. Bring to a boil, reduce heat, and simmer, stirring occasionally, for 5 minutes. Stir in the scallops with their liquid and bring to a boil, stirring occasionally. Top with the feta cheese and pine nuts. Serve immediately.

cranberry chicken

There are many ways to liven up chicken breast, but serving it with a sweet and tangy cranberry relish is one of the easiest and most nutritious. Several different phytochemicals found in cranberries are now being studied for their antioxidant properties and have been linked to lower risk of chronic disease. If you can't find a commercially prepared cranberry relish, chutney, or sauce, try the simple Cranberry Chutney on page 118. MAKES 4 SERVINGS | PER SERVING: 347 CALORIES, 9 G. TOTAL FAT (1 G. SATURATED FAT), 49 G. CARBOHYDRATES, 21 G. PROTEIN, LESS THAN 1 G. DIETARY FIBER, 569 MG. SODIUM.

Canola oil spray

2 tablespoons extra-virgin olive oil

2 tablespoons Dijon mustard

½ teaspoon salt, or to taste

½ teaspoon freshly ground black pepper, or to taste

Four 3-ounce skinless, boneless chicken breast halves

¾ cup cranberry relish, chutney, or whole-berry sauce

1 tablespoon finely minced scallions, trimmed

1 tablespoon red wine vinegar

■ Preheat the oven to 375 degrees. Lightly coat an 11 × 7-inch baking pan with canola oil spray.

■ In a medium bowl, whisk together the oil, mustard, salt, and pepper. Transfer half the mixture to a small cup or bowl and set aside. Brush the remaining mixture on the chicken pieces, coating all sides. Discard any of this mixture not used on the chicken. Place the chicken in the prepared pan. Roast the chicken for 10 to 15 minutes on each side, until cooked through, turning once. Remove the chicken from the oven.

■ Meanwhile, in a microwave-safe bowl, whisk the cranberry relish, scallions, and vinegar with the reserved mustard mixture. Heat in a microwave oven on high for 30 seconds or until warm. Season to taste with salt and pepper. Spoon the warm sauce over the chicken and serve.

chicken with tomatoes, honey, and cinnamon

Subtle notes of cinnamon, honey, and ginger enliven this unpretentious chicken and tomato dish. Try it alongside Braised Collard Greens with Garlic and Shallots (page 30), Broccoli, Cherry Tomato, and Watercress Salad (page 54), and Brown Rice with Scallions and Fresh Herbs (page 72). **MAKES 4 SERVINGS | PER SERVING: 256 CALORIES, 9 G. TOTAL FAT (1 G. SATURATED FAT), 30 G. CARBOHYDRATES, 19 G. PROTEIN, 4 G. DIETARY FIBER, 362 MG. SODIUM.**

2 tablespoons olive oil

1 large onion, finely chopped

2 (1¼ pounds total) skinless chicken breasts with ribs, halved

½ cup water

2½ pounds ripe plum tomatoes, peeled, seeded, and chopped

¼ teaspoon ground turmeric

1 teaspoon ground cinnamon

1 teaspoon ground ginger

3 tablespoons honey

½ teaspoon salt, or to taste

■ In a Dutch oven or large, heavy pan, heat the olive oil over medium-high heat. Sauté the onion until golden, about 6 minutes. Remove the onion with a slotted spoon and transfer to a plate. Add the chicken and sauté, turning frequently, until browned on all sides, about 8 minutes. Transfer the chicken to the plate with the onions and set it aside.

■ Add the water to the pan and bring to a boil, scraping the bottom of the pan with a wooden spoon to loosen any browned bits of chicken. Add the tomatoes and cook over medium heat, stirring often, for about 8 minutes, until soft. Stir in the turmeric, cinnamon, ginger, honey, and salt. Return the chicken and onion to the pot, cover tightly, and gently simmer over low heat for about 50 minutes, until the chicken is very tender. Serve hot.

cornish hens with orange sauce

Cornish hens are ready-made for the New American Plate. Their small size keeps your meal's proportion of meat in check, allowing you to fill the rest of your plate with healthy plant-based options. In this recipe, an orange-lime marinade brings out the hens' natural flavor to the fullest and marries well with such recipes as Quinoa Pilaf with Peas and Sage (page 77), steamed kale, and Gingered Carrots with Golden Raisins and Lemon (page 25). **MAKES 4 SERVINGS | PER SERVING: 234 CALORIES, 5 G. TOTAL FAT (1 G. SATURATED FAT), 21 G. CARBOHYDRATES, 27 G. PROTEIN, 2 G. DIETARY FIBER, 108 MG. SODIUM.**

2 Cornish hens

Salt and freshly ground black pepper

4 tablespoons orange marmalade

1 teaspoon freshly squeezed lime juice

1 cup fat-free, reduced sodium chicken broth

2 sliced oranges, for garnish

■ Preheat the oven to 375 degrees.

■ Rinse the hens and trim any excess fat. Season the birds' cavities with salt and pepper. Place a rack in a shallow roasting pan and place the hens on the rack, breast side up. Set aside.

■ In a small bowl, mix together the orange marmalade, lime juice, and broth. Spoon ¼ of the marinade over the hens. Roast the hens, basting every 15 minutes with the remaining marinade, until done, about 1 hour 15 minutes. (The hens are done when the juices run clear when the thigh is pricked with a fork.) Remove from the oven and let the hens cool for 15 minutes.

■ Cut each hen in half lengthwise and place each half on an individual serving plate. Transfer any pan juices to a small microwave-safe cup and skim off the fat. Heat in a microwave oven and then pour over the birds. Garnish with orange slices and serve.

tarragon turkey breast

Tarragon is a fragrant herb with a taste reminiscent of anise. Despite its presence in many American spice racks, it is sometimes overlooked in favor of more familiar seasonings. Reach for this versatile herb when preparing poultry, salad, or tomato sauce. The delicate flavor of this marinated turkey breast is particularly good when matched with Tarragon-Mustard Sauce (page 111). For a modern twist on a classic Thanksgiving pairing, try this recipe with Cranberry Chutney (page 118). Use leftovers for sandwiches or in recipes such as Butternut Squash and Barley Casserole with Turkey (page 131) or Sweet Potato and Apple Stew with Turkey and Cranberries (page 138). For easy clean-up, line the roasting pan with aluminum foil. **MAKES 10 SERVINGS | PER SERVING: 220 CALORIES, 1 G. TOTAL FAT (LESS THAN 1 G. SATURATED FAT), 2 G. CARBOHYDRATES, 47 G. PROTEIN, LESS THAN 1 G. DIETARY FIBER, 97 MG. SODIUM.**

MARINADE

¼ cup chopped shallots

1 tablespoon chopped fresh tarragon or 1 teaspoon dried

1 teaspoon grated orange zest

⅛ teaspoon salt

Generous dash of freshly ground black pepper

1 cup freshly squeezed orange juice

1 cup fat-free, reduced sodium chicken broth

. . . .

1 turkey breast (about 5 pounds), with ribs

½ cup chopped flat leaf parsley, loosely packed

¼ cup chopped shallots

1 tablespoon finely chopped fresh tarragon or 1 teaspoon dried crumbled leaves

■ To prepare the marinade, combine the shallots, tarragon, orange zest, salt, pepper, orange juice, and broth in a small bowl.

■ With a paring knife, carefully loosen the skin from the turkey (but do not remove). Place the turkey in a 2-gallon sealable plastic bag or large cooking bag and pour in the marinade. Marinate the turkey in the refrigerator for 6 to 12 hours.

■ Preheat the oven to 325 degrees.

■ Drain the turkey and discard the marinade. Mix the parsley with the shallots and tarragon. Stuff the mixture under the turkey skin.

■ Place the turkey on a wire rack in a shallow roasting pan. Bake until the internal temperature of the turkey reaches 170 degrees on a meat thermometer inserted into the thickest part of the breast (not touching the bone), about 2 hours. Cool for 15 minutes. Remove the skin.

■ Slice and serve the turkey or refrigerate for later use.

chili burgers

People put all kinds of things on burgers, but it's what's in this New American Plate burger that makes it special: juicy sirloin and rich refried beans, seasoned with garlic, chili powder, and jalapeño. Be careful to mix with a light touch. If the meat gets compacted, it will toughen when cooked. Try these patties on whole wheat buns with sliced tomato, onion, and well-drained fresh salsa. Serve with a side of Southwestern Black Bean Salad with Barley (page 58) or deliciously light Fresh Corn Bisque (page 205). With a 3-ounce burger, you need the side dishes to fill the plate. **MAKES 4 SERVINGS | PER SERVING: 95 CALORIES, 3 G. TOTAL FAT (1 G. SATURATED FAT), 6 G. CARBOHYDRATES, 13 G. PROTEIN, 2 G. DIETARY FIBER, 444 MG. SODIUM.**

½ pound extra-lean ground sirloin

½ cup canned fat-free refried beans

2 tablespoons onion, finely chopped

1 garlic clove, minced

1 jalapeño chile, seeded and minced*

2 teaspoons chili powder

½ teaspoon salt

⅛ teaspoon freshly ground black pepper

Canola oil spray

*Note: Wear rubber gloves to handle fresh chiles, and keep your hands away from your eyes.

■ In a bowl, lightly mix together the meat and beans with a fork until well combined. Mix in the onion, garlic, jalapeño, chili powder, salt, and pepper. Gently form the mixture into four 4-inch patties.

■ Coat a large nonstick skillet with canola oil spray and place over medium heat. Cook the burgers, turning them once, about 5 to 7 minutes per side or until a meat thermometer inserted in their centers registers 160 degrees. The burgers crumble easily, so handle them carefully, using a wide spatula. Serve immediately.

lime and ginger pork loin

A tangy marinade tenderizes the pork and infuses it with bold flavor. You can achieve a healthy proportion of plant foods—and create a delicious, satisfying dinner—by filling the rest of your New American Plate with steamed carrots, Broccoli with Scallion Dressing and Hazelnuts (page 20), and Orange Rice Pilaf with Dried Fruit (page 72). **MAKES 4 SERVINGS | PER SERVING: 216 CALORIES, 7 G. TOTAL FAT (3 G. SATURATED FAT), 11 G. CARBOHYDRATES, 26 G. PROTEIN, LESS THAN 1 G. DIETARY FIBER, 117 MG. SODIUM.**

⅓ cup freshly squeezed lime juice

2 tablespoons honey

2 teaspoons Dijon mustard

1 teaspoon ground ginger

1 garlic clove, minced

1 pound center-cut boneless pork loin, trimmed of fat and cut in ½- to ¾-inch slices

■ In a shallow baking dish or pan, mix together the lime juice, honey, mustard, ginger, and garlic. Place the pork in the pan with the marinade and turn the slices once to coat. Cover the pan and marinate the pork in the refrigerator for 30 minutes.

■ Heat a nonstick skillet over medium-high heat for about 30 seconds. Remove the pork from the marinade (saving the marinade) and put the pork in the skillet. Lightly brown the meat for about 2 minutes per side. Pour the marinade over the pork, bring to a boil, cover, and reduce the heat to low. Simmer until the pork is done, about 5 to 6 minutes for 1/2-inch slices or 8 to 9 minutes for 3/4-inch slices. Be careful not to overcook. Pork should be cooked through with no pink showing at all.

■ Remove the meat from the skillet and arrange on a serving platter. Boil the marinade for 30 to 40 seconds and then pour it over the meat. Serve immediately.

chili burgers

spiced braised lamb with apricots and carrots

The sweet and tangy flavor of dried apricots complements the exotic spices in this fragrant lamb stew. Serve over brown rice or whole wheat couscous. Round out your New American Plate with Curried Cauliflower with Chickpeas and Green Peas (page 26) and some steamed green beans. **MAKES 4 SERVINGS | PER SERVING: 289 CALORIES, 9 G. TOTAL FAT (4 G. SATURATED FAT), 26 G. CARBOHYDRATES, 25 G. PROTEIN, 4 G. DIETARY FIBER, 422 MG. SODIUM.**

1 tablespoon chopped peeled fresh ginger

4 garlic cloves, chopped

1½ teaspoons paprika

1½ teaspoons ground cumin

1 teaspoon ground turmeric

½ teaspoon ground coriander

½ teaspoon ground cardamom

⅛ teaspoon dried red pepper flakes, or to taste

⅛ teaspoon ground cloves

Canola oil spray

1 pound lamb meat, preferably from the leg, trimmed of fat, cut into 1-inch cubes

2 teaspoons canola oil, divided

1¼ cups chopped onion

1 can (14.5 ounces) diced tomatoes in juice

⅓ cup chopped dried apricots

¼ teaspoon salt

½ cup water, plus additional as needed

2 carrots, peeled and cut into ½-inch slices

½ cup frozen peas, thawed

½ cup plain lowfat yogurt

1 tablespoon chopped fresh cilantro, or to taste

■ In a food processor or blender, combine the ginger and garlic. Process until the mixture is the consistency of a paste, scraping down the sides with a rubber spatula as needed. Set aside. In a small bowl, stir together the spices.

■ Lightly coat a large nonstick skillet with canola oil spray. Brown the lamb over medium-high heat, stirring often, about 5 minutes. Transfer the lamb to a plate.

■ In a large pot, heat 1 teaspoon of the canola oil over medium-high heat. Add the onion and sauté, stirring, for 4 minutes. Add the remaining canola oil and the garlic-ginger paste and cook, stirring, for 1 minute. Reduce the heat to medium. Add the spice mixture and cook, stirring, for 1 minute.

■ With a slotted spoon, transfer the lamb to the pot. Add the tomatoes with juice, apricots, salt, and ½ cup water. Bring the mixture to a boil and reduce the heat. Cover and simmer for 25 minutes, stirring occasionally. Add the carrots, cover, and simmer for 15 to 25 minutes, stirring occasionally, until the meat and carrots are tender. Add water as needed if the mixture seems too dry.

■ Stir in the peas. Cover and cook for 2 minutes. Add the yogurt and cilantro and cook, stirring often, about 1 minute longer. Serve immediately.

spicy tomato-pepper pot roast
We've increased the proportion of vegetables to meat to bring this spicy, Cajun-style pot roast closer in line with foods that belong on the New American Plate. To achieve a meal that packs an even bigger phytochemical punch, serve it with Brown Rice with Scallions and Fresh Herbs (page 72), Roasted Asparagus with Garlic (page 19), and steamed peas. Leftovers of this pot roast make delicious sandwiches. MAKES 8 SERVINGS | PER SERVING: 200 CALORIES, 5 G. TOTAL FAT (2 G. SATURATED FAT), 8 G. CARBOHYDRATES, 28 G. PROTEIN, 2 G. DIETARY FIBER, 239 MG. SODIUM.

2 pounds top round of beef (about 1½ inches thick) in one piece, trimmed of fat

2 teaspoons olive oil

1¼ cups chopped onion

½ cup chopped celery

1 cup coarsely chopped red bell pepper

¾ cup coarsely chopped green bell pepper

2 large garlic cloves, minced

1 teaspoon paprika

⅛ teaspoon freshly ground black pepper, or to taste

¼ teaspoon salt, or to taste

1 can (14.5 ounces) diced tomatoes in juice

⅓ cup chopped flat leaf parsley, loosely packed

3 tablespoons tomato paste

1 tablespoon packed light brown sugar (optional)

1 tablespoon chopped fresh thyme or 1 teaspoon dried thyme

2 teaspoons Worcestershire sauce

¼ teaspoon hot pepper sauce, or to taste

1 bay leaf

⅓ pound fresh okra, trimmed and sliced into ½-inch pieces (optional)

■ Preheat the oven to 325 degrees.

■ In a large nonstick skillet over medium-high heat, brown the meat on all sides, about 3 to 4 minutes per side. Transfer the meat to a plate and allow the skillet to cool slightly. Rinse the skillet under hot water and dry. In the same skillet, heat the olive oil over medium-high heat. Add the onion and celery and sauté, stirring often, for 2 minutes. Add the red and green bell pepper and sauté, stirring often, for 5 minutes, until soft. Add the garlic, paprika, black pepper, and salt and sauté for 1 minute. Remove the skillet from the heat. Stir in the tomatoes with juice, parsley, tomato paste, brown sugar, thyme, Worcestershire sauce, hot pepper sauce, and bay leaf.

■ Pour ½ of the sauce into a 13 × 9-inch baking dish. Place the meat in the dish and pour the remaining sauce over the top. Cover the dish with two layers of aluminum foil and press the edges to seal. Bake for 1½ hours. Remove from the oven and remove the foil carefully (the steam trapped inside will be extremely hot). Set the foil aside. Cool the pot roast slightly and transfer it to a cutting board. Slice the meat across the grain. Place the sliced meat back in the baking dish and top it with okra, if using. Spoon sauce over the top. With cooking mitts, carefully cover the baking dish with the foil and press the edges to seal. Bake for 30 minutes, until the meat and okra are tender. Remove the bay leaf before serving.

sauces, dressings, and marinades

Most of the time, "accessories" like sauces, salsas, dressings, marinades, and chutneys get little, if any, thought. Yet often it is these little things that make the difference between an ordinary meal and one that makes us sit up and pay attention. So this is the chapter to turn to when you want to do something "extra" to give your food a fresh look. When company suddenly calls, this is the chapter that will help you turn the staples you have on hand into festive dishes. And this is the chapter that will inspire you to try your own variations on the theme of sauces and other add-on touches that maximize both enjoyment and health benefits.

You will find yourself turning to this chapter for a variety of other purposes, of course. Marinades are important flavor enhancers for many foods, but they also have an important health feature when used with meat, poultry, or fish. When those foods are cooked at high temperatures, carcinogens are formed, but the use of a marinade before cooking can significantly reduce that risk, according to most researchers.

Vegetables often seem to need something to give them a little excitement. Sometimes a vegetable is overly familiar ("carrots, *again?*"). Sometimes it may be unfamiliar or unpopular, but you want to serve it because it's rich in phytochemicals other vegetables don't have. But pair these vegetables—Brussels sprouts, for example, or bitter salad greens like arugula or mâche—with a flavorful and rich-tasting sauce or salad dressing, and you've made the dull or suspicious worthy of heightened anticipation. Asian-Style Peanut Sauce (page 110) adds exotic allure to simply cooked broccoli or Brussels sprouts,

and Hoisin Vinaigrette (page 121) can turn any vegetable into a newfound favorite.

If you have long relied on store-bought versions of salsas, dressings, and chutneys, or on "instant mix" versions of sauces and marinades, you may not readily imagine the rewards of trying one of the homemade versions in this chapter. But if you give some of these recipes a try, you will find that not even a "gourmet" commercial product can surpass its freshly made counterpart. Think of the recipes in this chapter as flavor *enhancers* that bring out the best of the foods they are paired with, rather than masking them. Try, for example, Strawberry-Almond Chutney (page 116) or Cranberry Chutney (page 118) to add zest—and some healthful components—to a simple main dish. Other chutneys, like Sweet Curried Tomato Chutney (page 117), do double duty as toppings for vegetables with a strong character, like Brussels sprouts or cabbage.

Salsas and dressings are two other types of condiments usually bought in bottles for convenience. But the commercially processed products often contain too much sugar or fat and too few healthful benefits. On the other hand, Pineapple, Corn, and Mango Salsa (page 114), for example, is fresh and delicious and offers a cornucopia of health-boosting ingredients as well as full and zesty flavor.

Some of the marinades in this chapter work equally well as dressings. Many of the dressings and vinaigrettes can be served as sauces for vegetables (especially those with strong flavors), or drizzled over grilled or sautéed poultry or fish to add pizzazz. The recipes that follow are all multitaskers that can easily change roles.

roasted red pepper sauce
This sauce is fabulous on seafood of any kind. It can also be used on pasta, tossed with black or green olives. The red peppers give it a beautiful color and a wealth of vitamins A and C.

MAKES 10 SERVINGS | PER SERVING: 14 CALORIES, LESS THAN 1 G. TOTAL FAT (LESS THAN 1 G. SATURATED FAT), 2 G. CARBOHYDRATES, LESS THAN 1 G. PROTEIN, LESS THAN 1 G. DIETARY FIBER, 131 MG. SODIUM.

½ large yellow onion, cut into 8 or 10 pieces

1 teaspoon extra-virgin olive oil

1 jar (12 ounces) roasted red bell peppers, drained and chopped

1 tablespoon tomato paste

1 cup fat-free, reduced sodium vegetable broth

1 teaspoon balsamic vinegar

¼ teaspoon salt (optional)

½ teaspoon dried oregano (optional)

1 tablespoon minced fresh basil or flat leaf parsley (optional)

■ In a covered microwave-safe container, combine the onion and olive oil. Microwave on high (100% power) for 2 to 3 minutes, until the onion is very soft, stirring once after cooking 1 minute. In a blender or food processor, combine the cooked onion, bell peppers, tomato paste, broth, and vinegar and blend until smooth. Pour the mixture into a saucepan. Add the salt and oregano to taste. Heat the mixture to a low boil and cook for about 2 minutes. Just before serving, stir in the basil. Store in a covered container in the refrigerator.

mushroom sauce
You can use this versatile sauce with eggs, grains, meats, roasted vegetables, and tofu. The beef broth intensifies the earthy flavor of the mushrooms, and the mustard adds a high note. This is another sauce that adds strong taste without adding fat. MAKES 10 SERVINGS | PER SERVING: 18 CALORIES, 1 G. TOTAL FAT (LESS THAN 1 G. SATURATED FAT), 2 G. CARBOHYDRATES, 1 G. PROTEIN, LESS THAN 1 G. DIETARY FIBER, 56 MG. SODIUM.

2 teaspoons olive oil, divided

1 garlic clove, minced

1 shallot, minced

8 ounces mushrooms, cleaned and sliced

1 cup fat-free, reduced sodium beef broth

½ teaspoon dried thyme

1 teaspoon Dijon mustard

1 tablespoon chopped flat leaf parsley

Freshly ground black pepper

■ In a medium skillet, heat 1 teaspoon of the olive oil over medium-high heat. Add the garlic and shallot and sauté, stirring constantly, for about 1 minute, until lightly browned. Add the mushrooms and cook, stirring, for about 5 to 6 minutes, or until the mushrooms are browned and their water has completely evaporated. Add the broth, thyme, and mustard. Bring to a boil and cook for about 8 minutes, until the liquid is reduced by about half. Remove the skillet from the heat.

■ Using a food processor or blender, process about 3 tablespoons of the mushrooms, adding only enough cooking liquid to make a thick paste. Return the puréed mushrooms to the skillet and place it over medium-high heat. When the sauce returns to a boil, stir in the parsley, the remaining 1 teaspoon of olive oil, and pepper to taste. Serve immediately or refrigerate and reheat just before serving.

chunky tomato-vegetable sauce

A weekend afternoon is the perfect time to prepare this easy sauce and let it simmer, giving off a mouthwatering aroma. It's chock-full of beta-carotene from carrots as well as lycopene from cooked tomatoes. This recipe makes 16 servings, so freeze what you don't use soon after cooking. MAKES 16 SERVINGS | PER SERVING: 51 CALORIES, 1 G. TOTAL FAT (LESS THAN 1 G. SATURATED FAT), 8 G. CARBOHYDRATES, 2 G. PROTEIN, 2 G. DIETARY FIBER, 346 MG. SODIUM.

1 tablespoon olive oil

1 medium onion, chopped

3 garlic cloves, minced

1 large green bell pepper, seeded and chopped

1½ cups grated carrots

8 ounces mushrooms, cleaned and sliced

2 cans (28 ounces each) whole peeled tomatoes in juice

1 can (15 ounces) tomato sauce

2 teaspoons dried basil, or to taste

1 teaspoon dried oregano, or to taste

Salt and freshly ground black pepper

■ In a large saucepan, heat the olive oil over medium heat. Add the onion and garlic and sauté, stirring often, for 3 minutes. Add the bell pepper, carrots, and mushrooms and sauté, stirring often, for 10 minutes or until the vegetables are tender. Add the tomatoes and juice and the tomato sauce. Season with the basil, oregano, and salt and pepper to taste. With a large spoon or potato masher, break up the tomatoes. Bring the sauce to a boil, reduce heat to low, and simmer for 2 hours, stirring occasionally. Don't cover tightly, but do use a splatter screen or partially cover the sauce with a lid. Adjust the seasonings to taste before serving.

cucumber-yogurt sauce with dill

This cooling sauce goes well with Falafel-Style Chickpea Patties (page 191), grilled salmon, or vegetables. Cucumbers are a natural companion to yogurt, as is fresh dill, which is far superior in flavor to the dried form. MAKES 8 SERVINGS | PER SERVING: 47 CALORIES, 3 G. TOTAL FAT (LESS THAN 1 G. SATURATED FAT), 3 G. CARBOHYDRATES, 2 G. PROTEIN, LESS THAN 1 G. DIETARY FIBER, 91 MG. SODIUM.

¾ cup plain nonfat yogurt

⅓ cup lowfat mayonnaise

½ cup seeded and coarsely chopped peeled cucumbers

¼ cup chopped fresh dill or 1 tablespoon dried dill

1½ teaspoons grated lemon zest

Salt and freshly ground black pepper to taste

■ In a medium bowl, whisk together all of the ingredients. Cover and refrigerate for at least 1 hour before serving. The sauce can be made up to 2 days in advance. Stir well before using.

asian-style peanut sauce

Peanut sauce is wonderful when tossed with noodles and vegetables or served on the side with satay, the Southeast Asian appetizer of meat or poultry cooked on small skewers. A little of this sauce goes a long way. Just a bit will enliven cooked whole grains such as quinoa, bulgur, or brown rice. Mix some with blanched vegetables. Spread a thin layer on chicken during the last 20 minutes of roasting. Marinate chicken and meat in the sauce for 2 to 8 hours and marinate fish for 30 minutes to 1 hour. This sauce will keep in the refrigerator for 5 days. **MAKES ABOUT 28 SERVINGS | PER SERVING: 29 CALORIES, 2 G. TOTAL FAT (LESS THAN 1 G. SATURATED FAT), 1 G. CARBOHYDRATES, 1 G. PROTEIN, 0 G. DIETARY FIBER, 75 MG. SODIUM.**

½ cup fat-free, reduced sodium chicken or vegetable broth

½ cup creamy peanut butter

2 tablespoons reduced sodium soy sauce

2 teaspoons minced garlic, or to taste

3 tablespoons rice vinegar

2 teaspoons sugar

¼ cup finely minced fresh cilantro (optional), loosely packed

½ teaspoon cayenne, or to taste

■ In a small saucepan over high heat, bring the broth to a boil and then immediately remove it from the heat.

■ In a blender, combine the hot broth, peanut butter, soy sauce, and garlic. Blend the mixture until smooth. Add the vinegar and sugar and blend again until smooth. Transfer the mixture to a bowl and stir in the cilantro, if using. Season to taste with the cayenne.

■ If using as a sauce, let the mixture stand at room temperature for 1 hour or cover and refrigerate for up to 1 day to allow the flavors to fully develop. Before serving, heat the sauce over medium heat until hot. Transfer to a pitcher and drizzle 2 teaspoons of the sauce in the center of each plate. Place a piece of cooked fish, chicken, or meat on top and drizzle 1 teaspoon of the sauce over the top.

■ If using as a marinade, place the mixture in a shallow, wide pan and add the fish, chicken, or meat, turning the pieces so that all of the sides are coated. When the meat has marinated, discard the marinade; used marinade cannot be used as a sauce for food safety reasons. Cook meat according to recipe directions, being careful not to char.

pear sauce

This easily prepared sauce goes well with Gingerbread (page 253) and with pork, chicken, or turkey dishes. Pears provide dietary fiber—a bit more than apples of equal size. **MAKES 10 SERVINGS | PER SERVING: 42 CALORIES, 1 G. TOTAL FAT (0 G. SATURATED FAT), 10 G. CARBOHYDRATES, LESS THAN 1 G. PROTEIN, 2 G. DIETARY FIBER, 4 MG. SODIUM.**

2 cans (15 ounces each) pears in their own juice

1 teaspoon ground cinnamon

¼ teaspoon ground ginger

⅛ teaspoon ground nutmeg

■ Drain the pears, reserving the juice. In a blender or food processor, purée the pears with the spices, adding reserved juice, as needed, to produce the consistency of applesauce. Serve warm. The sauce can be made in advance and stored up to 2 days in the refrigerator. To reheat, stir and heat on low in the microwave until the sauce is warm.

curried fruit sauce

This sauce is dense in flavor as well as in consistency. Its blend of sweet, earthy, and hot elements stands up to strong-tasting foods. The banana gives it a rich texture you won't find in other sauces. You can serve this sauce with lamb, chicken, shrimp, fish, tofu, or mixed vegetables. **MAKES 16 SERVINGS | PER SERVING: 30 CALORIES, 1 G. TOTAL FAT (LESS THAN 1 G. SATURATED FAT), 5 G. CARBOHYDRATES, 1 G. PROTEIN, LESS THAN 1 G. DIETARY FIBER, 39 MG. SODIUM.**

1 tablespoon olive oil

2 large shallots, finely chopped

½ cup thinly sliced leek, well rinsed (white part only)

⅔ cup finely chopped celery

2 cloves garlic, minced

2½ tablespoons curry powder

1 medium sweet apple (such as Fuji or Gala), peeled, cored, and diced

1 medium banana, diced

1 tablespoon tomato paste

1 cup fat-free, reduced sodium chicken or vegetable broth

¼ cup evaporated fat-free milk

Salt and freshly ground black pepper

■ In a nonstick skillet, heat the olive oil over medium-high heat. Sauté the shallots, leek, celery, and garlic, stirring often, for 5 minutes. Add the curry powder, apple, and banana and continue to sauté, stirring often, for another 5 minutes. Stir in the tomato paste and broth, bring to a boil, reduce heat to low, and simmer for 10 minutes. Remove from heat and allow to cool slightly. In a blender or food processor, purée the sauce in batches. Return the sauce to the skillet and place over medium heat. Add the milk and stir until the sauce is hot. Season to taste with salt and pepper. Serve immediately. The sauce can be stored in the refrigerator up to 3 days and reheated.

tarragon-mustard sauce

You'll love this smooth sauce drizzled over a green salad, vegetables, sliced roast chicken, or Tarragon Turkey Breast (page 101). It can also be used in a turkey or chicken salad with halved red grapes as a sweet contrast or a few slivered almonds for crunch. It would also work well as a dip for raw vegetables at your next party. **MAKES 13 SERVINGS | PER SERVING: 23 CALORIES, 2 G. TOTAL FAT (LESS THAN 1 G. SATURATED FAT), 1 G. CARBOHYDRATES, 1 G. PROTEIN, LESS THAN 1 G. DIETARY FIBER, 54 MG. SODIUM.**

½ cup lowfat sour cream

2 tablespoons lowfat mayonnaise

1 tablespoon Dijon mustard

½ teaspoon minced fresh tarragon or ¼ teaspoon dried tarragon

3 tablespoons fat-free milk

⅛ teaspoon ground turmeric

Pinch of cayenne

Salt to taste

■ In a small bowl, combine all of the ingredients. Blend vigorously with a wire whisk. Store in a covered container in the refrigerator for 2 to 3 days.

cilantro sauce

cilantro sauce

Cilantro, also known as coriander or Chinese parsley, is a dainty plant that packs a powerful aroma and flavor. It is rich in coriandrol, which researchers believe may help prevent cancer. You can serve it with baked white fish, steamed vegetables, or whole grains. **MAKES 6 SERVINGS | PER SERVING: 42 CALORIES, 2 G. TOTAL FAT (LESS THAN 1 G. SATURATED FAT), 5 G. CARBOHYDRATES, 1 G. PROTEIN, 1 G. DIETARY FIBER, 149 MG. SODIUM.**

1 tablespoon olive oil

1 medium onion, chopped

2 celery ribs, chopped

2 medium carrots, peeled and chopped

1 teaspoon minced peeled fresh ginger

1 can (14.5 ounces) fat-free, reduced sodium chicken broth

Salt and freshly ground black pepper

½ cup chopped fresh cilantro leaves, loosely packed

■ In a nonstick skillet, heat the olive oil over medium-high heat. Add the onion, celery, carrots, and ginger and sauté for 5 minutes, until the onion is translucent. Add the chicken broth, bring to a boil, reduce heat to low, and simmer, partially covered, for about 10 minutes, until the vegetables are tender. Season to taste with salt and pepper. In a blender or food processor, purée the mixture until smooth. Stir in the cilantro. Serve warm. The sauce can be stored up to 3 days in the refrigerator.

roasted garlic and shallot sauce

Roasting garlic and shallots makes them soft and spreadable, as well as bringing out their sweetness and making them milder to the taste. Garlic and shallots offer protective allyl sulfides. Low in fat, this sauce is high in flavor. **MAKES 10 SERVINGS | PER SERVING: 30 CALORIES, 2 G. TOTAL FAT (LESS THAN 1 G. SATURATED FAT), 3 G. CARBOHYDRATES, LESS THAN 1 G. PROTEIN, LESS THAN 1 G. DIETARY FIBER, 153 MG. SODIUM.**

15 large peeled garlic cloves or 1 unpeeled garlic head

2 large shallots, skins left on

Olive oil spray or canola oil spray

1 cup fat-free, reduced sodium chicken broth, divided

1 tablespoon reduced sodium soy sauce

1 tablespoon canola oil

2 teaspoons cornstarch

¼ teaspoon salt (optional)

Freshly ground black pepper (optional)

½ teaspoon dried tarragon or marjoram

■ Preheat the oven to 400 degrees.

■ In a small baking dish, combine the garlic with the shallots and coat with the olive oil spray. Bake for 25 to 30 minutes, until the garlic cloves are light brown and the shallots are soft when squeezed. Remove the garlic cloves and shallots from the pan to cool. If using the garlic head, remove the shallots but continue to roast the garlic for 15 more minutes, until the cloves are soft when squeezed.

■ Remove and discard the skins from the shallots. If using the whole garlic head, cut it in half horizontally and squeeze the cut edges together to push the garlic out. In a food processor or blender, combine the shallots, garlic, ½ cup of the chicken broth, and the soy sauce. Process the mixture until smooth. Add the remaining chicken broth and continue processing.

■ In a small saucepan, heat the canola oil over medium heat. Whisk in the cornstarch. When the cornstarch is well blended in and the oil is bubbling slightly, pour in the garlic-shallot mixture. Bring to a low boil and cook for 1 to 2 minutes, stirring occasionally, until thickened. Add the salt, pepper to taste, and tarragon. Serve immediately over chicken, fish, or steamed vegetables. Store in a covered container in the refrigerator for 2 to 3 days.

five-pepper salsa

A pepper lover's dream come true, this colorful salsa gives a spicy Southwestern kick to vegetable, bean, or meat dishes. Red bell peppers provide 14 times as much beta-carotene as the less-ripe green variety. **MAKES 6 SERVINGS | PER SERVING: 100 CALORIES, 9 G. TOTAL FAT (1 G. SATURATED FAT), 4 G. CARBOHYDRATES, LESS THAN 1 G. PROTEIN, 1 G. DIETARY FIBER, 2 MG. SODIUM.**

½ cup diced red bell pepper

½ cup diced green bell pepper

½ cup diced yellow bell pepper

½ cup diced orange bell pepper

½ medium red onion, diced

½ jalapeño chile, seeded and diced*

1 garlic clove, finely minced

4 tablespoons extra-virgin olive oil

2 tablespoons red wine vinegar

¼ cup minced fresh cilantro, loosely packed

Salt to taste

*Note: Wear rubber gloves to handle fresh chiles, and keep your hands away from your eyes.

■ In a medium bowl, mix all of the ingredients. Refrigerate for at least 1 hour before serving to allow the flavors to meld.

pineapple, corn, and mango salsa

Tropical fruits are married here to corn, onions, and tomatoes to make a tangy salsa to accompany grilled fish, chicken, or tofu. Mango's vitamins A, C, and E and pineapple's vitamin C work with phytochemicals such as red onion's organosulphur compounds and tomato's lycopene to protect health. Even the parsley contains flavones, a type of phytochemical. **MAKES 10 SERVINGS | PER SERVING: 31 CALORIES, LESS THAN 1 G. TOTAL FAT (LESS THAN 1 G. SATURATED FAT), 8 G. CARBOHYDRATES, LESS THAN 1 G. PROTEIN, 1 G. DIETARY FIBER, 5 MG. SODIUM.**

1 can (8 ounces) crushed pineapple in juice, drained

½ medium mango, peeled and diced*

½ cup frozen corn, thawed

½ cup chopped fresh tomato

¼ cup minced flat leaf parsley, loosely packed

3 tablespoons minced red onion

Salt to taste

Pinch of cayenne, or to taste

Pinch of cumin, or to taste

■ In a medium bowl, mix the pineapple, mango, corn, tomato, parsley, and onion. Season to taste with the salt, cayenne, and cumin. Store in a covered container in the refrigerator for 1 to 2 days.

*Note: To cube a mango easily, hold the fruit vertically, small end up, on a cutting board and slice twice from top to bottom, cutting as close as possible to each side of the flat pit. Score through the fleshy side of each half both lengthwise and crosswise without cutting through the skin. Hold each half fleshy side up and press the skin up in the center, so it turns inside out. Slice the cubes of flesh away from the skin. Trim any remaining flesh from the pit.

five-pepper salsa

strawberry-almond chutney

This chutney unlocks strawberries' full potential to please. It starts out sweet, but the mild curry flavor, white wine vinegar, and ginger keep it from being cloying and turn it into a fitting—and nutritious—accompaniment for fish, poultry, or meat. The almonds add crunch and another subtle flavor to this unusual condiment. Strawberries are rich sources of vitamin C, dietary fiber, and the phytochemical ellagic acid. MAKES 28 SERVINGS | PER SERVING: 45 CALORIES, 1 G. TOTAL FAT (0 G. SATURATED FAT), 9 G. CARBOHYDRATES, LESS THAN 1 G. PROTEIN, 1 G. DIETARY FIBER, 3 MG. SODIUM.

½ cup golden raisins

2 teaspoons minced peeled fresh ginger

3 tablespoons packed dark brown sugar, or to taste

½ teaspoon curry powder

½ cup fruit-sweetened strawberry preserves

1 medium navel orange, peeled and chopped

½ cup red or white wine vinegar

½ cup freshly squeezed orange juice

4 cups diced fresh strawberries

½ cup sliced almonds, toasted*

*Note: To toast the almonds, put them in a small skillet over medium heat, shaking or stirring frequently until lightly browned, about 2 to 3 minutes. Immediately transfer the nuts to a small dish and cool.

■ In a large, nonaluminum saucepan over high heat, combine all the ingredients except the fresh strawberries and almonds and bring the mixture to a boil. Reduce the heat to medium and cook uncovered, stirring frequently, for 15 minutes, until the mixture is slightly thickened and syrupy.

■ Add the strawberries, bring to a boil, reduce the heat to low, and simmer uncovered, stirring occasionally, for 10 minutes, until the mixture thickens.

■ Remove the pan from the heat and stir in the almonds. Transfer the chutney to a serving bowl. Cover and refrigerate for at least 1 hour before serving. Can be stored in a covered container in the refrigerator for 1 to 2 days.

sweet curried tomato chutney

This densely sweet-sour chutney follows the Asian concept of *umami,* or taste pungency, and can add a new dimension to chicken, fish, or meats—or even to mild-tasting steamed vegetables such as cauliflower or squash. Its health qualities start with vitamin C from tomatoes and organosulphur compounds from onion and garlic. Additional phytochemicals come from curry powder, with turmeric's phytochemical curcumin, which fights inflammation, and chili powder, which contains the antioxidant capsaicin. **MAKES 20 SERVINGS | PER SERVING: 14 CALORIES, 0 G. TOTAL FAT (0 G. SATURATED FAT), 4 G. CARBOHYDRATES, LESS THAN 1 G. PROTEIN, LESS THAN 1 G. DIETARY FIBER, 2 MG. SODIUM.**

2 large, ripe tomatoes

½ cup chopped onion

1 tablespoon minced peeled fresh ginger

2 garlic cloves, minced

1 to 2 tablespoons sugar, or to taste

2 tablespoons red wine vinegar

¼ cup golden raisins

1 teaspoon chili powder

1 teaspoon curry powder

½ teaspoon paprika

¼ teaspoon ground cinnamon

¼ teaspoon ground allspice

Salt to taste

■ In a large pot, bring some water to a boil. Using a paring knife, make an X opposite the stem on each tomato. Using a slotted spoon, place tomatoes in the boiling water until skins start to peel away—about 30 to 60 seconds, depending on size. Remove and place in a bowl of ice water, or under cold running water, to stop the cooking. When the tomatoes are cool enough to handle, remove the skins and chop.

■ In a medium saucepan, combine all the ingredients. Set the pan over medium-high heat and bring the mixture to a boil. Reduce the heat to low and simmer for 20 to 25 minutes, until the tomatoes break down and the mixture becomes thick. Serve the chutney warm or chilled. The sauce can be stored up to 5 days in the refrigerator and reheated.

cranberry chutney

This chutney mixes cranberries with apples, oranges, dried currants, and onion for a marvelous relish to enhance any poultry dish. Harvest vegetables, such as sweet potatoes and winter squash, also combine well with these flavors. The variety of fruits adds more healthful substances to the cancer-fighting procyanidins found in cranberries. **MAKES 32 SERVINGS | PER SERVING: 32 CALORIES, LESS THAN 1 G. TOTAL FAT (LESS THAN 1 G. SATURATED FAT), 8 G. CARBOHYDRATES, LESS THAN 1 G. PROTEIN, LESS THAN 1 G. DIETARY FIBER, 2 MG. SODIUM.**

½ cup white grape juice

½ cup packed light brown sugar, or to taste

1 teaspoon ground cinnamon

½ teaspoon ground cumin

¼ teaspoon ground cloves

1 bay leaf

1 medium sweet apple (such as Golden Delicious), peeled, cored, and finely chopped

1 medium onion, finely chopped

1 medium navel orange, peeled and finely chopped

1 bag (12 ounces) fresh or frozen cranberries

½ cup dried currants

■ In a Dutch oven or large, heavy pan, combine the grape juice, sugar, cinnamon, cumin, cloves, and bay leaf. Bring the mixture to a boil over medium-high heat. Add the apple, onion, orange, cranberries, and currants. Return to a boil, reduce the heat, and simmer uncovered, stirring occasionally, for about 30 minutes, until the cranberries are soft. Remove the bay leaf. Spoon the hot chutney into sterilized glass jars. Cover immediately with 2-part canning tops, cool, and refrigerate. Or store in a plastic container in the refrigerator. Once sealed, the chutney will keep for about 1 month. Once opened, use within a couple of weeks. Always store chutney in the refrigerator.

papaya-lime marinade

In Polynesian-style foods, like this marinade, lime is frequently used for flavor. Here, it accents the sweetness of the papaya. You can use this as a marinade for fish or chicken—or try it when grilling tofu, mushrooms, or vegetables. It can also be used as a fat-free dressing for salad. **MAKES 5 SERVINGS | PER SERVING: 25 CALORIES, LESS THAN 1 G. TOTAL FAT (LESS THAN 1 G. SATURATED FAT), 6 G. CARBOHYDRATES, LESS THAN 1 G. PROTEIN, 1 G. DIETARY FIBER, 414 MG. SODIUM.**

1½ cups unsweetened papaya juice*

1 tablespoon reduced sodium soy sauce

1 tablespoon freshly squeezed lime juice

½ teaspoon minced peeled fresh ginger

¼ teaspoon dried red pepper flakes, or to taste

½ teaspoon salt

*Note: If you don't have papaya juice, peel and seed 1 papaya and purée it in a blender with enough water to equal 1½ cups total.

■ In a blender or food processor on low speed, blend all of the ingredients until smooth. Transfer the mixture to a nonmetal baking dish or bowl. Add the food to be grilled to the marinade and turn several times until thoroughly coated. Cover and refrigerate for up to 1 hour, occasionally turning the food so the marinade is evenly distributed. When ready to grill, drain the food to be grilled, pat it dry with paper towels, and discard the marinade.†

†Note: Never baste with used marinade or serve used marinade as a sauce. It may be contaminated by potentially harmful bacteria and could lead to food-borne illnesses.

cranberry chutney

rosemary-orange marinade and sauce

Rosemary and orange blend to create a mild and versatile marinade or sauce. This recipe also works well at room temperature as a salad dressing. It makes enough marinade for ¾ to 1 pound of fish, chicken, meat, vegetables, or tofu. The orange juice brings you vitamin C, the rosemary provides carnosol, a phytochemical relevant to fighting cancer, and the orange zest contributes limonene, another cancer-fighting plant substance. **MAKES 4 SERVINGS | PER SERVING: 61 CALORIES, 4 G. TOTAL FAT (LESS THAN 1 G. SATURATED FAT), 6 G. CARBOHYDRATES, 1 G. PROTEIN, LESS THAN 1 G. DIETARY FIBER, 116 MG. SODIUM.**

1 tablespoon grated orange zest

1 tablespoon extra-virgin olive oil

¼ cup finely chopped fresh rosemary

½ cup freshly squeezed orange juice

2 tablespoons balsamic vinegar

1 cup fat-free, reduced sodium chicken broth (optional; use if serving as a sauce)

■ To use as a marinade for grilled food, blend all of the ingredients except the broth in a blender or food processor. Pour the marinade into a large bowl, add the food to be grilled, and turn several times until thoroughly coated. Refrigerate marinated chicken or meat for 1 hour or overnight; refrigerate marinated vegetables for 30 minutes. When ready to grill, drain the food to be grilled and discard the marinade.*

■ To use as a sauce, blend all of the ingredients including the broth in a blender or food processor. In a small saucepan over medium-high heat, bring the sauce to a boil. Reduce the heat and simmer about 10 minutes, until the liquid is reduced to a thin sauce. Strain the sauce through a fine sieve and serve immediately. Store tightly covered in the refrigerator for up to 3 days.

*Note: Never baste with used marinade or serve used marinade as a sauce. It may be contaminated by potentially harmful bacteria and could lead to food-borne illnesses.

yogurt marinade with ginger and coriander

Indian cuisine inspires this smooth and spicy marinade for chicken or fish. Yogurt tenderizes the food as it marinates. This recipe can also be used as a sauce to enliven steamed vegetables, such as broccoli, cauliflower, and carrots. **MAKES 4 SERVINGS | PER SERVING: 62 CALORIES, 1 G. TOTAL FAT (LESS THAN 1 G. SATURATED FAT), 8 G. CARBOHYDRATES, 5 G. PROTEIN, 0 G. DIETARY FIBER, 65 MG. SODIUM.**

1½ cups plain lowfat yogurt

2 tablespoons freshly squeezed lemon juice

¼ teaspoon cayenne

2 teaspoons minced garlic

2 teaspoons ground coriander

1 teaspoon ground turmeric

2 teaspoons minced peeled fresh ginger

Salt and freshly ground white pepper to taste

■ In a blender or food processor, blend all of the ingredients at low speed until well combined.

■ If using as a sauce, use immediately or store covered in the refrigerator for 1 to 2 days.

■ If using as a marinade, transfer the mixture to a nonmetal baking dish or bowl. Add the food to be grilled to the marinade and turn several times until thoroughly coated. Cover and refrigerate for up to 1 hour, occasionally turning the food so the marinade is evenly distributed. When ready to grill, drain the food to be grilled, pat it dry with paper towels, and discard the marinade.*

*Note: Never baste with used marinade or serve used marinade as a sauce. It may be contaminated by potentially harmful bacteria and could lead to food-borne illnesses.

herb-garlic marinade

A tasty melange of herbs and garlic add a dimension of flavor to grilled meat. The garlic supplies beneficial allyl sulfides, while the herbs add the phytochemicals carnosol, luteolin, and quercetin. To get the greatest reward from the garlic's health-protecting compounds, chop or mince it, and then let it stand for 10 minutes before adding it to other ingredients or cooking it. This recipe makes enough marinade for ¾ to 1 pound of fish, chicken, or meat. If desired, make additional marinade for basting. **MAKES 4 SERVINGS | PER SERVING: 36 CALORIES, 3 G. TOTAL FAT (LESS THAN 1 G. SATURATED FAT), 1 G. CARBOHYDRATES, LESS THAN 1 G. PROTEIN, LESS THAN 1 G. DIETARY FIBER, LESS THAN 1 MG. SODIUM.**

½ cup rice vinegar or white wine vinegar

1 tablespoon canola oil

¼ cup finely chopped onion

1 small bay leaf

2 sprigs fresh rosemary, thyme, or oregano, chopped, or ½ teaspoon dried rosemary, thyme, or oregano

2 garlic cloves, finely minced

½ teaspoon freshly ground black pepper

■ In a small nonmetal bowl, combine all of the ingredients and stir until well blended. Add the food to be grilled to the marinade and turn several times until thoroughly coated. Cover and refrigerate for at least 30 minutes, occasionally turning the food so the marinade is evenly distributed. When ready to grill, drain the food to be grilled and discard the marinade.*

*Note: Never baste with used marinade or serve used marinade as a sauce. It may be contaminated by potentially harmful bacteria and could lead to food-borne illnesses.

hoisin vinaigrette

Especially good for cruciferous vegetables that have a strong flavor, like Brussels sprouts and broccoli, this vinaigrette gets its Asian inflection from thick, sweet hoisin sauce, hot Chinese-style mustard, and fresh ginger. Many grocery stores stock the Asian ingredients used in this recipe, or you can find them in Asian markets. **MAKES 12 SERVINGS | PER SERVING: 20 CALORIES, 1 G. TOTAL FAT (0 G. SATURATED FAT), 2 G. CARBOHYDRATES, 0 G. PROTEIN, 0 G. DIETARY FIBER, 120 MG. SODIUM.**

¼ cup hoisin sauce

¼ cup Chinese cooking wine or rice vinegar

¼ cup fat-free, reduced sodium chicken or vegetable broth

1 tablespoon toasted sesame oil

1 tablespoon finely minced peeled fresh ginger

1 tablespoon reduced sodium soy sauce

2 teaspoons hot Chinese-style mustard, or to taste

Salt and freshly ground black pepper

■ In a blender or food processor, blend all of the ingredients except the salt and pepper until smooth. In a nonstick saucepan over low heat, gently heat the mixture until the sauce begins to simmer. Season to taste with salt and pepper. Serve the vinaigrette immediately with or on top of cooked vegetables, or store in a covered container in the refrigerator for up to 2 days. Reheat the chilled vinaigrette before using.

lime-peanut dressing

Lime is a common ingredient in Southeast Asian cooking. Its freshness lightens the peanut base of this salad dressing, which is made even more piquant with hoisin sauce and mint. Lime has the sound-alike phytochemical limonene, common to all citrus fruits, especially in their peels. Add a bit of grated lime zest if you want a stronger lime taste. This dressing would go well with strongly flavored greens such as mâche or radicchio and can also be used as a sauce on vegetables. **MAKES 8 SERVINGS | PER SERVING: 22 CALORIES, LESS THAN 1 G. TOTAL FAT (0 G. SATURATED FAT), 4 G. CARBOHYDRATES, LESS THAN 1 G. PROTEIN, 0 G. DIETARY FIBER, 103 MG. SODIUM.**

3½ tablespoons freshly squeezed lime juice

3 tablespoons hoisin sauce

¼ cup finely minced fresh cilantro, loosely packed

2 tablespoons finely minced fresh mint

½ tablespoon creamy peanut butter

■ In a small bowl, combine all of the ingredients. Blend vigorously with a wire whisk until well combined and smooth. Store in a covered container in the refrigerator for 3 to 4 days. Whisk thoroughly before serving.

orange-honey vinaigrette

This lowfat salad dressing can be made spicier by adding more than just a dash of cayenne. But as is, it is light and sweet and especially well suited to leafy greens. **MAKES 4 SERVINGS | PER SERVING: 51 CALORIES, 3 G. TOTAL FAT (LESS THAN 1 G. SATURATED FAT), 6 G. CARBOHYDRATES, LESS THAN 1 G. PROTEIN, LESS THAN 1 G. DIETARY FIBER, LESS THAN 1 MG. SODIUM.**

2 tablespoons cider vinegar

2 tablespoons freshly squeezed orange juice

1 tablespoon honey

1 tablespoon canola oil

⅛ teaspoon onion powder

Dash of cayenne, or to taste

Salt to taste

■ In a small bowl, combine all of the ingredients. Blend vigorously with a wire whisk. Serve over salad or fresh cut-up vegetables. Store in a covered container in the refrigerator for up to 1 week. Whisk thoroughly before serving.

dijon-herb dressing

Dijon mustard is wonderful in this creamy salad dressing, which also includes aromatic fresh basil and parsley, both of which have cancer-fighting properties from terpenes and flavonoids. **MAKES 5 SERVINGS | PER SERVING: 45 CALORIES, 4 G. TOTAL FAT (LESS THAN 1 G. SATURATED FAT), 2 G. CARBOHYDRATES, LESS THAN 1 G. PROTEIN, 0 G. DIETARY FIBER, 230 MG. SODIUM.**

3 tablespoons Dijon mustard

1 tablespoon white wine vinegar

1 tablespoon extra-virgin olive oil

2 tablespoons chopped fresh basil or 2 teaspoons dried basil

1 tablespoon chopped fresh flat leaf parsley

2 to 3 tablespoons half-and-half

■ In a small bowl, combine all of the ingredients except the half-and-half and blend with a wire whisk until well combined and smooth. Blend in the half-and-half and serve. Store in a covered container in the refrigerator for 2 to 3 days. Whisk thoroughly before serving.

apple vinaigrette with fresh herbs

Vinaigrettes often taste too sour. The apple juice in this one rounds out the sharpness of the vinegar, mustard, and onion. Fresh rosemary, thyme, and mint imbue it with inviting aromas as well as protective phytochemicals. Serve over a tossed salad. **MAKES 14 SERVINGS | PER SERVING: 76 CALORIES, 8 G. TOTAL FAT (1 G. SATURATED FAT), 1 G. CARBOHYDRATES, LESS THAN 1 G. PROTEIN, LESS THAN 1 G. DIETARY FIBER, 33 MG. SODIUM.**

½ cup apple cider vinegar

2 sprigs fresh rosemary

4 sprigs fresh thyme

¼ cup tightly packed fresh mint leaves

¼ cup unsweetened apple juice

½ cup extra-virgin olive oil

2 tablespoons minced red onion

1 tablespoon Dijon mustard

Salt and freshly ground black pepper

■ In a medium saucepan over medium-high heat, combine the vinegar, rosemary, thyme, and mint and bring to a boil. Remove the pan from the heat, cover, and allow to steep for 20 minutes. Strain the vinegar into a bowl and discard the herbs. Whisk in the apple juice, olive oil, onion, mustard, and salt and pepper to taste. Store in a covered container in the refrigerator for up to 5 days. Whisk thoroughly before serving.

asian-style dressing with scallions

This pungent vinaigrette can enliven a salad or steamed vegetables. Ginger and scallions combine to create a forceful flavor, yet the dressing is light and lowfat. **MAKES 6 SERVINGS | PER SERVING: 25 CALORIES, 2 G. TOTAL FAT (LESS THAN 1 G. SATURATED FAT), 1 G. CARBOHYDRATES, LESS THAN 1 G. PROTEIN, LESS THAN 1 G. DIETARY FIBER, 111 MG. SODIUM.**

1 tablespoon canola oil

¼ teaspoon minced peeled fresh ginger or a dash of ground ginger

2 scallions, trimmed and minced

½ cup fat-free, reduced sodium chicken broth

1 tablespoon rice vinegar

1 teaspoon reduced sodium soy sauce

½ teaspoon sugar

Freshly ground black pepper

1 teaspoon freshly squeezed lemon juice, or to taste

■ In a small saucepan, heat the canola oil over medium-high heat. Add the ginger and stir until it begins to color, about 30 seconds. Add the scallions and stir for a few seconds. Add the broth, vinegar, soy sauce, and sugar and bring to a boil. Boil for 30 seconds and stir in some pepper. Remove from the heat and cool slightly. Taste the dressing and add the lemon juice and more pepper, if desired, to get a tart, peppery flavor that appeals to you. Let cool completely and serve over cooked vegetables. Can be stored covered in the refrigerator for 3 to 4 days.

new american beef stew

one-pot meals on the plate

One-pot meals are the original convenience food for make-from-scratch cooks around the world. Virtually every cuisine features them, from Italian lasagna to the classic French boeuf bourguignonne, from Indian curry to Japanese sukiyaki. One-pot meals take many forms, including stews, casseroles, chilis, pilafs, stir-fries, entrée salads, and egg dishes like omelets and frittatas. You could serve a different one every night of the week without repetition. Some one-pot meals, such as stews and chilis, can be made ahead and refrigerated, often developing a deeper flavor in the process. Some can also be frozen for later use. Check Food Storage and Handling (page 268) for guidelines on freezing foods.

Because one-pot meals typically contain a variety of ingredients, their look, aroma, texture, and flavor become multilayered—and often make the dish more interesting than the old-fashioned meat-potato-vegetable meal. A medley of vegetables and whole grains or beans, as well as some animal protein, can offer a rainbow of colors, textures that vary from crunchy to soft, and a wide range of flavors. In many parts of Asia, cooks recognize as many as eight individual flavors: hot, sour, salty, sweet, bitter, pungent, astringent, and *umami,* which is sometimes translated as "mouthfeel." The richest-tasting dishes incorporate many if not all of these flavors. Sweet Potato and Pear Stir-Fry with Chicken and Chile Sauce (page 155), for example, contains all eight components, but a dish need not contain all eight in order to achieve a rich, complex flavor. Some recipes contain no meat, yet are so rich in taste that the lack of animal protein is not missed. Mushroom-Pepper Gumbo (page 146) has a meaty flavor, thanks to its portobello mushrooms. This gumbo's combination of rich flavor with a lighter, healthier character is also due to an innovative modification to the traditional flour-and-oil roux, which uses no oil. Another surprisingly rich-flavored meatless dish is Sweet Potato Chili with Peanuts (page 186). In addition to terrific depth of flavor, this chili has a lush medley of colors and textures. As a result, the cookbook team members called this dish a winner despite its lack of meat. In fact, one team member (who is a tough judge of dishes outside the mainstream) exclaimed, upon trying this chili, "I don't eat chili, but this, I like!"

One-pot meals are an easy way to make the transition to the New American Plate's two-thirds vegetable to one-third meat proportion. All the one-pot recipes in the chapters that follow adhere to that model, but you can also adjust your own favorite one-pot recipes, either gradually over time or in one fell swoop.

Remember: the number of servings in each recipe relates to USDA standard serving sizes. Depending on individual needs, you may choose to serve larger portions. (See Introduction, pages 7–10.) ▪

casseroles

When we think of one-pot meals, casseroles are often the first thing that comes to mind. The casserole has a long history but had its American heyday in the 1950s. Unfortunately, cooks too often relied on leftovers and "instant" sauces (especially cans of condensed mushroom and cream of chicken soup). Overuse of such "shortcuts" gave the casserole a bad reputation, and it fell out of favor. Today, revamped casseroles are enjoying a new popularity.

High-fat ingredients like cream have been replaced with reduced-fat substitutes like lowfat sour cream, nonfat yogurt, and nonfat evaporated milk. Rather than butter and cream, cornstarch and arrowroot are frequently used to thicken the casserole's base, making a lighter sauce that still retains flavor. Many recipes call for tomato-based or Asian-style sauces instead of traditional cream-based versions.

Different cooking techniques have updated and improved the traditional casserole. Most old-fashioned casseroles were made the slow-bake way, which often caused vegetables to lose their texture and color. The long bake also leached the vegetables' water content into the sauce, making the dish soupy. These problems can be avoided in several ways. You can precook major ingredients on top of the stove, then combine all the ingredients in a casserole dish and bake just long enough for the flavors to meld. Butternut Squash and Barley Casserole with Turkey (page 131) uses this strategy. Greek-Style Potato and Green Bean Casserole with Lamb (page 134) employs a variation of that strategy, with vegetables that can stand up to a more leisurely baking time.

Today, "no-bake" casseroles, such as Penne with Eggplant, Tomatoes, and Tuna (page 127), can be made quickly on top of the stove, often by combining cooked pasta or another grain with vegetables that have been lightly steamed or sautéed. In the final stage, the dish is bound together by a sauce.

penne with eggplant, tomatoes, and tuna

Tuna is a good source of omega-3 fatty acids, the "good fat" that has received so much scientific attention for its potential to protect against a variety of chronic diseases. This simple casserole comes together on the stovetop. It combines tuna with tomatoes (a source of both vitamin C and the antioxidant lycopene) and eggplant (rich in fiber, folate, several minerals, and a family of phytochemicals called anthocyanosides, believed to help fight heart disease and cancer). **MAKES 4 SERVINGS | PER SERVING: 362 CALORIES, 7 G. TOTAL FAT (1 G. SATURATED FAT), 57 G. CARBOHYDRATES, 20 G. PROTEIN, 6 G. DIETARY FIBER, 370 MG. SODIUM.**

8   ounces penne pasta, preferably whole wheat

1   small eggplant (1 pound), peeled

Olive oil spray

1   small red onion, finely chopped

4   medium tomatoes, seeded and chopped

1   can (6 ounces) water-packed solid tuna, well drained

2   tablespoons chopped green olives

2   tablespoons capers, rinsed, drained, and coarsely chopped

2   tablespoons chopped fresh basil

2   tablespoons chopped flat leaf parsley

Salt and freshly ground black pepper

¼   cup toasted whole wheat bread crumbs or freshly grated Parmesan cheese (optional)

■ Preheat the oven to 375 degrees.

■ Prepare the pasta according to the package directions. While it's cooking, cut the eggplant lengthwise into 3/4-inch slices, then into 3/4-inch cubes. On a nonstick baking sheet, arrange the eggplant in a single layer. Coat the pieces well with olive oil spray. Bake for 15 minutes, stirring once to turn the cubes, until the eggplant is soft but holds its shape.

■ Coat a large nonstick skillet with olive oil spray and heat over medium heat. Add the eggplant, onion, and tomatoes. Cook for about 5 minutes, stirring occasionally, until the tomatoes are soft. Add the tuna, breaking it into pieces and stirring it into the sauce. Add the olives, capers, basil, and parsley. Cook the mixture, stirring, until heated through. Season to taste with salt and pepper.

■ Drain the cooked pasta, but leave some of the water still clinging to it. Immediately add the pasta to the sauce. Stir to combine well. Sprinkle the mixture with the bread crumbs or cheese. Serve immediately.

portobello mushroom jambalaya with chicken

Here is a classic casserole with the proportions of ingredients adjusted just slightly for health. Most recipes for jambalaya call for rice with onion, peppers, and tomatoes, along with some combination of meats (usually chicken, ham, sausage, crawfish, and/or shrimp). This version concentrates on getting the distinctive seasonings right, and using a combination of portobello mushrooms and chicken to provide the satisfying, stick-to-your-ribs quality for which jambalaya is known. The earthy flavor of portobello mushrooms also adds an extra, unexpected layer of depth to the dish. **MAKES 6 SERVINGS |** PER SERVING: 422 CALORIES, 8 G. TOTAL FAT (1 G. SATURATED FAT), 60 G. CARBOHYDRATES, 21 G. PROTEIN, 7 G. DIETARY FIBER, 791 MG. SODIUM.

2 tablespoons canola oil

2 large onions, chopped

1 medium green bell pepper, seeded and chopped

1 small garlic clove, minced

⅓ cup all-purpose flour

1 pound skinless, boneless chicken breast, cut into ½-inch pieces

2 cups long-grain brown rice

1 can (28 ounces) diced tomatoes in juice, drained

2 cups fat-free, reduced sodium chicken broth

½ teaspoon dried thyme

1 teaspoon salt

⅛ teaspoon cayenne

¼ teaspoon freshly ground black pepper

1 package portobello mushrooms (about 6 ounces), cleaned and sliced

2 cups water

3 scallions, trimmed and chopped

■ In a Dutch oven or large, heavy pan, heat the canola oil over medium-high heat. Sauté the onions, bell pepper, and garlic for about 4 minutes, until soft. Remove the pan from the heat.

■ Put the flour in a large sealable plastic bag. Add the chicken and shake the bag to coat the chicken with the flour. Remove the chicken pieces, shaking off the excess flour, and add them to the pan. Cook over medium heat for 4 minutes, stirring frequently, until the chicken pieces are opaque and the flour has colored in places.

■ Stir in the rice. Add the tomatoes, broth, thyme, salt, cayenne, and black pepper. Bring the liquid to a boil, reduce the heat, cover, and simmer for 30 minutes.

■ Add the mushrooms, arranging them on top of the rice mixture. Pour in the water. Return to a boil, reduce heat to low, and cover partially. Simmer for about 20 to 30 minutes, or until the rice is done. Stir in the scallions and remove from heat. Let cool for 5 minutes and serve.

butternut squash and barley casserole with turkey

To update the classic 1950s casserole so it belongs on the New American Plate, we scrapped the instant soup mixes and cream. Now this simple one-dish method of cooking is a no-fuss way to get more variety into your diet. This recipe includes ingredients you might not use every day: butternut squash, aromatic sage, tangy feta, and satisfying barley.

MAKES 4 SERVINGS | PER SERVING: 369 CALORIES, 8 G. TOTAL FAT (4 G. SATURATED FAT), 52 G. CARBOHYDRATES, 26 G. PROTEIN, 13 G. DIETARY FIBER, 534 MG. SODIUM.

Canola oil spray

2 teaspoons olive oil

1 medium green bell pepper, seeded and diced

½ cup minced onion

½ cup pearl barley, rinsed and drained

1 teaspoon dried sage

Freshly ground black pepper

1 can (15 ounces) fat-free, reduced sodium chicken broth

1 cup (about ½ pound) cubed cooked or leftover turkey breast

2 medium butternut squash (about 1½ pounds each), halved lengthwise, peeled, seeded, and cut into ½-inch cubes

½ cup crumbled feta cheese

■ Coat a 4-quart baking dish with canola oil spray.

■ In a large saucepan, heat the olive oil over medium-high heat. Add the bell pepper and onion. Sauté for 2 minutes. Add the barley, sage, and black pepper and stir to combine well. Add the broth and bring to a boil. Reduce the heat to low and simmer, covered, for 45 minutes. Add the turkey and squash and continue to simmer for 15 minutes more or until all of the broth is absorbed and the squash is tender. If the mixture seems too dry, add an additional ¼ cup of broth or water.

■ Preheat the oven to 350 degrees.

■ Transfer the mixture to the prepared baking dish and top with the cheese. Bake, uncovered, for about 30 minutes, until the cheese is golden.

green peppers stuffed with rice, beans, and feta

This recipe for stuffed peppers was a big hit at AICR tastings. Beans and rice are a classic protein combination. Basmati rice is an aromatic long-grain rice noted for its nutty flavor. Brown basmati rice is less polished and retains more nutrients. Matching it with the sweetness of corn and the salty tang of feta cheese results in a delightful variety of flavors and textures.

MAKES 4 SERVINGS | PER SERVING: 360 CALORIES, 12 G. TOTAL FAT (4 G. SATURATED FAT), 50 G. CARBOHYDRATES, 13 G. PROTEIN, 9 G. DIETARY FIBER, 466 MG. SODIUM.

Olive oil spray

4 medium green bell peppers

2 cups cooked brown basmati rice
(⅔ cup dry)

1 cup canned pinto beans, rinsed and drained

¾ cup finely chopped onion

¾ cup fresh, frozen (thawed), or canned corn kernels, drained

½ cup crumbled reduced fat feta cheese

¼ cup pine nuts, toasted*

½ teaspoon dried basil

Salt and freshly ground black pepper

1 tablespoon freshly squeezed lemon juice

2 teaspoons extra-virgin olive oil

*Note: To toast the pine nuts, put them in a small skillet over medium-high heat and stir constantly for 1 to 2 minutes until lightly browned. Immediately transfer the nuts to a small dish and cool.

■ Put an oven rack in the middle of the oven. Preheat the oven to 375 degrees. Spray an 8-inch square baking dish with the olive oil spray.

■ Cut the tops off of the bell peppers and remove the seeds. Reserve the tops. If necessary to help the bell peppers stand upright, trim a slice off the bottom, taking care not to cut through the pepper wall. Set the peppers aside.

■ In a large bowl, combine the rice, beans, onion, corn, cheese, pine nuts, and basil. Season to taste with salt and pepper. Spoon the filling into the bell peppers, packing the filling lightly and mounding the tops. Then place the peppers in the prepared baking dish and cover with the reserved pepper tops. Place the baking dish on the middle rack in the oven. Add water to the baking dish to a depth of 1½ inches.

■ Bake the bell peppers for about 45 to 50 minutes, until they are soft when pierced with a knife. Remove the pepper tops and discard. In a small bowl, whisk together the lemon juice and olive oil and spoon over the peppers. Let cool for 20 minutes before serving.

greek-style potato and green bean casserole with lamb

A tangy yogurt sauce adds a distinctively Greek character to this simple one-dish meal. The lamb is used to add flavor without overwhelming the other ingredients. **MAKES 4 SERVINGS | PER SERVING: 377 CALORIES, 7 G. TOTAL FAT (3 G. SATURATED FAT), 44 G. CARBOHYDRATES, 36 G. PROTEIN, 7 G. DIETARY FIBER, 753 MG. SODIUM.**

1 pound lean lamb (preferably from the leg or shoulder), trimmed of fat and cut into ¾-inch pieces

2 cups plain lowfat yogurt

4 garlic cloves, crushed

2 teaspoons grated peeled fresh ginger

1 tablespoon plus 1 teaspoon sweet paprika

1 teaspoon salt, or to taste

½ teaspoon freshly ground black pepper, or to taste

Olive oil spray

2 medium onions, chopped

2 large tomatoes, seeded and chopped

2 large yellow-fleshed potatoes (such as Yukon Gold), peeled and cut into 1-inch pieces

1 pound fresh green beans, trimmed and halved crosswise

■ In a large bowl, combine the lamb, yogurt, garlic, ginger, paprika, salt, and pepper and stir until well mixed. Cover and refrigerate for 2 to 4 hours.

■ Preheat the oven to 350 degrees.

■ Generously coat a large ovenproof skillet with olive oil spray and heat over medium-high heat. Add the onions and tomatoes and sauté over medium-high heat for about 10 minutes, stirring often, until they are soft.

■ Add the marinated lamb and stir to combine.

■ Add the potatoes and green beans. Cover the skillet and bring to a slow boil over medium heat.

■ Transfer the skillet to the oven. Bake for about 45 to 50 minutes, until the lamb and potatoes are tender. Serve immediately.

spinach lasagna with red pepper sauce

This lasagna earns its place on the New American Plate because it's packed with spinach, peppers, and other vegetables that add flavor, fiber, and nutrients without adding fat or many calories. Roasted red peppers enrich the tomato sauce with a deep, smoky character. The vegetables supply flavonoids, carotenoids, lutein, zeaxanthin, saponins, and lycopene. Many scientists believe it is the interaction among such phytochemicals that strengthens our bodies against chronic diseases.

MAKES 9 SERVINGS | PER SERVING: 350 CALORIES, 13 G. TOTAL FAT (5 G. SATURATED FAT), 42 G. CARBOHYDRATES, 18 G. PROTEIN, 6 G. DIETARY FIBER, 640 MG. SODIUM.

3 tablespoons olive oil, divided

2 medium onions, one thinly sliced, one chopped

4 garlic cloves, chopped, divided

1 jar (12 ounces) roasted red peppers, drained and chopped

½ tablespoon crushed dried basil

1 can (28 ounces) tomato sauce

1 cup water, divided

3 packages (10 ounces each) frozen chopped spinach, thawed and squeezed dry

1 container (15 ounces) lowfat ricotta cheese

1 cup (4 ounces) shredded reduced-fat mozzarella cheese

12 sheets oven-ready lasagna noodles (not regular lasagna noodles)

¼ cup freshly grated Parmesan cheese

■ In a Dutch oven or large, heavy pan, heat 1 tablespoon of the olive oil over medium-high heat. Sauté the sliced onion and half of the garlic for about 4 minutes, stirring often, until the onion is translucent. Add the peppers, basil, tomato sauce, and ½ cup of the water. Bring to a boil, reduce heat, and simmer for 20 minutes. Cool slightly and then purée in a blender or food processor in batches.

■ Preheat the oven to 350 degrees.

■ In a large nonstick skillet, heat the remaining 2 tablespoons of olive oil over medium-high heat. Sauté the chopped onion and remaining garlic for about 4 minutes, stirring often, until the onion is translucent. Add the spinach and the remaining ½ cup of water. Cook for 10 minutes, stirring occasionally, until the water evaporates and the spinach and onion are tender. Meanwhile, combine the ricotta and mozzarella cheeses in a bowl.

■ Spoon ¼ of the puréed sauce to cover the bottom of a 13 × 9-inch baking dish. Arrange 3 sheets of pasta over the sauce. Cover with ⅓ of the spinach. Spread ⅓ of the cheese mixture over the top. Sprinkle on 1 tablespoon of the Parmesan cheese. Repeat this process twice, starting with the sauce. For the final (fourth) layer, arrange the remaining pasta over the cheeses and top with the remaining sauce and Parmesan cheese.

■ Cover the lasagna with foil and bake for 45 minutes. Remove the lasagna from the oven and let it stand uncovered for 15 minutes before serving. To serve, cut into 9 squares.

stews

Stews are probably the original one-pot meal, made by slowly simmering food barely covered with a liquid such as broth. This method of cooking was commonly used to tenderize tough pieces of meat. But cooks discovered that long, slow cooking also allows the flavors of the ingredients in a stew to fully develop and intermingle, producing a deep, complex taste.

Historically, the proportion of meat to vegetables in a stew varied depending on the economic circumstances of the household. Wealthier families ate stews with a generous proportion of meat, while poor or economizing families used meat sparingly, to add flavor, and relied on vegetables to provide the filling bulk. Today, health is often the primary reason for focusing on a variety of nonmeat ingredients to provide flavor. As with the other one-pot meals, the stews in this chapter have been updated to reflect the healthier two-thirds to one-third proportion of the New American Plate. The New American Beef Stew (page 137) is studded with more vegetables than old-fashioned versions, but has enough beef to ensure a hearty, deep flavor. With its unexpected color and varied textures, Sweet Potato and Apple Stew with Turkey and Cranberries (page 138) is a refreshing change from more traditional stews, and an easy dish to prepare.

Although some stews are baked, Brazilian-Style Seafood Stew (page 140) is cooked stovetop, in surprisingly little time given its complex flavors. Mushroom-Pepper Gumbo (page 146) is also prepared stovetop, and produces a deep, meaty flavor without the less healthful aspects of classic gumbos.

new american beef stew

We've packed the traditional beef stew with more vegetables, including some that might surprise you. But that's what New American Plate cooking is all about: maximizing flavor by maximizing variety. In this recipe such familiar beef stew ingredients as carrots, onions, and tomatoes share the pot with leeks, green beans, and kale. By adding the green beans and kale at the last minute, you give the whole dish more substance, and the greater variety of vegetables means a greater mix of nutrients and phytochemicals. So beef stew becomes health food as well as comfort food. **MAKES 6 SERVINGS | PER SERVING: 400 CALORIES, 10 G. TOTAL FAT (2 G. SATURATED FAT), 58 G. CARBOHYDRATES, 26 G. PROTEIN, 12 G. DIETARY FIBER, 606 MG. SODIUM.**

2 tablespoons olive oil

1 pound lean beef stew meat, cut into 1-inch cubes

2 large onions, chopped

4 medium carrots, cubed

2 cups diced leeks, rinsed well

6 garlic cloves, finely chopped

2 cans (14.5 ounces each) diced tomatoes in juice

2 cans (6 ounces each) tomato paste

2 cans (14.5 ounces each) fat-free, reduced sodium beef broth

3 tablespoons dried oregano

2 cups water

2 large potatoes, cubed

1¼ pounds frozen green beans

2 cups chopped kale

Salt and freshly ground black pepper

■ In a large pot or stockpot, heat the olive oil over medium-high heat. Add ½ the beef and sauté for about 5 minutes, stirring, until browned on all sides. Remove the beef from the pot and set it aside. Repeat procedure with the remaining beef. In the same pot, sauté the onions for about 5 minutes, stirring often until translucent. Remove the onions from the pot and set aside. Add the carrots, leeks, and garlic, and sauté for about 5 minutes, stirring often, until barely tender. Return the beef and onions to the pot. Add the tomatoes with juice, tomato paste, broth, oregano, and water, and bring to a boil. Reduce the heat to low and simmer for about 1 hour, until the beef is almost tender. Add the potatoes and bring back to a boil. Lower heat, cover partially, and simmer for about 15 minutes, until the potatoes are barely tender. Add the green beans and kale and cook for another 6 to 8 minutes, until the kale is tender. Season to taste with salt and pepper and serve.

sweet potato and apple stew with turkey and cranberries

This homey, satisfying dish combines several harvesttime foods, each of which boasts an impressive profile of health-protective substances. Root vegetables like carrots, rutabagas, and sweet potatoes are loaded with vitamins A and C. Apples and cranberries contain many members of a family of phytochemicals known as flavonoids, which have proven to be the most potent antioxidants yet discovered. The different health benefits of the ingredients in this stew, like their different flavors, reinforce each other. This stew is a good way to use leftovers from Thanksgiving.

MAKES 4 SERVINGS | PER SERVING (DOES NOT INCLUDE ALMONDS): 369 CALORIES, 13 G. TOTAL FAT (LESS THAN 2 G. SATURATED FAT), 41 G. CARBOHYDRATES, 25 G. PROTEIN, 9 G. DIETARY FIBER, 319 MG. SODIUM.

1 tablespoon canola oil

1 medium onion, chopped

1 large carrot, peeled and cut into ¾-inch slices

1 celery rib, cut into ¾-inch slices

1 medium rutabaga, peeled and cut into 1-inch pieces

1½ cups fat-free, reduced sodium chicken broth

1 bay leaf

2 large sweet apples (such as Crispin or Red Delicious), peeled and cut into 1-inch pieces

2 medium orange-flesh sweet potatoes (about 1 pound total), peeled and cut into bite-sized pieces

2 cups (about 10 ounces) diced cooked turkey breast

½ cup fresh, frozen, or dried cranberries

½ teaspoon dried thyme

Salt and freshly ground black pepper

3 tablespoons chopped almonds, toasted* (optional)

*Note: To toast the almonds, put them in a small skillet over medium heat, shaking or stirring frequently until lightly browned, about 2 to 3 minutes. Immediately transfer the nuts to a small dish and cool.

■ Preheat the oven to 375 degrees.

■ In a Dutch oven or large, heavy ovenproof pan, heat the canola oil over medium-high heat. Add the onion and sauté for about 4 minutes, until tender. Add the carrot, celery, and rutabaga, reduce heat to medium-low, cover tightly, and cook for 10 minutes, until the vegetables are barely tender. Add the broth and bay leaf and cover.

■ Transfer the stew to the oven. Bake for 10 minutes. Add the apples, sweet potatoes, turkey, cranberries, and thyme. Cover and bake for 15 to 20 minutes, until the vegetables and cranberries are tender and the turkey is heated through.

■ Remove the bay leaf and season to taste with salt and pepper. Sprinkle with the almonds, if desired, and serve.

cinnamon and raisin couscous with chicken

A classically North African blend of sweet and savory, this stew combines the natural sugars of raisins and carrots with aromatic notes of cinnamon, ginger, and cumin. In this, as in so many New American Plate recipes, the chicken imparts flavor and texture to the dish without becoming the focus of the meal. Couscous is a fluffy, fine-grained, and quick-cooking form of pasta common to North Africa and the Middle East; look for whole wheat couscous, which is becoming more widely available.

MAKES 4 SERVINGS | PER SERVING: 350 CALORIES, 3 G. TOTAL FAT (LESS THAN 1 G. SATURATED FAT), 51 G. CARBOHYDRATES, 29 G. PROTEIN, 6 G. DIETARY FIBER, 383 MG. SODIUM.

- 1 large onion, finely chopped
- 2 large carrots, peeled and cut into ¾-inch slices
- ½ small fennel bulb, cut lengthwise into ½-inch slices, or 1 large celery rib, cut into 1-inch pieces
- 1 pound skinless, boneless chicken breast, cut into ¾-inch pieces
- ½ cup raisins
- 1½ teaspoons ground cumin
- 1 teaspoon ground cinnamon
- 1 teaspoon ground ginger
- ½ teaspoon salt, or to taste
- ¼ teaspoon freshly ground black pepper, or to taste
- 2½ cups water
- 1 medium zucchini, cut into ¾-inch slices
- ⅔ cup couscous, preferably whole wheat

■ In a large, heavy pan or Dutch oven, combine the onion, carrots, fennel, chicken, raisins, cumin, cinnamon, ginger, salt, pepper, and water, and bring to a boil over medium-high heat. Reduce the heat, cover, and simmer for 20 minutes. Add the zucchini. Cover and simmer for 5 minutes. Stir in the couscous. Cover and simmer for 8 to 12 minutes or until the liquid is absorbed. Remove from the heat and let cool for 5 minutes before serving.

brazilian-style seafood stew

This revamp of a traditional Brazilian recipe is more a vegetable stew with seafood than a seafood stew. Changing the proportions of the dish so that it fits nicely on the New American Plate allows each of its many flavorful ingredients more time in the spotlight. Here, the colorful bell peppers and fresh herbs mingle in a spicy tomato–coconut milk base. Chile and lime boost these complex flavors so they can hold their own against the fish and shrimp. **MAKES 6 SERVINGS | PER SERVING: 319 CALORIES, 10 G. TOTAL FAT (2 G. SATURATED FAT), 33 G. CARBOHYDRATES, 24 G. PROTEIN, 2 G. DIETARY FIBER, 220 MG. SODIUM.**

¾ pound skinless white fish fillets (such as halibut, cod, or red snapper), cut into 1-inch pieces

Salt and freshly ground white pepper

3 tablespoons olive oil, divided

2 tablespoons freshly squeezed lime juice

3 garlic cloves, finely minced

1½ cups chopped onion

½ cup chopped green bell pepper

½ cup chopped red bell pepper

½ cup chopped orange bell pepper

1 fresh serrano chile, seeded and diced,* or ¾ teaspoon cayenne, or to taste

1 garlic clove, mashed

1 can (14.5 ounces) diced tomatoes in juice

¾ cup unsweetened reduced fat coconut milk

½ cup finely chopped fresh cilantro, loosely packed, divided

½ cup finely chopped fresh chives, loosely packed, divided

¾ pound medium shrimp, peeled and deveined

3 cups hot cooked long-grain brown rice

*Note: Wear rubber gloves to handle fresh chiles, and keep your hands away from your eyes.

■ Sprinkle the fish with salt and pepper and let it stand a few minutes. In a large bowl, whisk together 2 tablespoons of the olive oil and the lime juice. Stir in the minced garlic cloves. Add the fish and stir to coat on all sides. Let it stand for 15 minutes.

■ In a large pot, heat the remaining 1 tablespoon of oil over medium heat. Add the onion, bell peppers, chile, and mashed garlic. Sauté for about 5 minutes, stirring often, until the onion is translucent. Mix in the tomatoes with juice, coconut milk, ½ of the cilantro, ½ of the chives, the shrimp, and the fish and its marinade. Bring liquid to a simmer and cook gently for 5 to 7 minutes, until the fish and shrimp are opaque in the center. Take care not to overcook the seafood. Season to taste with salt and pepper.

■ Place ½ cup of hot cooked rice in each of 6 shallow bowls. Ladle the stew on top of the rice. Sprinkle with the remaining cilantro and chives, and serve.

pineapple and pork stew

Pork goes well with many fruits. In this stew, inspired by Caribbean cooking, the slight natural sweetness of pork is paired with the bracing zip of pineapple. Pineapple's dual nature—both sweet and tangy—adds layers of flavor to this dish, as do touches of chile, ginger, and garlic. MAKES 4 SERVINGS | PER SERVING: 355 CALORIES, 11 G. TOTAL FAT (3 G. SATURATED FAT), 42 G. CARBOHYDRATES, 23 G. PROTEIN, 4 G. DIETARY FIBER, 522 MG. SODIUM.

¾ pound boneless pork loin, trimmed of fat and cut in 1-inch cubes

2 tablespoons all-purpose flour

Canola oil spray

1 tablespoon canola oil

1 medium onion, sliced

1 medium green bell pepper, seeded and chopped

1 garlic clove, minced

1 small fresh chile pepper (such as jalapeño), seeded and minced*

1 cup water

1 tablespoon Worcestershire sauce

½ teaspoon ground ginger

¾ teaspoon salt

¼ teaspoon freshly ground black pepper

1 can (8 ounces) sliced pineapple in juice

1 large tomato, seeded and diced

¼ medium cucumber, peeled, seeded, and diced

2 cups cooked brown rice

*Note: Wear rubber gloves to handle fresh chiles, and keep your hands away from your eyes.

■ In a medium bowl, toss the pork with the flour to coat. Generously coat a deep skillet with canola oil spray. Over medium-high heat, sauté the meat for about 5 minutes, stirring often, until brown on all sides. Transfer the meat to a plate. Do not clean the skillet.

■ Add the canola oil to the skillet. Sauté the onion, pepper, garlic, and chile for 3 to 4 minutes, stirring often over medium heat, scraping up the browned floury bits, until the onion is translucent. Return the meat to the skillet. Add the water, Worcestershire sauce, ginger, salt, and pepper. Drain the juice from the pineapple into the skillet. Bring to a boil, cover, reduce the heat, and simmer for 30 minutes until the pork is almost tender.

■ Stack the pineapple slices and cut them into 8 sections. Add the pineapple, tomato, and cucumber to the stew. Simmer uncovered for 10 minutes. When the liquid has thickened slightly and the meat is tender, ladle the stew over the rice and serve. The stew keeps 2 to 3 days, covered, in the refrigerator.

lentil and potato stew with veal and rosemary

This simple "peasant" stew combines several satisfying ingredients—lentils, carrots, celery, potatoes, and veal—for a hearty wintertime meal. Red lentils may be attractive when cooked, but they have lost their seed coat and with it goes significant nutritious value. The green lentils used in this recipe deliver folate, fiber, and many of the vitamins the body needs each day. Garnish this dish with shaved carrots to add color and texture. **MAKES 4 SERVINGS | PER SERVING: 394 CALORIES, 10 G. FAT (LESS THAN 2 G. SATURATED FAT), 49 G. CARBOHYDRATES, 28 G. PROTEIN, 10 G. DIETARY FIBER, 522 MG. SODIUM.**

2 tablespoons extra-virgin olive oil

½ pound lean veal stew meat, cut into ¾-inch cubes

1 large onion, finely chopped

1 medium carrot, chopped

1 medium celery rib, chopped

1 garlic clove, minced

1 cup green lentils, picked over and rinsed

4 cups fat-free, reduced sodium beef or vegetable broth, divided

1 bay leaf

1 teaspoon finely chopped fresh rosemary or ½ teaspoon dried rosemary

3 new potatoes, roughly chopped

Salt and freshly ground black pepper

Thinly shaved carrot, for garnish

Chopped flat leaf parsley, for garnish

■ In a deep, heavy pot, heat the olive oil over medium heat. Sauté veal cubes with the onion, carrot, celery, and garlic for about 5 minutes, stirring often, until the onion is golden.

■ Add the lentils, 3½ cups of the broth, bay leaf, and rosemary. Bring to a boil, cover, and reduce the heat to low. Simmer for 45 to 60 minutes, until the veal is tender. Add the potatoes and the remaining broth. Cover and cook until the potatoes are tender, about 20 minutes. Remove the bay leaf. Season to taste with salt and pepper. Ladle into 4 serving bowls, garnish generously with the shaved carrot and parsley, and serve hot.

fourteen-vegetable stew with pork

Hearty and satisfying, this stew boasts an impressive variety of healthy ingredients with a wide range of nutrients and health-protective phytochemicals, textures, and flavors. And recipes do not get much easier. If you have a Dutch oven and a good chopping knife, you are halfway done. MAKES 4 SERVINGS | PER SERVING: 355 CALORIES, 7 G. TOTAL FAT (LESS THAN 1 G. SATURATED FAT), 56 G. CARBOHYDRATES, 23 G. PROTEIN, 15 G. DIETARY FIBER, 376 MG. SODIUM.

1 tablespoon olive oil

½ pound pork tenderloin, cut into ¾-inch pieces

1 medium orange-flesh sweet potato (about 8 ounces), peeled and cut into 1-inch pieces

1 medium white-skinned waxy potato, peeled and cut into 1-inch pieces

1¼ cups shelled fresh or frozen lima beans (not baby limas)

2 medium carrots, cut into 1-inch pieces

4 cups small cauliflower florets (about ½ a medium head)

1½ cups chopped green cabbage (about ¼ head)

1 cup diced Spanish onion

1 medium green bell pepper, seeded and cut into 1-inch pieces

4 ounces fresh green beans, trimmed, cut in half

1 medium celery rib, cut into 1-inch slices

2 medium tomatoes, seeded and coarsely chopped

3 cups peeled and cubed eggplant (about ½ a small eggplant)

6 white button mushrooms, cleaned and halved

1 large garlic clove, finely chopped

1 bay leaf

¼ cup coarsely chopped flat leaf parsley, loosely packed

1 cup tomato juice

1 tablespoon tomato paste

1 teaspoon paprika

1 teaspoon dried oregano

1 teaspoon dried basil

1 teaspoon Worcestershire sauce

Salt and freshly ground black pepper

Dash of cayenne, or to taste

■ In a large Dutch oven or large, heavy pan, heat the olive oil over medium-high heat and sauté the pork for about 5 minutes, stirring often, until browned on all sides. Transfer the pork to a plate. In the same pan, layer the vegetables, pork, and seasonings in the following order: sweet potato, white potato, lima beans, carrots, cauliflower, cabbage, onion, bell pepper, green beans, celery, tomatoes, eggplant, mushrooms, pork, garlic, bay leaf, and parsley.

■ In a small bowl mix the tomato juice, tomato paste, paprika, oregano, basil, Worcestershire sauce, salt and black pepper to taste, and cayenne. Pour over the vegetables.

■ Cover and bring the liquid to a boil over medium-high heat. Reduce the heat and simmer for about 30 minutes, until the pork and vegetables are tender. Adjust the seasonings and remove the bay leaf. Cool for at least 20 minutes before serving.

mushroom-pepper gumbo

While a gumbo without okra may not be a gumbo in the traditional sense, most people—especially those who aren't overly fond of okra's distinctive texture—will welcome this New American Plate twist on an old favorite. A generous amount of portobello mushrooms provides a meaty heft to the dish. And instead of the traditional thickener—roux, which is high in fat—lightly toasted flour alone is used. This technique, developed by famed chef Paul Prudhomme and his sister, Enola, is faster and easier than making a roux, yet it adds a depth of flavor to the already rich-tasting cooking liquid. Earthy filé powder, which is stocked in the spice section of many supermarkets, is a traditional Creole seasoning made from sassafras leaves. Don't be put off by the instructions. This recipe requires many simple steps, but they go quickly. **MAKES 5 SERVINGS | PER SERVING: 301 CALORIES, 7 G. TOTAL FAT (LESS THAN 1 G. SATURATED FAT), 50 G. CARBOHYDRATES, 11 G. PROTEIN, 5 G. DIETARY FIBER, 737 MG. SODIUM.**

⅔ cup all-purpose flour

2 tablespoons canola oil, plus 1 teaspoon more if needed

¾ pound portobello mushrooms, cleaned, stems removed, and cut into large chunks (about 4 cups)

½ cup coarsely chopped mild onion (such as Bermuda or shallots)

2 large green bell peppers, seeded and cut into eighths

¼ cup minced fresh chives or scallions, trimmed, green part only

¼ cup diced celery

1 tablespoon minced garlic

Salt

½ teaspoon dried thyme

¼ teaspoon freshly ground black pepper, or to taste

¼ teaspoon cayenne, or to taste

3 bay leaves

2 quarts fat-free, reduced sodium chicken broth

Hot pepper sauce, to taste

3 cups hot cooked rice, either a mix of long-grain brown and wild rice, or all brown rice

2 tablespoons finely chopped fresh chives or 1 tablespoon dried chives, for garnish

Filé powder, to accompany gumbo (optional)

■ In a nonstick skillet over medium-low heat, heat the flour for about 10 to 12 minutes, stirring constantly, until it turns a light peanut butter color. Immediately transfer the toasted flour to a small bowl and set it aside to cool near the stove.

■ In a large skillet or medium stockpot, heat the 2 tablespoons of canola oil over high heat until very hot. Working in batches so the skillet is not overcrowded, sauté the mushrooms until the water they release has evaporated and they are tender. Remove the sautéed mushrooms with a slotted spoon and set them aside near the stove.

■ Add the onion and bell pepper to the skillet and sauté for about 2 minutes, adding an additional 1 teaspoon of canola oil, if necessary. Add the chives, celery, and garlic and cook for 1 minute more, or until all the vegetables are lightly sautéed. Reduce heat to medium-low. Sprinkle the toasted flour over the vegetables and quickly stir in, scraping the bottom of the skillet to keep the flour from burning. Stir in salt to taste, thyme, black pepper, cayenne, and bay leaves.

■ Slowly add the broth, whisking or stirring constantly to blend to a smooth, lump-free mixture. Return the mushrooms to the skillet and bring to a boil. Immediately reduce the heat and simmer gently for about 10 minutes.

■ Adjust the seasonings to taste by adding more salt, black pepper, and cayenne, if necessary. Remove the bay leaves. Add the hot pepper sauce and adjust to taste.

■ When ready to serve, divide the cooked rice evenly among 5 bowls. Spoon equal amounts of the gumbo over the rice. Garnish with the chopped chives. Serve with filé powder in a separate bowl for individuals to spoon into the gumbo.

stir-fries

Although stir-fries are associated with East Asian cooking, the technique of using high heat and constant stirring to cook food quickly is as familiar to Western cooks as the sauté. Although traditional stir-fry recipes sometimes involve much dicing and chopping, these steps can easily be streamlined by using precut vegetables found in the produce or salad bar sections of markets. There is also a health bonus in buying small bags of different vegetables for a stir-fry: a greater variety of vegetables will increase the number of different types of phytochemicals and other nutrients in the stir-fry.

Once the ingredients are cut into small, uniform pieces, the cooking process of a stir-fry is quick and easy. But there are a few tricks worth keeping in mind if you aren't experienced with this technique. The key rule is to cook meats or fish just until cooked through, and the vegetables until tender yet still crisp. For a handy guide to take you smoothly and successfully through each step, you can refer to the section on stir-frying in the Cooking Methods chapter (page 265). Although we think of stir-fries as Asian in nature, the mix-it-up strategy of fusion cooking can be seen in several of the stir-fry recipes that follow. Zucchini and Portobello Stir-Fry with Chicken (page 156) uses vegetables and seasonings associated with Italian cooking, but cooked in the traditional Eastern style. The unexpected combination of vegetables and fruit in Sweet Potato and Pear Stir-Fry with Chicken and Chile Sauce (page 155) adopts the Southeast Asian practice of using fruit in a savory dish, unifying the whole with the basic seasonings of the region: ginger, soy sauce, a splash of fish sauce, and a dash of red pepper.

Allow these dishes to inspire you to experiment with new pairings. The simplest way is to serve a stir-fry with a nontraditional grain. Although stir-fries are traditionally served with steamed rice, other cooked grains can be used as well: rice or bean thread noodles, quinoa, couscous, or pasta.

broccoli and straw mushroom stir-fry with shrimp

This stir-fry is loaded with broccoli, a favorite of parents and nutrition scientists everywhere. Parents know it's loaded with vitamins and minerals, and scientists have recently discovered it is a source of powerful phytochemicals, which seem to bolster the body's defenses against cancer. Stir-frying is perfect for broccoli because this quick-cooking method discourages the kind of overcooking that can bring out a bitter taste. By making sure to cook the broccoli florets until they are just tender, you'll bring out the best in this light, flavorful stir-fry. Straw mushrooms can be found in the Asian section of most supermarkets. **MAKES 4 SERVINGS | PER SERVING: 356 CALORIES, 9 G. TOTAL FAT (LESS THAN 1 G. SATURATED FAT), 38 G. CARBOHYDRATES, 35 G. PROTEIN, 9 G. DIETARY FIBER, 790 MG. SODIUM.**

¼ cup fat-free, reduced sodium chicken broth

2 tablespoons reduced sodium soy sauce

⅛ teaspoon toasted sesame oil

Canola oil spray

1 large garlic clove, minced

2 teaspoons finely chopped peeled fresh ginger

4 cups small broccoli florets (about 1 pound)

1 large red bell pepper, seeded and diced

1 can (15 ounces) straw mushrooms, rinsed and drained

1 pound medium shrimp, peeled and deveined

2 cups hot cooked brown rice

¼ cup unsalted roasted peanuts

■ In a small bowl, whisk together the chicken broth, soy sauce, and sesame oil. Set it aside. Coat a large nonstick skillet with canola oil spray and heat over high heat until hot. Stir-fry the garlic and ginger for 15 seconds, until fragrant. Add the broccoli and pepper and stir-fry for 2 minutes, until the broccoli is bright green. Add the mushrooms, shrimp, and broth mixture. Cook for about 3 to 4 minutes, stirring, until the shrimp are pink and cooked through. Serve immediately over the rice. Sprinkle with the peanuts.

citrus-braised tofu with vegetables

Animal proteins are often high in saturated fat. For quality protein without this disadvantage, many cooks look to tofu. Some people think tofu is mushy or flavorless. It doesn't have to be that way. By buying the firm or extra firm variety, pressing out the excess water, and cooking the tofu until it turns a rich golden brown, you'll dispel any illusions about tofu's "mushiness." And by stir-frying it with a variety of distinctly flavorful ingredients, you'll demonstrate how well tofu absorbs the flavors of different foods to bring a dish together. The tofu should be prepared 45 minutes in advance, so plan accordingly.

MAKES 5 SERVINGS | PER SERVING: 360 CALORIES, 8 G. TOTAL FAT (1 G. SATURATED FAT), 62 G. CARBOHYDRATES, 11 G. PROTEIN, 3 G. DIETARY FIBER, 150 MG. SODIUM.

1 pound firm or extra-firm tofu

2 tablespoons toasted sesame oil, divided

12 baby carrots, peeled and halved lengthwise

1 medium red onion, diced

1 medium red bell pepper, seeded and diced

1½ teaspoons minced peeled fresh ginger

1 garlic clove, minced

1 can (6 ounces) orange juice concentrate, thawed and diluted with 2 cans of water

1 tablespoon freshly squeezed lime juice

1 tablespoon light soy sauce

2 teaspoons grated orange zest

½ teaspoon dried basil

Pinch of dried red pepper flakes (optional)

1 cup trimmed fresh or frozen cut green beans

6 ears canned baby corn, drained and cut into 1-inch pieces

1½ tablespoons cornstarch

Salt and freshly ground black pepper

1 package (7 ounces) thin rice noodles, soaked in hot water until pliable, then drained

■ Cut the tofu block horizontally into 2 slabs. Place the two pieces side by side on a cutting board covered with plastic wrap. Place another cutting board on top, and put 2 to 4 heavy cans on the top board to weight the tofu evenly. Let the tofu stand for 45 minutes. Remove the cans and the top board and blot the tofu well with paper towels. Cut the tofu into 3/4-inch cubes. If not using immediately, arrange them on a baking sheet covered with paper towels, then cover with plastic wrap. Refrigerate for up to 24 hours. Blot the tofu with paper towels before cooking.

■ In a large nonstick skillet, heat 2 teaspoons of the sesame oil over medium-high heat. Add half of the tofu. Cook for about 10 minutes, turning gently every 2 minutes, until golden. Transfer the tofu to a plate. Heat 2 more teaspoons of the sesame oil in the skillet and repeat the procedure with the remaining tofu.

■ Add the remaining 2 teaspoons of the sesame oil to the skillet. Add the carrots, onion, bell pepper, ginger, and garlic and stir-fry for 2 minutes. Set aside 2 tablespoons of the orange juice mixture in a small bowl and add the remaining orange juice mixture, lime juice, and soy sauce to the skillet. Stir in the tofu, orange zest, basil, and red pepper flakes. Bring the mixture to a boil. Reduce the heat and simmer for about 2 minutes. Add the green beans and corn. Cook for about 4 minutes, or until the beans are crisp but tender. Mix the remaining 2 tablespoons of the orange juice mixture with the cornstarch until completely blended and stir it into the stir-fry. Cook on medium-high heat for 1 to 2 minutes, stirring, until slightly thickened. Season to taste with salt and pepper. To serve, divide the prepared rice noodles among 6 wide, shallow bowls. Ladle the stir-fry over the noodles.

orange and sesame stir-fry with bow tie pasta

Bursting with color and flavor, this stir-fry comes with a twist—the addition of juicy orange segments at the end of cooking. Try toasting the sesame seeds for heightened flavor. Then for one final surprise, serve this stir-fry over whole wheat pasta instead of the usual rice. A traditional preparation with unusual and healthy ingredients makes for an interesting one-dish meal.

MAKES 4 SERVINGS | PER SERVING: 370 CALORIES, 7 G. OF TOTAL FAT (1 G. SATURATED FAT), 57 G. CARBOHYDRATES, 22 G. PROTEIN, 7 G. DIETARY FIBER, 292 MG. SODIUM.

½ cup freshly squeezed orange juice

2 tablespoons reduced sodium soy sauce

1 tablespoon toasted sesame oil

1 teaspoon cornstarch

8 ounces bow tie pasta, preferably whole wheat

Canola oil spray

2 garlic cloves, minced

1 tablespoon finely grated peeled fresh ginger

1 cup scallions, trimmed and chopped

1½ cups sliced mushrooms

⅓ pound asparagus, trimmed and cut into 1-inch pieces (about 1 cup)

1 orange, peeled, halved, seeded, and split into segments

1 cup (about 5 ounces) cooked turkey or chicken breast or thigh, or lean beef, cut into bite-sized pieces, or 2 cups black beans, rinsed and drained

1 tablespoon sesame seeds, toasted*

*Note: To toast the sesame seeds, put them in a small skillet over medium heat for 1 to 2 minutes, stirring constantly, until the seeds are light brown. Watch carefully: sesame seeds can burn quickly. Immediately transfer the seeds to a small dish and cool.

■ In a small bowl, stir together the orange juice, soy sauce, sesame oil, and cornstarch until completely blended. Set this sauce aside.

■ Cook the pasta according to the package instructions. Rinse the pasta with cold water and drain well.

■ Lightly coat a large nonstick skillet with canola oil spray and heat over medium-high heat. Add the garlic and ginger and stir-fry for about 1 minute, until lightly colored. Add the scallions and mushrooms and stir-fry for about 2 minutes. Add the asparagus and stir-fry for about 2 minutes.

■ Stir the sauce and add to the skillet. Cook for 1 to 2 minutes, stirring constantly, until the vegetables are crisp but tender and the sauce thickens. Add the pasta and orange pieces, stirring lightly until all the ingredients are combined. Add the meat and cook until heated through. Sprinkle with the sesame seeds and serve.

three-pepper tofu stir-fry

In this recipe, marinating the tofu infuses it with flavors of pineapple, ginger, sesame, and garlic. If you don't have time to marinate it overnight, don't worry—a quick one-hour soak will do the trick. Then the fully flavored tofu is mixed with three different kinds of bell pepper, each with its own degree of sweetness and distinctive color. The result is a dish that is surprisingly complex yet takes just a few minutes to cook. MAKES 4 SERVINGS | PER SERVING: 354 CALORIES, 12 G. TOTAL FAT (1 G. SATURATED FAT), 50 G. CARBOHYDRATES, 15 G. PROTEIN, 4 G. DIETARY FIBER, 535 MG. SODIUM.

MARINADE

½ cup pineapple juice

1 tablespoon packed light brown sugar

2 tablespoons reduced sodium soy sauce

¼ teaspoon toasted sesame oil

1 tablespoon hoisin sauce

½ teaspoon ground ginger

1 teaspoon chopped garlic

. . . .

1 pound extra firm tofu, well drained, patted dry, and cut into ¾-inch cubes

1 tablespoon plus 1 teaspoon canola oil, divided

½ medium purple onion, sliced

½ medium yellow bell pepper, seeded and chopped

½ medium green bell pepper, seeded and chopped

1 medium red bell pepper, seeded and chopped

1 scallion, trimmed and sliced

1 celery rib, sliced

1 tablespoon reduced sodium soy sauce

1 cup fresh or canned pineapple chunks, drained

1 teaspoon cornstarch

3 tablespoons chopped walnuts, toasted*

¼ cup chopped fresh cilantro, loosely packed, for garnish

2 cups hot cooked brown rice

*Note: To toast the walnuts, put them in a small skillet over medium-high heat and stir frequently for 2 to 3 minutes, until lightly browned. Immediately transfer the nuts to a small dish and cool.

■ In a large bowl, mix together the marinade ingredients and add the tofu. Refrigerate for 1 hour or up to 24 hours. Remove the tofu from the marinade and reserve the marinade. Gently pat the tofu dry with paper towels. In a large nonstick skillet, heat 1 tablespoon of the canola oil over medium-high heat. Add the tofu and cook about 10 minutes, turning gently with a spatula every few minutes to brown all of the sides evenly.

■ When the tofu has browned, transfer it to a bowl. Add the remaining 1 teaspoon of canola oil to the skillet and heat over medium-high heat until hot. Stir-fry the onion, bell peppers, scallion, and celery in the soy sauce until the bell peppers are crisp but tender. Stir-fry the pineapple to heat through. Add the cornstarch to the reserved marinade and stir until completely blended. Add the marinade to the skillet. Quickly return the tofu to the skillet and stir gently until the marinade has turned clear and thick, about 2 to 3 minutes. Transfer to a serving dish and sprinkle with the walnuts and garnish with the cilantro, if desired. Serve over the brown rice.

sweet potato and pear stir-fry with chicken and chile sauce

In some parts of Southeast Asia, fruit is used to supply the sweet element in the delicate balance of hot-sour-salty-bitter-sweet flavors that cooks strive to achieve. The pears used in this stir-fry, for example, add a delicate sweetness and crunch. This recipe calls for a few extra minutes of prep time to prepare the sweet potatoes for stir-frying, but the flavor they impart to the dish is well worth the effort. Mirin, a sweet Japanese rice wine used for cooking, can be found in the Asian section of many supermarkets and in Asian markets, as can Thai or Vietnamese fish sauce, which adds a unique pungency to the dish. **MAKES 6 SERVINGS | PER SERVING: 370 CALORIES, 7 G. TOTAL FAT (LESS THAN 1 G. SATURATED FAT), 54 G. CARBOHYDRATES, 24 G. PROTEIN, 7 G. DIETARY FIBER, 754 MG. SODIUM.**

MARINADE

- 2 tablespoons reduced sodium soy sauce
- 1 teaspoon sugar
- 1 tablespoon mirin or sake or dry white wine
- 1 pound boneless, skinless chicken breast or thigh, cut into thin bite-sized pieces

SAUCE

- 2 teaspoons cornstarch
- 1 cup fat-free, reduced sodium chicken broth
- 1½ tablespoons Vietnamese or Thai fish sauce or reduced sodium soy sauce, or to taste
- ¼ teaspoon dried red pepper flakes, or to taste

. . . .

- 2 large orange-flesh sweet potatoes, peeled and cut into 1-inch pieces
- 2 tablespoons canola oil, divided
- 2 large garlic cloves, minced
- 2 tablespoons peeled and minced fresh ginger
  Pinch of cayenne
- 1 medium yellow bell pepper, seeded and cut into bite-sized pieces
- 1 medium red bell pepper, seeded and cut into bite-sized pieces
- ½ cup canned whole water chestnuts, drained and sliced
- 1 large Asian pear or Bosc pear, peeled, cored, and thinly sliced
- 1 bag (6 ounces) baby spinach leaves
- 3 cups hot cooked brown rice
- ¼ cup chopped fresh cilantro, loosely packed, for garnish

■ To prepare the marinade, combine the soy sauce, sugar, and mirin in a glass, plastic, or nonreactive metal pan large enough to hold the chicken. Add the chicken, tossing to coat all sides, and marinate for up to 30 minutes at room temperature, or cover and refrigerate for 1 hour or up to 8 hours. If chilled, bring the chicken to room temperature before beginning to stir-fry.

■ To prepare the sauce, in a small bowl or measuring cup, stir or whisk the cornstarch with the broth until completely blended. Stir in the fish sauce and red pepper flakes. Set the sauce aside.

■ In a large pot, add the sweet potatoes with water to cover. Bring to a boil, reduce the heat, and simmer for about 3 minutes, until the sweet potatoes are fairly resistant when pierced with a fork. Drain the sweet potatoes into a colander and set aside. Remove the chicken from the marinade and pat it dry with a paper towel. Discard the marinade.

■ In a large, heavy skillet or wok, heat 1 tablespoon of the canola oil over medium-high heat. Add the garlic, ginger, and cayenne and stir-fry for 30 seconds, or until the garlic is golden. Add the chicken to the skillet and stir-fry for about 3 to 4 minutes, until just cooked through or until the juices run clear. Transfer the contents of the skillet to a bowl.

■ In the same skillet, heat the remaining 1 tablespoon of canola oil over medium-high heat. Add the drained sweet potatoes, bell peppers, and water chestnuts. Stir-fry for about 3 minutes, until the bell peppers and the sweet potatoes are not quite tender. Add the cooked chicken, pear, and spinach. Stir-fry, stirring constantly, just until the spinach is wilted, about 2 to 3 minutes.

■ Stir the sauce and add to the skillet. Cook, stirring constantly, for 2 to 3 minutes, just until the sauce becomes clear and thickened. Immediately remove from the heat. Use a slotted spoon to serve the stir-fry mixture over the rice. Garnish with the cilantro. Pass the sauce to add separately, as desired.

zucchini and portobello stir-fry with chicken

This recipe pairs a method of preparation traditionally regarded as Asian (stir-frying) with ingredients traditionally regarded as Italian (zucchini, portobello mushrooms, oregano, and Parmesan). The quick cooking that these ingredients get from stir-frying allows their flavors to remain distinct and recognizable even as they contribute to the dish's deep, nuanced character. As with all recipes on the New American Plate, we have focused on the vegetables, with the portobello mushrooms providing extra substance and richness. MAKES 4 SERVINGS | PER SERVING: 364 CALORIES, 11 G. TOTAL FAT (2 G. SATURATED FAT), 32 G. CARBOHYDRATES, 34 G. PROTEIN, 3 G. DIETARY FIBER, 303 MG. SODIUM.

2 tablespoons extra-virgin olive oil

1 pound skinless, boneless chicken breast or thigh, cut into ¾-inch pieces

2 large red bell peppers, seeded and cut into 1-inch pieces

2 large zucchini, halved lengthwise and sliced diagonally into ½-inch pieces

4 garlic cloves, finely minced

4 large portobello mushrooms (about 1 pound), cleaned, stems removed, and cut into 1-inch pieces

2 teaspoons dried basil

2 teaspoons dried oregano

½ teaspoon dried red pepper flakes, or to taste

1 cup fat-free, reduced sodium chicken broth

¼ cup freshly grated Parmesan cheese

Salt and freshly ground black pepper

2 cups hot cooked brown rice

■ Place a large skillet or medium stockpot over high heat. Add the olive oil and heat it until very hot. Add the chicken and stir-fry for about 5 minutes, until it loses its pink color. With a slotted spoon, remove the chicken from the skillet and set it aside. Add the bell pepper, zucchini, and garlic to the skillet. Stir-fry for about 2 minutes, until the vegetables are crisp but tender. Add the mushrooms and stir-fry for about 2 minutes, until the liquid released from the mushrooms evaporates.

■ Return the chicken to the skillet and add the basil, oregano, red pepper flakes, and chicken broth. Cook for about 4 minutes, stirring, until the chicken is completely cooked through. Remove the pan from the heat. Add the cheese, season to taste with salt and pepper, and toss ingredients together. Serve immediately over the brown rice.

sweet and sour mixed vegetables with pork

Pork with pineapple is a classic pairing, as anyone who's enjoyed a holiday ham studded with sliced pineapple can tell you. In this stir-fry, the pineapple brings out the flavor of the pork and intensifies the tastes of the dish's many other ingredients. In return, the carrots, onion, broccoli, and baby corn keep the sweetness of the pineapple in check. The result is a balanced and intriguing flavor. **MAKES 4 SERVINGS | PER SERVING: 409 CALORIES, 9 G. TOTAL FAT (2 G. SATURATED FAT), 61 G. CARBOHYDRATES, 25 G. PROTEIN, 6 G. DIETARY FIBER, 158 MG. SODIUM.**

¾ pound boneless pork loin, trimmed of all visible fat

1 can (20 ounces) pineapple chunks in juice

2 tablespoons Worcestershire sauce

1 tablespoon cornstarch

4 teaspoons canola oil, divided

1 garlic clove, finely chopped

1 teaspoon minced peeled fresh ginger

2 cups small broccoli florets

1 medium carrot, peeled and thinly sliced on the diagonal

1 medium onion, cut into ½-inch slices

8 ears canned baby corn, drained

2 cups bean sprouts

Salt and freshly ground black pepper

2 cups cooked brown rice

■ Wrap the pork in foil and put it in the freezer for 20 to 30 minutes, until very firm but not frozen. Remove the pork and cut it into very thin strips, about ⅛ inch by 1 inch. Set aside.

■ Drain the juice from the pineapple into a measuring cup. (There should be slightly less than 1 cup of juice.) Measure out ¾ cup of the pineapple chunks and set aside. Reserve the remaining pineapple for another use. Stir the Worcestershire sauce into the juice. Add the cornstarch and stir until the mixture is well combined.

■ In a wok or large skillet, heat 2 teaspoons of the canola oil over medium-high heat. Add the garlic and ginger and stir-fry for about 20 seconds, until fragrant, taking care not to burn the garlic or ginger. With a slotted spoon, transfer the garlic and ginger to a small dish and set aside.

■ Add the remaining oil and heat over high heat until hot. Add the pork and stir-fry about 2 minutes, until white. Add the broccoli, carrot, onion, corn, and bean sprouts. Season with salt and pepper. Stir-fry for about 4 to 5 minutes, until the broccoli and carrot are crisp but tender. Stir in the ginger and garlic and the ¾ cup of pineapple.

■ Stir the pineapple juice mixture and add it to the pan. Cook 2 to 3 minutes, stirring constantly, until the liquid has thickened into a sauce. Season to taste with salt and pepper. Serve immediately over hot brown rice.

pilafs

Pilaf is a fancy name for a one-pot meal with rice or another grain as its base. The traditional pilaf, which originated in the Middle East over seven hundred years ago, is cooked so the rice grains are fluffy but separate, rather than sticking together. In Iran and other parts of the Middle East, rice is often combined with fruits like quince, sour cherry, and pomegranate. Different combinations are used in other parts of the world. Pilafs contain meat and vegetables in Central Asia, fish in Turkey, and curry or other strong spices in India. In some culinary traditions, pilafs contain many different kinds of vegetables, fruits, and nuts as well as meat.

In the New World, the pilaf underwent changes in both character and ingredients. Perhaps the most traditional American pilaf is Hoppin' John, which combines rice with black-eyed peas and other vegetables, plus some form of pork for flavor.

Pilafs can be prepared with a wide variety of grains, offering you an opportunity to use more healthful whole grains rather than refined versions. Other grains used in pilafs include barley; bulgur, which is common in Syria and Armenia; and kasha, or buckwheat groats. They all make hearty and flavorful pilafs. For a light, delicate pilaf, some cooks prefer quinoa, a small, ivory grain originally grown by the Incas.

Pilafs are an excellent way to transition from the high-fat, less healthful, meat-dominated entrée so common today. The revamped pilafs in this chapter, with their two-thirds to one-third proportion and their high-fiber, low-fat content, fit beautifully into the ideal diet for reducing the risk of cancer and other chronic health problems.

As with stews and casseroles, pilafs can easily include a wide variety of vegetables; if these are cooked separately and added to the grains at the last minute, their crunch nicely contrasts with and complements the soft texture of cooked grains. When it includes fruit with vegetables and a whole grain, a pilaf will offer a richer, more interesting taste as well as a wider range of phytochemicals. Recipes that contain fruit—in an echo of Middle Eastern pilafs—include Couscous and Lamb Pilaf with Dried Fruits and Nuts (page 159).

couscous and lamb pilaf with dried fruits and nuts
Couscous is a light, fluffy pasta resembling a grain. It is a dietary staple in many Mediterranean countries. This recipe pairs it with other classic Mediterranean ingredients—plump golden raisins, apricots, toasted nuts, and tender lamb—in a pilaf scented with cumin, cinnamon, coriander, and mint. Look for whole wheat couscous, which is becoming increasingly available in supermarkets. MAKES 8 SERVINGS | PER SERVING: 350 CALORIES, 11 G. TOTAL FAT (2 G. SATURATED FAT), 48 G. CARBOHYDRATES, 13 G. PROTEIN, 5 G. DIETARY FIBER, 338 MG. SODIUM.

½ teaspoon ground cumin

½ teaspoon ground cinnamon

1 teaspoon ground coriander, divided

1 teaspoon salt, plus more to taste

6 ounces lamb tenderloin, trimmed of visible fat

2 tablespoons canola oil, divided

1 box (10 ounces) couscous, preferably whole wheat

½ cup dried apricots, cut into slivers

½ cup golden raisins

3 cups boiling water, divided

2 cups frozen green peas, thawed

Freshly ground white pepper

½ cup unsalted shelled pistachios or slivered almonds, toasted*

¼ cup minced fresh mint leaves, for garnish

*Note: To toast the nuts, put them in a small skillet over medium-high heat and stir frequently for 2 to 3 minutes, until lightly browned. Immediately transfer the nuts to a small dish and cool.

■ Mix together the cumin, cinnamon, ½ teaspoon of the coriander, and 1 teaspoon salt. Rub this spice mixture into the lamb. Cover the lamb and let stand for 30 to 60 minutes in the refrigerator.

■ Meanwhile, in a medium saucepan, heat 1 tablespoon of the canola oil over medium-high heat. Add the couscous and cook, stirring, for 1 to 2 minutes, until the grains turn translucent and shiny. Remove the pan from the heat. Add the remaining ½ teaspoon of coriander and the apricots and raisins, and mix well. Pour in 2 cups of the boiling water and stir briskly. Immediately cover the pan with a tight-fitting lid. Let it stand for 7 minutes.

■ Stir the couscous with a fork to fluff the grains. Add the remaining 1 cup of boiling water. Put the peas on top of the couscous. Cover and let it stand for 5 to 8 more minutes, or until liquid is absorbed.

■ Cut the lamb into ¼-inch-thick slices, then into bite-sized pieces. In a skillet, heat the remaining 1 tablespoon of canola oil over medium-high heat. Add the lamb and sauté 5 to 7 minutes, until browned and cooked through. With a slotted spoon, transfer the meat to a paper towel.

■ Stir the couscous to fluff the grains and season to taste with salt and white pepper. Transfer to a serving bowl. Top with the lamb and nuts. Sprinkle with mint and serve.

red pepper, tomato, and chicken pilaf

This healthy revamp of a classic chicken pilaf stays true to its roots in simplicity and convenience. Using bottled roasted red peppers is a convenient, quick way to add extra flavor without adding extra time. **MAKES 6 SERVINGS | PER SERVING: 229 CALORIES, 4 G. TOTAL FAT (LESS THAN 1 G. SATURATED FAT), 32 G. CARBOHYDRATES, 17 G. PROTEIN, 3 G. DIETARY FIBER, 441 MG. SODIUM.**

1⅔ cups quick-cooking brown rice

1 small onion, chopped

1 tablespoon extra-virgin olive oil

1 can (14.5 ounces) stewed tomatoes

1 can (14.5 ounces) fat-free, reduced sodium chicken or vegetable broth

1 teaspoon paprika

½ teaspoon dried oregano

½ teaspoon freshly ground black pepper

1 jar (7 ounces) roasted red peppers, drained and chopped

¾ pound skinless, boneless chicken breast, cut into 1-inch pieces

1 bay leaf

Salt (optional)

½ cup frozen green peas

■ Preheat the oven to 375 degrees.

■ In a 2-quart casserole dish, combine the rice, onion, oil, tomatoes, broth, paprika, oregano, black pepper, roasted red peppers, chicken, bay leaf, and salt, if using. Stir, then cover and bake the casserole for 40 minutes.

■ Stir in the peas and continue to bake, uncovered, for an additional 10 minutes, until all of the broth is absorbed. Remove the bay leaf and serve.

kasha pilaf with squash and chicken

Pilafs are a great way to introduce new flavors to the daily diet. This recipe calls for kasha, or roasted buckwheat kernels, a nutritional powerhouse bursting with fiber, minerals, and the phytochemical rutin, believed to help lower cholesterol. Kasha has a pleasant toasted, nutty flavor, but it lacks gluten, the protein that holds grains like wheat and barley together during cooking. That's why kasha is usually prepared by coating it with egg, heating it to "bake" the egg protein onto the grains, and simmering it in chicken broth until the liquid is absorbed. **MAKES 4 SERVINGS | PER SERVING: 389 CALORIES, 13 G. TOTAL FAT (3 G. SATURATED FAT), 40 G. CARBOHYDRATES, 31 G. PROTEIN, 6 G. DIETARY FIBER, 713 MG. SODIUM.**

1 cup kasha

1 large egg, lightly beaten

2 cups fat-free, reduced sodium chicken broth, plus more to thin pilaf, if needed

2 tablespoons extra-virgin olive oil

1 cup chopped onion

1 cup chopped red bell pepper

1 cup chopped zucchini

1 cup chopped yellow squash

2 cups cubed cooked chicken

1½ tablespoons reduced sodium soy sauce, or to taste

Salt and freshly ground black pepper

2 tablespoons sliced almonds, for garnish

■ Cook the kasha according to the package instructions, using the egg and broth.

■ Meanwhile, in a large nonstick skillet, heat the olive oil over medium-high heat. Add the onion, bell pepper, zucchini, and yellow squash and sauté for 5 minutes, until the vegetables are tender. Add the chicken and soy sauce and cook for 1 minute. Add the cooked kasha to the skillet and season to taste with salt and pepper. If the mixture is too dry, thin it with additional broth. Garnish with the almonds.

entrée salads

At one time a salad was a simple first course or side dish—some lettuce dressed with oil and vinegar, and perhaps garnished with a few cucumber and tomato slices. Today, a salad can be substantial enough to be an entrée or even a meal in itself. In addition to leafy greens and chopped vegetables, a salad that is filling enough to serve for dinner might contain pasta or another grain, beans, or some cooked meat or fish. Hard-cooked eggs, nuts, chickpeas, anchovies, olives, cheese, and fruit might also be added.

Entrée salads make an easy meal when time is limited. They are especially refreshing in warm weather, when a heavy meal would be out of place. They also offer the opportunity to use a wide variety of vegetables.

The endless possibilities for entrée salad ingredients mean you can improvise at the last minute, creating a salad straight from your refrigerator, freezer, and cupboards. Although we usually think of fresh produce when it's time to make a salad, many canned ingredients can also be used, from beans, marinated artichoke hearts and hearts of palm, corn, and beets to canned chicken, salmon, and tuna fish. (For maximum taste and minimum sodium, canned vegetables and beans should be drained, rinsed, and drained again before using.) Frozen peas and corn need only to be defrosted before being added to the salad bowl. Leftover meat or chicken, thinly diced or sliced, works well with most salad ingredients. A freshly cooked (or even leftover) grain, such as pasta, rice, bulgur, or quinoa, will add both soft texture and filling heartiness.

Although an entrée salad can be made with ingredients at hand, recipes help, especially when you're in a salad "rut" or time pressures have temporarily disconnected your imagination. Use dark leafy greens as a base. From old standbys (romaine, red- or green-leaf lettuce, spinach, and Bibb or Boston lettuce) to so-called gourmet greens (arugula, frisée, mâche) to less well-known options (mustard greens, Swiss chard, broccoli rabe) there is a wide variety of greens to choose from. You can combine two to four of these greens in one salad to create a more interesting mix of flavors and textures. Mixing greens will also guarantee a wider range of vitamins, minerals, and phytochemicals. You can now buy a variety of bags containing different mixed greens, often with other salad ingredients included.

When selecting salad ingredients, keep in mind the importance of color: different colors look good together, and they signal a wider range of nutrients. Instead of the usual green bell pepper, try the orange, red, or yellow versions; red instead of yellow onion; red instead of pale green cabbage; and carrots to add as a grated garnish. Grapes, slices of apple, and segments of orange or grapefruit will add a bright note as well as a contrasting juiciness to the salad. Don't forget fresh herbs, which add depth of flavor as well as important phytochemicals. Mint, basil, cilantro, and flat leaf parsley are classic salad herbs.

Whatever ingredients you use, follow the two-thirds to one-third proportion of plant-based foods to meat or other protein that is used to create the healthy New American Plate.

fruit and nut salad with pork

This fruit salad is a study in contrasts: the satisfying crunch of nuts amid a sweet and tangy medley of berries, peaches, and citrus fruits. It's also pleasing to the eye: the brilliant color of each fruit stands out against the pale strips of julienned pork. Pork has a slight natural sweetness all its own, which is why so many different world cuisines put pork and fruit together. Here, pork provides the protein that turns this fruit salad into a main dish. **MAKES 4 SERVINGS | PER SERVING: 353 CALORIES, 13 G. TOTAL FAT (2 G. SATURATED FAT), 44 G. CARBOHYDRATES, 20 G. PROTEIN, 7 G. DIETARY FIBER, 42 MG. SODIUM.**

1½ cups sliced fresh strawberries

1½ cups fresh blueberries

1½ cups sliced fresh peaches

1½ cups sliced fresh or canned pineapple

2 kiwis, peeled and diced

½ pound cooked pork, julienned

1½ tablespoons honey

1½ tablespoons freshly squeezed lime juice

3 tablespoons freshly squeezed orange juice

3 tablespoons chopped hazelnuts or Brazil nuts, toasted*

2 tablespoons slivered almonds, toasted*

Fresh mint leaves, for garnish

*Note: To toast the nuts, put them in a small skillet over medium-high heat and stir frequently for 2 to 3 minutes, until lightly browned. Immediately transfer the nuts to a small dish and cool.

■ In a serving bowl or on a serving platter, combine all of the fruit. (You can also serve the salad in hollowed-out shells of cantaloupe or watermelon.) Arrange the pork strips over the fruit.

■ In a small bowl, whisk together the honey, lime juice, and orange juice. Drizzle over the fruit and pork. Top with the toasted nuts, garnish with the fresh mint leaves, and serve.

papaya, red pepper, and pecan salad with chicken

Sweet papaya and crisp red bell pepper are the real stars of this salad—although the deliciously tangy dressing, made with lime juice, honey, garlic, and mustard, gives them both a run for their money. The toasted pecans add crunch and flavor.

MAKES 4 SERVINGS | PER SERVING: 360 CALORIES, 17 G. TOTAL FAT (2 G. SATURATED FAT), 33 G. CARBOHYDRATES, 24 G. PROTEIN, 7 G. DIETARY FIBER, 122 MG. SODIUM.

8 cups torn romaine lettuce leaves

2 medium, ripe papaya, peeled, halved, seeded, and cubed

1 large red bell pepper, halved, seeded and sliced into ¼-inch pieces

2 scallions, trimmed and sliced, white part only

¼ cup freshly squeezed lime juice

2 tablespoons fat free, reduced sodium chicken broth

1 tablespoon honey

2 garlic cloves, minced

1 teaspoon Dijon mustard

3 tablespoons extra-virgin olive oil

Salt and freshly ground black pepper

¾ pound cooked boneless, skinless chicken breast, cut into bite-sized pieces

¼ cup chopped pecans, toasted*

*Note: To toast the pecans, put them in a small skillet over medium-high heat and stir frequently for 2 to 3 minutes, until lightly browned. Immediately transfer the nuts to a small dish and cool.

■ In a large salad bowl, combine the lettuce, papaya, bell pepper, and scallions. In a measuring cup or small bowl, whisk together the lime juice, broth, honey, garlic, and mustard. Slowly add the olive oil in a thin stream and whisk the dressing until it is well blended. Season to taste with salt and pepper.

■ Pour the dressing over the salad, add the chicken, and toss until well combined. Top with the pecans and serve.

bean, corn, and pepper salad with chicken

Bold colors and flavors combine in this satisfying salad. There's something for everyone: crunchy jicama, the zing of lime juice, sweet and tender corn, and a nourishing backdrop of black beans and salsa. **MAKES 6 SERVINGS | PER SERVING: 395 CALORIES, 15 G. TOTAL FAT (2 G. SATURATED FAT), 40 G. CARBOHYDRATES, 29 G. PROTEIN, 7 G. DIETARY FIBER, 691 MG. SODIUM.**

1½ cups cooked brown rice

3 cups cubed cooked skinless chicken breast

1 can (15 ounces) corn, drained

1 can (15.5 ounces) black beans, rinsed and drained

1 medium green bell pepper, seeded and diced

1 medium red bell pepper, seeded and diced

½ cup peeled and diced jicama

⅓ cup extra-virgin olive oil

1 tablespoon freshly squeezed lime juice, or to taste

¾ cup chunky salsa

3 drops hot pepper sauce, or to taste (optional)

2 to 4 tablespoons water

Salt and freshly ground black pepper

Green leafy lettuce leaves

¼ cup finely chopped fresh cilantro or flat leaf parsley, loosely packed, for garnish

¼ cup lowfat shredded cheddar cheese, for garnish

■ In a large bowl, combine the rice, chicken, corn, beans, bell peppers, and jicama. Gently toss until well mixed and set aside.

■ In a medium bowl, whisk together the olive oil and lime juice until well blended. Mix in the salsa and hot pepper sauce. Add enough water to thin the consistency so the dressing can be thinly drizzled over the salad. Drizzle the dressing over the chicken mixture and toss to coat the salad ingredients evenly. Cover the salad and refrigerate for 1 to 3 hours so the flavors can meld. Bring the salad to room temperature and check the seasonings before serving. Season to taste with salt and pepper. Drain off any excess dressing. Place the salad in a serving bowl lined with lettuce leaves, sprinkle the top of the salad with cilantro and cheese, and serve.

corn and quinoa salad with chicken

Although corn is commonly referred to as a vegetable, it is technically a grain. For that matter, although quinoa (pronounced "*keen*-wah") is commonly referred to as a grain, it's technically a fruit. (The individual "grains" are actually seeds.) Whatever their botanical classification, putting these two foods together makes good sense—and good flavor. Quinoa is rich in a family of substances called saponins, which appear to fight a wide range of chronic diseases. With tomato, red onion, chile, and chunks of roasted chicken, this cool salad makes a great summertime meal. **MAKES 4 SERVINGS | PER SERVING: 367 CALORIES, 7 G. TOTAL FAT (1 G. SATURATED FAT), 60 G. CARBOHYDRATES, 20 G. PROTEIN, 6 G. DIETARY FIBER, 334 MG. SODIUM.**

1 cup quinoa, well rinsed and drained

2½ cups cold water

2 cups drained canned corn

1 cup (3 ounces) roasted or grilled skinless chicken breast, cut into ½-inch pieces

2 medium tomatoes, seeded and chopped

1 cup finely chopped red onion

2 small jalapeño chiles, seeded and minced (optional)*

1 cup chopped fresh cilantro, loosely packed

Juice of 2 oranges

1 teaspoon ground cumin

2 teaspoons extra-virgin olive oil

Salt and freshly ground black pepper

*Note: Wear rubber gloves to handle fresh chiles, and keep your hands away from your eyes.

■ In a large saucepan, cook the quinoa with water according to package directions. Uncover and cool slightly.

■ In a large bowl, combine the quinoa, corn, chicken, tomatoes, onion, jalapeños, and cilantro. In a separate bowl, combine the orange juice, cumin, and oil. Add to quinoa mixture. Toss to coat. Season to taste with salt and pepper. Serve warm or slightly chilled.

salade niçoise

We haven't had to tinker too much with the traditional salade niçoise. In many ways, this classic French salad typifies New American Plate fare: a wide variety of nutrient-rich plant foods, with a bit of animal protein added for flavor. **MAKES 4 SERVINGS | PER SERVING: 323 CALORIES, 10 G. TOTAL FAT (1 G. SATURATED FAT), 31 G. CARBOHYDRATES, 28 G. PROTEIN, 7 G. DIETARY FIBER, 462 MG. SODIUM.**

16 romaine lettuce leaves, torn into large pieces

2 cans (6.5 ounces each) chunk light tuna in water, drained, or ¾ pound fresh cooked tuna, flaked

1¼ pounds new potatoes, cooked and halved

1 pound trimmed fresh green beans or 1 package (10 ounces) frozen green beans, cooked until crisp but tender

1 tablespoon capers, rinsed and dried

2 hard-boiled eggs, quartered

3 medium ripe tomatoes, cut into 6 wedges each

4 anchovy fillets, well rinsed and dried (optional)

¼ cup Niçoise olives

8 very thin slices red onion

2 tablespoons red wine vinegar

1 garlic clove, finely minced

2 tablespoons plus 1 teaspoon extra-virgin olive oil

Salt and freshly ground black pepper

■ Arrange the lettuce leaves to cover a large serving platter. Mound the tuna in the center of the platter and arrange the potato halves in a ring around the tuna. Arrange the cooked beans around the potatoes and sprinkle the capers over the potatoes. Alternate the hard-boiled eggs, tomato wedges, and anchovies around the beans. Sprinkle the olives over the salad and arrange the onion on top.

■ In a small bowl, combine the vinegar and garlic. Whisk in the olive oil. Season to taste with salt and pepper. Pour the dressing over the salad, making sure to moisten the tuna well.

spinach and orange salad with shrimp

As with most dishes on the New American Plate, this refreshing salad takes color as its cue for maximizing flavor and health. A vibrant array of different colors means different tastes, textures, and protective phytochemicals. Here, dark green spinach offsets red bell peppers, red onions, and juicy slices of orange. **MAKES 4 SERVINGS | PER SERVING: 300 CALORIES, 11 G. TOTAL FAT (2 G. SATURATED FAT), 33 G. CARBOHYDRATES, 21 G. PROTEIN, 8 G. DIETARY FIBER, 254 MG. SODIUM.**

1 pound uncooked large shrimp

12 cups baby spinach leaves, stems removed, loosely packed

3 navel oranges, peeled, halved, and thinly sliced

2 large red bell peppers, seeded and julienned

8 very thin slices red onion

1 cup freshly squeezed orange juice

Juice of 1 lime (optional)

¼ teaspoon ground turmeric

½ teaspoon dried oregano

2½ tablespoons extra-virgin olive oil

Salt and freshly ground black pepper

Lime wedges, for garnish

■ Bring a large saucepan filled with cold water to a boil over medium-high heat. Add the shrimp and cook 3 to 4 minutes, until they are pink and curled. Drain them promptly. As soon as the shrimp are cool enough to handle, peel and devein them. Halve each shrimp lengthwise and set them aside.

■ Arrange ¼ of the spinach as a bed on each of 4 dinner plates. Arrange ¼ of the orange slices on each bed of spinach. Arrange ¼ of the red peppers on top of each salad. Arrange ¼ of the shrimp over the peppers in each salad. Separate the onion into rings and arrange over the shrimp.

■ In a small bowl, whisk together the orange juice, lime juice, turmeric, and oregano. Whisk in the olive oil until well blended. Season to taste with salt and pepper. Spoon the dressing over each salad, garnish with the lime wedges, and serve. The salads can be assembled and the dressing made up to 4 hours ahead. Cover the salads with plastic wrap and refrigerate. Dress and garnish just before serving.

layered black bean and spinach salad

This Southwest-inspired recipe looks great in the salad bowl and tastes great on the plate. The layered effect is easy to create, but your guests don't have to know that. Black beans provide the protein, along with a satisfying mouthfeel that contrasts nicely with the crisp spinach and bell peppers. **MAKES 6 SERVINGS | PER SERVING: 360 CALORIES, 21 G. TOTAL FAT (4 G. SATURATED FAT), 32 G. CARBOHYDRATES, 16 G. PROTEIN, 13 G. DIETARY FIBER, 624 MG. SODIUM.**

6 tablespoons extra-virgin olive oil or canola oil

3 tablespoons freshly squeezed lemon juice

3 tablespoons rice vinegar

1 tablespoon prepared mustard

Salt and freshly ground black pepper

12 cups baby spinach leaves, stems removed, loosely packed

3 cups halved cherry or grape tomatoes

1 medium yellow bell pepper, seeded, cut into quarters and thinly sliced

1 medium red bell pepper, seeded, cut into quarters and thinly sliced

2 cans (15 ounces each) black beans, drained and rinsed

1 cup shredded reduced fat sharp cheddar cheese

1 medium avocado, peeled, pitted, and sliced into ½-inch pieces

■ In a small bowl, whisk together the olive oil, lemon juice, vinegar, and mustard. Season to taste with salt and pepper. Set this dressing aside.

■ In a deep, clear glass bowl, layer the salad as follows: 6 cups of spinach leaves, 1½ cups of tomatoes, ½ of the yellow bell pepper, ½ of the red bell pepper, ½ of the beans, and ½ cup shredded cheese. Repeat the procedure. Top the salad with the avocado. To serve, pass the salad around the table, followed by the dressing.

frittatas

An omelet can qualify as a one-pot meal, whether eaten for breakfast, lunch, or dinner. Another hearty egg dish that will pass muster as a one-pot entrée is the frittata, which is easier to cook than the traditional French-style omelet. Unlike omelets, which are cooked quickly over rather high heat, frittatas are usually cooked very slowly over low to medium heat until firm, not runny like many omelets, and served open-faced rather than folded like the classic omelet. A frittata is usually turned so that both sides are cooked and browned, or the top is browned under a broiler. Frittatas are typically served in wedges, like a pizza. They work well as either an appetizer or a main dish, and because they taste great whether hot, warm, or at room temperature, they can be enjoyed year-round.

As with other dishes prepared according to the guidelines of the New American Plate, the frittatas that follow have been slimmed down from the traditional whole-egg version. But a more healthful pairing of whole eggs with egg whites need not affect the full-flavored character of the dish, especially if generous use is made of vegetables and seasonings.

Frittatas are associated with Italy and Spain, as in the Potato, Pepper, and Cherry Tomato Frittata (page 177). But they can be adapted to reflect a broader geography. Southwestern Vegetable Frittata with Avocado and Salsa (page 181) is as vibrant as the region it represents. Sesame-Ginger Frittata with Broccoli and Shrimp (page 178) proves how well a Mediterranean dish can adopt an Asian persona.

The frittatas in this section are perfect for a light meal, such as breakfast, or on a sweltering day that begs for less than weighty fare. Depending on individual tastes, they can be paired, for example, with a soup and leafy green salad, or a whole-grain bread and fruit salad.

potato, pepper, and cherry tomato frittata

This frittata can be thought of as a no-fuss omelet: no folding or flipping, just a quick sauté of healthy ingredients, after which you allow the eggs to set. Serve it with hot marinara sauce, and you've got a quick but satisfying main dish. In this recipe, egg whites are substituted for some whole eggs and the amount of vegetables is increased to make the frittata a healthy addition to your diet. The frittata is a particularly good choice when you want a filling but low calorie one-dish meal.

MAKES 4 SERVINGS | PER SERVING: 201 CALORIES, 10 G. TOTAL FAT (2 G. SATURATED FAT), 17 G. CARBOHYDRATES, 12 G. PROTEIN, 3 G. DIETARY FIBER, 290 MG. SODIUM.

4 large eggs

4 large egg whites

1 tablespoon olive oil

1 medium red potato, cut into ¼-inch slices or diced

1½ cups halved cherry or grape tomatoes

½ cup diced green bell pepper

½ cup diced onion

½ cup diced mushrooms

Salt and freshly ground black pepper

¼ teaspoon dried basil, crushed

¼ teaspoon dried oregano, crushed

½ cup bottled marinara sauce, heated (optional)

■ In a mixing bowl, whisk together the eggs and egg whites and set aside. Heat a nonstick skillet over medium-high heat, add the olive oil and swirl to coat the entire surface. Add the potato and sauté for 6 minutes, stirring occasionally, until tender but not too soft. Transfer the potato to a plate. Add the tomatoes, bell pepper, onion, and mushrooms to the skillet. Sauté for 4 minutes, stirring frequently, until vegetables are tender. Pour the beaten eggs over the vegetables in the skillet. Set the heat to low. Arrange the potatoes over the eggs in a circle. Season with salt and pepper, then basil and oregano. Cover and cook over low heat until the eggs are just set, about 3 to 5 minutes.

■ Gently slide the frittata onto a serving dish. Top with heated marinara sauce, if desired, cut into 4 pieces, and serve hot.

sesame-ginger frittata with broccoli and shrimp

The frittata is of Italian origin, but we add interest by bringing other cuisines into the mix. This Asian-influenced version uses toasted sesame oil and a sauce with ginger and soy to flavor broccoli, shrimp, sprouts, and red onion. The result is a study in delicate contrasts. **MAKES 4 SERVINGS | PER SERVING: 168 CALORIES, 5 G. TOTAL FAT (1 G. SATURATED FAT), 13 G. CARBOHYDRATES, 19 G. PROTEIN, 2 G. DIETARY FIBER, 430 MG. SODIUM.**

2 cups ½-inch pieces of broccoli florets

2 or 3 scallions, trimmed and finely chopped

1 cup finely chopped red onion

1 cup fresh bean sprouts

5 ounces peeled cooked shrimp, cut into ½-inch pieces (about 1½ cups)

¼ teaspoon toasted sesame oil

¼ teaspoon freshly ground black pepper

3 large eggs

4 large egg whites

2 tablespoons all-purpose flour

1 tablespoon cornstarch

1 tablespoon cold water

1 tablespoon reduced sodium soy sauce

1 teaspoon rice vinegar

1 small garlic clove, minced

½ teaspoon grated peeled fresh ginger

½ teaspoon sugar

½ cup fat-free, reduced sodium chicken broth

Canola oil spray

■ In a medium bowl, combine the broccoli, scallions, onion, bean sprouts, shrimp, sesame oil, and pepper. In another bowl, whisk the eggs, egg whites, and flour for about 2 minutes, until the lumps are almost gone. Pour this over the vegetable mixture, mix well with a fork, and set it aside.

■ Preheat the broiler.

■ In a small bowl, mix the cornstarch into the 1 tablespoon cold water to dissolve and place it near the stove. In a small pan, bring the soy sauce, vinegar, garlic, ginger, sugar, and broth to a boil over medium heat. Stir the cornstarch mixture, pour it into the hot liquid, and whisk 1 to 2 minutes, until the sauce is thick and translucent.

■ Coat a large, ovenproof, nonstick skillet with canola oil spray. Heat the skillet over medium-low heat. Stir the egg and vegetable mixture and pour it into the skillet, smoothing the mixture into an even layer. Cook for about 4 minutes, until the eggs are set and the bottom is browned. Place the skillet under the broiler for about 2 minutes, until the top is browned and the center is almost dry.

■ Loosen the frittata from the skillet with a spatula and slide it onto a serving dish. Cut the frittata into quarters and serve with the warm sauce spooned over the wedges.

apple and leek frittata

In this easy to make but surprisingly full-flavored frittata, the mild onion flavor of leeks merges with the sweetness of crunchy diced apple against a golden, pillowy backdrop of eggs and rosemary. The leek-apple combination provides a healthy range of protective phytochemicals. And the calorie count is low. **MAKES 4 SERVINGS | PER SERVING: 124 CALORIES, 5 G. TOTAL FAT (2 G. SATURATED FAT), 10 G. CARBOHYDRATES, 10 G. PROTEIN, 2 G. DIETARY FIBER, 122 MG. SODIUM.**

4 large eggs

4 large egg whites

   Canola oil spray

1 large sweet apple (such as Fuji), peeled, cored, and diced

1 medium leek, tough outer leaves removed, rinsed well and thinly sliced

   Salt and freshly ground black pepper

1 teaspoon minced fresh rosemary

1 tablespoon minced fresh chives

■ In a medium bowl, whisk together the eggs and egg whites and set them aside.

■ Coat a large nonstick skillet with canola oil spray and place over medium-high heat. Add the apple and leek and sauté for about 5 minutes, until the apple is tender but not too soft. Pour the eggs over the apple and leek mixture. Season with salt and pepper, then with the rosemary and chives. Cover and cook over low heat for about 3 to 5 minutes, just until the eggs are set. Loosen the frittata from the pan with a spatula and gently slide onto a serving plate. Cut into quarters and serve.

southwestern vegetable frittata with avocado and salsa

This frittata features classic favorites from the American Southwest: black beans, avocado, salsa, jalapeño, and cilantro. Together, their bold flavors and brilliant colors create a meal that's as attractive as it is delicious. With the amount of egg yolk reduced and the amount of vegetables and beans increased, this frittata ends up being a perfect low-calorie one-dish meal for the New American Plate. **MAKES 4 SERVINGS | PER SERVING: 160 CALORIES, 8 G. TOTAL FAT (1 G. SATURATED FAT), 11 G. CARBOHYDRATES, 12 G. PROTEIN, 3 G. DIETARY FIBER, 427 MG. SODIUM.**

2 large eggs

4 large egg whites

1 tablespoon canola or olive oil

½ cup diced red bell pepper

¼ cup diced onion

½ small jalapeño chile, seeded and finely minced*

½ cup drained and rinsed canned black beans

Salt and freshly ground black pepper

¼ cup grated soy cheese or reduced fat sharp cheddar cheese

¼ medium avocado, thinly sliced

½ cup chunky salsa or pico de gallo

2 tablespoons chopped cilantro, for garnish

*Note: Wear rubber gloves to handle fresh chiles, and keep your hands away from your eyes.

■ In a medium bowl, beat the eggs and egg whites together and set aside.

■ In a large skillet, heat the canola oil over medium-high heat. Add the bell pepper, onion, jalapeño, and black beans and sauté for 5 minutes. Be careful not to mash the beans. Lower the heat to medium. With a wooden spoon, spread the vegetables and beans until evenly distributed over the bottom of the skillet. Pour in the eggs and spread the mixture with the spoon to distribute the eggs evenly across the vegetables and beans. Season with salt and pepper. Cover and cook for about 2 to 3 minutes, just until the eggs are set. Remove the pan from the heat and sprinkle with the cheese. Cover and allow the cheese to melt. Loosen the frittata from the pan with a spatula and gently slide it onto a plate or platter. Cut into quarters and top with the avocado slices and salsa. Garnish with the cilantro and serve.

chilis

Many people think of chili as a meat dish, probably because *chile con carne*, America's first introduction to the dish, means "chili with meat" in Spanish. But numerous versions, including meatless options, have been developed since chili's popularity spread across the country.

The exact origin of chili is shrouded in mystery and controversy, but culinary historians seem to agree that chili first took hold in Texas in the 1800s. Many Texans believe it criminal to make chili with beans, but others consider kidney and other types of beans an essential ingredient. As chili's popularity grew over the past two hundred years, so did countless variations. Some Southwestern chilis call for rattlesnake or armadillo meat, Cincinnati chili contains spaghetti, Hawaiian versions have been known to include the fish mahi mahi, and one Asian-style version contains adzuki, a sweet red bean.

Everyone seems to have a particular viewpoint on what goes into a chili, generating heated debates—over beans versus no beans, for example—as demonstrated by chili contests. Most chili lovers have one favorite recipe that they rely on. But this one-pot meal offers an opportunity to think creatively and use nontraditional ingredients and seasonings.

The chilis in this chapter are innovative, but more important, they are also more healthful than most of the old standbys. The proportion of meat has been scaled back to allow for a larger proportion of vegetables and other plant-based foods or, as with Vegetable Chili (page 185), the meat has been totally eliminated. Meatless chilis are usually more economical, but they can be just as hearty and flavorful as their more traditional cousins.

spicy chili with ground beef over spaghetti

Served over spaghetti, "Cincinnati chili" is one hearty dish. Often, it's topped with cheese and crumbled crackers. In this New American Plate takeoff on the classic recipe, you increase the proportion of beans, tomatoes, peppers, and spices while using just enough ground beef to provide a robust, meaty flavor. This shift in proportion provides body without weighing down the meal with calories and fat. A bit of cocoa powder adds a deep, rich flavor that mingles nicely with the more standard spices—chili powder, cumin, and oregano. **MAKES 6 SERVINGS | PER SERVING (DOES NOT INCLUDE GARNISHES): 375 CALORIES, 7 G. TOTAL FAT (2 G. SATURATED FAT), 60 G. CARBOHYDRATES, 21 G. PROTEIN, 15 G. DIETARY FIBER, 573 MG. SODIUM.**

1 tablespoon canola oil

1½ cups chopped onion, divided

3 garlic cloves, finely chopped

2 jalapeño chiles, seeded and finely chopped*

½ pound lean ground beef

1 tablespoon chili powder, or to taste

1 tablespoon unsweetened cocoa powder

2 teaspoons ground cumin

2 teaspoons dried oregano

1 can (15 ounces) kidney beans, drained and rinsed

1 can (14.5 ounces) diced tomatoes in juice

1 cup mild tomato salsa

Salt and freshly ground black pepper

12 ounces spaghetti, preferably whole wheat

3 ounces shredded reduced fat cheddar cheese, for garnish

Crumbled soda crackers, for garnish

*Note: Wear rubber gloves to handle fresh chiles, and keep your hands away from your eyes.

■ In a Dutch oven or large, heavy pan, heat the canola oil over medium-high heat. Add 1 cup of the onion, garlic, and jalapeños and sauté for about 4 minutes, stirring often, until the onion is translucent.

■ Add the meat and cook for about 3 minutes, breaking up the meat with a wooden spoon, until just browned. Stir in the chili powder, cocoa, cumin, and oregano. When the seasonings are fragrant, in about 30 seconds, add the beans, tomatoes with juice, and salsa. Bring to a boil, reduce heat, cover, and simmer the chili for about 10 minutes, stirring frequently. Season to taste with salt and pepper.

■ Meanwhile, cook the spaghetti according to the package directions.

■ Serve the chili over the spaghetti. Top each serving with equal parts of the remaining onion and the cheese and crackers.

three-bean chili with corn and turkey

People who dismiss beans as chili "filler" have it backward. Unlike meat, beans are a great source of fiber, and they provide plant protein, vitamins, and minerals with only a fraction of the fat found in beef and chicken. But it's their recently discovered roster of protective phytochemicals that has so many nutrition researchers excited about beans: natural substances like isoflavones, saponins, phytosterols, and protease inhibitors, all of which seem to help bolster the body's defenses in different ways. This recipe uses beans to provide a hearty base. In a neat twist, it's the turkey that acts as "filler," lending a bit of texture to round out the dish. MAKES 8 SERVINGS | PER SERVING: 435 CALORIES, 8 G. TOTAL FAT (1 G. SATURATED FAT), 62 G. CARBOHYDRATES, 29 G. PROTEIN, 13 G. DIETARY FIBER, 581 MG. SODIUM.

2 tablespoons canola oil

2 cups chopped onion

2 garlic cloves, finely chopped

1 large red bell pepper, seeded and coarsely chopped

2 tablespoons chili powder

¼ teaspoon cayenne, or to taste

1 tablespoon ground cumin

1 teaspoon dried oregano

½ teaspoon ground cinnamon (optional)

3 cans (15 ounces each) of 3 different types of beans (such as kidney beans, black beans, or chickpeas), rinsed and drained

1 cup frozen or drained canned corn

1 can (28 ounces) crushed tomatoes

1 cup reduced sodium tomato or vegetable juice

Salt and freshly ground black pepper

3 cups (about 15 ounces) diced cooked turkey

Hot sauce (optional)

4 cups cooked brown rice

■ In a large, deep pot, heat the canola oil over medium-high heat. Stir in the onion, garlic, and bell pepper. Sauté about 4 minutes, stirring often, until the onion is translucent, the garlic is golden, and the bell pepper is softened. Add the chili powder, cayenne, cumin, oregano, and cinnamon and cook for 30 seconds, stirring constantly. Stir in the beans, corn, tomatoes, and tomato juice. Bring to a boil, reduce the heat to medium-low, and simmer gently, partially covered, for 45 minutes, stirring occasionally. Season to taste with salt and pepper.

■ Stir in the turkey and simmer until heated through. Adjust the seasonings by adding more salt and pepper and hot sauce to taste, if desired. Serve over cooked brown rice.

vegetable chili

Here's a chili that's bursting with a bumper crop of vegetables and herbs: tomatoes, onions, chile peppers, chives, beans, corn, and cilantro. Because of this tremendous variety, you can be sure that each bowl is packed with phytochemical power. Any kind of canned diced tomatoes can be used, depending on your taste. Likewise, canned Great Northern beans or chickpeas can be used instead of kidney beans or black beans. Serve with a dollop of lowfat sour cream or reduced fat cheddar cheese and Whole Corn and Green Chile Muffins (page 231) on the side. MAKES 6 SERVINGS | PER SERVING: 408 CALORIES, 6 G. TOTAL FAT (LESS THAN 1.5 G. SATURATED FAT), 77 G. CARBOHYDRATES, 17 G. PROTEIN, 20 G. DIETARY FIBER, 627 MG. SODIUM.

2 tablespoons canola oil

1 large onion, chopped

3 garlic cloves, chopped

3 cans (14.5 ounces each) diced tomatoes in juice

1 can (4 ounces) diced mild green chiles, drained

½ jalapeño chile, seeded and finely chopped*

2 to 3 tablespoons chili powder

1 tablespoon ground cumin

1 tablespoon dried chives

1 large bay leaf

1 can (15 ounces) red kidney beans, drained and rinsed

1 can (15 ounces) black or cannellini (white kidney) beans, rinsed and drained

1 large green bell pepper, seeded and cut into ½-inch pieces

1 large red bell pepper, seeded and cut into ½-inch pieces

1 can (15 ounces) corn, drained

1½ ounces semisweet chocolate, chopped (optional)

Salt and freshly ground black pepper

¼ cup chopped fresh cilantro leaves, loosely packed

Hot sauce (optional)

*Note: Wear rubber gloves to handle fresh chiles, and keep your hands away from your eyes.

■ In a large, heavy pot, heat the canola oil over medium-high heat. Add the onion and garlic and sauté, stirring often, for about 5 minutes, until the onion is translucent and the garlic is golden.

■ Add the tomatoes with juice, green chiles, jalapeño, chili powder, cumin, chives, and bay leaf. Cook over medium heat for 10 minutes, stirring occasionally. Add the beans, bell peppers, corn, and chocolate. Bring to a boil, reduce the heat to medium-low, and simmer partially covered for about 35 minutes, stirring occasionally, until the chili is thick. Season to taste with salt and pepper. Stir in the cilantro and adjust the seasonings by adding chili powder or hot sauce. Remove the bay leaf before serving.

sweet potato chili with peanuts

Here's a chili with no meat and no beans. This richly satisfying variant uses the mellow flavors and textures of sweet potatoes and carrots as a base. Perfect for autumn, this earthy chili benefits from the addition of roasted peanuts, which soften the acidity of the tomatoes and provide a gentle hint of sweetness in every chunky bite. Serve this chili over long-grain brown rice, if you like.

MAKES 10 SERVINGS | PER SERVING: 385 CALORIES, 15 G. TOTAL FAT (2 G. SATURATED FAT), 55 G. CARBOHYDRATES, 11 G. PROTEIN, 8 G. DIETARY FIBER, 409 MG. SODIUM.

2 tablespoons canola oil

1 medium onion, chopped

2 medium carrots, peeled and thinly sliced

1 medium green bell pepper, seeded and chopped

1 medium red bell pepper, seeded and chopped

2 to 4 garlic cloves, minced, to taste

1½ to 2 pounds orange-flesh sweet potatoes, peeled and cut into bite-sized chunks (about 4 cups)

1½ cups unsalted roasted peanuts

1 can (28 ounces) crushed tomatoes in juice

1 can (6 ounces) tomato paste

2 cans (4 ounces each) diced mild green chiles with liquid

4 to 6 tablespoons chili powder, or to taste

1 tablespoon ground cumin, or to taste

1 tablespoon sugar

Salt and freshly ground black pepper

■ In a large, heavy pot, heat the canola oil over medium heat. Add the onion, carrots, and bell peppers and sauté, stirring occasionally, for about 8 minutes, until vegetables are golden. Add the garlic and sauté, stirring constantly, for 30 seconds, until fragrant. Stir in the sweet potatoes, peanuts, tomatoes and juice, tomato paste, chiles and their liquid, chili powder, cumin, and sugar.

■ Bring to a boil, then reduce the heat to low immediately and simmer gently, stirring occasionally, for 15 to 25 minutes, until the sweet potatoes are just tender. Halfway through the cooking process, adjust the seasonings, adding more chili powder and cumin if desired. Season to taste with salt and pepper and serve.

fresh plum tart

around the plate

Appetizers, soups, breads or muffins, and desserts play minor but important roles in our meals, providing diversity and extra appeal. Appetizers create a flourish to a special occasion or celebratory meal. For many people, breads and muffins are reliable breakfast and snack staples. Soups are versatile multitaskers, serving as starters to a sit-down meal, convenient elements of a workday lunch, and soothing comforts when we are under the weather. And desserts have the happy task of providing a delectable conclusion to a meal.

Because these components play a peripheral rather than central role in a meal, too often less attention is given to whether they are as healthful as they are delicious. As a result, an appetizer or dessert, for example, can undo a good portion of the healthful benefits of a meal and add unwanted fat-enriched or sugar-laden calories.

The cookbook team was determined to avoid that pitfall but at the same time to produce dishes rich in flavor, texture, and eye appeal. As you try the recipes that follow, you will be pleased to discover it is possible to pair good taste and good health.

Remember: the number of servings in each recipe relates to USDA standard serving sizes. Depending on individual needs, you may choose to serve larger portions. (See Introduction, pages 7–10.) ■

part 3

appetizers

Because we live in a grab-and-go culture, too often eating on the run, the concept of an appetizer to start a meal might seem as antiquated as white cotton gloves and spats. But appetizers can play several important roles at the dinner table.

Appetizers can serve as the prelude to special meals at holiday time, when we're entertaining, or on other festive or celebratory occasions. Broiled Asparagus with Sesame Sauce (page 196) and Spinach-Stuffed Mushrooms with Feta (page 199), for example, are perfect candidates for a sit-down starter to a special meal. In a more informal setting, such as a cocktail party or buffet, you might want to prepare Falafel-Style Chickpea Patties (page 191), a spicy finger food, and serve it with Cucumber-Yogurt Sauce with Dill (page 109). These patties can also double as a light lunch, whether tucked into a pita pocket or as an accompaniment to soup and a salad.

Serving appetizers is also a great way to help slow down the pace of the day, so that a meal can be given the attention it deserves and truly be enjoyed. Appetizers can brighten the spirits when we're in the doldrums, and they can be alternatives to high-calorie processed snack foods like chips and crackers, which typically contain harmful saturated fats or trans fats. Spicy Toasted Almonds (page 198) and Bruschetta with Green Pea and Roasted Garlic Spread (page 195) both fall into the category of healthful snack foods.

Dips for crackers or assorted raw vegetables are so popular for both entertaining and snacking that a variety of prepared dips can be found in markets today. But consider making one from scratch for the freshest flavor and maximum nutritional value.

The dips in this chapter range widely in taste, texture, and seasonings, from Roasted Red Pepper Hummus (page 200) and Roasted Eggplant Spread (page 199) to White Bean and Sun-Dried Tomato Dip (page 201) and Spinach and Feta Dip (page 200). Most of these dips can be made in a blender or food processor and take only minutes. Many of the recipes call for ingredients you most likely already have on hand, and so can be made easily when company arrives unexpectedly.

You will find that most of the appetizers in this chapter can take on multiple roles. For example, one of the cookbook team members likes to pair a red and a green dip for Christmas entertaining. Some of us depend on the dips and vegetables for healthful eat-at-your-desk snacks that avoid the fats and calories of processed snacks. A few others use the dips as sandwich spreads, and the spreads as dips. You will find that most of the appetizers in this chapter are multitaskers, with the capability to serve many different needs in your hectic life.

falafel-style chickpea patties

Falafel is a Middle Eastern mixture of chickpeas and spices that's deep-fried. Here is a lowfat version of this spicy favorite that fits the New American Plate. For a festive occasion or whenever you need a little eating adventure, serve this finger food on a tray with a bowl of Cucumber-Yogurt Sauce with Dill (page 109). Or tuck a couple of these light, delicate patties into a whole wheat pita pocket for an extraordinary sandwich. Add lettuce, tomato, cucumber, and onion, along with the cucumber-yogurt sauce. **MAKES 12 SERVINGS (2 PATTIES PER SERVING) | PER SERVING: 86 CALORIES, 2 G. TOTAL FAT (LESS THAN 1 G. SATURATED FAT), 14 G. CARBOHYDRATES, 3 G. PROTEIN, 3 G. DIETARY FIBER, 24 MG. SODIUM.**

1 tablespoon olive oil

1 small onion, finely chopped

2 garlic cloves, minced

2 cups cooked chickpeas or 1 can (15 ounces) chickpeas, rinsed and drained

½ cup cilantro leaves, loosely packed

½ cup loosely packed flat leaf parsley

1 cup cooked brown rice

1 teaspoon curry powder

⅛ teaspoon cayenne, or to taste

1 tablespoon freshly squeezed lemon juice

¼ cup dry bread crumbs, preferably whole wheat

Salt

Olive oil spray

■ In a medium nonstick skillet, heat the olive oil over medium-high heat. Sauté the onion and garlic for about 4 minutes, stirring often, until the onion is soft and the garlic is golden. Let the onion mixture cool.

■ In a food processor or blender, combine the sautéed onion mixture and chickpeas. Pulse to coarsely chop the chickpeas. Add the cilantro, parsley, rice, curry powder, and cayenne. Pulse again until all of the ingredients are finely chopped and evenly distributed.

■ Transfer the mixture to a bowl. Add the lemon juice, bread crumbs, and salt to taste. With your hands, knead the mixture until it is like a moist dough. Form the chickpea mixture (about 2 tablespoons per patty) into 24 patties.

■ Heat a griddle or cast iron skillet over medium heat and coat it lightly with olive oil spray. Place some of the patties in the pan 1 inch apart. Cook for 4 minutes until browned in places. Turn gently with a spatula and cook for another 3 to 4 minutes to lightly brown the second side. Repeat until all the patties are cooked, using more olive oil spray if necessary to keep the patties from sticking. Serve hot or at room temperature.

tabbouleh-filled cherry tomatoes

Traditional Middle Eastern tabbouleh consists of bulgur mixed with chopped tomatoes, onions, parsley, mint, olive oil, and lemon juice. For this easy and attractive appetizer, cherry tomatoes become the shells for a whole-grain filling. Don't confuse cherry tomatoes with grape tomatoes; cherry tomatoes are bigger and thus better for stuffing. **MAKES ABOUT 15 SERVINGS (3 TOMATOES PER SERVING) | PER SERVING: 39 CALORIES, 1 G. FAT (LESS THAN 1 G. SATURATED FAT), 6 G. CARBOHYDRATES, 1 G. PROTEIN, 1 G. DIETARY FIBER, 45 MG. SODIUM.**

½ cup uncooked bulgur

¼ teaspoon salt

¾ cup boiling water

1 tablespoon plus 1 teaspoon extra-virgin olive oil

1 tablespoon freshly squeezed lemon juice, or to taste

1 garlic clove, minced

3 tablespoons scallions, trimmed and chopped

2 tablespoons chopped flat leaf parsley

2 tablespoons chopped fresh mint

Salt and freshly ground black pepper

42 to 45 cherry tomatoes

■ In a small bowl, combine the bulgur and salt. Pour in the boiling water, cover, and let stand for 30 minutes. Stir in the olive oil, lemon juice, garlic, scallions, parsley, mint, and salt and pepper to taste. Cover and refrigerate for at least 2 hours or up to 2 days.

■ Slice the tops off the tomatoes and gently remove and discard the seeds and pulp. If desired, slice a tiny piece from the bottom of each tomato so that they will sit upright. Stuff each tomato with about 1½ teaspoons of the tabbouleh mixture. Slightly pack down the filling and mound the tops. Refrigerate until ready to serve.

bruschetta with green pea and roasted garlic spread

Bruschetta is Italian garlic bread. In its simplest form, slices of bread are rubbed with garlic and brushed with olive oil, then grilled. In this recipe, a thick spread pairs the mild flavor of roasted garlic with the sweetness of petite peas for a rich taste and more health protection. MAKES 24 SERVINGS (1 SLICE PER SERVING) | PER SERVING: 56 CALORIES, 1 G. TOTAL FAT (LESS THAN 1 G. SATURATED FAT), 8 G. CARBOHYDRATES, 2 G. PROTEIN, 1 G. DIETARY FIBER, 105 MG. SODIUM.

1 large head of garlic

4 teaspoons olive oil, divided

1 package (10 ounces) frozen petite peas, thawed

¼ cup freshly grated Parmesan cheese

Dash of cayenne, or to taste

Salt and freshly ground black pepper

1 baguette (about 10 ounces), preferably whole wheat, diagonally sliced into twenty-four ½-inch-thick slices

■ Preheat the oven to 375 degrees.

■ Separate the cloves of garlic, peel the skins from the cloves, and trim the ends. In a small bowl, toss the peeled garlic cloves with 1 teaspoon of the olive oil to coat. Fold an 18-inch-long sheet of foil (shiny side out) in half to form a 9-inch-long piece. Put the garlic cloves in the center and fold the foil over them. Fold the edges of the foil a few times to form a tightly sealed packet. Place the packet in the oven with the folded side up. Bake for about 35 minutes, until the garlic is tender. Remove from the oven, unwrap the packet, and let the garlic cool slightly.

■ In a food processor or a blender, combine the garlic, peas, cheese, cayenne, and salt and pepper to taste. Process the mixture until smooth.

■ Transfer the mixture to a microwave-safe bowl. Microwave on high (100% power) for about 30 to 60 seconds, until warm (or cover and refrigerate until ready to serve, then heat in the microwave). Preheat the broiler. Brush both sides of the bread slices lightly with the remaining olive oil and arrange on a baking sheet. Broil about 6 inches from the heat source for 30 to 60 seconds on each side, until lightly toasted. Spread each slice of bread with 2 teaspoons of the garlic-pea mixture. Serve immediately.

broiled asparagus with sesame sauce

Asparagus is an elegant vegetable as well as a healthy choice. It has significant amounts of vitamin C and folate and the phytochemical glutathione. Glutathione helps remove carcinogens from the body. Your guests should each have a small plate, knife, and fork to eat this sophisticated, Asian-inspired appetizer. It could also be served as one of two vegetables on the New American Plate. **MAKES 6 SERVINGS (3 ASPARAGUS SPEARS PER SERVING) | PER SERVING: 55 CALORIES, 3 G. TOTAL FAT (LESS THAN 1 G. SATURATED FAT), 5 G. CARBOHYDRATES, 2 G. PROTEIN, 2 G. DIETARY FIBER, 169 MG. SODIUM.**

ASPARAGUS

1 tablespoon toasted sesame oil

1 teaspoon finely minced garlic

¼ teaspoon grated peeled fresh ginger

Dash of cayenne

18 thick asparagus spears (about 1 pound), trimmed

Generous dash of salt

SAUCE

2 tablespoons reduced sodium soy sauce

1 teaspoon sugar

¼ teaspoon finely minced garlic

⅛ teaspoon grated peeled fresh ginger

¼ teaspoon toasted sesame oil

2 teaspoons toasted sesame seeds*

*Note: To toast the sesame seeds, put them in a small skillet over medium heat for 1 to 2 minutes, stirring constantly, until the seeds are light brown. Watch carefully: sesame seeds can burn quickly. Immediately transfer the seeds to a small dish and cool.

■ Preheat the broiler. Line a jellyroll pan with foil.

■ In a small bowl, mix the sesame oil with the garlic, ginger, and cayenne. In a shallow bowl, toss the asparagus in the oil mixture to coat. Place the asparagus in a single layer in the prepared pan. Sprinkle the asparagus lightly with salt.

■ To prepare the sauce, mix the soy sauce, sugar, garlic, and ginger in a small bowl, stirring to dissolve the sugar. Stir in the sesame oil and set the sauce aside.

■ Broil the asparagus about 6 inches from the heat source for about 8 to 12 minutes, turning once or twice, until lightly browned. The asparagus should be tender, but not mushy. Place the asparagus on a serving platter. Stir the sauce and drizzle over the asparagus. Sprinkle with the sesame seeds and serve hot or at room temperature.

spicy toasted almonds

Nuts contain healthy mono- and polyunsaturated fats, vitamin E, protein, magnesium, potassium, and dietary fiber. The trick is to eat nuts in moderation because they are high in calories. Set these crunchy, spiced almonds out in little bowls as appetizers, or have them on hand as a filling snack. A small handful of nuts, or 1/3 cup, is considered one serving. MAKES 6 SERVINGS (^{1}/3 CUP PER SERVING) | PER SERVING: 264 CALORIES, 23 G. TOTAL FAT (2 G. SATURATED FAT), 8 G. CARBOHYDRATES, 9 G. PROTEIN, 5 G. DIETARY FIBER, 314 MG. SODIUM.

1 tablespoon dried thyme

1 teaspoon kosher or sea salt

1/8 teaspoon cayenne, or to taste

2 teaspoons canola oil

2 cups unblanched whole almonds

Canola oil spray

■ Preheat the oven to 400 degrees.

■ In a large, shallow bowl, combine the thyme, salt, cayenne, and canola oil. Set it aside. Place the almonds in a medium bowl and lightly coat them with canola oil spray while tossing with a fork.

■ Lightly coat a rimmed baking sheet with canola oil spray. Transfer the almonds to the sheet and spread them evenly across the surface. Place the baking sheet in the center of the oven. Toast the almonds for about 8 minutes, until they are lightly browned and fragrant. Occasionally shake the pan to shift the almonds and prevent them from scorching. (Be careful not to let the almonds get too dark.)

■ Remove the almonds from the oven and immediately add them to the seasoning mixture. Stir the mixture for just a minute to coat the nuts thoroughly. Taste and adjust the seasonings, if needed. Serve warm or at room temperature. The nuts can be stored airtight at room temperature for up to 2 weeks. If desired, reheat in a 350 degree oven for 3 to 5 minutes, stirring once, before serving.

spinach-stuffed mushrooms with feta

This warm appetizer will make any occasion special. The healthy spinach filling has a zesty taste, and the baked mushrooms make for an elegant presentation. This dish would make a great starter to a Mediterranean-style main course, such as Penne with Eggplant, Tomatoes, and Tuna (page 127). MAKES 20 SERVINGS (1 MUSHROOM PER SERVING) | PER SERVING: 25 CALORIES, 1 G. TOTAL FAT (LESS THAN 1 G. SATURATED FAT), 3 G. CARBOHYDRATES, 2 G. PROTEIN, 1 G. DIETARY FIBER, 59 MG. SODIUM.

Olive oil spray

2 teaspoons olive oil

⅓ cup chopped shallots

1 package (10 ounces) frozen chopped spinach, thawed and well drained

1 large egg white, beaten

½ cup fresh whole wheat bread crumbs (from about 1 slice of bread)

⅓ cup reduced fat feta cheese

1 tablespoon freshly grated Parmesan cheese

Generous dash of ground nutmeg

Salt and freshly ground black pepper

20 medium mushrooms (each about 1½ inches in diameter), cleaned and stems scooped out

■ Preheat the oven to 350 degrees. Coat a jellyroll pan with olive oil spray.

■ In a nonstick skillet, heat the olive oil over medium-high heat. Add the shallots and sauté for about 5 minutes, stirring often, until golden. Transfer the shallots to a medium bowl and mix in the spinach. Stir in the egg white, bread crumbs, feta cheese, Parmesan cheese, and nutmeg; season mixture with salt and pepper, and stir to combine.

■ Stuff each mushroom with 1 rounded tablespoon of the spinach mixture, mounding the filling. Place the mushrooms, cap side down, in the prepared jellyroll pan. Bake for 20 minutes, until mushrooms are tender. Serve warm.

roasted eggplant spread

This thick and mellow purée—a cousin of the well-known Middle Eastern baba ghanouj—has a wonderful texture and rich flavor, yet it's low in fat. Use it as a dip with whole wheat pita wedges, or spread it on hearty whole-grain bread or focaccia for a sandwich topped with sliced tomatoes, roasted green or yellow squash slices, pepper strips, or onions. If you plan to serve this dip at a party, double or triple the recipe. MAKES 6 SERVINGS (2 TABLESPOONS PER SERVING) | PER SERVING: 32 CALORIES, LESS THAN 1 G. TOTAL FAT (LESS THAN 1 G. SATURATED FAT), 6 G. CARBOHYDRATES, 1 G. PROTEIN, 2 G. DIETARY FIBER, 6 MG. SODIUM.

1 large eggplant

1 medium tomato, peeled, seeded, and chopped

¼ cup chopped flat leaf parsley, loosely packed

1 tablespoon minced scallions, trimmed

2 teaspoons freshly squeezed lemon juice

1 teaspoon extra-virgin olive oil

Salt and freshly ground black pepper

■ Preheat the oven to 400 degrees.

■ Put the eggplant in a baking dish and bake for 45 to 55 minutes.

■ Let the eggplant cool and then cut it in half lengthwise. Scrape the insides of the eggplant into a blender or food processor and discard the skin. Purée the eggplant, leaving it slightly chunky. Add the remaining ingredients, including salt and pepper to taste, and process until just combined. Serve with sliced raw vegetables or pita wedges.

roasted red pepper hummus

This tangy appetizer takes only minutes to prepare. Toasted wedges of whole wheat pita bread are one good vehicle for this dip. Or use it as a spread on sandwiches, piling on a variety of colorful vegetables for a phytochemical feast. You may substitute 1¼ cups cooked beans for each 15-ounce can. Tahini, a Middle Eastern paste made from sesame seeds, is rich in syringic acid, a powerful antioxidant. This acid, working with the lignans and other phenolic acids in sesame, is believed to protect against skin cancer. Look for tahini in the ethnic section of your supermarket. **MAKES 24 SERVINGS (2 TABLESPOONS PER SERVING) | PER SERVING: 50 CALORIES, 2 G. TOTAL FAT (LESS THAN 1 G. SATURATED FAT), 7 G. CARBOHYDRATES, 2 G. PROTEIN, 2 G. DIETARY FIBER, 104 MG. SODIUM.**

- 1 jar (7 ounces) roasted red peppers, drained
- 1 can (15 ounces) chickpeas, drained and rinsed
- 1 can (15 ounces) cannellini (white kidney) beans, drained and rinsed
- ¼ cup tahini (sesame paste)
- 2 garlic cloves, minced
- 2 tablespoons freshly squeezed lemon juice, or to taste
- 1 teaspoon ground cumin
- Salt and freshly ground black pepper

■ In a food processor or blender, combine all of the ingredients except the salt and pepper. Process the mixture until smooth. Season to taste with salt and pepper. Serve chilled or at room temperature with warmed whole wheat pita wedges.

spinach and feta dip

This super-easy dip requires no cooking, and the flavor is outstanding. The horseradish adds zip, but spinach is the star ingredient. This dark leafy green contains the phytochemical lutein, which helps protect the eyes and may help ward off skin and colon cancer. Scottish Crackers (page 240), whole wheat pita wedges, and fresh vegetables go well with this dip. Double the recipe if you're expecting a crowd. **MAKES 8 SERVINGS (2 TABLESPOONS PER SERVING) | PER SERVING: 28 CALORIES, 1 G. TOTAL FAT (LESS THAN 1 G. SATURATED FAT), 2 G. CARBOHYDRATES, 2 G. PROTEIN, LESS THAN 1 G. DIETARY FIBER, 184 MG. SODIUM.**

- 4 cups stemmed fresh spinach, loosely packed
- ½ cup coarsely crumbled reduced fat feta cheese (about 2 ounces)
- 2 scallions, trimmed and chopped
- ¼ cup fat-free mayonnaise
- 2 teaspoons drained prepared white horseradish
- 1 teaspoon freshly squeezed lemon juice
- ¼ cup chopped fresh dill
- Salt and freshly ground black pepper

■ In a food processor or blender, finely chop the spinach. Add the cheese and scallions. Process the mixture until well blended. Add the mayonnaise, horseradish, and lemon juice and process to blend until smooth. Add the dill and process for another 15 seconds. Season the dip to taste with salt and pepper. Although this dip keeps for 2 to 3 days in the refrigerator, it loses some of its zing after 24 hours. It is best served at room temperature to experience the full flavor.

white bean and sun-dried tomato dip

Beans are so versatile. Because their flavor is mild, this fiber- and nutrient-rich, lowfat food can be used in many dishes, including dips. You could serve this smooth, well-seasoned dip with Scottish Crackers (page 240) or celery sticks. You can also use it as a spread on sandwiches. **MAKES 20 SERVINGS (2 TABLESPOONS PER SERVING) | PER SERVING: 37 CALORIES, 1 G. TOTAL FAT (LESS THAN 1 G. SATURATED FAT), 5 G. CARBOHYDRATES, 2 G. PROTEIN, 1 G. DIETARY FIBER, 57 MG. SODIUM.**

- 1 jar (12 ounces) roasted red peppers, drained
- 1 can (15 ounces) white beans, drained and rinsed
- 10 oil-marinated sun-dried tomato halves, coarsely chopped
- 2 garlic cloves, chopped
- 3 tablespoons lowfat mayonnaise
- 1 teaspoon dried oregano
- 1 teaspoon ground cumin
- ¼ teaspoon chili powder or dash of cayenne

  Salt and freshly ground black pepper

■ Using a food processor or blender, process the roasted peppers until smooth. Add the beans, tomatoes, garlic, mayonnaise, oregano, cumin, and chili powder. Blend the mixture to a smooth purée. Season to taste with salt and pepper. The dip is best if it sits at room temperature an hour before serving. It keeps for up to 3 days, tightly covered, in the refrigerator. The dip can be served cold or at room temperature.

chickpea dip with cilantro

Cilantro, garlic, and lemon juice enliven the taste of chickpeas in this easy, Mexican-style dip. There is just a touch of reduced fat sour cream and lowfat mayonnaise for a creamy texture. For a party appetizer, surround a bowl of this dip with an assortment of sliced vegetables (like carrots, radishes, different-colored bell peppers, sugar snap peas, broccoli, cauliflower, zucchini, and jicama), baked tortilla chips, or Scottish Crackers (page 240). **MAKES 8 SERVINGS (2 TABLESPOONS PER SERVING) | PER SERVING: 50 CALORIES, 1 G. TOTAL FAT (LESS THAN 1 G. SATURATED FAT), 8 G. CARBOHYDRATES, 2 G. PROTEIN, 1 G. DIETARY FIBER, 110 MG. SODIUM.**

- 1 cup canned chickpeas, rinsed and drained
- ¼ cup lowfat sour cream or plain lowfat yogurt, plus more to thin dip
- ¼ cup chopped fresh cilantro, loosely packed
- 1 small garlic clove, chopped
- 1 tablespoon freshly squeezed lemon juice, or to taste
- 1 tablespoon lowfat mayonnaise, plus more to thin dip

  Salt and freshly ground white pepper (optional)

  Hot pepper sauce (optional)

■ In a food processor or blender, process the chickpeas with the ¼ cup sour cream, cilantro, garlic, lemon juice, and 1 tablespoon mayonnaise until smooth. If the dip is too thick, gradually add additional teaspoons of sour cream and mayonnaise, just until the desired consistency is reached. Transfer the mixture to a container with a tightly fitting lid. Season to taste with salt, white pepper, and hot pepper sauce, if desired. Cover and refrigerate for at least 1 hour and up to 24 hours before serving to allow the flavors to meld. Bring the dip to room temperature before serving.

southwestern red pepper dip

Once you try this lower-fat, lower-salt dip, you will never again want a commercial dip or one made from salty seasoning mixes and sour cream. The roasted red peppers give it an earthy, peppery taste that's not hot. Place this dip in an attractive bowl on a platter, and surround it with a variety of cut-up vegetables or baked tortilla chips. It can also be used as a sandwich spread. **MAKES 18 SERVINGS (2 TABLESPOONS PER SERVING) | PER SERVING: 42 CALORIES, 2 G. TOTAL FAT (1 G. SATURATED FAT), 5 G. CARBOHYDRATES, 2 G. PROTEIN, LESS THAN 1 G. DIETARY FIBER, 117 MG. SODIUM.**

1 package (3 ounces) or about 30 sun-dried tomato halves (not packed in oil)

2 jars (7 ounces each) roasted red peppers, drained

2 garlic cloves, finely chopped

1½ teaspoons ground cumin, or to taste

1 teaspoon freshly squeezed lemon juice, or to taste

¼ cup chopped fresh cilantro, loosely packed

¼ cup chopped scallions, trimmed

4 ounces reduced fat cream cheese, softened

Salt and freshly ground black pepper

Hot pepper sauce (optional)

■ Put the dried tomatoes in a medium bowl and add enough very hot water to cover. Let the tomatoes soak for 5 minutes. Drain well, reserving 3 tablespoons of the soaking liquid.

■ In a food processor or blender, process the tomatoes, red peppers, garlic, cumin, lemon juice, cilantro, and scallions until smooth and well blended.

■ Add the cream cheese and purée the mixture, scraping down the sides of the bowl occasionally and adding enough of the reserved tomato-soaking liquid to thin the dip to the desired consistency. Season to taste with salt, pepper, and hot pepper sauce, if desired. Adjust the seasoning, adding more cumin or lemon juice if needed.

■ Transfer the dip to a container. Cover the dip and refrigerate for 6 to 24 hours before using to allow flavors to meld. Bring the dip to room temperature before serving.

curried spinach dip

Either fresh or frozen chopped spinach may be used in this exotic, Indian-style dip that's a snap to make. However, fresh spinach will give the dip a lighter, brighter shade of green and a fresher taste. When it is ready to serve, surround the bowl containing the dip with a variety of cut-up vegetables for a colorful, festive, and healthful display. Pappadams, the thin crackers found in Indian markets, also go well with this dip, as do whole-grain crackers. **MAKES 16 SERVINGS (2 TABLESPOONS PER SERVING) | PER SERVING: 26 CALORIES, 1 G. TOTAL FAT (LESS THAN 1 G. SATURATED FAT), 2 G. CARBOHYDRATES, 1 G. PROTEIN, LESS THAN 1 G. DIETARY FIBER, 24 MG. SODIUM.**

2 teaspoons curry powder, or to taste

1 teaspoon ground cumin, or to taste

1 package (9 ounces) uncooked baby spinach, or 1 package (10 ounces) frozen chopped spinach, thawed, drained, and squeezed dry

¾ cup reduced fat sour cream

½ cup plain nonfat yogurt

2 garlic cloves, finely minced

Salt and freshly ground black pepper (optional)

■ In a small nonstick skillet over medium-high heat, combine the curry powder and cumin and stir for 30 to 45 seconds, just until fragrant. Transfer the spices to a small bowl.

■ In a food processor or blender, combine the spinach, sour cream, yogurt, and garlic. Process the mixture until it is smooth. Blend in 1/3 of the curry mixture. Add more curry mixture to taste. Process until well blended. Season to taste with salt and pepper.

■ Transfer the dip to a container with a cover. Cover and refrigerate for at least 1 hour and up to 24 hours to allow flavors to meld. Bring the dip to room temperature before serving.

southwestern red pepper dip

soups

Soups may be the most versatile of all dishes. They can be hot or cold, chunky or smooth, thin or robust. They can be served as starters meant to stimulate the appetite for what follows or as meals in themselves, accompanied with whole-grain bread and a salad.

As those who are trying to lose weight know, having soup at the beginning of a meal can take the edge off your hunger and help to reduce the portion size of the entrée. And since soups are usually lower in fat and calories than entrées, this can allow you to reduce the overall calorie count for a meal without feeling deprived.

Soups make a good mid-morning or mid-afternoon snack. They are far more nutritious and lower in calories than the usual crackers, chips, or candy. And on chilly winter days, a hearty soup can make a great breakfast that is comforting as well as filling and that takes no longer to eat than a bowl of cereal and milk.

Best of all, soups are an easy way to eat more vegetables, whole grains, and beans. Soup made with a variety of vegetables, or in which a main ingredient is lentils, beans, or a grain like barley or brown rice, will contain a wide variety of health-protective vitamins, minerals, and phytochemicals.

Because canned soup was one of the first commercially processed foods available, it has become an American icon. It's so easy to empty a can of soup into a pan, add water or milk, and heat. But many canned soups are very high in sodium and fat and therefore may contribute to health problems like high blood pressure and excess weight. And canned soup is often watery, and may sometimes have the lingering taste of metal. Homemade soup, on the other hand, is an entirely different food. It can be made flavorful by adding herbs or spices rather than relying on salt or fat.

We often think of making soup from scratch as a time-consuming chore, but it needn't take much of your attention. Most soups can be cooked slowly and gently at a simmer without constant checking, leaving you free to do other things. Preparation time is required simply to cut up the vegetables and perhaps sauté them to bring out their flavor. (Kitchen appliances such as a hand-chopper or a food processor can dramatically cut down the time needed to prepare the vegetables.) Puréeing, which is used to make some of the soups that follow—for example, Easy Gazpacho (page 220), Chilled Cantaloupe Soup with Mint (page 223), and Roasted Red Pepper and Corn Soup (page 206)—requires only a few minutes in the blender.

An added benefit of making your own soups is that the slow simmering will fill your home with delectable aromas, evoking all sorts of pleasant memories.

The bottom line is that homemade soups can make a significant contribution to your pleasure, nutrition, and health protection with a minimum investment of effort.

fresh corn bisque

Bisque usually describes a smooth, rich soup made with cream. Although there's no cream in this healthy soup, evaporated lowfat milk makes the texture creamy. For optimum taste, use the sweetest, freshest corn of your local crop. Adding the optional shrimp embellishes this dish wonderfully for dinner company. **MAKES 4 SERVINGS | PER SERVING: 152 CALORIES, 2 G. TOTAL FAT (LESS THAN 1 G. SATURATED FAT), 27 G. CARBOHYDRATES, 9 G. PROTEIN, 3 G. DIETARY FIBER, 76 MG. SODIUM.**

4 ears fresh corn

1 small onion, finely chopped

1 medium yellow potato (such as Yukon Gold), peeled and cut into ½-inch cubes

4 cups cold water

½ to ¾ cup evaporated lowfat milk

Pinch of cayenne, or to taste

Salt and freshly ground black pepper

¼ cup scallions, trimmed and chopped

12 medium shrimp, cooked, peeled, and deveined, for garnish

■ On a cutting board, cut the corn kernels from each cob and transfer the kernels to a Dutch oven or large, heavy pan. Scrape the corncobs over the pot with the back of a knife to extract the milk and any remaining corn and add the cobs to the pot. Add the onion, potato, and cold water and bring to a boil. Reduce the heat to low, cover, and simmer for about 15 minutes, until the vegetables are tender. Remove the cobs and discard. Strain the soup into a bowl, reserving the cooked vegetables. (There should be about 4 cups of broth.) Take out ½ cup of the vegetables and set aside for later use. Cool the remaining vegetables slightly.

■ In a blender or food processor, purée all but the reserved ½ cup of cooked vegetables with 2 cups of the broth in batches until the mixture is smooth.* Return the vegetable purée to the pot. Mix in ½ to ¾ cup of evaporated milk, depending on the thickness of the purée. Reheat over medium heat and season to taste with cayenne and salt and pepper.

■ Divide the soup into four bowls. Garnish the chowder with the reserved cooked vegetables, the scallions, and the shrimp, and serve.

*Note: Refrigerate or freeze the remaining corn broth to use in making vegetable soup.

roasted red pepper and corn soup
The yellow corn floating in this deep red soup is a scrumptious sight. And red bell pepper—high in both beta-carotene and vitamin C—is a wonderfully nutritious vegetable. A garnish of cilantro would add more Southwestern flavor, while basil would bring out the sweetness of the vegetables. **MAKES 4 SERVINGS | PER SERVING: 156 CALORIES, 4 G. TOTAL FAT (LESS THAN 1 G. SATURATED FAT), 27 G. CARBOHYDRATES, 5 G. PROTEIN, 4 G. DIETARY FIBER, 597 MG. SODIUM.**

2 red bell peppers, seeded and quartered

1 large sweet onion, peeled and cut into ½-inch wedges

2 garlic cloves, peeled and halved

½ teaspoon dried thyme

1 tablespoon extra-virgin olive oil

1 can (14.5 ounces) fat-free, reduced sodium chicken broth

1 can (15.5 ounces) Italian-style plum tomatoes in juice

1 can (11 ounces) corn kernels, drained

Freshly ground black pepper

¼ cup cilantro leaves or coarsely chopped fresh basil leaves, loosely packed, for garnish

■ Preheat the oven to 400 degrees.

■ In a 13 × 9-inch baking dish, combine the peppers, onion, garlic, thyme, and olive oil and toss to coat the vegetables. Bake for 35 to 40 minutes, stirring occasionally, until the vegetables are tender and lightly browned. Cool slightly. Stir in the chicken broth and tomatoes with juice.

■ Working in batches, purée the mixture. Transfer the purée to a large saucepan over medium heat and bring to a simmer. Add the corn and simmer about 3 minutes, until heated through. Season to taste with pepper, ladle into bowls, garnish with cilantro or basil, if desired, and serve.

carrot and apple soup

carrot and apple soup

The orange color of carrots reflects the presence of plenty of carotenoids, a family of antioxidants believed to fight cancer and bolster disease immunity. Beta-carotene is one well-known carotenoid, but there are over 500 more. This soup, rich in carrots, makes an excellent starter for an autumn meal. **MAKES 6 SERVINGS | PER SERVING: 92 CALORIES, 4 G. TOTAL FAT (LESS THAN 1 G. SATURATED FAT), 15 G. CARBOHYDRATES, 3 G. PROTEIN, 4 G. DIETARY FIBER, 84 MG. SODIUM.**

1 tablespoon canola oil

1 medium onion, chopped

1 medium leek, white part only, rinsed well and chopped

1 pound carrots, peeled and cut into ½-inch slices

1 tart apple (such as Granny Smith), peeled, cored, and chopped

3 cups fat-free, reduced sodium chicken broth

Milk or additional fat-free, reduced sodium chicken broth, to thin soup (optional)

Salt and freshly ground black pepper

3 tablespoons minced fresh mint leaves, for garnish

■ In a Dutch oven or large, heavy pan, heat the canola oil over medium-high heat until hot. Add the onion and leek and sauté for about 4 minutes, until the onion is translucent.

■ Mix in the carrots and apple. Reduce the heat to medium-low, cover, and cook for 5 minutes, stirring often. Add the broth, cover, and bring to a boil over high heat. Then reduce heat to low and simmer for about 30 minutes, until the carrots are very soft. Remove the pot from the heat and set the soup aside to cool slightly. In a blender or food processor, purée the soup in batches until smooth. Return soup to pan and heat to very hot before serving. If the soup is too thick, add milk or more broth, as desired. Season to taste with salt and pepper and serve, garnishing each serving with mint.

vegetable and rice soup

When you're pressed for time, this soup makes a quick, healthy meal that doesn't sacrifice taste. Preparation takes about 20 minutes. Brown rice is a nutritious whole grain, and the cruciferous vegetables broccoli and cauliflower are packed with cancer-protective phytochemicals. **MAKES 6 SERVINGS | PER SERVING: 99 CALORIES, 2 G. TOTAL FAT (LESS THAN 1 G. SATURATED FAT), 16 G. CARBOHYDRATES, 5 G. PROTEIN, 2 G. DIETARY FIBER, 398 MG. SODIUM.**

5 cups fat-free, reduced sodium chicken broth

½ cup quick-cooking brown rice

1 cup small broccoli florets

1 cup small cauliflower florets

1 medium carrot, peeled and sliced

1 cup drained canned diced tomatoes

2 teaspoons dried basil

1 teaspoon dried oregano

1 teaspoon ground cumin

Salt and freshly ground black pepper

3 tablespoons freshly grated Romano or Parmesan cheese

■ In a large saucepan, bring the chicken broth to a boil. Stir in the brown rice. Cover, reduce heat to low, and cook for 5 minutes. Add the vegetables, basil, oregano, and cumin, and simmer for about 5 minutes, just until the vegetables are tender. Season to taste with salt and pepper. Ladle the soup into bowls, sprinkle the soup with the grated cheese, and serve.

green lentil and swiss chard soup

It's hard to believe that there is no fat in this rich, satisfying, and quick soup. Preparation takes about 1 hour, but involves only 10 minutes of actual work. You can purée the apple for a smoother texture. The Swiss chard is a good source of vitamins A and C and many phytochemicals, as are many greens. You could add even more vegetables to this soup, like chopped cabbage or tomatoes, to increase the textures, colors, and nutritional benefits. **MAKES 5 SERVINGS | PER SERVING: 170 CALORIES, 0 G. TOTAL FAT, 33 G. CARBO-HYDRATES, 12 G. PROTEIN, 8 G. DIETARY FIBER, 567 MG. SODIUM.**

1 cup green lentils, picked over and rinsed

1 medium onion, finely chopped

1 large carrot, finely chopped

1 garlic clove, minced

1 teaspoon dried thyme

1 bay leaf

4½ cups fat-free, reduced sodium chicken or vegetable broth

1 medium leek, well rinsed, trimmed, and chopped

2 cups chopped Swiss chard leaves, loosely packed

Canola oil spray

1 large sweet apple (such as Fuji), peeled, cored, and diced

Salt and freshly ground black pepper

3 or 4 large pretzels, broken into small pieces, for garnish

■ In a Dutch oven or large, heavy pan over medium-high heat, combine the lentils, onion, carrot, garlic, thyme, bay leaf, and broth. Bring the mixture to a boil, reduce heat to low, cover, and simmer for about 35 to 45 minutes, until the lentils are tender. Add the leek. Simmer for 20 minutes, then stir in the Swiss chard and simmer for another 5 minutes.

■ Meanwhile, lightly coat a medium nonstick skillet with canola oil spray and place over medium-high heat. Add the apple and sauté for about 3 or 4 minutes, stirring often, until the apple is golden on all sides.

■ Remove the bay leaf from the lentil mixture and stir in the apple. For a smoother soup, let the apple cool slightly and purée it in a blender, then combine it with the soup. Season to taste with salt and pepper, garnish with pretzel pieces, and serve.

roasted chestnut soup

Cooked, unsweetened chestnuts, imported from France or Italy, are available in several forms. The combination of broken pieces and whole nuts sold in a plastic pouch usually costs less than whole chestnuts in a jar. Bags of frozen roasted chestnuts sold in their shell are best of all, if you can find them. Once you discover the creamy, nutty flavor of chestnuts, you'll always want to have some on hand to toss with cooked vegetables or crumble into soups. Chestnuts deliver vitamin C and fiber. Their phytochemical makeup is yet to be defined. **MAKES 4 SERVINGS | PER SERVING: 286 CALORIES, 5 G. TOTAL FAT (2 G. SATURATED FAT), 55 G. CARBOHYDRATES, 6 G. PROTEIN, 5 G. DIETARY FIBER, 313 MG. SODIUM.**

2 teaspoons canola oil

1 celery rib, chopped

1 large shallot, chopped

12 to 14 ounces packaged unsweetened cooked chestnuts

1 small potato, peeled and chopped

½ teaspoon dried thyme

1 can (15 ounces) fat-free, reduced sodium chicken broth

2 cups water

1 cup reduced fat milk

Salt and freshly ground black pepper

Small bunch of fresh dill, minced, for garnish

■ In a large saucepan, heat the canola oil over medium-high heat. Sauté the celery and shallot for about 4 minutes, until the shallot is translucent and soft. Add the chestnuts, potato, thyme, broth, and water. Bring to a boil, then reduce heat to low and cook for about 40 minutes, partially covered, until the potatoes and chestnuts are very soft. Remove the saucepan from the stove and allow the soup to cool slightly. Purée the soup until creamy using an immersion blender in the saucepan, or by transferring the soup to a blender and puréeing it in batches before returning it to the saucepan. Stir or blend in the milk and season to taste with salt and pepper. Reheat before serving.

■ Serve in individual bowls, garnishing with the dill. The soup keeps for up to 3 days in the refrigerator. (Once refrigerated, this soup becomes very thick. To restore the consistency of a creamy soup, add equal amounts of milk and chicken broth when reheating.)

potato and watercress soup with shrimp
Watercress is full of vitamins, minerals, and other health-protective substances. Compared with light-colored lettuce, darker leafy greens like watercress have more beta-carotene, vitamin C, and folate (a B vitamin linked to lower risk of cancer and heart disease). The shrimp add interest to this otherwise understated soup. Chill this in the summer, or serve it hot when the weather is cool. **MAKES 4 SERVINGS | PER SERVING: 152 CALORIES, 3 G. TOTAL FAT (2 G. SATURATED FAT), 25 G. CARBOHYDRATES, 7 G. PROTEIN, 2 G. DIETARY FIBER, 609 MG. SODIUM.**

1 tablespoon olive oil

1 small onion, chopped

1 bunch watercress, tough lower stems removed

3 medium potatoes (about 1 pound), peeled and diced

4 cups fat-free, reduced sodium chicken broth

Salt and freshly ground black pepper

8 large shrimp, cooked, peeled, deveined, and halved

■ In a Dutch oven or large, heavy pan, heat the olive oil over medium-high heat. Stir in the onion and sauté for about 4 to 5 minutes, until it is translucent. Do not let the onion turn brown. Add the watercress, stirring for about 2 minutes, until it is wilted, and then add the potatoes and chicken broth. Bring the soup to a boil and then reduce the heat and simmer, covered, for about 20 minutes, until the vegetables are soft. Remove the pot from the heat and allow the soup to cool slightly. In a blender or food processor, purée the soup in batches until it is creamy and smooth.

■ Season the soup to taste with salt and pepper. Return to pot and reheat. Ladle the soup into individual bowls. Arrange 4 shrimp halves on the surface of each serving of soup, and serve. Alternatively, pour the soup into a container and refrigerate it until well chilled, at least 4 hours and up to 2 days. Serve cold, topped with the shrimp.

broccoli and potato soup with parmesan
When fall settles in, you'll reach for the comfort of this thick, nourishing soup. The ingredients are all familiar, and preparation takes less than half an hour. Broccoli provides the phytochemical sulforaphane, a strong anticancer agent. **MAKES 5 SERVINGS | PER SERVING: 176 CALORIES, 5 G. TOTAL FAT (2 G. SATURATED FAT), 26 G. CARBOHYDRATES, 9 G. PROTEIN, 3 G. DIETARY FIBER, 462 MG. SODIUM.**

1 tablespoon olive oil

1 medium onion, chopped

1 medium leek, green part only, well rinsed, trimmed, and chopped

Pinch of dried red pepper flakes

3 medium potatoes, peeled and cut into ½-inch cubes (about 3 cups)

3 cups small broccoli florets, divided

2 cans (15 ounces each) fat-free, reduced sodium chicken broth

3 tablespoons freshly grated Parmesan cheese

½ cup evaporated fat-free milk

Salt and freshly ground black pepper

Chopped flat leaf parsley, for garnish

■ In a Dutch oven or large, heavy pan, heat the olive oil over medium heat and sauté the onion, leek, and red pepper flakes for 5 to 7 minutes, stirring often, until the onion and leek are tender and just beginning to turn golden. Add the potatoes, 2 cups of the broccoli florets, and the chicken broth. Bring the mixture to a boil. Reduce the heat, cover, and simmer for 10 to 12 minutes, until the potatoes are tender. Remove the pot from the heat and allow the soup to cool slightly. In a blender or food processor, purée the soup in batches until it is creamy, and return it to the pot over medium heat. Add the remaining broccoli florets, cover, and simmer for about 3 minutes, until the broccoli florets are just tender. Turn off the heat and stir in the Parmesan cheese and evaporated milk. Season to taste with salt and pepper, garnish with parsley, and serve.

potato and watercress soup with shrimp

butternut squash, tomato, and watercress soup

A Portuguese dish called *potaje de berros* is the inspiration for this puréed vegetable soup. The multicolored vegetables—red, yellow, orange, white, and green—indicate the presence of many health-protective phytochemicals; carotenoids abound. One-quarter of a butternut squash provides an entire day's worth of vitamin A, plus a healthy dose of vitamin C, iron, calcium, and fiber. **MAKES 6 SERVINGS | PER SERVING: 111 CALORIES, 5 G. TOTAL FAT (LESS THAN 1 G. SATURATED FAT), 16 G. CARBOHYDRATES, 3 G. PROTEIN, 3 G. DIETARY FIBER, 167 MG. SODIUM.**

2 tablespoons olive oil

2 large tomatoes, seeded and chopped

1 small onion, chopped

1 small garlic clove, sliced

2 small carrots, chopped

1 cup peeled and chopped butternut squash

1 medium potato, peeled and chopped

1 bunch watercress, including stems, coarsely chopped

2 cups fat-free, reduced sodium chicken broth

4 cups water

Salt and freshly ground black pepper

⅔ cup thawed frozen corn kernels, for garnish

■ In a large saucepan, heat the olive oil over medium-high heat. Sauté the tomatoes, onion, and garlic for about 12 minutes, stirring occasionally, until the onions are translucent.

■ Add the carrots, squash, potato, watercress, and chicken broth. Bring to a boil, reduce heat to low, and simmer, uncovered, for 30 minutes. Add the water and return the mixture to a boil. Reduce heat and simmer, uncovered, for about 10 minutes, until the vegetables are very soft. Remove the saucepan from the heat and let the soup sit for 15 minutes to cool slightly.

■ In a blender or food processor, purée the soup in batches and return to the saucepan. Season to taste with salt and pepper. Reheat soup. Ladle the soup into bowls and garnish with the corn kernels. (The boiling hot soup heats the corn, eliminating the need to cook it separately before adding.)

summer squash soup

This light soup, full of yellow summer squash, makes a simple starter for a delightful summer dinner on the patio. Yellow and orange vegetables and fruits contain powerful antioxidants like vitamin C, as well as two kinds of phytochemicals, carotenoids and bioflavonoids. Research shows that these foods help protect your heart, eyes, and immune system. They are also being studied for their ability to reduce cancer risk. The onions add organosulfides and also bolster the sweetness of the elegant soup. MAKES 10 SERVINGS | PER SERVING: 72 CALORIES, 3 G. TOTAL FAT (LESS THAN 1 G. SATURATED FAT), 10 G. CARBOHYDRATES, 3 G. PROTEIN, 3 G. DIETARY FIBER, 235 MG. SODIUM.

2 tablespoons canola oil

3 pounds yellow summer squash, sliced

3 large onions, sliced

1 tablespoon dried thyme leaves

3 cans (14.5 ounces each) fat-free, reduced sodium chicken broth

3 to 5 cups water

Freshly ground black pepper

Finely chopped fresh chives, for garnish

■ In a Dutch oven or large, heavy pan, heat the canola oil over medium heat. Add the squash, onions, and thyme. Cover and cook over medium-low heat, stirring often, for about 30 minutes, until the vegetables are tender. Add the broth and 3 cups of water, bring to a boil, reduce heat, and simmer, uncovered, for 30 minutes. Remove the pot from the heat and let the soup cool slightly. In a blender or food processor, purée the soup in batches and return it to the pot. Thin with additional water, if necessary. Season to taste with pepper, garnish with chives, and serve. The soup can be refrigerated for 2 to 3 days, and then reheated over medium-low heat when ready to serve.

mushroom and barley soup

This combination of mushrooms, barley, and carrots makes a high-fiber, "stick to your ribs" soup. Soup is ideal for delivering nutrients and phytochemicals. This soup is rich in vitamin B6, terpenes, carotenoids, and fiber. It is a comforting dish for cool-weather days. MAKES 6 SERVINGS | PER SERVING: 123 CALORIES, 3 G. TOTAL FAT (LESS THAN 1 G. SATURATED FAT), 21 G. CARBOHYDRATES, 5 G. PROTEIN, 4 G. DIETARY FIBER, 632 MG. SODIUM.

1 tablespoon canola oil, divided

1 medium onion, chopped

2 celery ribs, chopped

½ cup pearl barley, rinsed and drained

6 cups fat-free, reduced sodium chicken or vegetable broth, divided

5 cups (about ¾ pound) chopped button mushrooms

2 teaspoons Worcestershire sauce

3 medium carrots, peeled and diced

Salt and freshly ground black pepper

Cayenne

■ In a large soup pot, heat ½ tablespoon of the canola oil over medium heat. Add the onion and celery and sauté for 3 minutes. Add the barley and stir constantly for 2 minutes. Add 4 cups of the broth and bring the mixture to a boil. Reduce heat to low, cover, and simmer for 40 minutes.

■ Meanwhile, in a nonstick pan, heat the remaining canola oil over medium-high heat. Add the mushrooms and sauté for 6 minutes, stirring constantly, until mushrooms are tender. Add the Worcestershire sauce and stir constantly for 1 minute. Remove the mushrooms from the heat. Stir in the carrots and set aside. After the barley has simmered for 40 minutes, add the mushrooms and carrot mixture and the remaining 2 cups of broth. Bring to a boil, then reduce heat to low and simmer, covered, for 30 more minutes, until vegetables and barley are very tender and all flavors are melded. Season to taste with salt, black pepper, and cayenne. Serve hot, or refrigerate and use within 3 to 4 days. When reheating, thin the soup with more broth or water, as desired.

black bean soup with onion and cilantro

black bean soup with onion and cilantro

This recipe will become a favorite. The ingredients are simple and inexpensive, and the soup is full of flavor. It also takes less than 45 minutes to make. If you prefer a mild soup, you can leave out the red pepper flakes. The garnishes of cilantro and red onion provide extra flavor and visual appeal. **MAKES 4 SERVINGS | PER SERVING: 229 CALORIES, 5 G. TOTAL FAT (LESS THAN 1 G. SATURATED FAT), 36 G. CARBOHYDRATES, 13 G. PROTEIN, 13 G. DIETARY FIBER, 679 MG. SODIUM.**

1 tablespoon olive oil

1 medium onion, chopped

6 scallions, trimmed and chopped

2 garlic cloves, finely chopped

1 teaspoon ground cumin

1 teaspoon dried oregano

2 cans (15.5 ounces each) black beans, undrained

2 cups water

½ teaspoon dried red pepper flakes

1 bay leaf

½ cup orange juice

Salt and freshly ground black pepper

Chopped red onion, for garnish

Fresh cilantro leaves, for garnish

■ In a Dutch oven or large, heavy pan, heat the olive oil over medium-high heat. Sauté the onion and scallions for about 3 minutes, until translucent. Stir in the garlic, cumin, and oregano, and sauté for 1 minute.

■ Add the beans in their liquid, water, red pepper flakes, and bay leaf. Bring the soup to a boil and then reduce the heat and simmer, uncovered, for 20 minutes, until the onions are soft. Mix in the orange juice and season to taste with salt and pepper. Cook for 5 minutes more, then remove the pot from the heat and let the soup cool slightly.

■ Remove the bay leaf. Using a food processor or blender, purée about half of the soup in batches and return it to the pot. There should be whole beans and onions in a smooth liquid.

■ Serve hot in 4 bowls, each garnished with a little chopped red onion and some cilantro leaves.

pinto bean soup

Beans are the richest plant sources of protein. They are also good sources of dietary fiber, iron, folate, and phytochemicals. Because they are so filling, they can help you make the transition to a New American Plate style of eating. This simple, hearty soup can be put together in less than an hour. **MAKES 4 SERVINGS | PER SERVING: 200 CALORIES, LESS THAN 1 G. TOTAL FAT (LESS THAN 1 G. SATURATED FAT), 38 G. CARBOHYDRATES, 12 G. PROTEIN, 13 G. DIETARY FIBER, 287 MG. SODIUM.**

2 cans (15 ounces each) pinto beans, rinsed and drained

2 medium tomatoes, seeded and chopped

1 celery rib, sliced

1 medium onion, chopped

1 bay leaf

1 can (15 ounces) fat-free, reduced sodium chicken or vegetable broth

Salt and freshly ground black pepper

■ In a large, heavy pan or Dutch oven, combine the beans, tomatoes, celery, onion, bay leaf, and broth. Cover and bring to a boil over medium-high heat. Reduce the heat and simmer until the vegetables are soft, about 20 minutes. Remove the pan from the heat and set the soup aside to cool slightly. Remove the bay leaf. In a blender or food processor, purée half of the soup until smooth, working in batches if necessary. Stir the purée into the remaining soup. Season to taste with salt and pepper, and serve.

bean and split pea chowder with chicken

Traditional chowders are made with seafood, potatoes, and corn. But great-tasting chowder, like this one, can be made with a small amount of poultry and almost any type of vegetable, grain, or bean. Increasing the amount and variety of vegetables enhances the body and taste of either a milk- or a broth-based chowder. Because time greatly improves the flavor of chowders, you may want to make more than you need so you'll have leftovers. **MAKES 8 SERVINGS | PER SERVING: 255 CALORIES, 5 G. TOTAL FAT (LESS THAN 1 G. SATURATED FAT), 35 G. CARBOHYDRATES, 18 G. PROTEIN, 7 G. DIETARY FIBER, 590 MG. SODIUM.**

2 tablespoons canola oil

1 cup finely chopped onion

1 red bell pepper, seeded and diced

2 celery ribs, diced

2 tablespoons chopped flat leaf parsley

1 teaspoon minced garlic

1 teaspoon dried cilantro leaves

1 teaspoon dried thyme

1 can (15.5 ounces) cannellini (white kidney) beans, rinsed and drained

½ cup yellow split peas, picked over and rinsed

½ cup lentils, picked over and rinsed

½ cup pearl barley

8 cups fat-free, reduced sodium chicken broth plus additional broth, if needed

1 large bay leaf

1 teaspoon salt, or to taste (optional)

1 teaspoon freshly ground black pepper, or to taste

1 cup cooked and diced skinless chicken breast

■ Heat a large, heavy pan or Dutch oven over high heat. Add the canola oil and reduce the heat to medium. Add the onion, bell pepper, celery, parsley, garlic, cilantro, and thyme. Sauté, stirring frequently, for about 5 minutes, until the onion is translucent and pale gold. Add the beans, split peas, lentils, barley, broth, bay leaf, salt, and pepper. Bring the mixture to a boil over medium-high heat. Reduce the heat to medium and simmer, stirring occasionally, for about 1 hour, until the lentils, split peas, and barley are tender. (If the liquid evaporates too quickly and the mixture becomes dry, add additional broth or water, about ½ cup at a time, until the chowder resembles a thick soup.) Add the chicken and simmer until heated through. Check the seasoning and add more salt and pepper, if desired. Remove the bay leaf before serving.

new england–style chowder

This healthy chowder keeps the full-bodied flavor of traditional New England clam chowder while maximizing ingredients such as onion, squash, and spinach that have cancer-fighting potential. To give it a thicker consistency, you can do one of three things. Either replace half of the lowfat milk with an equal amount of evaporated fat-free milk, or thicken the broth with a small amount of cornstarch. Or, for a lot of texture, purée a peeled, cooked potato in a blender with a little of the cooking liquid and stir it into the chowder.

MAKES 6 SERVINGS | PER SERVING: 253 CALORIES, 3 G. TOTAL FAT (1 G. SATURATED FAT), 32 G. CARBOHYDRATES, 25 G. PROTEIN, 3 G. DIETARY FIBER, 786 MG. SODIUM.

½ tablespoon olive oil

½ cup finely chopped onion

5 cans (6.5 ounces each) chopped clams, drained, 2 cups of juices reserved*

2 cups reduced fat milk

2 cups evaporated fat-free milk

1 cup peeled and diced potato

2 cups peeled and diced butternut squash

1 bay leaf

Salt and freshly ground black pepper

1 cup stemmed baby spinach leaves or chopped fresh spinach leaves, loosely packed

1 cup drained canned or thawed frozen corn kernels

½ teaspoon dried thyme

Paprika, for garnish

*Note: One pound of freshly shucked clams, chopped and with their juices reserved, can be used instead of canned clams. Use any juices from the shells plus enough bottled clam juice to make 2 cups. Or use 1 pound skinless fresh fish fillet, cut into ¾-inch pieces. Add 2 cups of bottled clam juice.

■ In a large, heavy pot or Dutch oven, heat the olive oil over medium-low heat. Add the onion and cook for 5 minutes, stirring often, until the onion is soft and golden. Add the reserved clam juice, reduced fat milk, evaporated milk, potato, squash, and bay leaf. Bring the mixture to a boil. Reduce the heat to low and simmer, partially covered, for about 15 minutes, just until the potatoes and squash are tender.

■ Remove the cooked potatoes and squash from the soup with a slotted spoon. Cool the vegetables slightly. In a blender or food processor, purée the potatoes and squash with a small amount of soup broth until smooth. Transfer the vegetable purée back to the chowder. Season to taste with salt and pepper. (The chowder may be made up to this point 1 day ahead and refrigerated, tightly covered, until it is ready for the final stage of preparation.)

■ Add the spinach, corn, clams, and thyme. Bring to a simmer for 1 to 3 minutes, just until the clams are heated through, being careful not to overcook them. Adjust the seasonings to taste, remove the bay leaf, and ladle the hot chowder into individual bowls. Lightly sprinkle each serving with paprika before serving.

easy gazpacho

The name of this Spanish soup derives from a word meaning "remainders" or "worthless things." This soup, however, is far from worthless. Researchers have found that gazpacho's tomatoes, garlic, and onions contain the phytochemicals lycopene, phenolic acids, quercetin, and more, making this chilled soup a potent health ally, as well as zesty and satisfying. Because this soup requires no cooking, it is a perfect summer dish.

MAKES 6 SERVINGS | PER SERVING: 68 CALORIES, 3 G. TOTAL FAT (LESS THAN 1 G. SATURATED FAT), 11 G. CARBOHYDRATES, 2 G. PROTEIN, 2 G. DIETARY FIBER, 447 MG. SODIUM.

1 large tomato, seeded and chopped

1 medium cucumber, peeled, seeded, and chopped

1 medium yellow onion, chopped

1 large roasted red bell pepper from a jar, seeded and coarsely chopped

2 large garlic cloves, minced

½ cup chopped fresh cilantro, loosely packed

2 tablespoons red wine vinegar

1 tablespoon extra-virgin olive oil

3 cups tomato juice or vegetable juice, divided

Salt and freshly ground black pepper

Hot pepper sauce (optional)

Any or all of the following for garnish: croutons; diced tomato; diced onion; minced fresh cilantro leaves; peeled, seeded, and diced cucumber

■ In a blender or food processor, combine the tomato, cucumber, onion, bell pepper, garlic, cilantro, vinegar, and olive oil. Add 1 cup of the tomato juice and purée to the desired degree of smoothness. Stir in the remaining tomato juice. Add salt, pepper, and hot pepper sauce to taste.

■ Refrigerate the mixture for at least 4 hours and up to 2 days. Before serving, check the seasoning again and add salt, pepper, and hot pepper sauce, if desired. (Cold soups usually need more seasonings than hot ones, but the spiciness of this one increases over time.)

■ Stir the soup and serve very cold in bowls or glasses. Add whichever of the garnishes you desire directly to the serving bowls, or pass the garnishes in separate bowls for each individual to add as desired.

chilled cantaloupe soup with mint

chilled cantaloupe soup with mint

In summer, this simple soup is a refreshing way to begin a meal. And you don't need to heat up the kitchen to make it. Garnished with strawberry and mint, this pretty, pastel-colored soup will impress your dinner companions. **MAKES 4 SERVINGS | PER SERVING: 85 CALORIES, 0 G. TOTAL FAT (0 G. SATURATED FAT), 22 G. CARBOHYDRATES, 1 G. PROTEIN, 1 G. DIETARY FIBER, 27 MG. SODIUM.**

4 cups cubed cantaloupe (about 1 large cantaloupe)

2 tablespoons honey, or to taste

3 tablespoons freshly squeezed lime juice, or to taste

⅛ teaspoon ground cardamom, or to taste (optional)

Sliced fresh strawberries, for garnish

¼ cup whole fresh mint leaves, for garnish

■ Put the cantaloupe in a wide, shallow, microwave-safe container. In a microwave oven, heat the melon on medium (50% power) for 2 minutes, or just until the melon softens slightly. Transfer the cantaloupe to a blender or food processor. Add the honey, lime juice, and cardamom and blend the mixture until smooth. Transfer to a bowl. Cover and refrigerate for 1 to 2 hours, until cold.

■ Before serving, taste and add more honey, cardamom, or lime juice as needed. Garnish each serving with strawberry slices and mint leaves.

chilled strawberry soup

When strawberries are in season, this is an elegant, light soup to serve your guests, and it requires little preparation time. You could also serve this soup as a cooling beverage on a hot June day. Strawberries are high in the phytochemical ellagic acid, which protects against cancer. **MAKES 4 SERVINGS | PER SERVING: 114 CALORIES, 1 G. TOTAL FAT (LESS THAN 1 G. SATURATED FAT), 27 G. CARBOHYDRATES, 2 G. PROTEIN, 6 G. DIETARY FIBER, 10 MG. SODIUM.**

5 cups sliced fresh strawberries (about 2 pounds)

¼ cup freshly squeezed orange juice

2 tablespoons fresh mint leaves, chopped

2 tablespoons honey, or to taste (optional)

4 fresh mint sprigs, for garnish

■ In a blender or food processor, purée the strawberries with the orange juice and mint leaves until smooth. Add the honey, if desired, and blend. Transfer to a bowl, cover, and refrigerate 1 to 2 hours, until cold. To serve, ladle the cold soup into 4 serving bowls and garnish with mint sprigs.

breads and muffins

Breads and muffins make great side dishes and can also serve as an alternative to cooked grains like pasta or rice. The benefits of eating whole grains are detailed in the Grains chapter (page 66), and eating whole-grain breads and muffins is another pleasurable way to get extra health benefits.

Unless you already appreciate the value and enjoyment of baking your own breads and muffins, you may ask why you should go to the trouble of baking when there are so many commercial versions and "instant" mixes available. The right question to ask is how good the store-bought products and mixes are for your health, weight, and psyche.

There are clear health benefits to making your own breads and muffins. Doing so helps avoid the hydrogenated oils used in so many store-bought versions—oils that contain dangerous trans fats. And although sugar in itself is not unhealthful, it does contain lots of extra calories with little nutritional value, and we Americans consume far too much of it in the processed foods we eat. And, of course, making our own baked goods rather than opting for commercial products is often a financial savings as well.

A less tangible benefit, but one worth mentioning, is that breads and muffins can be fun to make and even therapeutic. Many cooks find the preparation stage, especially if kneading is involved, helps work out the accumulation of everyday stress and acts as a psychological restorative. The baking process produces delectable aromas—a natural "aromatherapy"—that make the house smell homey and comforting.

Three classic myths that prevent many people from trying their hand at baking breads are

It takes too much time.
It's messy.
It's hard and complicated.

It's easy to dispel those myths: *They simply aren't true.* Although it's true that some bread recipes are complicated and time-consuming, many are not. The recipes in this chapter were chosen and developed to take very little of the cook's time. Some breads can be made speedily with a blender, and require minimal cleanup. You can approach them with confidence.

The breads and muffins in this chapter generally fall into two categories—savory and sweet. The savory breads are what we usually associate with morning toast, sandwiches, and complementary side dishes for a meal. There are several savory bread recipes and one savory muffin recipe to consider. The cookbook team is especially pleased to endorse these recipes because of their wholesomeness as well as great taste and texture.

Always looking for the maximum in health benefits, the cookbook team was challenged to find simple savory bread recipes that use the maximum amount of whole-grain flour possible while still retaining the texture and flavor that make bread so enjoyable. As we tested different types of savory breads, we discovered that our opinions varied, sometimes sharply, on which breads had the best flavor or texture. That is to be expected, since our personal tastes are as unique as our personalities.

But another cause for differences was the breads each of us was accustomed to eating. Some had grown up eating—and preferring—soft white breads made with refined flour. Finding a bread recipe that had a high percentage of whole-grain flour and would also receive a thumbs-up from those who love softer breads was a special challenge, but we succeeded. The three savory breads in this chapter each contain a high proportion of whole-grain flour. One, Heirloom Whole Wheat Bread (page 228), uses 100 percent whole wheat flour. It has great taste and texture, yet it requires no special experience or skill to make. It is versatile enough to be served at any meal of the day. The other two savory breads each contain a small percentage of refined flour. They are rich in the benefits of whole grains, but closer in texture and taste to commercial breads. They represent a good way to transition from soft white American-style bread to the more healthful whole-grain breads popular in Europe. Whole Wheat Bread with Herbs (page 226) is a classic all-purpose bread that can be enjoyed as toast, in sandwiches, or as an alternative to grain side dishes in a meal. Whole Wheat Bread with Onions (page 227) has a country-style texture that is achieved by kneading the dough, which can be done by hand or with a machine. This small but important investment of time and effort produces generous rewards. There is also one savory muffin recipe to consider: Whole Corn and Green Chile Muffins (page 231), which go great with soups, salads, chilis, and meats.

Straddling the middle between savory and sweet is Raisin Brown Bread (page 238). This bread, an almost-classic New England combination of cornmeal and whole wheat flour, has an interesting history. It is a simplified version of an early American yeast bread called Anadama Bread. According to legend, the name was born when an angry farmer, tired of the cornmeal porridge his wife served every day, added some flour and yeast to it in a desperate attempt to turn it into bread, cursing all along, saying, "Anna, damn 'er!" This bread is so easy to make,

yet so like old-fashioned brown bread, that it would make a perfect candidate for your first try at home-made bread.

In the sweeter category are several breads and muffins that can make great alternatives to traditional desserts and sweet treats. They are rich in whole grains, with a minimum of added sugar and the extra health protection of ingredients like fruit, seeds, and nuts. For example, Cranberry-Pumpkin Bread with Flaxseed (page 236) contains whole wheat pastry flour as well as all-purpose flour. The addition of this less familiar flour helps create a finer texture and lighter consistency than in most whole wheat breads that rely on yeast for better texture in quick breads. Apple-Spice Bread (page 235) offers the fresh tart taste of apples, the benefits of whole wheat flour, and the old-fashioned comfort of spices like cinnamon, allspice, and nutmeg. Carrot-Raisin Bread (page 239) is a good alternative to the typical sugary, high-calorie carrot cake, and works as either a dessert or a snack.

Even if you've never baked bread from scratch, the ease and simplicity of these recipes should tempt you to try. Besides the nutritional and therapeutic benefits we've already discussed, making your own bread has some additional bonuses. Homemade quick breads are especially valued as gifts: they symbolize time and caring attention. If you have children of grade-school age, another benefit to consider is that children generally love to help with baking—baking is fun, and the results are magical and tasty. (You don't need to tell them this, but baking also helps children acquire skills and concepts they need in school and in life: planning, organization, a little math, and the importance of accuracy and precision.) Research shows that children who learn to cook are more inclined to eventually cook for themselves and be less dependent on convenience and fast foods. Children will especially enjoy making muffins, as the mixing and baking take little time. We adults appreciate this benefit as well.

whole wheat bread with herbs

This hearty wheat loaf comes close to traditional European peasant-style bread. The major ingredient is stone-ground whole wheat flour, which is rich in nutrients and phytochemicals. In addition, the hefty amount of fiber means it is digested more slowly than breads made of refined flour and thus holds off hunger longer. This recipe, however, calls for a small amount of refined bread flour to soften the texture. Molasses lends a hint of dusky sweetness (use "unsulfured" molasses, which has a cleaner taste). This is a delicious transitional loaf for people accustomed to less dense breads made with refined flour. MAKES 14 SERVINGS | PER SERVING: 119 CALORIES, LESS THAN 1 G. TOTAL FAT (LESS THAN 1 G. SATURATED FAT), 26 G. CARBOHYDRATES, 5 G. PROTEIN, 4 G. DIETARY FIBER, 334 MG. SODIUM.

Canola oil spray

3½ cups whole wheat flour, preferably stone-ground

½ cup unbleached bread flour

2 teaspoons salt

1 tablespoon unsulfured molasses

2 cups warm water (105 to 115 degrees), divided

2 packages (2¼ teaspoons each) active dry yeast

¾ cup chopped walnuts (optional)

1 tablespoon dried basil

1 teaspoon dried oregano

2 teaspoons dried thyme

■ Lightly coat a 9 × 5-inch loaf pan with canola oil spray. Position a rack in the center of the oven. Turn the oven on to its lowest setting.

■ In a large, heat-proof bowl, combine the whole wheat and bread flours with the salt. Place the bowl in the oven to warm.

■ In a small bowl, mix the molasses into ½ cup of the warm water. Sprinkle the yeast over the liquid. Let stand 5 to 10 minutes, until foamy. (If the mixture fails to foam, start again with fresh packages of yeast.)

■ Remove the warmed bowl of flour from the oven. Preheat the oven to 450 degrees.

■ Stir the walnuts, basil, oregano, and thyme into the warm flour. Pour the yeast mixture and the remaining 1½ cups of warm water into the flour. Using a wooden spoon, mix until a sticky dough forms. The mixture will seem dry at first but will get wetter as you stir. It will partially pull away from the sides of the bowl but will remain sticky and too soft to knead. Turn the dough into the prepared pan. Cover the pan loosely with plastic wrap coated with canola oil spray, and then with a kitchen towel. Set the pan in a warm, draft-free place for 10 to 15 minutes, until the dough doubles in volume and is slightly below the edge of the pan.

■ Remove the towel and plastic wrap and bake the bread for 10 minutes. Reduce the heat to 425 degrees. Bake for 20 minutes, until a wooden toothpick inserted near the center comes out clean. The crust will be dark brown and hard. (If the loaf is very dark but still moist in the center, turn off the oven, remove the bread from the pan and let the bread sit in the oven, on the rack, for 5 minutes.) Transfer the bread from the oven to a wire rack to cool completely before slicing.

whole wheat bread with onions

Onions put a delicious spin on this whole wheat bread. Its texture and taste make it a great morning toast as well as a sandwich bread that complements a wide range of fillings, depending on whether the optional walnuts and raisins are used. This recipe calls for kneading, which can be done in a food processor, with a mixer and dough hook, or by hand. Although it takes a little time and effort, kneading greatly improves a bread's texture. To knead by hand, lightly sprinkle flour over the surface of a cutting board and place the dough on it, close to you. Rub some flour into the palms of your hands. Press the heels of your hands down into the dough, pushing it away from yourself. Then fold the dough in half, give it a quarter turn and repeat this process. If the dough seems to stick to the board or your hands, use a little more flour. **MAKES 16 SERVINGS | PER SERVING: 75 CALORIES, 3 G. TOTAL FAT (LESS THAN 1 G. SATURATED FAT), 10 G. CARBOHYDRATES, 3 G. PROTEIN, 1 G. DIETARY FIBER, 150 MG. SODIUM.**

Canola oil spray

3 tablespoons olive oil, divided

1 cup finely chopped onion

¾ cup lukewarm water (100 to 110 degrees)

1 tablespoon unsulfured molasses

2 packages (2¼ teaspoons each) active dry yeast

½ cup lukewarm fat-free milk (105 to 110 degrees)

1 large egg

2 teaspoons salt

1 tablespoon dried basil

½ teaspoon dried oregano

½ teaspoon dried thyme

2 cups whole wheat flour, preferably stone-ground

1½ to 2 cups unbleached bread flour, divided

½ cup chopped walnuts (optional)

1 cup raisins (optional)

■ Lightly coat two 8 × 4-inch loaf pans with canola oil spray and set them aside. Set the oven rack in the center of the oven.

■ In a small nonstick skillet, heat 1 tablespoon of the olive oil over medium-high heat. Add the onion and sauté for about 5 minutes, stirring often, until it is golden in color.

■ In a large bowl, combine the lukewarm water and the molasses. Sprinkle the yeast over the liquid. Let stand 5 to 10 minutes, until foamy. (If the mixture fails to foam, start again with fresh packages of yeast.) Stir in the milk, egg, onion (with its cooking oil), and the remaining 2 tablespoons of olive oil. Stir in the salt, herbs, and whole wheat flour until blended. Stir in 1 cup of the bread flour. Add the walnuts and raisins, if desired, and stir until combined. Stir in ½ cup more of the bread flour, until dough gathers easily into a ball. On a lightly floured board, knead the dough for 8 to 10 minutes, until it is smooth and elastic, adding additional flour 1 tablespoon at a time, if needed.

■ Coat a large bowl with canola oil spray. Place the dough in the bowl and turn it over to coat the dough with oil. Cover the bowl with a damp kitchen towel and let the dough rise in a warm, draft-free place for 30 to 45 minutes, until doubled in size.* Punch the dough down and shape it into two loaves with rounded tops. Place the loaves in the prepared pans. Cover the pans with the damp towel and let the dough rise for 30 to 45 minutes, until doubled in size.

■ Preheat the oven to 375 degrees.

■ Bake the bread for 25 to 35 minutes, until it is golden brown. Transfer the loaves from the pans to wire racks to cool completely.

*Note: A warm oven is an ideal place for dough to rise. Warm the oven slightly by turning it on at 200 degrees for 1 minute then turning it off. To keep the oven warm, place a covered pot of simmering water in the oven with the dough.

heirloom whole wheat bread

After we tested many recipes, this 100 percent whole-grain bread won the AICR cookbook team's vote for best taste, tenderness, and versatility. It is similar to the nutritious, rough-textured whole wheat breads that have nourished generations of Europeans, yet pleasing enough for Americans accustomed to soft white bread. The oat bran in this bread is a superb source of soluble fiber, and the stone-ground whole wheat flour adds healthful insoluble fiber. It's great for toasting, making sandwiches, or soaking up sauces and soups. Adding 2 tablespoons of olive oil to the dough will create a fuller flavor and crispier crust. **MAKES 16 SERVINGS | PER SERVING: 88 CALORIES, 1 G. TOTAL FAT (LESS THAN 1 G. SATURATED FAT), 19 G. CARBOHYDRATES, 4 G. PROTEIN, 3 G. DIETARY FIBER, 147 MG. SODIUM.**

Canola oil spray

3 cups whole wheat flour, preferably stone-ground

½ cup oat bran

1 teaspoon salt

2 cups warm water (105 to 115 degrees)

2 teaspoons honey

2 teaspoons active dry yeast

2 tablespoons extra-virgin olive oil (optional)

▪ Lightly coat a 9 × 5-inch loaf pan with canola oil spray and set it aside. Turn the oven on to its lowest setting. In a large, heat-proof bowl, mix together the flour, oat bran, and salt. Place the bowl in the oven to warm while preparing the yeast mixture.

▪ In a small bowl, combine the lukewarm water with the honey. Sprinkle the yeast over the liquid. Let stand for 5 to 10 minutes, until foamy. (If the mixture fails to foam, start again with fresh yeast.)

▪ Remove the warmed flour mixture from the oven. Add the yeast mixture and olive oil, stirring to combine thoroughly, and adding a bit more water if necessary to make a loose, sticky dough. Spoon the dough into the prepared pan. Cover it loosely with plastic wrap coated with canola oil spray, and then with a dish towel. Leave the pan in a warm place until the dough has risen about one-third, about 30 to 60 minutes.*

▪ Preheat the oven to 375 degrees.

▪ Bake the bread for 40 to 50 minutes, or until golden brown. Take the bread out of the oven and carefully remove it from the loaf pan. Place the bread upside down on the oven rack and bake it for 5 minutes more to crisp the crust and ensure the loaf is done. Transfer the bread from the oven to a wire rack to cool completely.

*Note: A warm oven is an ideal place for dough to rise. Warm the oven slightly by turning it on at 200 degrees for 1 minute, then turning it off. To keep the oven warm, place a covered pot of just simmering water in the oven with the dough.

whole corn and green chile muffins

The whole corn kernels, chiles, and cheese in these muffins make them moist, tender, and unforgettably delicious. They are indispensable as a side dish for any type of chili or other Southwestern-style food, and they also go well with salads, soups, and even eggs. **MAKES 12 SERVINGS | PER SERVING: 168 CALORIES, 7 G. TOTAL FAT (LESS THAN 1 G. SATURATED FAT), 22 G. CARBOHYDRATES, 5 G. PROTEIN, 2 G. DIETARY FIBER, 399 MG. SODIUM.**

Canola oil spray (optional)

½ cup whole wheat flour, preferably stone-ground

½ cup unbleached all-purpose flour

¾ cup cornmeal, preferably stone-ground

2 tablespoons sugar

1 tablespoon baking powder

1 teaspoon salt

¼ teaspoon cayenne, or to taste (optional)

1 large egg

¾ cup plus 2 tablespoons fat-free or lowfat milk

⅓ cup canola oil

1 can (8 ounces) salt-free whole kernel corn, well drained

1 can (4.5 ounces) diced green chiles, well drained, divided

½ cup shredded lowfat sharp cheddar cheese

■ Preheat the oven to 400 degrees. Lightly coat a 12-cup muffin pan with canola oil spray or line with paper liners and set it aside.

■ In a medium bowl, mix together the whole wheat flour, all-purpose flour, cornmeal, sugar, baking powder, salt, and cayenne. In a separate bowl, lightly beat the egg. Add the milk, canola oil, corn, and all but 2 tablespoons of the chiles, and mix together. Add the wet ingredients to the dry ingredients, stirring just until combined. Fill each muffin cup half full. Top each with 1 teaspoon of the cheese. Divide the remaining batter evenly among the muffin cups. Sprinkle each top with 1 teaspoon of the cheese and ½ teaspoon of the remaining green chiles.

■ Bake for 20 minutes, until a wooden toothpick inserted in the center of a muffin comes out clean. Cool in the pan on a wire rack for 5 minutes. Remove the muffins from the pan and continue cooling on the rack.

walnut-date muffins with rye

Whole-grain rye flour is used in pumpernickel bread and provides more dietary fiber than the refined version because it still has its bran. It also contains the mineral magnesium and the B vitamins niacin, thiamin, and folate. Whole-grain rye flour gives these muffins a hearty taste that contrasts well with the sweet dates. MAKES 12 SERVINGS | PER SERVING: 188 CALORIES, 4 G. TOTAL FAT (LESS THAN 1 G. SATURATED FAT), 35 G. CARBOHYDRATES, 5 G. PROTEIN, 3 G. DIETARY FIBER, 196 MG. SODIUM.

Canola oil spray (optional)

1 cup whole-grain rye flour

1 cup unbleached all-purpose flour

½ cup packed dark brown sugar

1 tablespoon baking powder

¼ teaspoon salt

½ cup chopped walnuts

2 large eggs

1 cup fat-free milk

6 tablespoons unsweetened applesauce

¾ cup chopped dates

■ Preheat the oven to 400 degrees. Lightly coat a 12-cup muffin pan with canola oil spray or line with paper liners and set it aside.

■ In a large bowl, combine the rye flour, all-purpose flour, brown sugar, baking powder, salt, and walnuts. Set the mixture aside. In a smaller bowl, lightly beat the eggs. Add the milk, applesauce, and dates. Add the wet ingredients to the dry ingredients and blend just until combined. Divide the batter among the muffin cups.

■ Bake for 20 to 25 minutes, until a wooden toothpick inserted into the center of 1 muffin comes out clean and the crusts are golden brown. Cool in the pan on a wire rack for 5 minutes. Remove the muffins from the pan and continue cooling on the rack.

flaxseed-raisin muffins

Muffins are an ideal opportunity to use flaxseed, which has phytoestrogens, a type of plant-based substance that may help protect cells against cancer development. This simple recipe takes practically no time to prepare and bake. Applesauce keeps these muffins moist while minimizing fat. With a 6-ounce cup of yogurt and some juice or a piece of fruit, one of these muffins can be part of a healthy, quick breakfast. Flaxseed is available in health food stores and many supermarkets. It must be ground for people to be able to digest it. MAKES 12 SERVINGS | PER SERVING: 231 CALORIES, 9 G. TOTAL FAT (LESS THAN 1 G. SATURATED FAT), 34 G. CARBOHYDRATES, 6 G. PROTEIN, 6 G. DIETARY FIBER, 197 MG. SODIUM.

Canola oil spray

1¼ cups unbleached all-purpose flour

¾ cup ground flaxseed

⅔ cup sugar

1 teaspoon baking soda

½ teaspoon ground cinnamon

¼ teaspoon ground nutmeg

¼ teaspoon salt

2 large eggs

2 tablespoons canola oil

½ cup unsweetened applesauce

1 cup fat-free buttermilk

½ cup golden raisins

■ Preheat the oven to 375 degrees. Lightly coat a 12-cup muffin pan with canola oil spray or line with paper liners and set it aside.

■ In a large bowl, blend the flour, flaxseed, sugar, baking soda, cinnamon, nutmeg, and salt together with a wooden spoon and set it aside. In a separate bowl, mix together the eggs, canola oil, applesauce, buttermilk, and raisins with a wire whisk. Add the wet ingredients to the dry ingredients, mixing just until combined. Divide the batter among the muffin cups.

■ Bake for 25 to 35 minutes, until a wooden toothpick inserted in the center of 1 muffin comes out clean. Cool in the pan on a wire rack for 5 minutes. Remove the muffins from the pan and continue cooling on the rack.

walnut-date muffins with rye

banana-orange bran muffins with pecans

If you are looking for a breakfast or dinner muffin sweetened only by fruit, this recipe comes close. The only added sugar comes from the bran flakes. (We couldn't locate a commercial bran flake without added sugar or sweeteners. If you find one, use it in this recipe and serve it for breakfast, too.) The whole wheat pastry flour, bran cereal, and mashed banana create a light batter that plays up the flavor of dried fruit and pecans. These muffins are a healthy breakfast, snack, or accompaniment to dishes such as Fruit and Nut Salad with Pork (page 165) or any green dinner salad. **MAKES 12 SERVINGS | PER SERVING: 176 CALORIES, 7 G. TOTAL FAT (LESS THAN 1 G. SATURATED FAT), 27 G. CARBOHYDRATES, 3 G. PROTEIN, 3 G. DIETARY FIBER, 175 MG. SODIUM.**

Canola oil spray (optional)

1 cup mashed ripe bananas (about 2 medium)

½ cup frozen orange juice concentrate, thawed

1 large egg

¼ cup canola oil

1½ cups bran flake cereal

1 cup whole wheat pastry flour

2 teaspoons baking powder

¼ teaspoon baking soda

¼ teaspoon ground cinnamon

⅛ teaspoon salt

½ cup diced dried cherries or dried apricots

¼ cup chopped toasted pecans*

*Note: To toast the pecans, put them in a small skillet over medium heat, shaking or stirring frequently until lightly browned, about 2 to 3 minutes. Immediately transfer the nuts to a small dish and cool.

■ Preheat the oven to 400 degrees. Lightly coat a 12-cup muffin pan with canola oil spray or line with paper liners and set it aside.

■ In a large bowl, whisk together the mashed bananas, orange juice concentrate, egg, and canola oil. Stir in the bran flakes. Let stand for about 15 minutes to soften the cereal. In a separate bowl, combine the flour, baking powder, baking soda, cinnamon, and salt. Add the dry ingredients to the cereal mixture and stir just until combined. Gently fold in the dried fruit and pecans. Divide the batter among the muffin cups.

■ Bake for 20 to 25 minutes, until a wooden toothpick inserted in the center of 1 muffin comes out clean. Cool in the pan on a wire rack for 5 minutes. Remove the muffins from the pan and continue cooling on the rack.

apple-spice bread

Grated apples give this bread a fresh, fruity taste. By leaving the peel on, you also get more dietary fiber, plus pectin and quercetin, two health-protective substances. The spices help blend the apples and the nutty taste of whole wheat flour into a terrific-tasting and healthful quick bread. **MAKES 10 SERVINGS | PER SERVING: 209 CALORIES, 5 G. TOTAL FAT (LESS THAN 1 G. SATURATED FAT), 39 G. CARBOHYDRATES, 4 G. PROTEIN, 2 G. DIETARY FIBER, 170 MG. SODIUM.**

Canola oil spray

2 medium tart apples (such as Granny Smith), cored and grated

3 tablespoons freshly squeezed lemon juice

1 cup whole wheat flour, preferably stone-ground

1 cup unbleached all-purpose flour

2 teaspoons baking powder

2 teaspoons ground cinnamon

½ teaspoon ground allspice

½ teaspoon ground ginger

¼ teaspoon salt

¼ teaspoon ground nutmeg (optional)

¾ cup packed light brown sugar

¼ cup unsweetened applesauce

3 tablespoons canola oil

1 large egg, lightly beaten

1 teaspoon vanilla extract

■ Preheat the oven to 350 degrees. Lightly coat a 9 × 5-inch loaf pan with canola oil spray and set aside.

■ In a medium bowl, toss the grated apples with the lemon juice to prevent browning. In a large bowl, combine the whole wheat flour, all-purpose flour, baking powder, cinnamon, allspice, ginger, salt, and nutmeg. Mix well and set aside. Add the brown sugar, applesauce, canola oil, egg, and vanilla extract to the apples. Mix well. Make a well in the center of the dry ingredients and pour the wet ingredients into it. Mix just until blended. Transfer the batter to the prepared pan.

■ Bake for about 1 hour, until a wooden toothpick inserted near the center comes out almost clean (to ensure moistness). Cool in the pan on a wire rack for 10 minutes. Remove the bread from the pan and continue cooling on the rack.

cranberry-pumpkin bread with flaxseed

Pumpkin's beta-carotene, a cancer-fighting antioxidant, is combined in this bread with another health protector, flaxseed. Researchers have found a type of omega-3 fatty acid, as well as the phytochemical lignans and dietary fiber, in flaxseed. Most health food stores and some supermarkets sell flaxseed. If you buy the seeds whole, they can be ground in an electric coffee grinder. Cranberries and whole wheat pastry flour round out this bread's health-packed ingredients. **MAKES 12 SERVINGS |** **PER SERVING: 206 CALORIES, 8 G. TOTAL FAT (LESS THAN 1 G. SATURATED FAT), 33 G. CARBOHYDRATES, 4 G. PROTEIN, 3 G. DIETARY FIBER, 221 MG. SODIUM.**

Canola oil spray
½ cup whole wheat pastry flour
½ cup unbleached all-purpose flour
½ cup ground flaxseed
⅔ cup packed light brown sugar
1 teaspoon baking soda
½ teaspoon salt
2 large eggs
1 cup canned pumpkin
¼ cup canola oil
½ cup unsweetened applesauce
¼ cup apple juice
½ teaspoon ground cinnamon
½ teaspoon ground ginger
¼ teaspoon ground nutmeg
1 cup dried cranberries

■ Preheat the oven to 350 degrees. Lightly coat an 8 × 4-inch loaf pan with canola oil spray and set it aside.

■ In a large bowl, combine the whole wheat pastry flour, all-purpose flour, flaxseed, sugar, baking soda, and salt, and set aside. In a medium bowl, lightly beat the eggs. Whisk in the pumpkin, canola oil, applesauce, apple juice, cinnamon, ginger, and nutmeg. Stir in the dried cranberries. Add the wet ingredients to the dry ingredients, mixing until all the dry ingredients are fully incorporated into the batter. Do not beat or overmix. Pour the batter into the prepared pan.

■ Bake for 50 to 60 minutes, until a wooden toothpick inserted into the center comes out clean. Cool in the pan on a wire rack for 10 minutes. Remove the bread from the pan and continue cooling on the rack.

raisin brown bread

Brown bread in America dates back to the days of the Puritan settlers in Massachusetts. This recipe uses the traditional cornmeal, buttermilk, and molasses combined with whole wheat flour. The raisins bring extra dietary fiber, resveratrol, and flavonoids as well as adding to this bread's rustic charm. **MAKES 12 SERVINGS | PER SERVING: 214 CALORIES, 5 G. TOTAL FAT (LESS THAN 1 G. SATURATED FAT), 41 G. CARBOHYDRATES, 4 G. PROTEIN, 2 G. DIETARY FIBER, 142 MG. SODIUM.**

Canola oil spray
1 cup raisins
½ cup packed dark brown sugar
3 tablespoons canola oil
⅓ cup unsweetened applesauce
½ cup cornmeal
¼ cup unsulfured molasses
1 large egg
1 cup fat-free or lowfat buttermilk
1 cup whole wheat flour, preferably stone-ground
1 teaspoon baking soda

■ Preheat the oven to 350 degrees. Coat an 8 × 4-inch loaf pan with canola oil spray and set aside.

■ In a small bowl, cover the raisins with boiling water. Let the raisins stand for 5 minutes and then drain. In a large bowl, blend the sugar, canola oil, and applesauce with a hand mixer until smooth. Add the cornmeal, molasses, egg, and buttermilk and mix to combine. Stir in the flour and baking soda just until combined. Add the raisins. Pour the mixture into the prepared pan.

■ Bake for 45 to 50 minutes, until a wooden toothpick inserted in the center comes out clean. Cool in the pan on a wire rack for 10 minutes. Remove the bread from the pan and continue cooling on the rack.

carrot-raisin bread

Plenty of carrots turn this bread into a powerhouse of beta-carotene, and pineapple, raisins, and rolled oats give it an intricate taste and texture. If you're trying to find a baked item that uses carrots but is less sugary than carrot cake, this is the recipe for you. It's good enough to eat for dessert. MAKES 12 SERVINGS | PER SERVING: 257 CALORIES, 6 G. TOTAL FAT (LESS THAN 1 G. SATURATED FAT), 48 G. CARBOHYDRATES, 5 G. PROTEIN, 3 G. DIETARY FIBER, 254 MG. SODIUM.

Canola oil spray

½ cup rolled oats

½ cup fat-free milk

1 cup whole wheat flour, preferably stone-ground

1¼ cups unbleached all-purpose flour

¾ cup packed light brown sugar

1 tablespoon baking powder

½ teaspoon baking soda

½ teaspoon ground cinnamon

¼ teaspoon salt

1¼ cups shredded carrots (about 3 medium)

½ cup raisins

1 can (20 ounces) crushed pineapple in juice, drained, with juice reserved

2 large eggs, lightly beaten

¼ cup canola oil

1 teaspoon vanilla extract

■ Preheat the oven to 350 degrees. Lightly coat a 9 × 5-inch loaf pan with canola oil spray.

■ In a medium bowl, combine the oats with the milk, mix well, and set aside. In a large bowl, combine the whole wheat flour, all-purpose flour, sugar, baking powder, baking soda, cinnamon, and salt. Mix well. Stir in the carrots and raisins, and set aside. To the oat mixture, add the pineapple and 4 tablespoons of the juice, eggs, canola oil, and vanilla extract. Mix well. Add the mixture to the dry ingredients and mix just until the dry ingredients are moistened. Pour the batter into the prepared pan.

■ Bake for 60 minutes, until a wooden toothpick inserted into the center comes out clean and the crust is golden brown. Cool in the pan on a wire rack for 10 minutes. Remove the bread from the pan and continue cooling on the wire rack.

scottish crackers

If you are trying to avoid refined flour, unhealthful fats (like the dangerous trans fats in commercial crackers), and sugars, these Scottish Crackers may seem like manna from heaven. Derived from an old recipe for Scottish oatcakes, these crackers are light, crisp, and delicious. They will satisfy you without raising your blood sugar to new heights. Try them with dips and appetizers, and for a treat, spread nut butter or jam on them. **MAKES ABOUT 24 CRACKERS | PER CRACKER: 50 CALORIES, 2 G. TOTAL FAT (LESS THAN 1 G. SATURATED FAT), 6 G. CARBOHYDRATES, 1 G. PROTEIN, 1 G. DIETARY FIBER, 73 MG. SODIUM.**

1⅓ cups quick-cooking rolled oats

⅔ cup whole wheat flour

½ to ¾ teaspoon salt

3½ tablespoons canola oil

4 to 6 tablespoons cold water

■ Preheat the oven to 375 degrees.

■ In a food processor, pulse the oats until they resemble very coarse flour. Add the flour, salt, and canola oil. Pulse until the mixture resembles coarse meal. Transfer the mixture to a medium bowl. Stir in just enough water to make the mixture cohere like pie crust dough. Form the dough into a ball.

■ Transfer the dough to a lightly floured cutting board and roll out to a thickness of about 1/8 inch. Use a 1 1/2- to 2-inch biscuit or other circular cutter to cut out the crackers. Arrange the crackers on a non-stick baking sheet. (They do not spread during baking so can be placed close together.)

■ Bake in the middle of the oven about 12 minutes, or until lightly colored. Turn over the crackers and bake about 12 minutes more, or until lightly colored on the second side. (Do not allow them to brown.)

■ Transfer the crackers to a wire rack and cool completely. Store in a metal container with a tight-fitting lid for 3 to 5 days.

desserts

Fruit is so perfectly nutritious and delectable that, in an ideal world, dessert would always be fruit. If you're accustomed to grabbing an orange to eat on the run, fruit may not seem like your idea of dessert. But don't sell fruit short as a dessert that you can look forward to at the end of a meal. Fruit cut into thin wedges and arranged in a star or pinwheel design on a pretty dish starts to look more like dessert. Take that concept a little further by alternating slices of fruits in contrasting colors. Try papaya and pear, or nectarine and kiwi, or mango and pineapple. Sprinkle blueberries or raspberries over the top. Now you have a *real* dessert.

In short, dessert depends more on a state of mind than on sugar, fat, and calories. It should taste, feel, and look special, like a reward. In other words, treatment and presentation are key. Fruit prettily arranged on an attractive dish makes us aware of sweet fragrances, glistening surfaces, and color contrasts. Our palates revel in contrast as well: a mixture of fruits that range from sweet to tart flavors and soft to crisp textures highlights each individual element.

It doesn't take much effort, or calories, to dress up a fruit. A drizzle of good balsamic vinegar over ripe strawberries both heightens and contrasts the fruit's sweetness. The cold tang of a dollop of sour cream or yogurt can enhance the taste of berries and other sweet fruits. A sprinkling of chopped nuts provides a nice, crunchy contrast to fruits with soft textures.

With an oven or grill, you can bring fruits to their ultimate in sweetness. Baking, for example, heightens the sweetness of apples and pears. But it's the grill that seems to bring out all the glory of fruits. With or without a marinade or sauce, firm fruits like just-ripe papaya, mango, plum, nectarine, peach, and pineapple become succulent with grilling. Try alternating types of fruits on skewers before grilling: Grilled Fruit Kebabs (page 260) will inspire variations on this theme.

Despite the varied pleasures of fruit, we occasionally yearn for some kind of baked treat. Fortunately, it's not necessary to ignore health and diet concerns to enjoy a rich-tasting, soul-satisfying dessert. Our cookbook team took up the challenge of researching, testing, and tasting recipes and developed a wide range of healthful but "real" desserts. (It was a tough job, but someone had to do it.)

These desserts minimize sugar without sacrificing flavor or the integrity of the recipe. All-purpose or refined flour is often replaced with whole-grain flour while still retaining quality and taste. Our New American Plate Pie Crust (page 243) contains whole wheat flour yet preserves a more traditional taste. This more healthful pie crust replaces unhealthful hydrogenated fats with canola oil, plus just enough butter to ensure a better flavor and flakiness.

Some of the desserts, like Banana-Oatmeal Cookies (page 257) and Maple-Fig Bars (page 259), are old-fashioned enough to conjure up childhood memories. Others, like Chocolate Angel Food Cake with Raspberries (page 249) and Meringue Tartlets with Strawberries and Shaved Chocolate (page 254), are elegant finales to any celebratory meal.

fresh plum tart

The sweet-tart taste of delectable black plums is accented with a brown sugar glaze in this sumptuous yet simple dessert. You can create a stylish "heaped" effect by standing each plum half on end, so the cut side faces in toward the middle of the pan and each piece supports the next. You could also add more plums, which would increase the tartness and raise the calorie count just slightly. Ready-made whole wheat crusts are available at most health food markets and some supermarkets, or use a double recipe of the New American Plate Pie Crust on page 243. This beautiful tart is easy to make for a casual meal, yet sophisticated enough to follow a fancy dinner. If desired, serve the tart with lowfat ice cream, frozen yogurt, or a light dusting of powdered sugar.

MAKES 12 SERVINGS | PER SERVING: 255 CALORIES, 10 G. TOTAL FAT (2 G. SATURATED FAT), 40 G. CARBOHYDRATES, 3 G. PROTEIN, 2 G. DIETARY FIBER, 103 MG. SODIUM.

1 prepared whole wheat pastry crust for 10- or 11-inch tart pan (or double the New American Plate Pie Crust recipe on page 243)

10 large black plums

1 cup finely ground lowfat vanilla wafers or biscotti cookies

½ cup packed light brown sugar

- Line a 10- or 11-inch tart pan that has a removable bottom with the pastry crust. Trim excess crust from edges. Refrigerate the crust for 30 minutes.

- Preheat the oven to 425 degrees.

- Cut the plums in half and discard the pits. When the pastry crust has chilled, sprinkle the cookie crumbs evenly over the bottom. Lay the plum pieces over the crumbs in concentric circles so the plums touch each other. Sprinkle the brown sugar evenly over the top of the plums.

- Bake for 15 minutes. Reduce the oven heat to 350 degrees and bake for an additional 1 hour 15 minutes to 1 hour 30 minutes, until the plums are soft and the juices cover the bottom of the pan. Let the tart cool to room temperature before serving.

new american plate pie crust

Unlike many pie crusts, this one uses some whole wheat flour (for extra nutrients and dietary fiber) and contains no trans fats, which are found in margarine, shortening, and any product that contains partially hydrogenated vegetable oil. You can use this crust recipe for any dessert pie; for a nondessert vegetable or quiche filling, use water instead of apple juice and omit the powdered sugar. **MAKES 1 CRUST FOR A 9-INCH PIE; 10 SERVINGS | PER SERVING: 93 CALORIES, 5 G. TOTAL FAT (1 G. SATURATED FAT), 10 G. CARBOHYDRATES, 1 G. PROTEIN, LESS THAN 1 G. DIETARY FIBER, 41 MG. SODIUM.**

¼ cup whole wheat flour

¾ cup unbleached all-purpose flour

1 tablespoon powdered sugar

⅛ teaspoon salt

1 tablespoon butter

3 tablespoons canola oil

1 to 2 tablespoons ice water or cold apple juice

■ In a food processor, combine the whole wheat flour, all-purpose flour, sugar, and salt. Pulse for a few seconds to combine. Add the butter and canola oil. Pulse again until the ingredients are well combined and the mixture resembles crumbs. With the food processor running, add the ice water, beginning with 1 tablespoon and adding more, one teaspoon at a time, until the dough starts to come together. Gather the dough into a ball and let it rest for a few minutes.

■ On a sheet of waxed paper, press the dough into a flattened disk. Cover the dough with another sheet of waxed paper and, using a rolling pin, roll the dough out into a 12-inch circle. Remove the top sheet of waxed paper and lift the bottom sheet to invert the dough over a 9-inch pie plate. Remove the waxed paper and gently press the dough down against the sides and bottom of the plate, pressing out any air bubbles. Crimp the edges by pinching between your thumb and forefinger. Refrigerate the dough while you prepare the filling. The dough can be covered and refrigerated overnight or can be tightly wrapped and frozen for up to 1 month.

cranberry-apple lattice pie

Cranberries are proving to have all kinds of health-protective qualities. They contain flavonoids, which may help decrease disease risk. Though they are most familiar in juices and relishes, cranberries also make a beautiful pie. The candied ginger, which is available in most supermarkets, adds a piquant sweetness. The minimal lattice crust on this cranberry-apple pie is not only attractive—it also allows you to avoid the high amount of fat in most full-crust pies. MAKES 10 SERVINGS | PER SERVING: 301 CALORIES, 9 G. TOTAL FAT (LESS THAN 1 G. SATURATED FAT), 56 G. CARBOHYDRATES, 4 G. PROTEIN, 4 G. DIETARY FIBER, 48 MG. SODIUM.

1 bag (12 ounces) fresh or frozen cranberries

3 medium yellow apples (such as Golden Delicious), peeled, cored, and chopped (about 5 cups)

1 cup raisins

¼ cup chopped candied (or crystallized) ginger

⅔ cup packed dark brown sugar

1½ teaspoons ground cinnamon

¼ teaspoon ground cloves

⅓ cup apple cider or frozen apple juice concentrate, thawed, divided

½ cup chopped walnuts

4 teaspoons cornstarch

Canola oil spray

Dough for 1 New American Plate Pie Crust (page 243) or other unbaked crust for a 9-inch pie

Unbleached all-purpose flour

1 large egg, lightly beaten

¼ cup granulated sugar

■ In a deep saucepan with a tight-fitting lid, combine the cranberries, apples, raisins, ginger, brown sugar, cinnamon, and cloves. Add ¼ cup of the cider and bring to a boil over medium heat. Reduce the heat to low and cook uncovered for about 5 minutes, or until some of the cranberries pop and the mixture is moist and bubbling. Stir well, cover, and cook for 4 to 5 minutes, until the cranberries are soft. Mix in the walnuts. In a small bowl, combine the cornstarch with the remaining cider and mix it into the cranberry mixture. Cook for about 2 minutes, stirring constantly, until thickened.

■ Lightly coat a 9-inch pie plate with canola oil spray and turn the filling into the pie plate, spreading it evenly. Let the filling stand and cool for about 30 minutes or cover with plastic wrap and refrigerate for up to 24 hours. Bring the chilled filling back to room temperature before you bake it.

■ Preheat the oven to 425 degrees. On a sheet of waxed paper, press the dough into a flattened square. Cover the dough with another sheet of waxed paper and, using a rolling pin, roll the dough out into a 6 by 10-inch rectangle. Remove the top sheet of waxed paper and cut the rolled-out pie crust into twelve ½-inch-wide strips. Place 6 strips evenly over the top of the pie, lightly flouring hands if sticky. One by one, weave through the remaining 6 strips at right angles to the first 6 strips to make a lattice. Trim away the overhanging crust from the edges of the pie. Use the remaining crust to make a border along the rim of the pie plate. Crimp the edges by pinching between your thumb and forefinger. Brush the crust with the beaten egg and then sprinkle the granulated sugar over the top of the pie, including the edges.

■ Set the pie on a baking sheet and bake for 10 minutes. Reduce the heat to 350 degrees and bake for 25 to 30 minutes more, until the crust is golden. If the rim of the crust starts to brown too quickly, cover it loosely with strips of foil.

■ Cool the pie on a wire rack for 20 minutes before serving. Serve warm or at room temperature.

pumpkin pie

This recipe for pumpkin pie uses a technique that helps create a particularly rich-tasting filling. Before the pumpkin is blended with other pie filling ingredients, it is cooked down slightly, which intensifies the pumpkin flavor and brings out its natural sweetness. That's why the filling requires less than the average amount of added sugar. The few minutes needed for this step are well worth taking. Sprinkling a flour and spice mixture over the bottom of the crust prevents the shell from becoming soggy and adds flavor, too. **MAKES 10 SERVINGS | PER SERVING: 194 CALORIES, 7 G. TOTAL FAT (1 G. SATURATED FAT), 29 G. CARBOHYDRATES, 6 G. PROTEIN, 2 G. DIETARY FIBER, 158 MG. SODIUM.**

Canola oil spray

2 cups canned pumpkin (one 15-ounce can and ¼ cup of another 15-ounce can)*

Dough for 1 New American Plate Pie Crust (page 243)

1½ teaspoons unbleached all-purpose flour

½ teaspoon ground nutmeg, divided

¾ teaspoon ground cinnamon, divided

1 can (12 ounces) evaporated fat-free milk

½ cup packed dark brown sugar

2 or 3 large eggs, lightly beaten†

¼ teaspoon salt

¼ teaspoon ground allspice

½ teaspoon vanilla extract

*Note: Any remaining canned pumpkin can be stored in a tightly covered container in the refrigerator for up to 5 days. It can be used as a side dish.

†Note: If you prefer a softer, more custardlike texture in your pie filling, use three eggs; if you like a firmer consistency, use two eggs.

■ Lightly coat the inside of a large, nonstick skillet or saucepan with canola oil spray. Add the pumpkin and cook over medium-high heat, stirring often with a wooden spoon so that all the pumpkin comes in contact with the pan, until the pumpkin is reduced to about 1³/4 cups, about 5 to 10 minutes. (This can be roughly gauged by "eyeballing" the amount or measuring the cooked-down pumpkin.) Transfer the pumpkin to a blender or food processor and let it cool slightly.

■ Set a baking rack in the middle of the oven. Preheat the oven to 400 degrees.

■ Meanwhile, roll out the dough. On a sheet of waxed paper, press the dough into a flattened disk. Cover the dough with another sheet of waxed paper and, using a rolling pin, roll the dough out into a 12-inch circle. Remove the top sheet of waxed paper and lift the bottom sheet to invert the dough over a 9-inch pie plate. Remove the waxed paper and gently press the dough down against the sides and bottom of the plate, pressing out any air bubbles. Crimp the edges by pinching between your thumb and forefinger. In a small bowl, combine the flour with ¹/4 teaspoon of the nutmeg and ¹/4 teaspoon of the cinnamon. Sprinkle the flour and spice mixture evenly over the bottom of the pie crust and set it aside. Chill prepared crust while preparing filling.

■ Gradually turn the blender or food processor to the highest speed and purée the pumpkin. Stop the motor and scrape down sides of the blender or processor with a rubber spatula. At medium speed, gradually add first the milk, then the sugar, then the eggs, blending only until each addition is incorporated into the mixture. Add the salt, the remaining ¹/4 teaspoon nutmeg, the remaining ¹/2 teaspoon cinnamon, the allspice, and vanilla extract and blend just until combined. Do not overmix. Pour the filling into the pie crust, scraping down the sides of the blender or processor with a rubber spatula.

■ Bake the pie for 15 minutes. Reduce the oven heat to 325 degrees and bake about 45 minutes more, until the filling looks set and a thin knife inserted into the center of the pie comes out almost clean. If the rim of the pie crust browns before the filling is set, cover it loosely with strips of foil.

■ Cool the pie on a wire rack before serving.

apple pie with granola topping

This is our updated, healthier makeover of the classic apple pie. Slice for slice, it cuts out as much as 200 calories, 16 grams of fat, and 5 grams of saturated fat when compared with a traditional recipe. Part of the savings comes from using a crumb topping instead of a top crust. **MAKES 10 SERVINGS | PER SERVING: 236 CALORIES, 9 G. TOTAL FAT (2 G. SATURATED FAT), 39 G. CARBOHYDRATES, 3 G. PROTEIN, 3 G. DIETARY FIBER, 89 MG. SODIUM.**

Dough for 1 New American Plate
Pie Crust (page 243)

FILLING

6 large tart apples (such as Granny Smith), peeled, cored, and thinly sliced (about 6 cups)

⅓ cup sugar

1 tablespoon unbleached all-purpose flour

2 teaspoons apple pie spice, or 2 teaspoons of a mixture of ground cinnamon, nutmeg, and cloves

Pinch of salt

TOPPING

¼ cup unbleached all-purpose flour

¼ cup whole wheat pastry flour

¼ cup quick-cooking rolled oats

3 tablespoons packed dark brown sugar

½ teaspoon ground cinnamon

Pinch of salt

½ tablespoon melted butter

1½ tablespoons canola oil

■ Preheat the oven to 350 degrees.

■ On a sheet of waxed paper, press the dough into a flattened disk. Cover the dough with another sheet of waxed paper and, using a rolling pin, roll the dough out into a 12-inch circle. Remove the top sheet of waxed paper and lift the bottom sheet to invert the dough over a 9-inch pie plate. Remove the waxed paper and gently press the dough down against the sides and bottom of the plate, pressing out any air bubbles. Crimp the edges by pinching between your thumb and forefinger. Chill dough while preparing filling.

■ Put the sliced apples in a large bowl. In a small bowl, mix together the remaining filling ingredients. Toss this mixture with the apples, coating them well. Spoon the apple mixture into the prepared crust.

■ In a large bowl, mix together the 1/4 cup all-purpose flour, whole wheat flour, oats, brown sugar, cinnamon, and salt until well combined. Using a pastry blender or fork, mix in the melted butter and canola oil until the mixture resembles crumbs. Sprinkle the topping evenly over the apples, pressing down gently. Bake for 45 to 60 minutes, until the apples are tender and bubbling. If the crust is browning too much, place crimped foil around the edges and continue baking. Cool on a wire rack. The pie can be served warm, at room temperature, or chilled.

pear crisp Bosc or Asian pears work beautifully in this dish because of their firm texture, but Bartletts work fine as well. Walnuts' healthful omega-3 fats, and the nutrients and phytochemicals from the whole grains, make this crisp an ideal autumn dessert. Leaving the pears unpeeled will not affect the texture. Although pear skin is delicate, it houses much of the nutrient value of the fruit. **MAKES 9 SERVINGS | PER SERVING: 164 CALORIES, 4 G. TOTAL FAT (LESS THAN 1 G. SATURATED FAT), 34 G. CARBOHYDRATES, 2 G. PROTEIN, 4 G. DIETARY FIBER, 3 MG. SODIUM.**

Canola oil spray

¼ cup rolled oats

1 tablespoon walnuts

3 tablespoons whole wheat flour

5 tablespoons unbleached all-purpose flour, divided

2½ tablespoons packed light brown sugar

⅛ teaspoon ground cinnamon

1 tablespoon plus 2 teaspoons canola oil

6 firm yet ripe pears (such as Bartlett), peeled (if desired), cored, and cubed into 1-inch pieces (about 6 cups)

¼ cup raisins

1 tablespoon freshly squeezed lemon juice

2 tablespoons granulated sugar

⅛ teaspoon ground nutmeg

Pinch of ground cloves

■ Preheat the oven to 375 degrees. Lightly coat an 8- or 9-inch round cake pan with canola oil spray.

■ In a food processor, pulse the oats and walnuts for 15 seconds. Add the whole wheat flour, 3 tablespoons of the all-purpose flour, brown sugar, and cinnamon. Process for 15 seconds. While the food processor is running, drizzle in the canola oil and process for 30 seconds, until the oil is completely integrated and the mixture resembles crumbs. Transfer the mixture to a bowl.

■ In another bowl, toss the pears with the raisins, lemon juice, granulated sugar, the remaining 2 tablespoons all-purpose flour, nutmeg, and cloves. Spoon the pear mixture into the prepared cake pan and cover the top with the oat mixture, pressing down gently. Bake for 45 to 50 minutes, until the topping is brown and the pears are bubbling. Serve hot.

chocolate angel food cake with raspberries

Because of its low fat content, angel food cake is known as a more healthful dessert than other cakes. This recipe dresses up plain angel food cake by flavoring it with cocoa and adding luxuriant red raspberries. These berries are low in calories and rich in vitamin C, and they contain lots of dietary fiber. Like all berries, they are rich in perillyl alcohol, a substance thought to fight cancer.

MAKES 12 SERVINGS | PER SERVING: 141 CALORIES, LESS THAN 1 G. TOTAL FAT (0 G. SATURATED FAT), 31 G. CARBOHYDRATES, 5 G. PROTEIN, 2 G. DIETARY FIBER, 104 MG. SODIUM.

1	cup cake flour
¼	cup nonalkalized cocoa powder
½	teaspoon ground cinnamon
¼	teaspoon salt
12	large egg whites, at room temperature
1	teaspoon cream of tartar
1¼	cups sugar
1	pint fresh raspberries, lightly rinsed, drained, and air-dried, divided

■ Set a rack in the center of the oven. Preheat the oven to 350 degrees.

■ Into a small bowl, sift together the flour, cocoa, cinnamon, and salt. In a large bowl, beat the egg whites with an electric mixer at medium speed for about 2 minutes, until foamy. Add the cream of tartar and beat the whites at high speed for about 3 minutes, until soft peaks form. Gradually add the sugar by sprinkling 2 tablespoons at a time over the egg whites and beating the mixture until the sugar is all blended in.

■ Sift ⅓ of the flour mixture over the egg whites. Using a rubber spatula, gently fold the dry ingredients into the egg whites just until combined. Repeat until all of the flour mixture is blended in. Do not overmix. There may still be white streaks in the batter. Spoon the batter into a deep 9-inch tube pan with a removable bottom, gently smoothing the batter to avoid large air pockets. Immediately place in the oven and bake for 50 minutes, until the cake feels springy when pressed in the middle with your fingertips and a tester inserted into the center comes out clean. Invert the pan and set it on a raised rack, or suspend it over the neck of a tall, heavy bottle.

■ When the cake is cool, turn the pan right-side up. Run a thin, sharp knife around the sides of the pan, including the center. Push up the bottom of the pan and remove the outside ring. Run a knife between the bottom of the pan and the cake. Invert a plate over the cake and, holding the plate firmly in place, turn the cake over so it rests on the plate. Lift away the pan bottom. Cover the cake with plastic wrap and let it rest overnight or for 12 hours on the counter or in the refrigerator. The cake keeps for up to 5 days.

■ To make the raspberry purée, place 1 cup raspberries in a food processor. Pulse until smooth. Strain to remove seeds.

■ To serve, slice the cake using a serrated knife and lay portions on plates. Drizzle cake slices with raspberry purée and top with remaining whole fresh raspberries.

nectarine and raspberry cobbler

When you want a fruit pie for dessert but don't feel like making a pie crust—or you want to use some fruit that's losing its freshness—cobbler is the answer. Fruit cobblers can also combine different fruits, each bringing a variety of phytochemicals that interact to protect health. This recipe is a colorful blend of juicy, fiber-rich raspberries, which deliver ellagic acid, a flavonoid believed to be a powerful cancer fighter, and nectarines, which contain cryptoxanthin. These fruits sweeten as they bake beneath a whole wheat biscuit crust. **MAKES 9 SERVINGS | PER SERVING: 193 CALORIES, 3 G. TOTAL FAT (2 G. SATURATED FAT), 41 G. CARBOHYDRATES, 3 G. PROTEIN, 5 G. DIETARY FIBER, 223 MG. SODIUM.**

Canola oil spray

6 cups thinly sliced nectarines (about 6 to 8 small)

2 cups fresh raspberries

½ cup sugar plus 1 tablespoon sugar, divided

½ cup whole wheat flour

½ cup unbleached all-purpose flour plus more for dusting

½ teaspoon ground cinnamon

2 teaspoons baking powder

¼ teaspoon baking soda

¼ teaspoon salt

2 tablespoons very cold unsalted butter, cut into small pieces

½ cup fat-free buttermilk

■ Preheat the oven to 450 degrees. Lightly coat an 8-inch square baking dish with canola oil spray. In a bowl, toss the nectarines and raspberries with ½ cup of the sugar, using your hands to distribute the sugar evenly. Pour the fruit, scraping the bowl with a rubber spatula, into the prepared baking dish.

■ In a medium bowl, combine the whole wheat flour, ½ cup of the all-purpose flour, the remaining 1 tablespoon of sugar, and the cinnamon, baking powder, baking soda, and salt. Cut the butter into the dry ingredients using a pastry blender or the tines of a fork. Work the mixture with the tips of your fingers just until it looks grainy. Mix in the buttermilk with a wooden spoon until a soft, moist dough forms. (The topping can also be prepared in a food processor, pulsing until dough is soft and moist but not overmixed.)

■ Lightly dust a work surface with flour. Gently pat the dough into a ¼-inch-thick rectangle using the heel of your hand. Sprinkle the dough lightly with flour, if it becomes too sticky. Dip the rim of a 2-inch biscuit cutter or drinking glass in flour and cut 9 rounds from the dough. Arrange the rounds in 3 rows on top of the fruit in the baking dish. The rounds should almost touch and should leave a border of fruit along the outer edges of the dish.

■ Bake the cobbler for 25 to 30 minutes, until the biscuits are lightly browned and the fruit is bubbling with juices. Cool on a wire rack for 20 minutes and serve warm.

gingerbread

This is a beautifully light version of traditional gingerbread made with whole wheat pastry flour, which has a finer texture than regular whole wheat flour. When it is substituted for part or all of the all-purpose flour in breads, cakes, and cookies, it adds dietary fiber, vitamins, and phytochemical protection. Already full of flavor from iron-rich molasses and sweet spices, this moist and flavorful gingerbread is made even more appealing when served with spicy Pear Sauce (see page 110). **MAKES 9 SERVINGS | PER SERVING: 245 CALORIES, 10 G. TOTAL FAT (1 G. SATURATED FAT), 37 G. CARBOHYDRATES, 4 G. PROTEIN, 3 G. DIETARY FIBER, 357 MG. SODIUM.**

Canola oil spray

1¾ cups whole wheat pastry flour

¼ cup packed light brown sugar

1½ tablespoons ground ginger

¼ teaspoon ground cinnamon

¼ teaspoon ground nutmeg

¼ teaspoon ground cloves

1½ teaspoons baking soda

½ teaspoon salt

½ cup dark unsulfured molasses

½ cup unsweetened applesauce

6 tablespoons canola oil

1 large egg

½ cup boiling water

Pear Sauce (page 110), warmed (optional)

■ Preheat the oven to 350 degrees. Lightly coat a 9-inch square pan with canola oil spray. In a medium bowl, sift together the flour, sugar, spices, baking soda, and salt.

■ In a separate, large bowl, whisk together the molasses, applesauce, canola oil, and egg until well blended. Add the dry ingredients and stir until well combined. Whisk in the boiling water and pour the batter into the prepared baking pan.

■ Bake for about 35 minutes, until the cake begins to pull away from the pan and a wooden toothpick inserted near the center comes out clean. Cool in the pan on a wire rack for 30 minutes. Invert the cake onto a platter and cool for about 15 minutes before serving.

■ Cut into 9 squares and serve warm or at room temperature with warm Pear Sauce. Gingerbread can be tightly wrapped in foil and kept for 2 to 3 days in the refrigerator.

meringue tartlets with strawberries and shaved chocolate

These elegant tartlets combine the luscious tastes of high-quality chocolate and fresh strawberries on top of a fat-free meringue—an alternative to high-fat shortcake. The meringues are not difficult to make. Cream of tartar, found in the baking section of your grocery store, allows them to achieve their stiff consistency. To make successful meringues, be sure to start with clean, dry, grease-free equipment and, if possible, bake them on a low-humidity day. If you prefer, substitute fresh or frozen sliced peaches for the strawberries. **MAKES 8 SERVINGS | PER SERVING: 68 CALORIES, 1 G. TOTAL FAT (LESS THAN 1 G. SATURATED FAT), 13 G. CARBOHYDRATES, 2 G. PROTEIN, 1 G. DIETARY FIBER, 65 MG. SODIUM.**

2 cups sliced fresh strawberries

¼ cup plus 1 tablespoon sugar, divided

4 large egg whites, at room temperature

Dash of cream of tartar

Dash of salt

2 tablespoons plus 2 teaspoons shaved good-quality dark chocolate

■ Preheat the oven to 250 degrees. Cover a baking sheet with parchment paper.

■ In a bowl, mix the strawberries with 1 tablespoon of the sugar. Refrigerate the strawberries until ready to use. In a large mixing bowl, combine the egg whites, cream of tartar, and salt and beat with an electric mixer at medium speed for about 1 minute, until the eggs are frothy. With the mixer at high speed, add the remaining ¼ cup sugar 1 tablespoon at a time, beating for 5 to 7 minutes, until stiff, glossy peaks form.

■ Drop the meringue onto the prepared baking sheet in eight 3- to 4-inch-diameter rounds, smoothing the edges. Bake for 1 hour. Turn the oven off, but leave the meringues in overnight or for about 12 hours. Do not open the oven door. If the meringues will not be served immediately, remove them from the oven and store in a tightly covered dry container until ready to serve.

■ When ready to serve, gently peel the meringues off the parchment paper. Top each meringue with ¼ cup strawberries and garnish with 1 teaspoon shaved chocolate, and serve.

rice pudding with pears and apples

For centuries people have turned to rice pudding for sweetness and solace. This updated version offers comfort and a few health benefits as well. The principles behind this makeover should be familiar by now: decrease the level of fat, salt, and sugar where taste allows; increase the presence of plant foods, in this case fruits; and always choose whole grains, in this case brown rice, for fiber and weight management. This pudding's creaminess comes from being cooked slowly for 1 hour. (The resulting texture and taste justify the wait.) You can reduce the sugar to taste and serve this for a slow-burning, energizing breakfast. **MAKES 8 SERVINGS | PER SERVING: 192 CALORIES, 2 G. FAT (1 G. SATURATED FAT), 38 G. CARBOHYDRATES, 6 G. PROTEIN, 3 G. DIETARY FIBER, 107 MG. SODIUM.**

4 cups lowfat milk*

1 cup brown rice

3 cinnamon sticks

Pinch of salt

3 tablespoons sugar

1 teaspoon vanilla extract

Pinch of ground nutmeg

¼ cup vanilla nonfat yogurt

2 tart apples (such as Granny Smith), peeled, cored, and diced

1 firm pear (such as Bosc), peeled, cored, and diced

Ground cinnamon, for garnish

*Note: For a softer consistency, use ½ cup more milk and cook an additional 10 minutes.

■ In a heavy, medium saucepan over medium heat, bring the milk, rice, cinnamon sticks, and salt just to a boil, being careful not to scald the milk. Immediately reduce the heat to low, cover, and gently simmer for about 1 hour, stirring occasionally, until the rice is tender and the milk almost completely absorbed. Stir in the sugar, vanilla extract, and nutmeg and continue cooking uncovered, stirring often, over low heat until the mixture is very thick, about 15 minutes. Remove the saucepan from the heat and remove the cinnamon sticks. Stir in the yogurt and 3/4 of the apples and pear. Transfer to a large serving bowl and top with the remaining fruit. Sprinkle with ground cinnamon and serve hot.

banana-oatmeal cookies

Most commercial oatmeal cookies probably aren't as healthy as they sound, thanks to plenty of sugar and fat. With banana to bind them and round out the taste, plus walnuts and raisins for a variety of textures and nutrients, these cookies are next in healthfulness to plain oatcakes cooked on a hot rock in Scotland—and a lot tastier. These cookies keep for 5 days and are great as a lunchbox treat. They soften over time; for a crisper texture, enjoy them when they are just cooled from the oven. **MAKES 24 SERVINGS | PER SERVING: 72 CALORIES, 3 G. TOTAL FAT (LESS THAN 1 G. SATURATED FAT), 11 G. CARBOHYDRATES, 1 G. PROTEIN, 1 G. DIETARY FIBER, 42 MG. SODIUM.**

Canola oil spray

¾ cup whole wheat flour, preferably stone-ground

¼ teaspoon salt

¼ teaspoon baking soda

½ teaspoon ground cinnamon

¼ teaspoon ground allspice

1 cup quick-cooking rolled oats

⅓ cup raisins

¼ cup chopped walnuts

1 large egg white

3 tablespoons canola oil

⅓ cup packed dark brown sugar

1 small banana, cut into pieces

1 teaspoon vanilla extract

■ Preheat the oven to 350 degrees. Coat a nonstick baking sheet with canola oil spray and set it aside.

■ In a large bowl, whisk together the flour, salt, baking soda, cinnamon, and allspice. Mix in the oats, raisins, and walnuts. In a blender on medium speed, blend the egg white with the oil and the sugar until smooth. Add the banana and the vanilla extract and blend until the banana is completely puréed. Stir the banana mixture into the dry ingredients until well combined.

■ Drop the batter by tablespoonfuls onto the prepared baking sheet, 1 inch apart, to make 24 cookies. Flatten the cookies slightly with wet fingers or the back of a wet spoon.

■ Bake the cookies for 15 to 18 minutes, until they are golden brown and almost firm to the touch. Cool on the baking sheet on a wire rack for about 3 to 5 minutes, then remove the cookies from the baking sheet and continue to cool them on the rack.

date-nut drops

Almonds, raisins, and dates enhance the taste, texture, and nutrient content of these simple meringues. They can be stored for several days in airtight containers lined with waxed paper; they make wonderful holiday gifts. **MAKES 25 SERVINGS | PER SERVING: 40 CALORIES, 1 G. TOTAL FAT (LESS THAN 1 G. SATURATED FAT), 8 G. CARBOHYDRATES, LESS THAN 1 G. PROTEIN, LESS THAN 1 G. DIETARY FIBER, 10 MG. SODIUM.**

Canola oil spray

1 large egg white, at room temperature

Pinch of salt

Pinch of cream of tartar

¼ teaspoon almond extract or vanilla extract

2 tablespoons granulated sugar

3 tablespoons packed dark brown sugar

½ cup chopped pitted dates

½ cup raisins

⅓ cup sliced almonds, toasted*

*Note: To toast the almonds, put them in a small skillet over medium-high heat and stir frequently for 2 to 3 minutes, until lightly browned. Immediately transfer the nuts to a small dish and cool.

■ Set one oven rack at the top third of the oven, and another at the bottom third. Preheat the oven to 300 degrees. Coat two nonstick baking sheets generously with canola oil spray.

■ In a clean, dry bowl, beat the egg white with the salt and cream of tartar until soft peaks form, about 3 minutes. Add the almond extract and, while continuing to beat, gradually sprinkle in the granulated sugar. Beat in the brown sugar 1 tablespoon at a time. Fold in the dates, raisins, and almonds.

■ Using a teaspoon, drop the mixture onto the prepared baking sheets, 3 inches apart, to make 25 cookies. Stagger the pans on the separate racks so the lower pan is not directly below the top pan. Bake for 10 minutes and then switch the pans to the opposite racks. Bake for 10 more minutes, until the cookies are light brown and firm and feel dry to the touch.

■ Turn off the oven and let the cookies sit in the oven for 20 minutes. Remove them from the oven and let them cool completely on the baking sheets. Using a metal spatula, gently remove the cookies from the sheets. Serve warm or at room temperature.

maple-fig bars

Light and chewy, these bars satisfy the most demanding sweet tooth with the natural sweetness of maple syrup and dried figs. These make wonderful holiday gifts or lunch box treats. **MAKES 30 SERVINGS |**

PER SERVING: 104 CALORIES, 2 G. TOTAL FAT (LESS THAN 1 G. SATURATED FAT), 20 G. CARBOHYDRATES, 2 G. PROTEIN, 1 G. DIETARY FIBER, 72 MG. SODIUM.

Canola oil spray

1 cup chopped dried figs

½ cup packed dark brown sugar

¼ cup canola oil

½ cup maple syrup

1 large egg

2 large egg whites

½ cup unsweetened applesauce

½ cup whole wheat pastry flour or whole wheat flour, preferably stone-ground

1½ cups unbleached all-purpose flour

¾ teaspoon baking powder

¾ teaspoon baking soda

¼ teaspoon salt

ICING

½ cup powdered sugar

1 tablespoon maple syrup

½ teaspoon maple flavoring (optional)

1 to 2 teaspoons water

■ Preheat the oven to 350 degrees and lightly coat a 13 × 9-inch baking dish with canola oil spray.

■ In a small bowl, whisk together the dried figs, brown sugar, canola oil, 1/2 cup maple syrup, egg, egg whites, and applesauce.

■ In a medium bowl, stir together the whole wheat flour, all-purpose flour, baking powder, baking soda, and salt. Add the wet ingredients and blend just until combined.

■ Spread the batter in the prepared baking dish. Bake for 30 minutes, until light brown and springy to the touch in the center. Cool in the pan on a wire rack for 1 hour.

■ In a small bowl, mix together the powdered sugar, 1 tablespoon of maple syrup, maple flavoring, and 1 teaspoon of the water. Use more water if necessary to allow icing to drizzle easily from a spoon. Lightly drizzle the icing over the cooled cake and cut into bars. Serve. The bars may be stored in a tightly covered container for 2 to 3 days.

date-walnut bars

Pair chewy, sweet dates with crunchy walnuts and whole wheat flour, and you have the makings of a sweet treat. These cookie bars are made moist with applesauce, which helps keep their fat content low. They are great for packing in a lunch box, or serve them with a fresh fruit salad for dessert. MAKES 16 SERVINGS | PER SERVING: 91 CALORIES, 4 G. TOTAL FAT (LESS THAN 1 G. SATURATED FAT), 14 G. CARBOHYDRATES, 2 G. PROTEIN, 1 G. DIETARY FIBER, 58 MG. SODIUM.

Canola oil spray

¾ cup whole wheat flour, preferably stone-ground

½ teaspoon baking powder

¼ teaspoon baking soda

⅛ teaspoon salt

1 large egg

¼ cup honey

3 tablespoons unsweetened applesauce

2 tablespoons canola oil

½ teaspoon grated orange zest

⅔ cup chopped dates

⅓ cup chopped walnuts

■ Preheat the oven to 350 degrees. Lightly coat an 8-inch square baking pan with canola oil spray. In a large bowl, mix together the flour, baking powder, baking soda, and salt. In a medium bowl, stir together the egg, honey, applesauce, canola oil, and orange zest. Stir the wet ingredients into the dry ingredients until blended. Stir in the dates and walnuts. Spread the mixture into the prepared pan.

■ Bake about 25 minutes, until a tester such as a toothpick inserted in the center comes out clean. Cool the cookie bars in the pan on a wire rack until completely cool. Cut into sixteen 2-inch squares. Store in a tightly covered container for 2 to 3 days.

grilled fruit kebabs

Grilling brings fruit's natural sugars to the forefront—and this recipe highlights their taste even more with a lovely cinnamon glaze that caramelizes during the grilling process. The result is an easy, elegant dessert in which various fruits supply different phytochemicals, including carotenoids, flavonoids, and monoterpenes, that interact to help protect your health. MAKES 8 SERVINGS | PER SERVING: 125 CALORIES, 4 G. TOTAL FAT (LESS THAN 1 G. SATURATED FAT), 25 G. CARBOHYDRATES, LESS THAN 1 G. PROTEIN, 4 G. DIETARY FIBER, 3 MG. SODIUM.

2 tablespoons canola oil

2 tablespoons freshly squeezed lemon juice

1 teaspoon ground cinnamon

Four 1-inch-thick slices pineapple, canned or fresh, cut into chunks

2 firm red apples (such as Fuji), cored and cut into 1-inch pieces

2 firm pears (such as Bosc), cored and cut into 1-inch pieces

2 firm-fleshed peaches, nectarines, or plums (or a mix), pitted and cut into 1-inch pieces

2 bananas, cut into 1-inch pieces

■ Prepare a barbecue grill to medium heat. In a small bowl, stir together the canola oil, lemon juice, and cinnamon. Spear the fruit onto 8 skewers. Brush the kebabs with the oil mixture and place them on the grill rack. Grill for 6 to 8 minutes, turning frequently, until the fruit starts to brown.

Cooking Methods

You can usually cook a food in more than one way. You can bake, boil, grill, microwave, roast, sauté, or steam a potato, for example. The cooked food's flavor, texture, appearance, and nutritional content will often depend on the method you choose, so try to select the best method to cook a food based on several factors: the length of time you have; the quality or cut of the raw ingredient; and the health concerns and food preferences of those who will be eating the finished product.

BAKING

Baking is usually associated with breads, cakes, cookies, pies, and pastries, but you can bake other foods, such as chicken, fish, and potatoes and other vegetables. (Roasting is essentially the same process, but that term is used in reference to meat, whole poultry, and, sometimes, vegetables: see page 264.) Most baking is done in a preheated oven at temperatures between 300 and 425 degrees, though higher or lower temperatures may be more suitable, depending upon the dish.

Foods can be baked covered or uncovered. The high temperature of the oven browns the surface of the food and causes its moisture to evaporate. If you don't want the food to be browned or to lose much moisture as it bakes, use a covered baking dish or cover the food with aluminum foil. To avoid steaming the food, cover loosely.

Potatoes should be pierced before baking to ensure they don't explode in the oven. Bake them directly on the oven rack at 400 degrees until they are tender, about 45 to 60 minutes.

BLANCHING

Blanching, also known as *parboiling,* is cooking food briefly in hot water. This technique is typically used to partially cook a food that will be fully cooked using another method. It is often used to prepare fresh vegetables for freezing, as blanching deactivates enzymes that would cause continued ripening and helps the vegetables retain their shape and color.

Blanching tomatoes will facilitate the removal of their skins, which is desirable when you are preparing tomato soup or sauce. Cut a cross on the bottom of the tomatoes. Using a slotted spoon, place tomatoes, no more than two at a time, in a large pot of boiling water until skins start to peel away—about 30 to 60 seconds, depending on size. Don't leave tomatoes in the water longer or they will become mushy and difficult to handle. Remove and place in a bowl of ice-cold water, or under cold running water, to stop the cooking. The skin should come off easily from the end where you made the cross.

Dark green vegetables such as broccoli can be blanched and then plunged into cold water to help enhance their color. Drop broccoli florets into boiling salted water for about 2 minutes. Remove them with a slotted spoon and drop them into a bowl of ice-cold water to stop the cooking. Drain immediately. The broccoli will be bright green and crisp, ready to use in salads, soups, pasta dishes, or stir-fry dishes.

You can also blanch strongly flavored or salty foods such as olives to remove some of the salt and to moderate the strong flavor.

BOILING

Boiling entails immersing foods completely in generous quantities of rapidly boiling liquids. The liquid used, usually water or broth, is very hot (212 degrees). Thus, boiling will cook the food relatively quickly compared with other methods. Food may be added to cold liquid that is then brought to a boil, or it may be added to the pot after the liquid is already boiling. Generally, foods that grow above the ground are added to boiling water, and foods that grow below the ground are added to cold water, which is then brought to a boil. Root vegetables should not be placed in boiling water, as they are likely to crack. The food will absorb the liquid during cooking, so be sure that the flavor of the cooking liquid is appropriate. The food will also usually lose flavor and nutrients to the cooking liquid, which is one reason it is not the best cooking method to use for vegetables (see the introduction to the Vegetables chapter, page 14, for information about better ways to cook vegetables).

Meats, fish, and delicate foods are not good choices for boiling because the agitation of the water will break or toughen them.

See also Simmering, page 264.

BRAISING

Braising is a slow cooking method that is best used for larger pieces of tougher cuts of meat. Braising is also a good way to prepare root vegetables as it maintains firmness. It involves first sautéing the food in a small amount of oil until it is browned and then adding a small amount of liquid (such as stock, water, or wine) to the pan, covering the pan, and cooking slowly in the oven or on top of the stove over low heat until the food is tender. This process may take several hours, depending on the type and size of the food being braised. Braising is similar to stewing (page 265), but stewing uses meat that is cut into bite-sized pieces, and typically uses more cooking liquid.

Braised foods are most tender when cooked at a low temperature (about 200 degrees) in a tightly covered pan. A tight seal is important to keep the steam inside the pan. To make sure the seal is tight, first cover the pan with aluminum foil and then place the pan lid over the foil. Use a shallow pan that fits the food easily with a little room for the liquid.

BROILING

Broiling is a cooking method that requires high heat coming from a heat source above the food. It works best with foods that do not need long cooking times and that will benefit from a browned exterior.

Good candidates for broiling include fish, chicken, chops, and burgers. To cook the food evenly, make sure that the pieces of meat are uniform in size and thickness. For instance, place chicken breasts in a plastic food bag and pound them to a uniform thickness with a meat mallet or the bottom of a heavy pan.

The intense heat required by broiling can lead to the formation of carcinogens, especially in meats. To reduce this problem, place the food a bit further from the heating element and use applicable strategies from the section on grilling (below).

GRILLING

Grilling is similar to broiling (see above) except that the heat source is below the food rather than above it. This cooking method can be done indoors with grilling appliances or outdoors on a charcoal or gas grill. In outdoor grilling, the choice of wood or charcoal can affect the flavor of the food.

Oil the grill grate before placing the food on it so the food won't stick. The easiest and safest way to oil the grill is to dip a paper towel in a bit of oil and wipe it over the grate while it is still cold.

The temperature in a covered grill can get very hot (over 500 degrees). Watch the food you are cooking very carefully, and use an oven mitt to open and close the grill. The fat that drips from the food onto the coals can cause the flame to flare up suddenly. Keep a spray bottle of water nearby to spray the coals if necessary.

Meat, poultry, and fish are naturals for grilling. Vegetables are especially delicious when cooked on the grill. Asparagus, corn on the cob, mushrooms, onions, peppers, and zucchini are good choices. Most will cook in fewer than 10 minutes on a hot grill. Vegetables can be marinated and threaded on skewers or placed on a grill pan coated with cooking spray. As with broiling, the food should be of uniform thickness so that it will cook evenly. Note that it is best to make separate skewers for meat and vegetables, since cooking times will vary. Intense heat, direct flame, and smoke can cause the formation of carcinogens on foods. These can be minimized by using the following strategies when you grill:

- Marinate the food before grilling. (If desired, make additional marinade for basting; do not reuse marinade for food safety reasons.)
- Turn the food often to avoid charring. Use tongs rather than a fork to help prevent juices from dripping onto the coals and causing flare-ups.
- Remove any char on the food before eating.
- Grill more vegetables and other plant foods and less fish, meat, and poultry. Researchers believe that fewer carcinogens form on plant-based foods.

MICROWAVING

Microwaving works best for reheating, but it can be successfully used to cook many foods. It is a cooking technique unlike all others, because the heat is generated by the food rather than by the oven. It is excellent for melting chocolate, softening brown sugar, and toasting nuts and seeds. When toasting nuts in the microwave, put nuts on a paper towel or plate and microwave on high until lightly browned. After 2 to 3 minutes, check for doneness every minute. Microwaving is a time-saving method both because of the speed at which the food is cooked and because cleanup is typically easier.

Ingredients with a high water content such as fruits and vegetables cook nicely in a microwave. Because of the speed, green vegetables will stay bright green and crisp if cooked properly. To cook broccoli, for example, rinse fresh stalks and shake off any excess water, but do not dry them completely. Place the broccoli in a covered, microwave-safe container, and cook on high (100%) power for 1 to 3 minutes, depending on the amount of broccoli and the size of the pieces. Potatoes "baked" in the microwave are actually steamed. Their texture will be different from that of potatoes baked in a conventional oven. To microwave a potato, pierce the skin with a fork in 3 or 4 places. Cook on high for 5 to 6 minutes.

To cook evenly, foods that are microwaved should be of uniform shape and thickness, and will often require periodic stirring. The container in which you are cooking the food will have to be turned frequently unless your microwave has a rotating tray in the center to ensure even cooking. Because microwaved foods do not brown and so will often not look "cooked," frequent testing for doneness is important.

It is also important to remember that foods cooked in a microwave will continue to cook when taken out of the oven, and so remain extremely hot. Be cautious when touching or eating food that has just come out of the microwave. Although the interior of the microwave oven is cool throughout the cooking process, the heat from the cooked food will make the plate on which the food is cooked feel very hot. Always use a potholder to remove the food from the oven.

POACHING

Poaching is best suited to delicate foods that do not need long cooking times, such as chicken, eggs, or fish. The food is cooked in a barely bubbling liquid (often described as "shivering"). Poached foods such as salmon are often served cold or at room temperature.

The flavor of the poaching liquid will affect the flavor of the cooked food. You can poach food in water, broth, fruit or vegetable juice, wine, or some other seasoned liquid. The poaching liquid can be used to create a sauce for the dish after the food is cooked, or can be used in vegetable dishes or soups.

If cooked properly, poached boneless, skinless chicken breasts are tender and moist. For even cooking, place chicken breasts in a plastic food bag and pound them to a uniform thickness with a meat mallet or the bottom of a heavy pan. Place the breast in cold water or seasoned liquid, and bring it to a boil. Remove the pan from the heat and cover it. Allow the chicken breast to sit in the liquid for 10 minutes. Check for doneness by cutting through the breast. When it is no longer pink inside, remove the breast and either serve it or wrap and refrigerate it for later use.

PRESSURE COOKING

Pressure cooking is back in vogue now that pressure cookers have been redesigned for both ease of use and safety. Pressure cookers can prepare food more rapidly because they cook at higher temperatures than can be achieved in covered pans on the stove. Foods cooked in pressure cookers also retain much of their flavor and will be very tender. Follow the manufacturer's directions for using a pressure cooker safely and effectively. When adapting recipes for use with a pressure cooker, in general you should use less liquid since there is no evaporation.

Foods such as dried beans, soups, and stews are good candidates for the pressure cooker—they will cook quickly and retain their flavor. Soup is best made early in the day and allowed to cool. Fat will come to the surface of soups made with meat or poultry. When the soup has cooled, the fat will be easy to skim off.

ROASTING

Roasting is similar to baking, but the term is usually applied to meat, poultry, and vegetables. Roasting is generally done uncovered. Roasted foods typically have a tasty, browned exterior. Roasting is an effective way to prepare root vegetables such as carrots, potatoes, and turnips. Toss the cut-up vegetables in a small amount of olive oil. Spread the vegetables out on a rimmed nonstick cookie sheet. Roast them in a preheated 400-degree oven, stirring occasionally, until they are soft and have browned spots. Sprinkle them with salt and pepper toward the end.

SAUTÉING

Sautéing is a quick cooking method that uses a small amount of oil over high or medium heat. Heat the oil in a pan and then add the food to be sautéed. The food should be patted dry with a paper towel before sautéing. Avoid crowding too much food in the pan to prevent a steamed product. The food should be cut into small, uniform pieces to ensure even cooking. It can be constantly stirred (see Stir-Frying, page 265), or allowed to brown on one side and then turned.

An advantage of sautéing meats is that the pan can be "deglazed" with a liquid such as stock, water, or wine to make a flavorful sauce. Remove the cooked food from the pan, and add the deglazing liquid to the pan while it is still over the heat. Scrape the browned bits from the bottom of the pan into the boiling liquid. Keep swirling and stirring until the liquid is "reduced" (boiled until syrupy); this intensifies the flavor. Pour this sauce over the sautéed food and serve.

SIMMERING

Simmering involves heating a liquid to the point at which bubbles rise gently to the surface and barely break. This is the best method for cooking fragile foods and for making tough foods more tender. Soups, stews, and some sauces are simmered to tenderize meat and to gently enhance flavor, and scorching of the pot is less likely than with boiling.

Since simmering water is held just slightly below the boiling point, foods will cook almost as quickly as if they were boiled.

STEAMING

Steaming involves boiling a liquid such as water or a seasoned broth in a closed pot to produce steam. The food is placed in a steamer basket or on a rack above the liquid. Because the liquid never touches the food, the food retains most of its nutrients and flavor. Steaming is a particularly healthy way to cook because no fat is added and any fat associated with the raw ingredient drips into the liquid.

Steaming is a gentle method especially suitable for delicately textured and flavored foods. Fish fillets and other seafood such as scallops and shrimp are good choices for steaming. A seasoned liquid will impart a flavor to the steamed food.

Most vegetables can be successfully steamed, including asparagus, broccoli, carrots, green beans, leeks, potatoes, and summer squash. Steam most vegetables until just crisp but tender and bright in color (steam potatoes until tender). Steamed vegetables are especially tasty if dressed with a light vinaigrette made with lemon juice or balsamic vinegar. See the Sauces, Dressings, and Marinades chapter (page 107) for vinaigrettes and sauces that go well with steamed vegetables.

STEWING

Stewing is usually a two-step process. Cut-up raw meats are usually browned in a small amount of oil and then covered with liquid and cooked slowly until tender (the browning step can be skipped, but it adds much more flavor to the final product). Veg-etables are often added after the meat has cooked for a while, as they take less time to cook. You can cook a stew on top of the stove in a covered pot or in a covered baking dish in the oven.

Stewing is used to prepare foods that require long, slow cooking for tenderness and to develop flavor, such as tougher cuts of meat. Stewing is similar to braising (see page 262), but the foods are typically cut up into smaller pieces and cooked in more liquid than is used in braising.

STIR-FRYING

Stir-frying is similar to sautéing (see page 264). In stir-frying, the pan is heated on high, a small amount of oil is added and heated, and the ingredients are added in order from longest to shortest cooking time. The food is stirred constantly during the cooking process to keep it from burning and to ensure it cooks evenly on all sides. Stir-frying is usually associated with Asian foods, but the method can be used with most ingredients that do not require long cooking times.

Although stir-frying is usually done in a wok, you can successfully stir-fry in a large skillet or sauté pan. Before beginning, have all the ingredients measured and ready to go. Cut the food up into bite-sized pieces to ensure even cooking.

To keep the food crisp but tender, add only as much food as will fit in an even layer in the pan. Spread it out and do not overcrowd the pan.

Ingredient Substitutions

These ingredient substitutions can be used when you are looking for a healthier alternative in a favorite recipe, or when you have either run out of an item or cannot find an item in the grocery store.

AS A HEALTHIER ALTERNATIVE

Instead of	Try
Bread crumbs (white bread)	Whole wheat bread crumbs or toasted wheat germ
Butter or margarine (for baking)	Equal parts canola oil and applesauce, mashed bananas, or prune purée
2 tablespoons butter or margarine (for cooking)	1 to 2 tablespoons canola oil or olive oil
2 ounces mild cheddar cheese	1 ounce reduced fat sharp or extra sharp cheddar cheese
1 ounce unsweetened baking chocolate	3 to 4 tablespoons cocoa powder plus 1 tablespoon oil and 1 tablespoon sugar
1 cup chocolate chips	½ cup mini chocolate chips or 1 cup of a combination of chopped dried fruit, such as cranberries, apricots, raisins, or cherries plus chopped nuts
Cream (in casseroles and desserts)	Nonfat evaporated milk
Cream (to thicken soups)	Puréed vegetables or potatoes
Sour cream (regular)	Nonfat or lowfat sour cream or plain yogurt
Clam juice	Equal parts fat-free, reduced sodium vegetable or chicken broth and water
All-purpose flour (in baking)	Whole wheat pastry flour (for quick breads) or equal parts whole wheat flour and all-purpose flour; try to increase the proportion of whole wheat flour to your taste

Instead of	Try
Frosting	Sliced fresh fruit, puréed fruit, or a dusting of powdered sugar
Frozen pie crust	New American Plate Pie Crust (page 243)
Mayonnaise (regular)	Nonfat or lowfat mayonnaise or plain yogurt
Meat/poultry in soups, stews, stir-fries	More vegetables, extra-firm tofu, smaller amounts of meat/poultry
Ground red meat	Ground turkey breast or less ground red meat plus finely chopped vegetables, crumbled firm tofu, tempeh, soy crumbles, beans
Evaporated milk (regular)	Nonfat evaporated milk
Sweetened condensed milk (regular)	Lowfat or fat-free sweetened condensed milk
White rice	Brown rice, bulgur, quinoa, kasha, or whole wheat couscous
High-fat (butter- or oil-based) sauce over fish/poultry/meat	Lowfat (fruit- or vegetable-based) sauce, such as Broccoli, White Bean, and Roasted Garlic Purée (page 20), Sweet Potato and Pumpkin Purée (page 43), or Pineapple, Corn, and Mango Salsa (page 114)
White sauce	Puréed and seasoned white beans
Wine	Fat-free, reduced sodium broth or apple juice

Instead of	Try
1 teaspoon baking powder	¼ teaspoon baking soda and ½ teaspoon cream of tartar
¾ cup dried beans	1 can (16 ounces) beans, rinsed and drained
1 cup buttermilk	1 tablespoon lemon juice or vinegar added to milk to make 1 cup, or 1 cup plain yogurt
Capers	Chopped green olives, chopped dill pickles
1 tablespoon cornstarch	2 tablespoons all-purpose flour

Instead of	Try
Dried cranberries	Dried cherries or raisins
Juice of 1 lemon	3 tablespoons fresh or bottled lemon juice
Pine nuts	Walnuts or combination of chopped walnuts and almonds
Fresh vegetables	Frozen (thawed) or canned (drained and rinsed) vegetables
Rice wine vinegar	White wine vinegar
Jicama	Water chestnuts

HERBS AND SPICES

In general, 1 tablespoon of chopped or minced fresh herbs can be replaced with 1 teaspoon of crumbled dried leaf herbs (such as oregano) or ½ teaspoon of ground dried herbs (such as sage).

Instead of	Try
Allspice	Cinnamon, mace, or cloves
Basil	Oregano or thyme
Bay leaf	Thyme
Cardamom	Ground ginger
Chervil	Tarragon or parsley
Chinese five-spice powder	Combination of anise seed, fennel seed, ground cinnamon, ground black pepper, and ground cloves
Chives	Scallions or leeks (pale green parts)
Cloves	Allspice
Cumin	Chili powder
Curry powder	Combination of ground ginger, cumin, coriander, fenugreek, turmeric, and fennel seed

Instead of	Try
2 tablespoons herbes de Provence	4 teaspoons each of dried thyme and marjoram, plus 1½ teaspoons dried summer savory, plus ¼ teaspoon each of dried rosemary and mint, plus ⅛ teaspoon fennel seeds, and a pinch each of dried sage and lavender flowers
Ground ginger	Cinnamon, mace, or nutmeg
Italian seasoning	Combination of oregano, basil, marjoram, rosemary, and cayenne
Poultry seasoning	Combination of sage, thyme, marjoram, savory, black pepper, and rosemary
Rosemary	Thyme, tarragon, or savory
Saffron	Turmeric (for color)
Sage	Poultry seasoning, savory, or marjoram
Savory	Thyme, marjoram, or sage

food storage and handling

Cooking extra food for later use saves time, money, and energy. Preparing several batches of spaghetti sauce, for example, and freezing them in individual containers gives you a quick option for several weekday meals: you can use the sauce in casseroles, meat loafs, soups, and stews as well as in pasta dishes.

Whether cooking once to eat twice or making a large batch of food to be frozen and used over a long period of time, proper storage of cooked food will ensure its taste, appearance, and safety. Following are a few simple guidelines.

General Guidelines

- Food safety should be your primary concern. Promptly serve, refrigerate, or freeze cooked foods. Perishable food should never be left out of the refrigerator for more than two hours. If a prepared stew sits out for one hour during dinner, it has only one more hour of safe time out of the refrigerator.
- Always use a thermometer to test for doneness when food is cooked the first time and when it is reheated. See table for safe cooking temperatures.
- Do not partially cook foods before storing them.
- Handle the food to be stored as little as possible after it is cooked to avoid introducing harmful bacteria.
- If you are making a double batch and plan to serve the second batch in a day or two, separate the amount you will be saving and refrigerate

SAFE COOKING TEMPERATURES

Food	Doneness temperature
Egg dishes	160°
Ground beef	160°
Ground chicken	165°
Chicken breast	170°
Chicken thigh	180°
Whole chicken or turkey	180°
Stuffing	165°
Casseroles	160°
Leftovers	165°

it immediately. (Freeze it if you will be storing it for longer than a day or two.)

- Use shallow containers in the refrigerator and freezer to ensure that foods will cool down quickly. Do not try to cool a pot of soup in the deep soup pot in which it was cooked. Pour the soup into smaller, shallow containers for cooling. Stir food while it is cooling to hasten the process.
- Foods will decline in quality (and, if not refrigerated, in safety) the longer they are stored. Even food that is well wrapped and stored properly will lose some of its quality.
- You cannot always tell if a food is spoiled just by smelling it or looking at it. When in doubt, throw it out.

Freezing Guidelines

- The freezer temperature should be 0 degrees or lower.
- Use spices and seasoning sparingly before freezing food because many will change during freezing. Reseason when you reheat the food. Pepper, garlic, and green pepper tend to get stronger and more bitter when frozen. Onion and paprika will also change flavor. Salt loses its flavor when frozen. Curry will develop an off flavor and odor when frozen.
- Do not add bread crumbs, grated cheese, or other toppings before freezing.
- Cheese, cooked potatoes, cream cheese, mayonnaise, meringues, and sour cream do not freeze well. Instead of including them in food to be frozen, add them when the food is being reheated.
- Casseroles can be frozen baked or unbaked. Reheated casseroles, soups, and stews should be cooked to 165 degrees.
- Most casseroles, soups, and stews can be frozen for up to three months without a loss in quality. Prepare them as usual, omitting potatoes and slightly undercooking the vegetables.
- It is best to cool foods thoroughly before freezing them, but it is not safe to cool foods at room temperature. Cool them in the refrigerator in a pan of ice water.
- Breads, cakes, muffins, and quick breads should be cooled on racks before freezing.
- Freeze pies before they are baked, and bake them without thawing.
- Package foods in the smallest containers possible or wrap as airtight as possible. Use heavy-duty aluminum foil, freezer paper, plastic wrap, or plastic freezer bags. For best results, use a commercially available vacuum sealer. The longer it takes for a food to freeze solid, the more bacteria grows and the more quality is lost, so it is best to divide foods into several

RECOMMENDED FREEZING TIMES

Food	Freeze up to
Frozen vegetables	8 months
Raw whole chicken	12 months
Raw poultry pieces	9 months
Cooked fish	4 to 6 months
Raw lean fish	6 months
Raw fatty fish	2 to 3 months
Cooked poultry	4 to 6 months
Cooked meat, soup, stew, vegetables	2 to 3 months
Juice	12 months

smaller containers or packages to freeze and leave space between packages until they are frozen solid.
- Be sure to date the food. Foods remain safe indefinitely in the freezer, but they will lose quality as time goes on. Recommended freezing times are given in the table above.
- Avoid overloading the freezer.
- "Freezer burn" is a dry spot on the food and affects only the food's quality. The food is still safe to eat. Cut away the dry spot and prepare as normal.
- Freezing does not kill harmful bacteria—it just slows down their growth.

Safe Defrosting Methods

- If you have time to plan ahead, defrost frozen food in the refrigerator. A large frozen item may take more than twenty-four hours to defrost. After the food is defrosted, it should be safe to eat for one or two days. Be sure to heat it to a safe temperature.
- Cold-water thawing is quicker than thawing in the refrigerator, but it requires more attention. Wrap the frozen food in leak-proof packag-

ing and immerse it in cold tap water. The water should be changed every thirty minutes until the food is thawed. Foods defrosted by this method should be cooked immediately.

- The quickest way to defrost frozen food is to microwave it on the microwave's defrost setting. Food thawed in the microwave should be cooked or reheated immediately. This is because microwaves do not heat food evenly, and some parts of the food may warm to an unsafe temperature during the defrosting process.
- Defrost breads, cakes, and muffins in their wrappers in the refrigerator for best results.

Refrigerator Storage Guidelines

- The refrigerator temperature should be 40 degrees or lower.
- Proper refrigeration only inhibits the growth of harmful bacteria. Refrigeration does not kill bacteria.
- Food can still spoil or lose quality when it is in the refrigerator.
- As a conservative rule, use cooked refrigerated foods within two days; however, cooked vegetables may be stored for up to five days in the refrigerator, and meat- and poultry-based casseroles, soups, and stews may be stored for up to three days. They must be reheated to 165 degrees to ensure safety.
- Slightly undercook pasta and rice so they do not become soggy or sticky when reheated. Cooked pasta and rice are potentially hazardous foods and should be refrigerated immediately. They can be stored in the refrigerator for up to four days if they are to be reheated.
- Cooked pieces of chicken can be stored in the refrigerator for three to four days.
- Chicken covered with gravy can be stored for one to two days in the refrigerator.
- Cooked ground beef or turkey is safe to keep for one to two days.
- Cooked pizza can be refrigerated for up to four days.
- Storage time for dips and salad dressings depends on the ingredients. If the dip is made with a dairy ingredient, check the package of the dairy ingredient for the expiration, "use by (or before)," or "sell by" date. For example, if a dip that contains sour cream, yogurt, or cottage cheese is made soon after an expiration or "use by" date, it probably should not be kept in the refrigerator for more than a day. If made soon after the "sell by" date, it may be refrigerated safely a day or two longer. Other dip ingredients, such as chopped vegetables, may release moisture into the dip or dressing and greatly reduce its quality. When saving dips and dressings that have been left out on the table during the meal, keep the two-hour rule for unrefrigerated foods in mind.
- Whether or not a food looks or smells questionable, follow this rule: When in doubt, throw it out.

cooking with vegetables and fruits

Vegetables

A wide variety of vegetables, with their arsenals of protective phytochemicals and nutrients, is essential for a health-protective diet. But for many people the frame of reference is the vegetables mom used to prepare—a bit mushy, drab, and bitter, and perhaps doused in cream sauce. These people have been missing out on the delight of well-prepared vegetables. Vegetables can be prepared with pleasing seasonings, glazes, and light sauces. Cooked until they are crisp but tender so their best, freshest flavors shine through, they can be enticing—not a chore to prepare and eat.

Lightly steaming certain vegetables, such as carrots and spinach, can actually increase the availability of some phytochemicals. And cooking or serving vegetables with a small amount of fat can increase the availability of fat-soluble phytochemicals such as lycopene and beta-carotene, found in tomatoes and carrots, respectively.

ARTICHOKES are often considered a delicacy. They contain cancer-protective silymarin and can be steamed, boiled, or baked, and can be eaten hot or cold. They are available year-round, but harvesting peaks in the spring. Look for compact artichokes with leaves—soft green in spring and olive green in winter—that are tightly closed. Store them in a plastic bag in the refrigerator for no more than four days. Canned artichokes should be rinsed to reduce the sodium content.

ARUGULA is a leafy green that is related to the mustard family. For an elegant addition to a tossed salad, select bright green leaves, avoiding those that are wilting. Larger leaves have a peppery flavor; smaller leaves are milder. Peak season is spring and early summer.

ASPARAGUS is available in a variety of colors: green, purple, or white, though green is by far the most familiar and widely available. Look for closed tips and cut ends that are not dried out. Rinse in cool water to remove any sand from the tops and stems. Trim asparagus before cooking by bending the stalk until the tough end snaps off. For grilling or roasting, thicker spears work best. The outer layer can be removed with a vegetable peeler. Peak season is early March to mid-June.

AVOCADO is actually a fruit. Although avocados are high in fat, most of this fat is the more healthful monounsaturated type. Select an avocado that is heavy for its size and unblemished. Plan ahead because it can take three to five days to ripen. A ripe avocado yields to gentle pressure. Store unripened avocados in a brown paper bag, preferably with a banana or an apple. These fruits emit ethylene gas, which speeds ripening. Fold over the top of the bag to close it loosely. Cut just before adding to a dish. If using mashed avocado, add a few drops of lime juice to prevent discoloration. They are available throughout the year.

BEETS are available in many colors, including red, gold, orange, and white. Select beets that still have leaves attached. Brightly colored leaves are a good indication of freshness. Store up to one week in the refrigerator. Greens should be removed from the bulbs before storing beets in the refrigerator. About 1 inch of stem should remain attached to decrease the loss of color and nutrients during cooking. Use beet greens within a day or two.

BOK CHOY is an Asian cabbage with a mild flavor. Choose bok choy with firm stalks and bright green leaves. Refrigerate in an airtight container up to four days. It is also available in smaller heads, sold as baby bok choy. Bok choy is available year-round.

BROCCOLI is a cruciferous vegetable (a member of the cabbage family) offering powerful cancer-protective isothiocyanates. Choose broccoli with tight florets and no brown or yellow spots. The stalks should be firm. Store unwashed in the refrigerator in an airtight bag for up to four days. To prepare broccoli for cooking, trim the tough end off the bottom of the stalk and discard. If you want to eat the stalk (which is mild and tender if prepared properly), peel the stalk with a paring knife and slice it thinly. Divide the head into bite-sized florets, and rinse slices and florets. Peak season is late fall to early spring.

BRUSSELS SPROUTS are like bite-sized green cabbages (in fact, they are members of the cabbage family). Select tightly packed firm heads that are heavy for their size and bright green. Choose sprouts of a similar size for uniform cooking. Smaller sprouts are the sweetest, while the large ones have a more assertive flavor. Brussels sprouts develop a strong flavor during storage, so buy only as many as you will prepare within three days. They are in season from late summer through early spring.

CABBAGE, which comes in dozens of varieties, is a cruciferous vegetable, in the same huge family with broccoli, Brussels sprouts, and many other vegetables. The common cabbage comes in green and red; green cabbages have thinner, sweeter leaves than red cabbages, and they cook more quickly.

Choose tightly packed heads that are heavy for their size and have crisp, firm leaves with no bruising. Cabbage can be wrapped tightly and refrigerated for up to one week. It can be cooked or eaten raw in slaw.

CARROTS are available in many varieties with a range of colors: orange, red, purple, yellow, and white, some of which are usually only found in farmers' markets or specialty produce stores. When purchasing them in bunches with the tops attached, look for greens with a bright color and no wilting. Carrots should be firm and without cracks. Carrots are rich in antioxidants, which can vary with the color. Orange carrots contain alpha- and beta-carotene, red carrots provide lycopene, purple ones have anthocyanins, and yellow ones contain xanthophylls. Store carrots in the refrigerator in a plastic bag, but avoid any proximity to apples, which emit a gas that can cause the carrots to taste bitter. Carrots are available throughout the year.

CAULIFLOWER is a cruciferous vegetable, like cabbage and broccoli. It has a milder, more cabbage-like flavor than broccoli. Select heads that have creamy white, tightly packed florets and that feel heavy for their size. The greens surrounding the heads should be crisp and not wilting. Refrigerate cauliflower, wrapped tightly, for up to five days. When cooked in water, cauliflower has a tendency to discolor. To prevent this, add a tablespoon of lemon juice to the water before beginning to cook the cauliflower. Or use a method in which it is not cooked in water, like steaming or stir-frying. The briefer the cooking period, the less chance cauliflower has of developing a strong aroma and unpleasant taste.

CELERY should have firm ribs that are free from bruising and cracks. Leaves should be bright and not wilted. The leafy tops can be used as flavorings for soups. To firm up limp celery, place the ribs in a container of water and refrigerate. Store celery in a plastic bag in the refrigerator for up to two weeks.

COLLARD GREENS have a cabbage-like flavor. Available year-round, they have large leaves with a center rib and a firm stalk. Avoid limp leaves or those with holes. Although they can be refrigerated in a plastic bag, collards become bitter with age so are best when used as fresh as possible. To prepare, remove the leaves from the tough stalks. They can be prepared in any way appropriate for spinach or cabbage.

CORN is becoming sweeter, thanks to the efforts of scientists who breed it for a high sugar content. Sweet (fresh) corn is available in white and in varying shades of yellow; some varieties are bicolored. Choose ears with intact, snug husks and brown silk. The peak season for corn is May through September. Corn should be purchased and cooked as close to harvest as possible for optimal sweetness.

CUCUMBERS should be firm, unblemished, and heavy for their size. Peel cucumbers that have been waxed. Although generally served raw, cucumbers can be cooked. Cucumbers are available year-round and can be wrapped and stored in the refrigerator for up to five days.

EGGPLANT is available in many shapes and sizes. The most common type of eggplant is large and purple. Japanese or Chinese eggplants resemble summer squash in shape. Choose a shiny eggplant that has a fresh-looking cap and is heavy for its size. The skin should be unblemished and bounce back when pressed. Eggplant is available year-round. Store in the refrigerator and use within two days since eggplant becomes bitter over time. Salt helps to improve the bitter taste.

ESCAROLE has a bright green, curly leaf and a bitter flavor. It can be cooked or served raw in salads; when using escarole in salads, it's generally best to use the base of each leaf, where the flavor is milder. Avoid escarole with dry, wilted, or brownish leaves. Be sure to wash escarole thoroughly to remove any sand or grit. Peak availability is from December to April.

FENNEL looks a little like a bunch of celery with a larger white bulb and feathery green leaves that resemble dill. Its flavor is similar to anise or licorice. The bulb can be cooked or thinly sliced and served raw in salads. The leaves can be used as an herb or garnish. The stalks are fibrous and are best cooked in soups. Fennel is available from the fall through the spring. Select bulbs that are clean with no brown areas. Refrigerate, tightly wrapped, for up to five days.

GREEN BEANS should have a bright color. Avoid those that appear limp or have dimples or blemishes. The beans should "snap" when broken. Thinner, younger beans will be more tender. They are available throughout the year. Refrigerate, tightly wrapped in a plastic bag, for up to five days. Steam until crisp but tender.

JICAMA looks like a rough brown turnip but has a juicy, crisp, white flesh. Select firm, unblemished jicama that are heavy for their size. Avoid those that appear dried, wrinkled or soft. Jicama are delicious raw in salads or quickly cooked in a stir-fry. Whole jicama can be stored unwrapped in the vegetable crisper in the refrigerator for up to two weeks. Use jicama in place of water chestnuts or chopped apple.

KALE, a cruciferous vegetable like broccoli, has deep green curly leaves and a cabbage-like flavor. Choose bunches with crisp, unblemished leaves. Smaller leaves are more tender and can be eaten raw in salads; larger leaves need to be cooked to soften them, and are excellent in soups.

KOHLRABI is an unusual-looking member of the cabbage family. It is often mistaken for a root vegetable, but the swollen part of the stem actually grows just above the ground. Select small kohlrabi with smooth skin. Kohlrabi tastes like a sweet turnip and is available from the spring through the fall. Store in the refrigerator, tightly wrapped, for up to four days. Enjoy steamed and added to stews, soups, and stir-fries.

LEEKS are members of the onion family and resemble very large scallions. Select small leeks with crisp, brightly colored leaves. To clean leeks, trim off the root and dark green leaves. Remove any tough outer leaves. Cut the leek lengthwise and open the layers. Place under cold running water to rinse out any dirt and sand. Pat the leek dry with paper towels. Leeks are available year-round and should be stored in a plastic bag in the refrigerator for up to five days.

MUSHROOMS are available in many different species, the most commonly used of which is the cultivated white (or button) mushroom. Choose mushrooms that are heavy for their size and have firm caps. Many mushrooms can be cleaned with a damp cloth or paper towel and a soft vegetable brush if needed. More soiled mushrooms can be rinsed quickly under cold running water and patted dry. Don't soak mushrooms in water as they will absorb it and become soggy. Store mushrooms in the refrigerator (not in the crisper) for a few days. Store loose mushrooms in a loosely closed paper bag. Leave prepackaged mushrooms in their original container.

MUSTARD GREENS have a pungent flavor. They are available fresh from December through March and can also be found frozen and canned. Look for crisp leaves that are bright green. Refrigerate in a tightly sealed plastic bag for up to one week. Season them and try sautéing them as a side dish.

OKRA is the young seedpod of a plant related to the hibiscus. It is a green, pointed pod with a ridged surface. Choose small, brightly colored pods that are tender and free from bruises. When the pods are cut, they release a clear, gummy liquid that helps thicken soups and stews. To prevent the release of this liquid, carefully trim the ends without cutting into the pod. Okra is available from May through October and can be stored in a plastic bag in the refrigerator for up to three days. It can be braised, baked, or fried.

ONIONS should show no signs of sprouting. Choose the sweeter varieties, such as Maui, Vidalia, and Walla Walla, to use raw in salads or for quick cooking. Use the stronger yellow and white varieties for soups and stews. Sweeter onions have a higher sugar and water content, and lower levels of sulfur compounds. These sulfur compounds irritate your eyes when you cut onions. Select onions that are heavy for their size and have no signs of moistness. They are available year-round and should be stored in a cool, dry place for up to two months. After cutting, refrigerate and use within four days.

PARSNIPS are root vegetables that have a sweet flavor and look like large, cream-colored carrots. Look for firm, medium-size parsnips. To prepare, peel before cutting. Parsnips are available year-round and can be kept in the refrigerator for up to two weeks.

PEPPERS include bell peppers and hot peppers (chiles). Bell peppers are available in a variety of colors and are mild in flavor. Green bell peppers are picked when they are immature and are acidic and a little bitter in flavor. If allowed to ripen, bell peppers can turn bright red, orange, or yellow and develop a distinctly sweet flavor. Select bell peppers with smooth, unblemished skins. They should feel heavy for their size. Bell peppers are available year-round and can be stored in the refrigerator for up to one week. Hot peppers, or chiles, are available in many varieties, including the medium-hot jalapeño and the hotter serrano. In general, the smaller chiles are hotter than the larger ones. Chiles can be bought fresh or dried; fresh chiles are green when immature and ripen to yellow or red. Removing the seeds and ribs from chiles significantly reduces their heat level. When cutting and seeding chiles, wear plastic or rubber gloves to prevent skin irritation, or wash your hands promptly; never touch your eyes. Fresh chile peppers should be firm and unwrinkled without black spots or cracks. Store, wrapped in paper towels in the refrigerator, for up to three weeks.

POTATOES come in many varieties, with different shapes, colors, and textures. Potatoes are often classified as waxy or starchy. The waxy varieties, such as new potatoes, round white, and round red, hold their shape and are often considered best for boiling and steaming, and the starchy varieties, such as russet, are preferred for baking, frying, and mashing, but there are no hard and fast rules. Starchy potatoes, when cooked and puréed, can also be used as a thickener for soups. Select potatoes that are firm, with no cuts, holes, or green areas. They should be heavy for their size. Store potatoes in a cool, dark place for no more than two weeks.

RADICCHIO has red leaves that are tender but firm with a slightly bitter flavor. Radicchio is available throughout the year. The leaves should be crisp with no browning. Refrigerate in a plastic bag for up to one week. Radicchio can be added to salads, but can also be sautéed or baked.

RADISHES are available in various shapes, colors, and sizes, from the familiar red, spicy globe radish to the long, white, mild daikon. Choose firm radishes that are smooth and brightly colored. To store them, trim off the stems and place the radishes in perforated vegetable bags in the vegetable crisper for up to five days.

RUTABAGAS are root vegetables with golden-brown skins with dark, purple-brown tops and firm, creamy, yellow-orange flesh. They have a sweet yet strong flavor, reminiscent of turnips. The skins are usually waxed and should be removed before cooking. Choose smaller rutabagas that are heavy for their size. Rutabagas are available year-round and can be refrigerated in a plastic bag for up to two weeks.

SCALLIONS (green onions) are seedling onions with white bulbs and long, green leaves. The white bulbs are more strongly flavored than the leaves, and some recipes call for using the white parts only. Look for unblemished bulbs with moist roots and fresh leaves. To prepare scallions, trim off the roots and tough tops of leaves. Store by wrapping in a plastic bag and refrigerating for up to five days.

SHALLOTS belong to the onion family, are shaped like garlic heads, and are covered with onion-like skin. They offer a mild onion flavor in soups, stews, and other recipes. They are available year-round. Select those that are dry and firm, with no sprouting. Store them in a cool, dry place for up to one week.

SPINACH should be bright green and unblemished. When purchasing packaged spinach, avoid packages with wet spots or slime. The small leaves of baby spinach are more tender than larger leaves, and are better eaten raw in salads. Fresh spinach is available year-round and can be stored in a plastic bag in the refrigerator for up to three days. Rinse thoroughly before using. When using frozen spinach, be sure to squeeze out as much liquid as possible.

SQUASH come in summer and winter varieties. Summer squash are picked when they are still immature, so they are tender and the seeds are soft. They are available in a number of varieties, including crookneck, pattypan, straightneck, and zucchini. Select smaller, firm squash that are heavy for their size and free from bruises. Summer squash can be stored in a plastic bag in the refrigerator for up to five days. It is available during the summer months. Squash plants also have edible flowers. The blossoms can be used as a garnish, or can be sautéed or even stuffed. Winter squash come in a wide range of varieties including acorn, banana, butternut, Hubbard, pumpkin, and spaghetti. These squash are allowed to mature before picking, resulting in thicker shells and larger seeds. They come in many shapes, and the flesh colors range from green to yellow to orange. Choose squash with hard shells and no bruising or mold. They should be heavy for their size. Store whole winter squash in a dark, cool, well-ventilated place for up to one month. These hard-shelled squash are often difficult to cut. It is helpful to pierce them several times with a knife, then microwave or bake them whole to soften them slightly before cutting.

SWEET POTATOES, though they are often called yams, are not the same as yams, which are tropical tubers and are not readily available. Select firm sweet potatoes with smooth, unblemished skins that are free from mold. They should be heavy for their size. Store sweet potatoes in a dark, cool, ventilated area for three to four weeks. To prepare sweet potatoes, scrub them well and peel them, if necessary (for example, if you are using them in a soup).

SWISS CHARD is usually sold in bunches. Look for firm stems and shiny, slightly crinkled leaves. The bunches should be heavy for their size. Avoid Swiss chard with limp leaves. The center rib and stems are best removed and cooked separately from the leaves, as they are tougher and require longer preparation. The leaves can be cooked as you would spinach or cabbage. Store in the refrigerator for up to three days, wrapped in a plastic bag.

TOMATOES are actually fruits. Today they are available in a wide range of shapes, sizes, and colors. Store tomatoes at room temperature away from direct sunlight. The most flavorful tomatoes are vine ripened, but these are not always available and they spoil quickly. In general, choose firm, fragrant, and brightly colored tomatoes that are heavy for their size. To ripen tomatoes, place them in a brown paper bag. Fold down the top of the bag to close it loosely. Tomatoes emit ethylene gas, which will speed their ripening. Don't refrigerate tomatoes unless they are ripe and in danger of spoiling, in which case store them unwrapped on a refrigerator shelf and use as soon as possible. To peel tomatoes for use in soups and sauces, see the blanching technique on page 261. Seed them by cutting in half horizontally and squeezing or scooping the seeds out with your finger. Tomatoes are available year-round, but the peak season is summer.

TURNIPS have white flesh and skin with a purple top. Choose turnips that are small and firm, with unblemished skin. If the greens are attached, they should be fresh and not wilted. Young turnips are tender and do not need to be peeled. Turnips are available year-round and can be tightly wrapped and stored in the refrigerator for up to two weeks. They can also be kept in a cool (55 degrees), dark area. Turnips can be boiled, steamed, mashed, stir-fried, or used raw in salads.

WATERCRESS has a sharp, peppery flavor. Select bunches with crisp stems and unblemished, bright green leaves. Avoid watercress with very thick stems. Watercress can be served raw in salads and sandwiches, but it also can be added to salads, sauces, soups, and stews. The leaves and thinner stems are best for salads and quick cooking. Watercress is available year-round and can be refrigerated in a plastic bag for up to five days.

Fruits

Fruits, like vegetables, are a rich source of nutrients, fiber, and a wide variety of phytochemicals. Because they contain so much water and fiber, their calorie count is low compared with other foods of equal volume. Finding new ways of integrating them into your diet is a major objective of this cookbook.

APPLES are available in many varieties, ranging in taste from sweet to tart. Some firmer-fleshed varieties, such as Rome Beauty and Granny Smith, are better for baking, and some sweeter ones, such as Red and Golden Delicious, Fuji, Gala, and Rome, are better for eating raw. Select firm apples with good color, avoiding fruit with bruises. Larger apples may be mealy. Apples can be stored at room temperature for several days or in the refrigerator for several weeks.

APRICOTS in the United States are mainly grown in California. There are hundreds of varieties, some of which are used to produce dried apricots. Select fragrant fruit with color ranging from yellow to orange. Ripe fruit yields to gentle pressure. Avoid mushy, blemished apricots and those with a green tint. Apricots ripen after harvest; store them in a closed paper bag to ripen. They should be eaten as soon as they are ripe because they are very perishable.

BANANAS should be unblemished with a uniform shape and color. Ripe bananas are golden yellow and have dark specks. They continue to ripen after harvest. Store bananas at room temperature. Ripe bananas can be refrigerated or frozen to prevent spoilage, but the skin will turn dark brown. Overripe bananas can be used in banana muffins and quick breads. Sprinkle sliced bananas with lemon juice to prevent them from turning brown.

BLUEBERRIES should be firm and deep purple or blue-black with a white or silvery cast, called a "bloom." Avoid moldy or green berries—they do not continue to ripen after picking. Refrigerate blueberries, unwashed, for up to five days, until ready to use. They are available from late May to early October.

CHERRIES should be brightly colored, firm, and plump. The most popular varieties of cherries are dark red to dark purple. Sour cherries are smaller and used for pies and preserves. Select unblemished cherries, preferably attached to stems. Avoid those that are too soft or too hard; they do not ripen after harvest. Cherries are available from May through August and can be stored in the refrigerator for two to three days.

CRANBERRIES should be firm and bright red. Avoid shriveled and decayed berries. Store in the refrigerator for up to two months or freeze for up to one year. Cranberries do not ripen after harvest. Fresh cranberries are available only from October through December; purchase extra and freeze them so you can enjoy them year-round.

GRAPES come in many colors and varieties. Look for plump grapes firmly attached to the stems, with good color for the variety. Avoid mushy or moldy grapes. Grapes may have a whitish cast or bloom, indicating freshness. They do not ripen after harvest. Refrigerate grapes for up to one week. They are available throughout the year.

KIWI is a small, oval fruit with fuzzy brown skin and bright green flesh. Select unblemished fruit. Ripen kiwi in a loosely closed paper bag. Ripe fruit will yield to gentle pressure. Refrigerate the fruit when ripe for up to three weeks. Kiwi is available year-round.

LEMONS should be firm and heavy for their size. Choose lemons that have thin skins. Avoid any that are bruised or green in color; they do not ripen after harvest. A large lemon yields about three to four tablespoons of juice and two to three tablespoons of zest— the colored part of the peel. To remove the zest, wash the lemon and use the fine side of a hand grater. Do *not* remove the white pith, which is quite bitter. Refrigerate lemons for two to three weeks.

LIMES should be firm, shiny, and heavy for their size, and uniformly green in color. They do not ripen after harvest. Avoid any that are spongy. Refrigerate limes for up to ten days. Lime juice, like lemon juice, helps keep cut vegetables and fruits, like pears and apples, from getting brown before you serve them.

MANGOES should yield slightly to pressure when ripe, and have a strong, sweet aroma. Select fruits with no blemishes. Mangoes become yellow with red areas as they ripen. The flesh is bright orange. They continue to ripen after harvest. To hasten ripening, place in a paper bag at room temperature. Ripe mangoes will keep in the refrigerator for up to five days. Only the flesh is edible. To cut the flesh away from the pit and peel, stand the fruit on one end. Slice vertically down one side of the pit. Repeat on the other side. With a paring knife, cut the flesh of each piece into cubes, but do not slice through the skin. Turn fruit inside out so that the cubed side is turned outward and slice cubes off the skin. Cut away the fruit that remains around the pit. Mangoes are in season from May through September.

MELONS come in many varieties. Among the most popular is *cantaloupe,* a sweet, orange-fleshed melon that should have a distinctive fruity aroma when ripe. The blossom end (the end with a small round bump) should be slightly soft. Avoid shriveled or bruised melons: the skin should be firm and greenish yellow with pale raised webbing. Store an uncut and unripe cantaloupe at room temperature; ripe melons, or those that have been cut, should be refrigerated. Wrap carefully to avoid absorption of other food odors. *Honeydew melons* should be well shaped with a creamy, yellow rind, and a slightly soft blossom end (the end with a small round bump). They have light green, juicy flesh. Choose melons that are heavy for their size. Store uncut and unripe melons at room temperature. When ripe, store in the refrigerator for up to five days. Peak months for honeydew are July through September. *Watermelons* should be well shaped and heavy for their size. A dull rind, dried stem, and yellowish underside indicate ripeness. Watermelons do not ripen after harvest. Store uncut watermelon at room temperature for up to one week. Store cut watermelon, tightly wrapped, in the refrigerator and use within one to two days. Watermelons are available from May to September.

NECTARINES belong to the same family as peaches, and the two can generally be interchanged in recipes. Ripe nectarines yield to gentle pressure and continue to ripen after harvest; they will not become sweeter, but they will increase in juiciness. Ripe nectarines have a brilliant yellow, smooth skin with red blushes. They can be refrigerated for up to five days. Unripe nectarines can be stored at room temperature for several days. The best nectarines are available in the summer.

ORANGES should be firm and heavy for their size. Avoid oranges with dull, rough, scarred, green, or spongy skin. Oranges do not ripen after harvest. Oranges are available year-round. Store them in the refrigerator for up to two weeks.

PAPAYAS are yellow to yellow-orange when ripe. Choose firm papayas with unblemished skin. They continue to ripen after harvest and are ready to eat when they yield to gentle pressure. Store unripe papayas at room temperature. Store ripe papayas in the refrigerator and use as soon as possible.

PEACHES should have creamy or yellow skins with varying amounts of blush, depending on the variety. Ripe peaches should yield to gentle pressure. Overripe peaches are excessively soft. Peaches continue to ripen after harvest; ripen them in a loosely closed paper bag. Refrigerate them when they are ripe for up to five days. Peaches are at their peak from May through October.

PEARS are available in many varieties, including Bartlett (most popular), Bosc (hold their shape well for baking and poaching), Comice (very sweet and too delicate to be cooked), and Seckel (small fruit with a spicy flavor). Select pears without bruises. They continue to ripen after harvest; ripen them in a loosely closed paper bag. Most pears yield to gentle pressure when they are ripe. Refrigerate ripe pears for two to three days. Pears are available from late July to early spring.

PLUMS are available in many varieties. Avoid plums that have broken or discolored skins or that appear soft. They should be firm, giving slightly to pressure when they are ripe. Plums continue to ripen after harvest. Store at room temperature until slightly soft. Then store in the refrigerator for up to four days.

RASPBERRIES should be dry and plump. Select firm red, black, or golden berries (depending on variety); check the package carefully for moldy, soft, or leaky berries. Store in the refrigerator. Use raspberries within a few days, as they are highly perishable. Raspberries are available May through November.

STRAWBERRIES should be bright red, firm, and plump, with caps intact. Avoid green or white berries, as well as wrinkled, leaky, or moldy ones. Strawberries do not ripen after harvest. Refrigerate strawberries for two to three days.

Whole Grains

Grains—especially whole grains—can add a new world of tastes, textures, and good nutrition to any diet. Unfortunately, many of us are just not familiar with the wonderful array of whole grains now available in the United States. We have introduced a variety of grains in this cookbook in order to get you started (see the Grains chapter, page 66). Once you become familiar with such grains as barley, bulgur, millet, and quinoa, you'll want to experiment with amaranth, kamut, spelt, and others.

Grains, in their natural form, have an outer layer called the *bran*. This component is high in B vitamins and trace minerals, and it is especially high in dietary fiber. The endosperm, or *kernel,* is where most of the protein and carbohydrate, as well as small amounts of vitamins, are located. It is often the only part that is eaten after the grain has been refined. The *germ* has the highest concentration of nutrition. It also contains fat, which is why wheat germ can turn rancid over time if not refrigerated. When buying grain in packages, be sure to check the freshness date. Grains should be stored in tightly sealed containers in a cool, dark place for one month. If kept in the refrigerator, they can be stored for four months or longer. Frozen grains can be stored indefinitely, except for oats and oat bran, which will become rancid within two to three months.

Whole grains have the germ and bran components intact. Compared with grains that have been refined, whole grains are high in dietary fiber, both soluble (the kind that helps lower cholesterol levels) and insoluble (the kind that promotes regularity). In addition, whole grains are good sources of B vitamins (riboflavin, thiamin, and niacin), vitamin E, iron, zinc, calcium, magnesium, selenium, and many phytochemicals.

To determine whether a processed product is made from refined or whole grains, take a look at the ingredient list. If the first ingredient listed is, for example, whole wheat, whole grain, or whole oats, there is more of this whole grain in the product than any other item.

BARLEY is a versatile grain that is often put in casseroles, salads, and soups. Barley generally absorbs the flavors of the foods with which it is combined. Hulled barley (with only the outer husk removed) is not widely available. Because it offers health benefits, you might ask your grocer to get some for you. Pearl barley, however, which has had the bran layer removed, is easy to find in supermarkets and can be prepared in about 45 minutes.

BROWN RICE has a heartier flavor and a chewier texture than white rice and can be a more satisfying alternative. Though regular brown rice takes longer than white rice to cook, it is available in a quick-cooking form. Brown rice contains more dietary fiber, vitamin E, and phytochemicals (such as oryzanol), because the germ and bran are left intact. Try brown rice mixed with vegetables and fresh herbs, in salads, and as a nutritious accompaniment to fish, poultry, and meat. Different varieties of brown rice, such as brown basmati rice, are also available.

BULGUR is whole wheat berries that have been steamed, dried, and then cracked into coarse, medium, or fine granules. The coarsest bulgur is used for pilafs, the medium granules are used for cereal, and the fine granules are used in tabbouleh. One cup of bulgur should be combined with 2½ cups of boiling liquid, covered, and allowed to steep for about 30 minutes until the liquid is absorbed. (One cup of dry bulgur yields three cups cooked.)

KASHA is roasted, hulled buckwheat kernels that are cracked into granules. The granules are coarse, medium, or fine and have a toasted flavor. Kasha, a good source of dietary fiber and iron, is frequently combined with vegetables and herbs. Many kasha recipes call for a beaten egg to be mixed with the granules before cooking to help the grains cohere and to enhance their flavor; the package the kasha comes in will have instructions for cooking it.

MILLET, which has been used as a grain since the Middle Ages, is generally found in health food stores. Its bland flavor allows it to absorb the flavors of seasonings well. It can be used as a breakfast cereal, as a base for a cold salad, or as a side dish and is a good source of B vitamins, iron, magnesium, and zinc. Be sure to serve it immediately after cooking, because the texture can solidify when it cools. To reheat leftover millet, sprinkle it with warm water and separate the grains with a fork. Then cover with a wet paper towel and warm on low power in your microwave.

OATS are an especially good source of soluble fiber. Rolled oats are the type that is most frequently seen in the supermarket. There are three types of rolled oats: old-fashioned (the grain is simply rolled), quick-cooking (the oats are sliced before they are rolled), and instant (the oats are precooked, dried, and then rolled very thinly for fast preparation). Steel-cut oats, usually imported from Ireland or Scotland, are cooked for a longer period of time and have a more chewy and dense texture. Oats also contain phytochemicals, including saponins.

QUINOA is actually a relative of leafy vegetables but is used as a grain in the United States. With a unique crunchy texture, quinoa is one of the best sources of plant protein. It should be rinsed well before cooking to eliminate the bitter outer coating. Browning in a dry skillet for several minutes before cooking gives quinoa a toasted flavor that greatly enhances its appeal. Try combining quinoa with fresh herbs and finely chopped vegetables.

WHOLE WHEAT PASTA is a good source of dietary fiber and is considerably higher in selenium than refined pasta. Whole wheat pasta offers a unique, chewy texture that mixes well with strong-flavored vegetable sauces. It is available in most supermarkets and health food stores. Avoid overcooking, which will lead to a mushy texture. Couscous is a tiny pasta made from semolina (coarse durum wheat). It is used in a variety of cuisines. To prepare, add couscous to boiling water, remove from heat, and let it sit to absorb the liquid. The final product is fluffy and is usually served with meat and vegetables, as a side dish, or as an accompaniment to curries and Mediterranean stews. Whole wheat couscous is higher in fiber, but it is sometimes difficult to find.

Beans

Beans and peas (sometimes grouped together as "legumes") are an integral and versatile part of the New American Plate. They are low in fat and high in dietary fiber, folate, and minerals such as iron, potassium, magnesium, and selenium. They serve as an excellent alternative to meat in a variety of dishes. The dietary fiber beans contain is largely soluble fiber, meaning that it is especially useful in helping control cholesterol levels in order to lower heart disease risk. (Insoluble fiber also helps promote regularity.) Finally, beans are filling and help promote weight management by satisfying hunger. When beans are combined with grains, complete proteins are formed. You do not, however, need to eat grains at the same time as beans to get this result, as previously thought.

Dried beans can be prepared at home with a little advance planning but very little effort. Put rinsed beans in a large pot and cover them with water. Let them stand for six or more hours or overnight. Drain them and rinse again. Cover the beans with water, bring to a boil, reduce heat to low. Simmer them until tender and then drain and use. Adding salt during the cooking process will toughen the beans. Choose dried beans that are whole and not broken. Since older beans may require longer cooking, be sure to store them in a tightly covered container, which should be labeled and dated.

If this preparation does not fit your schedule, use canned beans. Be sure to rinse and drain canned beans before using them. Whether you cook them yourself or use canned, beans can be added to soup, sprinkled on salads and pasta dishes, puréed into dips and spreads, and substituted for meat in burritos, casseroles, stews, and tacos.

Some common beans that are used in the recipes in this cookbook (or can be used in your own favorite recipes) are described below.

BLACK BEANS, also called turtle beans, have an earthy flavor and are frequently used in Brazilian, Cuban, Mexican, and Southwestern dishes. Black bean soup is a well-known dish prepared from these small beans. Black beans are often accompanied by rice.

BLACK-EYED PEAS, also called cowpeas, are ivory-colored peas with a small black "eye," or spot. They are excellent in many bean salads and are the key ingredient in the Southern dish Hoppin' John. Eating black-eyed peas on New Year's Day is supposed to bring good luck throughout the year.

CANNELLINI BEANS, also known as white kidney beans, have a smooth texture and are often puréed with herbs and spices to make a hearty sandwich spread. They are used in the classic Italian dish *pasta e fagioli*.

CHICKPEAS, also called garbanzo beans or *ceci*, are frequently found in salads, in Middle Eastern falafel, in Mediterranean dishes, and in vegetable curries and stews. They are the basis of hummus spread. They also can be roasted and lightly salted and eaten as a snack.

CRANBERRY BEANS, also called Roman beans, are beige with red streaks. They are sweet and delicate in flavor. They can be added to pasta dishes and salads.

FAVA BEANS, or broad beans, are large, flat beans that are used most frequently in Mediterranean recipes.

GREAT NORTHERN BEANS are white and creamy; they are popular in baked bean dishes.

GREEN PEAS are legumes, although they are often consumed as a vegetable when fresh or frozen. Fresh green peas can be added to a variety of dishes including casseroles, pastas, salads, and soups.

LENTILS have a mild, earthy taste. They are excellent in soups, stews, and some salads. They are traditionally used in Indian dishes, where they are known as *dal* and are frequently combined with tomatoes, onions, and seasonings. Unlike most other dried beans, lentils do not need to be soaked before cooking. Green lentils are actually brown, hold their shape well when cooked, and have greater nutritional value. Red lentils are more refined and cook more quickly.

LIMA BEANS are a very light green and are used extensively in soups and stews. They are available fresh, frozen, canned, and dried. They have a starchy texture, which is less prominent when they are smaller. Succotash is a Southern dish combining lima beans with corn, peppers, and tomatoes.

NAVY BEANS are small white beans that are frequently used in casseroles. They are typically used in Boston baked beans.

PINTO BEANS, which have a meaty texture and taste, are pale pink with streaks of brown before cooking. They turn red when cooked. Pinto beans are found frequently in Mexican dishes, such as burritos, and in baked beans. Typically, they are used in refried beans.

RED KIDNEY BEANS are firm with deep red skin. They are used frequently in chilis and Cajun bean dishes.

SOYBEANS contain high-quality protein. In addition, they are high in isoflavones, which are currently being studied for their possible role in health protection—they appear to be heart protective and possibly cancer protective. Soybeans are usually sold in bulk and should be stored in an airtight container. They can be used in soups, stews, chilis, and casseroles. Foods made from soy include miso, soy milk, soy flour, soy burgers, soy nuts, tempeh, and tofu. Edamame, which are fresh soybeans, have recently gained popularity as an appetizer or snack.

SPLIT PEAS are similar to lentils in flavor, and are used in soups and stews. They should not be soaked before cooking.

Herbs and Spices

Herbs and spices have been used throughout human history to add flavor to foods. However, researchers have found another reason to use these flavoring agents: herbs and spices provide phytochemicals that help protect our health. Each has its own profile of phytochemicals. The protection we get from turmeric's curcumin is different from the protection that carnosol in rosemary gives us, for example. Herbs and spices can be used to replace all or part of the salt we are accustomed to using in many dishes, an advantage to those watching their salt intake.

Herbs are the edible leaves of plants used to flavor food. Both dried and fresh herbs are perishable, though dried herbs keep for much longer. Fresh herbs should be washed well in cool water. Shake off the excess water and wrap the herbs lightly in a paper towel. Place them in a plastic bag and refrigerate for up to five days. Another way to store fresh herbs is to trim a quarter inch from the stem end and place them upright in a cup of water. Cover loosely with a plastic bag and refrigerate. They will last four or five days before the leaves start to turn brown.

Dried herbs, which may be crushed or ground, should be stored in tightly covered containers away from heat, light, and humidity. Properly stored, their shelf life is about six months.

Dried herbs should be added at the start of the cooking process to give them time to release their flavors. They are typically used in dry rubs, sauces, and soups. Fresh herbs are best used at the end of cooking or sprinkled on food after it is cooked. In general, 1 tablespoon of fresh, finely chopped herbs can be replaced with 1 teaspoon of crumbled dried leaf herbs (such as oregano) or half a teaspoon of dried ground herbs (such as sage).

Spices are the buds, flowers, fruits, roots, or seeds of plants that have been dried. They can be whole or ground. Spices should also be stored in tightly covered containers and protected from light, heat, and moisture. They lose their potency after about six months.

Whole spices will last longer than ground spices. You can grind your own spices in a coffee mill reserved just for that purpose, or you can use a special spice grinder. Toasting the whole spice before grinding will intensify its flavor.

Spice blends are a convenient way to add a more complex flavor to food. You can combine your favorite blends in advance to have on hand and use regularly. Some herbs associated with ethnic cuisines are as follows:

- Mexican: chili powder, cilantro, cumin, and garlic powder
- Italian: basil, garlic powder, oregano, and rosemary
- Chinese: ground dried red chiles, five-spice powder, ground ginger, and sesame seeds
- Thai: basil, ground dried red chiles, cilantro, ground lemongrass, and mint
- Greek: cinnamon, dill, garlic powder, mint, and oregano

For a table of herb and spice substitutions, see page 267.

ALLSPICE is a tiny berry, ground and used in braised meats, pies, puddings, sausages, and stewed fruits. This spice is also found in Jamaican jerk seasoning. Allspice contains eugenol.

ANISE SEED is a spice in the parsley family. It is used in breads, candies, cookies, and pastries. Buy the seeds whole and grind them at home. This spice contains limonene.

BASIL is a green, pungent herb used in pesto sauce and with eggplant, egg dishes, pasta, salads, and tomatoes. It is often an ingredient in Italian and Thai dishes. This herb contains monoterpenes.

BAY LEAVES, either whole or ground, are used in braised dishes, sauces, soups, stews, and stocks. Unlike other flavoring agents, whole bay leaves are removed at the completion of cooking. This herb contains eugenol.

CARAWAY SEEDS, a member of the parsley family, are used in cabbage dishes, cheese spreads, and rye breads. Popular in Eastern European cuisines, this spice contains limonene.

CARDAMOM is a member of the ginger family and is sold in pod, seed, or ground form. This aromatic spice is used in curries and baked goods and for pickling. Popular in Indian, Scandinavian, and Middle Eastern cuisines, cardamom contains limonene.

CELERY SEED is used in coleslaw, potato salad, salad dressings, and tomato-based dishes. This spice contains limonene.

CHERVIL, which has a very mild anise taste, is used in cheese and egg dishes, salads, and soups. This herb is often used in French cuisine. It contains flavonoids.

CHILI POWDER is used with ground meat and in sauces. This spice blend is common in Mexican and Southwestern cuisine. Chili powder is divided into two categories: one is a blend that contains chiles, as well as cumin, garlic powder, and salt, and the other is pure ground chiles. The intensity of the heat depends on the type of chile pepper used. Both types of chili powders are commonly used in Mexican and Southwestern cuisines. Chili powder contains capsaicin.

CHIVES are used in salads and soups, as well as in egg, fish, and potato dishes. This herb is a member of the allium family, along with garlic, leeks, and onions. Chives contain allyl sulfides.

CILANTRO, also called fresh coriander, is used in rice dishes, salads, sauces, soups, and stews. Popular in Mexican, Southwestern, and Asian cuisines, this pungent herb is the leaf of the coriander plant, also called Chinese parsley. Cilantro contains limonene and coriandrol and may help protect against liver and breast cancer. Coriander seed is the dried fruit of the plant, and is used in curry powder, for baking, and for pickling.

CINNAMON is used to flavor breads, cooked fruits, desserts, hot beverages, and sweet potatoes. It is available ground or as whole sticks; cinnamon sticks should be removed from cooked dishes before serving. This spice contains limonene.

CLOVES, which are available whole or ground, are used in cakes, cooked fruits, marinades, pastries, quick breads, sauces, and stocks. This spice contains several phytochemicals that may help fight heart disease and cancer. Cloves also contain flavonoids, including quercetin.

CUMIN is an ingredient found in spice mixtures, especially Indian and Mexican blends, such as curry powder and chili powder. It is available whole or ground, and is often used to flavor cheese dishes, meats, sauces, and stews. Cumin contains cuminaldehyde, which is thought to have strong anticancer effects.

CURRY POWDER is a blend of many spices, and the version found in supermarkets generally includes turmeric, cardamom, coriander, cumin, fenugreek, cinnamon, and white or black pepper. It is a staple of Indian cooking, although in India the particular combination of spices varies among regions and individual cooks. Curry powder can be used in soups and stews, in vegetable recipes, and in rubs for fish, poultry, and meat.

DILL is both an herb (its leaves, fresh or dried) and a spice (dill seed). It is used to season egg dishes, salads (including potato salad), and vegetables. Dill contains limonene.

FENNEL SEED, which has a strong anise or licorice flavor, is used to flavor fish, sausage, soups, and tomato sauce. Fresh fennel bulb is used as a vegetable (see page 273). This spice contains limonene.

FIVE-SPICE POWDER is used extensively in Asian cooking, and generally includes equal parts ground cinnamon, cloves, fennel seed, star anise, and Szechuan peppercorns. It is found in Asian markets and most supermarkets.

GARLIC is one of the most versatile flavoring agents. A member of the allium family (with onions, leeks, and scallions), it is used in its fresh and dried powdered forms to flavor meat, soups, stews, and vegetables. After chopping fresh garlic, let it rest for 10 to 15 minutes before cooking so that the phytochemicals (allyl sulfides) have a chance to develop.

GINGER has a very different taste depending on whether it is fresh or ground (it can also be preserved, candied, or pickled). Fresh gingerroot is often used in Indian and Asian cuisines. It is popular in stir-fry dishes as well as in some baked goods. Powdered ginger is used in a variety of breads including, of course, gingerbread. This spice contains the phytochemicals gingerol and zingerone.

HERBES DE PROVENCE is used in sauces, soups, and stews. This blend of dried herbs and spices includes, among others, bay leaf, fennel seeds, lavender, rosemary, savory, and thyme.

MACE, which comes from the same plant as nutmeg, is used to flavor baked goods, desserts, fish, fruit, meat, and vegetables. This spice contains eugenol and limonene.

MARJORAM, an herb in the mint family, is used in stuffing for poultry and meat. Often used in Italian cuisine, marjoram contains eugenol and limonene.

MINT is used to flavor carrots, lamb, peas, potatoes, and teas. Found in many Middle Eastern and Southeast Asian dishes, this herb contains limonene and luteolin, which may protect against breast cancer.

MUSTARD powder is made from mustard seeds that are finely ground. White mustard seeds are mild and are used as a pickling spice or in basic "deli" mustard. Brown mustard seeds are more pungent and are often used in Asian and African cooking. The strongest flavor comes from black mustard seeds. Black seeds are used in sauces, marinades, salad dressings, chutneys, and pickling brine.

NUTMEG is used in breads, cream sauces, custards, desserts, pastries, soups, and vegetables. This spice contains eugenol and limonene. Available whole and ground, nutmeg is pungent and sweet. Grating whole nutmeg as needed offers the best flavor.

OREGANO is frequently used in Mexican and Italian cooking. This herb is especially good with tomatoes and other vegetables and contains the phytochemical quercetin.

PAPRIKA is ground, dried red pepper ranging from sweet to pungent to mildly hot. It is used as a garnish and in Hungarian dishes such as chicken paprikash and goulash. This spice contains capsanthin and beta-carotene.

PARSLEY is popular as a garnish, but it is also used in sauces, soups, and vegetables and in salads such as tabbouleh. Curly leaf parsley is the most popular, but flat leaf parsley has a stronger flavor. This herb contains beta-carotene and limonene.

PEPPER is perhaps the most popular spice in American cooking. Grinding black peppercorns as needed at the table or the stove provides the most flavorful pepper taste. White pepper, which is less "peppery" than black, is sometimes used to prepare white dishes when the black pepper specks would detract from the appearance. Both black and white pepper contain piperine. Cayenne (ground red pepper) is a different spice: it is the powdered dried form of various chiles, and is spicy-hot.

ROSEMARY is quite pungent and should be used sparingly to flavor braised foods, poultry, and tomato dishes. This herb contains the phytochemical carnosol, which is anti-inflammatory and anti-carcinogenic.

SAFFRON is used sparingly to flavor and add rich yellow color to poultry, rice, and seafood dishes. Harvested by hand from the stigmas of a member of the crocus family, it is the most expensive spice in the world. Available in thread or powder form, it is often found in Spanish dishes such as paella. This spice is high in monoterpenes, which act as antioxidants. When saffron is not available, turmeric can be added instead for a bright yellow color (though the taste is not comparable).

SAGE, a member of the mint family, is used in stuffings for poultry and in bean, grain, and poultry dishes. It has a very assertive flavor and should be used sparingly. This herb contains luteolin, a cancer-fighting phytochemical.

SAVORY, a peppery herb, comes in two types: summer and winter savory. Winter savory is often used in soups and other hearty dishes. Summer savory is used in egg, fish, and vegetable dishes. Savory contains ursolic acid.

TARRAGON, which has a mild anise flavor, is used to flavor egg dishes, poultry, salad dressings, sauces, and vinegar. This herb contains limonene and rutin.

THYME, a member of the mint family, is popular in Mediterranean cuisines, where it is used in grain dishes, sauces, soups, stocks, and tomato dishes. This herb contains luteolin, which may protect against breast cancer.

TURMERIC, which is related to ginger, is the ingredient that gives curry powder its yellow color. This spice is also used in rice dishes to add color. Turmeric contains curcumin, an anti-inflammatory phytochemical.

the science behind the new american plate

Evaluating the Evidence

As the twentieth century dawned, a number of physicians began to publish papers noting that their cancer patients tended to eat the same foods: meat, alcohol, white bread, and fatty, sugary treats. Since these early papers were based only on observations, they could not prove an association between such foods and a cancer diagnosis. Nevertheless, they did inspire later scientists, who began serious investigation of the hypothesis that diet and nutrition play a role in the cancer process.

During the first half of the twentieth century, scientists began conducting cohort studies, which tracked the diets and cancer rates of large groups of individuals in isolated populations over extended periods of time, and case-control studies, which compared the diets of patients with cancer to those of similar individuals who were cancer-free. Preliminary results from these investigations appeared in scientific journals and tended to link increased cancer risk to diets low in vegetables and fruits and high in fat and meat. These epidemiological studies, while few in number, strengthened the case for a connection between diet and cancer.

Before long, however, scientists started to explore alternative theories about cancer's origins. With the discovery of DNA's structure in 1953, cancer researchers began to focus on the role of random genetic mutation, exposure to viruses, and overexposure to specific chemicals. Unlike expensive epidemiological investigations, which took years to produce results and relied upon subjects' self-reported dietary information, these new theories could be studied under strictly controlled laboratory conditions. Results were produced in weeks, not years, and at considerably less expense.

Although genetic theories of cancer's origins occupied the scientific spotlight over the next couple of decades, epidemiological investigations documenting the impact of diet among groups, countries, and populations continued. By the 1960s, it was becoming clear that cancer rates varied greatly between countries—and even between different regions within countries. Populations consuming diets high in vegetables and fruits and low in meat had consistently lower cancer rates than populations consuming more meat and fewer plant foods. Cancer rates were also found to change over time, and, perhaps most tellingly, to vary as people migrated from one country to another. A series of studies showed that cancer rates rose significantly among Japanese people who migrated to Hawaii and adopted Westernized diets, which were higher in meat and dairy products. These results argued strongly for a dietary role in the development of cancer.

Throughout the 1970s and 1980s, scientists ingeniously adapted the experimental methods previously reserved for studying the genetic changes that cancer produces and used these rigorous methods to investigate how dietary components influence those changes. They examined cells (*in vitro* studies), tissues (*in vivo* studies), and living organisms, looking for possible mechanisms—clear, demonstrable ways that components of the diet could influence different stages of the cancer process.

They observed that certain foods and food substances seem able to bolster the body's natural defenses against cancer. Certain dietary substances, such as the phytochemicals found in cruciferous vegetables, may help our bodies defuse the potentially harmful compounds that we're exposed to on a daily basis. These substances also seem to make it easier for our immune systems to flush harmful compounds from our bodies long before they spark the cancer process. Other substances, such as the antioxidants found in fruits and vegetables, seem to help counteract oxidation, the low-level genetic damage that occurs as a by-product of our metabolism.

More recently, this laboratory work has shown that diet and lifestyle also have indirect effects on hormonal and metabolic processes that may influence cancer risk. Overweight and obesity, for example, seem to increase cancer risk by changing how our bodies regulate the rate of cell reproduction; regular physical activity, on the other hand, seems to help "reset" the switches that control this vital metabolic function.

The first studies that systematically compiled and evaluated this mounting evidence appeared in the 1980s. These reports were vital, because they allowed the international scientific community its first opportunity to see how the data was shaping up. Importantly, both *The Causes of Cancer,* by Richard Doll and Richard Peto (1981), and the U.S. National Academy of Sciences report *Diet, Nutrition and Cancer* (1982) concluded by issuing urgent calls for more and better research. To answer these calls, the American Institute for Cancer Research (AICR) was established in 1982. AICR's dual mission, then and now, is to fund vital research on diet's role in cancer development and to educate the public about the results.

During the 1980s and 1990s, the number of studies on the diet/cancer link grew. Most were epidemiological, some were experimental, and more than a few were clinical trials, although researchers had difficulty adapting the format of the clinical trial (which is better suited to studying cancer *treatment*) to the multifaceted issue of cancer *prevention*. By the mid-1990s, the number of studies published in reputable scientific journals was staggering. But the epidemiological data did not always jibe with the laboratory work that revealed plausible links between diet and cancer at the cellular level. It was becoming increasingly difficult for scientists—much less for the public—to keep track of this often confusing and sometimes contradictory evidence.

What was needed, then, was a comprehensive, global attempt to weigh the evidence in a systematic and meaningful way; ideally, this effort would also integrate the epidemiological data with data from experimental studies. To that end, AICR and its British affiliate, the World Cancer Research Fund, commissioned a panel of scientists from Africa, Asia, Europe, and North and Central America to prepare a report that would examine the research and place it in the largest possible context.

The panel discussed and debated thousands of scientific studies related to the role of diet, physical activity, and weight management in cancer development. They received input from such official observer organizations as the World Health Organization, the International Agency for Research on Cancer, and the Food and Agriculture Organization of the United Nations.

It took the panel several years to complete the landmark WCRF/AICR report *Food, Nutrition and the Prevention of Cancer: A Global Perspective.* This report is the most comprehensive and authoritative examination to date of the evidence linking diet, physical activity, and weight management to cancer risk. Governments, public health agencies, and millions of individuals throughout the world have adopted the report's recommendations for lowering cancer risk.

To formulate these recommendations, the panel compiled the available evidence by cancer site (such as breast, colon, and prostate), by dietary constitu-

Chair
John D. Potter, MBBS, PhD
Fred Hutchinson Cancer Research Center
Seattle, WA, USA

Members
Adolfo Chavez, MD, MPH
Instituto Nacional de la Nutricion
Mexico City, Mexico

Junshi Chen, MD
Chinese Academy of Preventive Medicine
Beijing, China

Anna Ferro-Luzzi, MD
Istituto Nazional della Nutrizione
Rome, Italy

Tomio Hirohata, MD, DrSHyg
Nakamura University
Fukuoka City, Japan

W. P. T. James, CBE, MD, FRCP, FRSE
The Rowett Research Institute
Aberdeen, UK

Fred F. Kadlubar, PhD
National Center for Toxicological Research
Jefferson, AR, USA

Festo P. Kavishe, MD
UNICEF Office of the Regional Director of East Asia and Pacific Region
Phnom Penh, Cambodia

Laurence N. Kolonel, MD, PhD
University of Hawaii
Honolulu, HI, USA

Suminori Kono, MD, MSc
Kyushu University
Fukuoka City, Japan

Kamala Krishnaswamy, MD
Indian Council of Medical Research
Hyderabad, India

A. J. McMichael, MBBS, FFPHM, FAFPHM
London School of Hygiene and Tropical Medicine
London, UK

Sushma Palmer, DSc
Center for Communications, Health and the Environment
Washington, DC, USA

Lionel A. Poirier, PhD
National Center for Toxicological Research
Jefferson, AR, USA

Walter C. Willett, MD, DrPH
Harvard School of Public Health
Boston, MA, USA

Scientific adviser to AICR/WCRF
T. Colin Campbell, PhD
Cornell University
Ithaca, NY, USA

---

ent (such as vegetables, fruits, and starches), and by related factors (such as obesity, level of physical activity, and method of preparing food). For each potential link to cancer risk, the panel graded the available evidence as *convincing, probable,* or *possible.* (The panel also issued a grade of *insufficient* if little or no research existed.)

A link was considered *convincing* if a substantial number of epidemiological studies were strongly consistent and laboratory studies showed a clear, plausible mechanism that could explain how and why that dietary constituent or lifestyle factor may affect cancer risk. The expert panel concluded, for example, that there is convincing evidence of the following:

- That diets high in vegetables and fruits *decrease* the risk of cancers of the colon, rectum, stomach, lung, esophagus, mouth, and pharynx.
- That regular physical activity *decreases* the risk of colon cancer.
- That obesity *increases* the risk of endometrial cancer.
- That alcohol *increases* the risk of cancers of the liver, esophagus, larynx, mouth, and pharynx.

A link was considered *probable* if only a majority of the epidemiological studies were consistent (or the total number of epidemiological studies was smaller) and laboratory studies showed a clear, plausible mechanism. The expert panel concluded that the following links were probable:

- That diets high in vegetables and fruits *decrease* the risk of cancers of the breast, bladder, and larynx.
- That alcohol *increases* the risk of cancers of the breast, colon, and rectum.

- That meat *increases* the risk of colorectal cancer.
- That obesity *increases* the risk of breast and kidney cancer.

A link was considered *possible* if the epidemiological studies were generally supportive, but small in number or of limited quality. Laboratory studies may or may not have shown a clear mechanism. The expert panel concluded that the following link was possible:

- That diets high in vegetables and fruits *decrease* the risk of cancers of the liver, ovary, endometrium, cervix, prostate, thyroid, and kidney.

After weighing scientific evidence from around the globe, the panel concluded: "Cancer is mostly a preventable disease. The chief causes of cancer are use of tobacco and inappropriate diets." Further, the panel estimated that "between 30 percent and 40 percent of all cancers are preventable by feasible and appropriate diets and related factors."

In the WCRF/AICR report, the panel outlined practical ways to lower cancer risk. These recommendations have been distilled into a set of guidelines that collectively inform the New American Plate campaign and every aspect of AICR's ongoing mission to help Americans lower their cancer risk.

AICR'S DIET AND HEALTH GUIDELINES FOR CANCER PREVENTION

1. Choose a diet rich in a variety of plant-based foods.
2. Eat plenty of vegetables and fruits.
3. Maintain a healthy weight and be physically active.
4. Drink alcohol only in moderation, if at all.
5. Select foods low in fat and salt.
6. Prepare and store food safely.

And always remember . . .

Do not use tobacco in any form.

For more information and to order a copy of *Food, Nutrition and the Prevention of Cancer: A Global Perspective*, visit the American Institute for Cancer Research on the web at www.aicr.org.

Phytochemicals

Nutritionists used to focus mostly on the benefits of vitamins and minerals. But during the past decade, researchers have identified protective substances in fruits and vegetables called phytochemicals. Hundreds of individual phytochemicals have been discovered and more are identified all the time. Each fruit, vegetable, herb, spice, bean, or grain has its own profile of phytochemicals, which means that the protection you get from blueberries is different from the protection you get from broccoli. Thus the best way to get maximum benefit from phytochemicals is to eat a large variety of plant-based foods.

The following is a partial list of phytochemicals (including groups, subgroups, and individual compounds), their probable role in health protection, and some known food sources.

ALLIUM COMPOUNDS This group decreases the risk of gastrointestinal cancers, as well as other cancers. Allium compounds stimulate the body to produce powerful phase-2 enzymes, which remove toxins from the body.
Allyl sulfides: present in chives, garlic, leeks, and onions

CAROTENOIDS Carotenoids, including the well-known beta-carotene, are associated with antioxidant activity. An orange has more than twenty carotenoids. Some carotenoids may interfere with breast cancer proliferation and induce cancer cell death in other cancers, as well.
Lutein, zeaxanthin: present in avocado, corn, kale, romaine lettuce, and spinach
Lycopene: present in tomatoes and tomato products (especially those exposed to heat), guava, papaya, pink grapefruit, and watermelon

GLUCOSINOLATES This group may stimulate the production of anticancer enzymes, thereby increasing the body's natural ability to ward off cancer. They can also make estrogen less effective, possibly reducing the risk of breast cancer.

Indoles: present in bok choy, broccoli, Brussels sprouts, cauliflower, collard greens, and kale

Sulforaphane: present in broccoli

PHYTOESTROGENS These plant substances have a mild estrogenic effect and are currently being studied for their ability to decrease the cancer-promoting effects of hormones in hormone-sensitive cancers.

Isoflavones (daidzein, genistein): present in soy products

Lignans: present in flaxseed, soybeans, and whole grains

PLANT POLYPHENOLS AND FLAVONOIDS These substances have several functions. They act as antioxidants in the body and may decrease inflammation and the growth of tumor cells. They also decrease clot formation. More than 4,000 flavonoids have already been identified.

Phenolic acids

  Curcumin: present in turmeric

  Ellagic acid: present in cranberries, raspberries, and strawberries

Flavonoids

  Anthocyanins: present in blueberries, cherries, and red grapes

  Catechins: present in apples and tea

  Kaempferol: present in endive, grapefruit, leeks, radishes, and tea

  Quercetin: present in apples, broccoli, onions, oranges, and tea

  Resveratrol: present in purple grape juice and red grapes

  Silymarin: present in artichokes

  Tangeretin: present in citrus peel

PLANT STEROLS This group reduces cancer cell proliferation. Plant sterols may also help lower cholesterol levels.

Saponins: present in legumes

PROTEASE INHIBITORS This group slows tumor growth by decreasing enzyme production in cancer cells. Protease inhibitors are present in grains, legumes, seeds, and soy products.

TERPENES This group slows tumor progression and can detoxify cancer promoters.

Carnosol: present in rosemary and sage

Gingerol: present in ginger

Limonene: present in lemon peel

Perillyl alcohol: present in cherries

How to Find Reliable Nutrition Information

Nutrition misinformation is rampant. When separating fact from fiction with regard to diet and the risk of cancer and other diseases, look for a preponderance of research. One or two studies reported on the morning news do not provide the data needed to make dietary changes. Make sure the information is science based and that the source is reliable.

Before accepting nutrition information published in print or on the Internet as factual, ask these questions:

- Does the web site or publication state clearly who is responsible for the information?
- Is there an editorial board? What are the authors' credentials?
- Does the web site or publication have sponsorships and advertisers, or is it supported by private funding?
- Does the web site or publication sell the products that it promotes?
- Is the information current?
- Is the information based on scientific research and expert consensus or is it based on personal opinion?

In general, look for web sites and publications that are produced by the government (web sites ending in .gov) or by educational institutions (web sites ending in .edu). For information provided by non-profit organizations (web sites ending in .org), be sure to check the source of funding, whether by sponsorships or by private funding; this can help you determine what the organization's biases might be. Some web sites that are maintained privately (web sites ending in .com) also have reliable and reputable affiliations.

The following is a list of reputable resources that can familiarize you with current information and research in the areas of diet, nutrition, and food safety, and can help you make smart food choices.

NEWSLETTERS AND MAGAZINES

American Institute for Cancer Research Newsletter

Subscription address: *American Institute for Cancer Research Newsletter,* American Institute for Cancer Research, 1759 R Street, NW, Washington, DC 20009. Tel: 1-800-843-8114. Web: http://www.aicr.org. This free quarterly newsletter contains practical information about reducing cancer risk. It includes recipes. Selected articles from the newsletter are on the American Institute for Cancer Research (AICR) web site.

Environmental Nutrition

Subscription address: *Environmental Nutrition,* P.O. Box 420234, Palm Coast, FL 32142-0234. Tel: 1-800-829-5384. Web: http://www.environmentalnutrition .com. Food and nutrition news are translated into practical guidelines in this monthly newsletter.

FDA Consumer

Subscription address: *FDA Consumer,* Superintendent of Documents, P.O. Box 371954, Pittsburgh, PA 15250. Tel: 1-202-512-1800. Web: http://www.fda.gov/fdac. This magazine, produced by the U.S. Food and Drug Administration (FDA), contains information about food safety and nutrition. It is available free on the FDA web site or in print with a paid subscription.

Tufts University Health & Nutrition Letter

Subscription address: *Tufts University Health & Nutrition Letter,* P.O. Box 420235, Palm Coast, FL 32142-0235. Tel: 1-800-274-7581. Web: http://www.healthletter .tufts.edu. Food and nutrition news is translated into practical guidelines.

TELEPHONE HOTLINES

American Dietetic Association

1-800-366-1655. This association of registered dietitians maintains a Consumer Nutrition Information Line that offers direct access to objective, credible food and nutrition information. The Consumer Nutrition Information Line provides recorded messages with timely, practical nutrition information as well as referrals to registered dietitians. Messages are available 24 hours daily. Messages and accompanying Nutrition Fact Sheets (in English and Spanish) change monthly.

American Institute for Cancer Research

1-800-843-8114. Staffed by registered dietitians, the American Institute for Cancer Research hotline provides personal answers to a wide variety of nutrition and health questions, especially those relating to diet and cancer.

U.S. Department of Agriculture

1-888-674-6854. The U.S. Department of Agriculture's Meat and Poultry Hotline provides information on safe food handling, preparation of meat products, food storage, recall advisories, and labeling of meat and poultry products.

WEB SITES

American Dietetic Association

http://www.eatright.org. This web site provides helpful information for consumers under the Food & Nutrition Information category. The Find a Dietitian feature enables users to locate registered dietitians in their community.

American Institute for Cancer Research

http://www.aicr.org. This web site includes the latest research on diet and cancer, free publications to order or read online, recipes, and press information.

Food and Nutrition Information Center

http://www.nal.usda.gov/fnic. The National Agricultural Library's Food and Nutrition Information Center provides information and links to topics such as food composition and nutrients, vitamins and minerals, food allergies, food preservation, shopping, meal planning, and food labels.

Food Lover's Companion

http://eat.epicurious.com/dictionary/food. This dictionary from the Epicurious web site contains more than 4,000 food terms.

FoodSafety

http://www.foodsafety.gov. This web site is a gateway to government food safety information, maintained by the Food and Drug Administration. It contains information on safe food handling and food preparation, as well as product-specific information. It covers topics such as drinking water safety, eggs, dairy products, and refrigerated ready-to-eat products.

MEDLINEplus

http://www.medlineplus.gov. MEDLINEplus contains health information from the National Library of Medicine that is authoritative and up-to-date. The site has extensive information on more than 600 diseases and conditions, with links to the latest news and research, directories, dictionaries, and organizations. Search under topics such as Food Contamination/Poisoning, Food Safety, Nutrition, and Pesticides for recent research and news.

Nutrition.gov

http://www.nutrition.gov. Nutrition.gov is a federal resource that provides easy access to online federal government information on nutrition, healthy eating, physical activity, and food safety.

Tufts University Nutrition Navigator

http://www.navigator.tufts.edu. The Tufts University Nutrition Navigator is an online rating and review guide: Tufts nutritionists review nutrition sites. Site reviews are updated quarterly to ensure that ratings take into account the ever-changing Internet and nutrition research environments.

Nutritional Analysis

Each recipe in this cookbook has been analyzed by registered dietitians using Esha Food Processor software. Data are provided for calories, total fat, saturated fat, carbohydrates, protein, dietary fiber, and sodium.

All numbers have been rounded up or down to the closest gram (or to the closest milligram, in the case of sodium).

If a recipe gives an amount range for an ingredient, such as 5 to 6 cups of sliced apples, the nutritional analysis is for the smaller amount.

Herbs and spices are not included in the nutritional analysis, nor is any ingredient that is listed as "optional," "to taste," or as a garnish.

index

Acorn Squash Stuffed with Apricots and Cornbread, 41
Activity, physical, 287, 288
Alcohol, 286, 288, 289
Allium compounds, 289
Allspice, 283
Allyl sulfides, 3, 121, 283, 289
Almonds
  Couscous and Lamb Pilaf with Dried Fruits and Nuts, 159
  Date-Nut Drops, 258
  Spicy Toasted Almonds, 198
  Strawberry-Almond Chutney, 116
American Dietetic Association, 291
American Institute for Cancer Research (AICR)
  diet and health guidelines of, 289
  expert panel of WCRF and, 288
  founding of, 287
  hotline of, 291
  mission of, 287
  newsletter of, 291
  research of, 2–3, 287–89
  web site of, 291–92
Angel Food Cake, Chocolate, with Raspberries, 249
Angel Hair Pasta with Sesame-Peanut Sauce, 79
Anise seed, 283
Anthocyanins, 2, 290
Anthocyanosides, 127
Antioxidants
  importance of, 2, 287
  sources of, 37, 50, 73, 98, 117, 127, 138, 200, 209, 236, 272, 285, 289
Appetizers
  Broiled Asparagus with Sesame Sauce, 196

Bruschetta with Green Pea and Roasted Garlic Spread, 195
  Chickpea Dip with Cilantro, 201
  Curried Spinach Dip, 202
  Falafel-Style Chickpea Patties, 191
  Roasted Eggplant Spread, 199
  Roasted Red Pepper Hummus, 200
  role of, 190
  Southwestern Red Pepper Dip, 202
  Spicy Toasted Almonds, 198
  Spinach and Feta Dip, 200
  Spinach-Stuffed Mushrooms with Feta, 199
  Tabbouleh-Filled Cherry Tomatoes, 192
  White Bean and Sun-Dried Tomato Dip, 201
Apples, 276
  Apple and Leek Frittata, 180
  Apple Pie with Granola Topping, 247
  Apple-Spice Bread, 235
  Apple Vinaigrette with Fresh Herbs, 123
  Carrot and Apple Soup, 209
  Cranberry-Apple Lattice Pie, 244
  Cranberry Chutney, 118
  Curried Fruit Sauce, 111
  Curried Sweet Potato and Apple Pilaf, 71
  Green Lentil and Swiss Chard Soup, 210
  Grilled Fruit Kebabs, 260
  Honey-Roasted Parsnips with Sweet Potatoes and Apples, 33
  Mushrooms with Apple-Herb Stuffing, 23
  Red Cabbage with Apples, 22
  Rice Pudding with Pears and Apples, 256

Sweet Potato and Apple Stew with Turkey and Cranberries, 138
Apricots, 276–77
  Acorn Squash Stuffed with Apricots and Cornbread, 41
  Couscous and Lamb Pilaf with Dried Fruits and Nuts, 159
  Quinoa with Dried Cranberries, Apricots, and Pecans, 77
  Spiced Braised Lamb with Apricots and Carrots, 105
Artichokes, 271
Arugula, 271
  Arugula Salad with Radicchio and Blue Cheese, 52
Asian-Style Dressing with Scallions, 123
Asian-Style Peanut Sauce, 110
Asian-Style Salmon with Sautéed Carrots and Leeks, 90
Asian-Style Stir-Fried Vegetables, 17
Asparagus, 19, 196, 271
  Broiled Asparagus with Sesame Sauce, 196
  Orange and Sesame Stir-Fry with Bow Tie Pasta, 152
  Roasted Asparagus with Garlic, 19
  Shrimp Curry with Asparagus and Snap Peas, 94
Avocados, 271
  Layered Black Bean and Spinach Salad, 175
  Southwestern Vegetable Frittata with Avocado and Salsa, 181

Baked Fish with Tomatoes, Spinach, and Olives, 88
Baking, 261
Balsamic Glaze, Brussels Sprouts with, 21

Bananas, 277
  Banana-Oatmeal Cookies, 257
  Banana-Orange Bran Muffins with
    Pecans, 234
  Curried Fruit Sauce, 111
  Grilled Fruit Kebabs, 260
Barley, 58, 67, 73, 279
  Bean and Split Pea Chowder with
    Chicken, 218
  Butternut Squash and Barley
    Casserole with Turkey, 131
  Lemon Barley, 73
  Mushroom and Barley Soup, 215
  Southwestern Black Bean Salad
    with Barley, 58
Basil, 283
Bay leaves, 283
Beans
  Bean and Split Pea Chowder with
    Chicken, 218
  Bean, Corn, and Pepper Salad with
    Chicken, 169
  Black Bean Soup with Onion and
    Cilantro, 217
  Black-Eyed Pea, Corn, and Spinach
    Salad, 60
  Broccoli, White Bean, and Roasted
    Garlic Purée, 20
  Chili Burgers, 102
  Citrus-Braised Tofu with
    Vegetables, 151
  Curried Cauliflower with Chickpeas
    and Green Peas, 26
  dried, 280–81
  Falafel-Style Chickpea Patties, 191
  Greek-Style Potato and Green Bean
    Casserole with Lamb, 134
  Green Beans with Tomatoes and
    Herbs, 34
  Green Peppers Stuffed with Rice,
    Beans, and Feta, 132
  Layered Black Bean and Spinach
    Salad, 175
  New American Beef Stew, 137
  nutritional value of, 184, 217, 280
  Pinto Bean Soup, 217
  Roasted Red Pepper Hummus, 200
  Salade Niçoise, 171
  Shrimp with Grapefruit and Black
    Bean Salsa, 53

Southwestern Black Bean Salad
  with Barley, 58
Southwestern Vegetable Frittata
  with Avocado and Salsa, 181
Spicy Chili with Ground Beef over
  Spaghetti, 183
standard serving size for, 9
Three-Bean Chili with Corn and
  Turkey, 184
Three-Bean Salad with Cilantro-
  Chile Dressing, 61
varieties of, 281–82
Vegetable Chili, 185
White Bean and Sun-Dried Tomato
  Dip, 201
White Bean and Tomato Salad with
  Parsley, 60
Bean sprouts
  Sesame-Ginger Frittata with
    Broccoli and Shrimp, 178
  Sweet and Sour Mixed Vegetables
    with Pork, 157
Beef
  Chili Burgers, 102
  ground, 268, 270
  New American Beef Stew, 137
  Orange and Sesame Stir-Fry with
    Bow Tie Pasta, 152
  Spicy Chili with Ground Beef over
    Spaghetti, 183
  Spicy Tomato-Pepper Pot Roast, 106
Beets, 271–72
  peeling, 19
  Roasted Beets with Dill Dressing, 19
Bell peppers, 37, 274
  Asian-Style Stir-Fried Vegetables, 17
  Bean, Corn, and Pepper Salad with
    Chicken, 169
  Brazilian-Style Seafood Stew, 140
  Bulgur Pilaf with Red Peppers and
    Herbs, 74
  Classic Ratatouille, 46
  Easy Gazpacho, 220
  Five-Pepper Salsa, 114
  Green Peppers Stuffed with Rice,
    Beans, and Feta, 132
  Grilled Fresh Vegetables with
    Dijon-Herb Sauce, 44
  Kasha Pilaf with Squash and
    Chicken, 163

Layered Black Bean and Spinach
  Salad, 175
Mushroom-Pepper Gumbo, 146
Papaya, Red Pepper, and Pecan
  Salad with Chicken, 166
Potato, Pepper, and Cherry Tomato
  Frittata, 177
Quinoa Pilaf with Peas and Sage, 77
Red Pepper, Tomato, and Chicken
  Pilaf, 160
Roasted Red Pepper and Corn Soup,
  206
Roasted Red Pepper Hummus, 200
Roasted Red Pepper Sauce, 108
Snow Pea and Carrot Pilaf, 68
Southwestern Black Bean Salad
  with Barley, 58
Southwestern Red Pepper Dip, 202
Southwestern Vegetable Frittata
  with Avocado and Salsa, 181
Spicy Tomato-Pepper Pot Roast, 106
Spinach and Orange Salad with
  Shrimp, 172
Spinach Lasagna with Red Pepper
  Sauce, 135
Sweet Potato and Pear Stir-Fry with
  Chicken and Chile Sauce, 155
Sweet Potato Chili with Peanuts,
  186
Three-Pepper Tofu Stir-Fry, 153
Tilapia with Sweet Peppers, 93
Tricolored Peppers with Fresh
  Herbs, 37
Vegetable Chili, 185
Whole Wheat Pasta with Zucchini,
  Mushrooms, and Basil, 83
Zucchini and Portobello Stir-Fry
  with Chicken, 156
Beta-carotene, 206, 209, 212, 236, 239,
  284, 289
Bisque, Fresh Corn, 205
Black beans, 281
  Bean, Corn, and Pepper Salad with
    Chicken, 169
  Black Bean Soup with Onion and
    Cilantro, 217
  Layered Black Bean and Spinach
    Salad, 175
  Shrimp with Grapefruit and Black
    Bean Salsa, 53

Southwestern Black Bean Salad with Barley, 58

Southwestern Vegetable Frittata with Avocado and Salsa, 181

Three-Bean Salad with Cilantro-Chile Dressing, 61

Vegetable Chili, 185

Black-eyed peas, 281

Black-Eyed Pea, Corn, and Spinach Salad, 60

Blanching, 261–62

Blueberries, 50, 277

Fruit and Nut Salad with Pork, 165

Mixed Greens with Blueberries and Feta, 50

Boiling, 262

Bok choy, 272

Braised Collard Greens with Garlic and Shallots, 30

Braised Escarole with Garlic, 29

Braised Kohlrabi, 26

Braising, 262

Bran Muffins, Banana-Orange, with Pecans, 234

Brazilian-Style Seafood Stew, 140

Breads. *See also* Muffins; Stuffing

Apple-Spice Bread, 235

Bruschetta with Green Pea and Roasted Garlic Spread, 195

Carrot-Raisin Bread, 239

Cranberry-Pumpkin Bread with Flaxseed, 236

defrosting, 270

freezing, 269

Gingerbread, 253

Heirloom Whole Wheat Bread, 228

kneading, 227

making, 224

Raisin Brown Bread, 238

Scottish Crackers, 240

store-bought, 224

types of, 224–25

Whole Wheat Bread with Herbs, 226

Whole Wheat Bread with Onions, 227

Broccoli, 148, 272

blanching, 261

Broccoli and Potato Soup with Parmesan, 212

Broccoli and Straw Mushroom Stir-Fry with Shrimp, 148

Broccoli, Cherry Tomato, and Watercress Salad, 54

Broccoli, White Bean, and Roasted Garlic Purée, 20

Broccoli with Scallion Dressing and Hazelnuts, 20

microwaving, 263

Sesame-Ginger Frittata with Broccoli and Shrimp, 178

Sweet and Sour Mixed Vegetables with Pork, 157

Vegetable and Rice Soup, 209

Broiled Asparagus with Sesame Sauce, 196

Broiling, 262

Brown Rice with Scallions and Fresh Herbs, 72

Bruschetta with Green Pea and Roasted Garlic Spread, 195

Brussels sprouts, 21, 22, 50, 272

Brussels Sprouts Salad with Garlic-Lemon Dressing, 50

Brussels Sprouts with Balsamic Glaze, 21

Brussels Sprouts with Shallots and Nutmeg, 22

buying, 14

Buckwheat. *See* Kasha

Bulgur, 67, 279–80

Bulgur Pilaf with Red Peppers and Herbs, 74

Tabbouleh-Filled Cherry Tomatoes, 192

Burgers, Chili, 102

Butternut squash, 214

Butternut Squash and Barley Casserole with Turkey, 131

Butternut Squash, Tomato, and Watercress Soup, 214

New England–Style Chowder, 219

Cabbage, 272

Cabbage and Carrot Slaw with Roasted Peanuts, 57

Red Cabbage with Apples, 22

Cakes

Chocolate Angel Food Cake with Raspberries, 249

defrosting, 270

freezing, 269

Gingerbread, 253

Cancer

genetic theories of, 286

geographic variation in, 286

prevention of, 2–3, 287–90

role of diet and lifestyle in, 2–3, 286–89

Cantaloupes, 278

Chilled Cantaloupe Soup with Mint, 223

Capsaicin, 117, 283

Capsanthin, 284

Caraway seeds, 283

Carbohydrates, 8

Carcinogens, 86, 90, 92, 107, 263

Cardamom, 283

Carnosol, 120, 121, 285, 290

Carotenoids, 2, 209, 214, 215, 289

Carrots, 54, 272

Asian-Style Salmon with Sautéed Carrots and Leeks, 90

Asian-Style Stir-Fried Vegetables, 17

Black-Eyed Pea, Corn, and Spinach Salad, 60

Cabbage and Carrot Slaw with Roasted Peanuts, 57

Carrot and Apple Soup, 209

Carrot-Raisin Bread, 239

Chunky Tomato-Vegetable Sauce, 109

Cilantro Sauce, 113

Gingered Carrots with Golden Raisins and Lemon, 25

Grilled Fresh Vegetables with Dijon-Herb Sauce, 44

Jicama and Orange Salad with Mint, 62

Mushroom and Barley Soup, 215

New American Beef Stew, 137

Snow Pea and Carrot Pilaf, 68

Spiced Braised Lamb with Apricots and Carrots, 105

Sweet and Spicy Carrot Salad with Pine Nuts, 54

Sweet Potato Chili with Peanuts, 186

Casseroles

Butternut Squash and Barley Casserole with Turkey, 131

Casseroles (continued)
cooking temperature for, 268
freezing, 269
Greek-Style Potato and Green Bean
Casserole with Lamb, 134
Green Peppers Stuffed with Rice,
Beans, and Feta, 132
Penne with Eggplant, Tomatoes,
and Tuna, 127
Portobello Mushroom Jambalaya
with Chicken, 128
preparing, 126
refrigerating, 270
Spinach Lasagna with Red Pepper
Sauce, 135
Catechins, 290
Cauliflower, 26, 272
Curried Cauliflower with Chickpeas
and Green Peas, 26
preparing, 15
Vegetable and Rice Soup, 209
Cayenne, 285
Celery, 272
Celery seed, 283
Cereal, standard serving size for, 9
Cheese
Arugula Salad with Radicchio and
Blue Cheese, 52
Butternut Squash and Barley
Casserole with Turkey, 131
Greek-Style Scallops, 97
Green Peppers Stuffed with Rice,
Beans, and Feta, 132
Layered Black Bean and Spinach
Salad, 175
Mixed Greens with Blueberries and
Feta, 50
Pear Salad with Ricotta Cheese and
Toasted Pistachios, 65
Southwestern Red Pepper Dip, 202
Spinach and Feta Dip, 200
Spinach Lasagna with Red Pepper
Sauce, 135
Spinach-Stuffed Mushrooms with
Feta, 199
standard serving size for, 9
Whole Corn and Green Chile
Muffins, 231
Cherries, 277
Chervil, 283

Chestnuts, 211
Chestnut and Dried Fruit Stuffing, 85
Roasted Chestnut Soup, 211
Chicken
Bean and Split Pea Chowder with
Chicken, 218
Bean, Corn, and Pepper Salad with
Chicken, 169
breasts, poaching, 264
Chicken with Tomatoes, Honey,
and Cinnamon, 100
Cinnamon and Raisin Couscous
with Chicken, 139
cooking temperature for, 268
Corn and Quinoa Salad with
Chicken, 170
Cranberry Chicken, 98
freezing, 269
Kasha Pilaf with Squash and
Chicken, 163
Orange and Sesame Stir-Fry with
Bow Tie Pasta, 152
Papaya, Red Pepper, and Pecan
Salad with Chicken, 166
Portobello Mushroom Jambalaya
with Chicken, 128
Red Pepper, Tomato, and Chicken
Pilaf, 160
refrigerating, 270
Sweet Potato and Pear Stir-Fry with
Chicken and Chile Sauce, 155
Zucchini and Portobello Stir-Fry
with Chicken, 156
Chickpeas, 281
Chickpea Dip with Cilantro, 201
Curried Cauliflower with Chickpeas
and Green Peas, 26
Falafel-Style Chickpea Patties, 191
Roasted Red Pepper Hummus, 200
Three-Bean Salad with Cilantro-
Chile Dressing, 61
Chiles, 274
Fettuccine with Figs and Chiles, 80
Five-Pepper Salsa, 114
Southwestern Vegetable Frittata
with Avocado and Salsa, 181
Spicy Chili with Ground Beef over
Spaghetti, 183
Sweet Potato Chili with Peanuts, 186
Vegetable Chili, 185

Whole Corn and Green Chile
Muffins, 231
Chili powder, 283
Chilis
Chili Burgers, 102
history of, 182
with meat vs. meatless, 182
Spicy Chili with Ground Beef over
Spaghetti, 183
Sweet Potato Chili with Peanuts, 186
Three-Bean Chili with Corn and
Turkey, 184
Vegetable Chili, 185
Chilled Cantaloupe Soup with Mint,
223
Chilled Strawberry Soup, 223
Chives, 283
Chocolate
Chocolate Angel Food Cake with
Raspberries, 249
Meringue Tartlets with
Strawberries and Shaved
Chocolate, 254
Chowders
Bean and Split Pea Chowder with
Chicken, 218
New England–Style Chowder, 219
Chunky Tomato-Vegetable Sauce, 109
Chutneys
Cranberry Chutney, 118
Strawberry-Almond Chutney, 116
Sweet Curried Tomato Chutney, 117
Cider-Glazed Sweet Potatoes with
Cranberries, 42
Cilantro, 113, 283
Chickpea Dip with Cilantro, 201
Cilantro Sauce, 113
Cinnamon, 283
Cinnamon and Raisin Couscous
with Chicken, 139
Citrus-Braised Tofu with Vegetables,
151
Clams
New England–Style Chowder, 219
Classic Ratatouille, 46
Cloves, 283
Cobbler, Nectarine and Raspberry,
250
Coconut milk
Brazilian-Style Seafood Stew, 140

Curried Cauliflower with Chickpeas
and Green Peas, 26
Collard greens, 30, 273
Braised Collard Greens with Garlic
and Shallots, 30
Color, importance of, 164
Cookies
Banana-Oatmeal Cookies, 257
Date-Nut Drops, 258
Date-Walnut Bars, 260
Maple-Fig Bars, 259
Cooking methods, 261–65
Cooking temperatures, 268
Coriander seed, 283
Coriandrol, 113, 283
Corn, 273
Bean, Corn, and Pepper Salad with
Chicken, 169
Black-Eyed Pea, Corn, and Spinach
Salad, 60
Corn and Quinoa Salad with
Chicken, 170
Fresh Corn Bisque, 205
Green Peppers Stuffed with Rice,
Beans, and Feta, 132
Kale with Sweet Corn, 29
New England–Style Chowder, 219
Pineapple, Corn, and Mango Salsa,
114
Roasted Red Pepper and Corn Soup,
206
Southwestern Black Bean Salad
with Barley, 58
Three-Bean Chili with Corn and
Turkey, 184
Three-Bean Salad with Cilantro-
Chile Dressing, 61
Vegetable Chili, 185
Whole Corn and Green Chile
Muffins, 231
Cornbread, Acorn Squash Stuffed
with Apricots and, 41
Cornish Hens with Orange Sauce, 100
Couscous, 159, 280
Cinnamon and Raisin Couscous
with Chicken, 139
Couscous and Lamb Pilaf with
Dried Fruits and Nuts, 159
Crackers, Scottish, 240
Cranberries, 98, 244, 277

Cider-Glazed Sweet Potatoes with
Cranberries, 42
Cranberry-Apple Lattice Pie, 244
Cranberry Chicken, 98
Cranberry Chutney, 118
Cranberry-Pumpkin Bread with
Flaxseed, 236
Quinoa with Dried Cranberries,
Apricots, and Pecans, 77
Sweet Potato and Apple Stew with
Turkey and Cranberries, 138
Whole Wheat Stuffing with
Cranberries and Walnuts, 84
Crisp, Pear, 248
Cryptoxanthin, 250
Cucumbers, 273
Cucumber-Yogurt Sauce with Dill,
109
Easy Gazpacho, 220
Cumin, 283
Cuminaldehyde, 283
Curcumin, 117, 285, 290
Curried Cauliflower with Chickpeas
and Green Peas, 26
Curried Fruit Sauce, 111
Curried Spinach Dip, 202
Curried Sweet Potato and Apple
Pilaf, 71
Curry, Shrimp, with Asparagus and
Snap Peas, 94
Curry powder, 283–84

Daidzein, 290
Dates
Date-Nut Drops, 258
Date-Walnut Bars, 260
Walnut-Date Muffins with Rye, 232
Defrosting methods, 269–70
Deglazing, 264
Desserts
Apple Pie with Granola Topping, 247
Banana-Oatmeal Cookies, 257
Carrot-Raisin Bread, 239
Chocolate Angel Food Cake with
Raspberries, 249
Cranberry-Apple Lattice Pie, 244
Date-Nut Drops, 258
Date-Walnut Bars, 260
Fresh Plum Tart, 242
fruit as, 241

Gingerbread, 253
Grilled Fruit Kebabs, 260
Maple-Fig Bars, 259
Meringue Tartlets with
Strawberries and Shaved
Chocolate, 254
minimizing sugar in, 241
Nectarine and Raspberry Cobbler,
250
Pear Crisp, 248
Pumpkin Pie, 246
Rice Pudding with Pears and
Apples, 256
Diet guidelines, 10, 289
Dijon-Herb Dressing, 122
Dijon-Herb Sauce, 44
Dill, 284
Dips
Broccoli, White Bean, and Roasted
Garlic Purée, 20
Chickpea Dip with Cilantro, 201
Curried Spinach Dip, 202
Roasted Eggplant Spread, 199
Southwestern Red Pepper Dip, 202
Spinach and Feta Dip, 200
storing, 270
Tarragon-Mustard Sauce, 111
White Bean and Sun-Dried Tomato
Dip, 201

Easy Gazpacho, 220
Eggplant, 273
Classic Ratatouille, 46
Penne with Eggplant, Tomatoes,
and Tuna, 127
Roasted Eggplant Spread, 199
Eggs
Apple and Leek Frittata, 180
omelets vs. frittatas, 176
Potato, Pepper, and Cherry Tomato
Frittata, 177
Salade Niçoise, 171
Sesame-Ginger Frittata with
Broccoli and Shrimp, 178
Southwestern Vegetable Frittata
with Avocado and Salsa, 181
Ellagic acid, 116, 223, 250, 290
Entrée salads
Bean, Corn, and Pepper Salad with
Chicken, 169

Entrée salads (*continued*)
Corn and Quinoa Salad with Chicken, 170
Fruit and Nut Salad with Pork, 165
Layered Black Bean and Spinach Salad, 175
Papaya, Red Pepper, and Pecan Salad with Chicken, 166
preparing, 164
Salade Niçoise, 171
Spinach and Orange Salad with Shrimp, 172
Environmental Nutrition, 291
Escarole, 29, 273
Braised Escarole with Garlic, 29
Eugenol, 283, 284

Falafel-Style Chickpea Patties, 191
Fat, saturated, 3, 151
FDA Consumer, 291
Fennel, 273
Fennel seed, 284
Fettuccine
Fettuccine with Figs and Chiles, 80
Whole Wheat Fettuccine with Citrus Sauce, 82
Fiber, 280
Figs
Fettuccine with Figs and Chiles, 80
Maple-Fig Bars, 259
Filé powder, 146
Fish
Asian-Style Salmon with Sautéed Carrots and Leeks, 90
Baked Fish with Tomatoes, Spinach, and Olives, 88
Brazilian-Style Seafood Stew, 140
cooking methods for, 86–87
freezing, 269
Grilled Ginger Tuna, 92
omega-3 fats in, 86
overconsumption of, 1, 86
Penne with Eggplant, Tomatoes, and Tuna, 127
portion size for, 1, 3, 9, 86
Salade Niçoise, 171
Steamed Fish with Black Bean and Garlic Sauce, 89
Tilapia with Sweet Peppers, 93
Fish sauce, 155

Five-Pepper Salsa, 114
Five-spice powder, 90, 284
Flavones, 114
Flavonoids, 2, 138, 215, 244, 283, 290
Flaxseed, 236
Cranberry-Pumpkin Bread with Flaxseed, 236
Flaxseed-Raisin Muffins, 232
Flour
refined vs. whole wheat, 226
rye, 232
Food and Nutrition Information Center, 292
Food Lover's Companion, 292
Food safety, 267–70, 292
FoodSafety (web site), 292
Fourteen-Vegetable Stew with Pork, 145
Freezing guidelines, 269
Fresh Corn Bisque, 205
Fresh Plum Tart, 242
Frittatas
Apple and Leek Frittata, 180
Potato, Pepper, and Cherry Tomato Frittata, 177
preparing, 176
Sesame-Ginger Frittata with Broccoli and Shrimp, 178
Southwestern Vegetable Frittata with Avocado and Salsa, 181
Fruits. *See also individual fruits*
Chestnut and Dried Fruit Stuffing, 85
Couscous and Lamb Pilaf with Dried Fruits and Nuts, 159
Curried Fruit Sauce, 111
as dessert, 241
Fruit and Nut Salad with Pork, 165
Grilled Fruit Kebabs, 260
health benefits of, 2–3, 288, 289
listing of, 276–79
Orange Rice Pilaf with Dried Fruit, 72
standard serving size for, 9

Garlic, 121, 284
Bruschetta with Green Pea and Roasted Garlic Spread, 195
Herb-Garlic Marinade, 121
Roasted Garlic and Shallot Sauce, 113
Gazpacho, Easy, 220

Genistein, 290
Ginger, 284
Gingerbread, 253
Gingered Carrots with Golden Raisins and Lemon, 25
Steamed Greens with Ginger and Water Chestnuts, 30
Gingerol, 284, 290
Glucosinolates, 290
Glutathione, 196
Grains. *See also* Breads; Pasta; *individual grains*
Mixed Grains with Garlic and Scallions, 73
nutritional value of, 66, 279
storing, 279
varieties of, 66–67, 279–80
whole vs. refined, 279
Grapefruit, Shrimp with Black Bean Salsa and, 53
Grapes, 277
Greek-Style Potato and Green Bean Casserole with Lamb, 134
Greek-Style Scallops, 97
Green beans, 273
Citrus-Braised Tofu with Vegetables, 151
Greek-Style Potato and Green Bean Casserole with Lamb, 134
Green Beans with Tomatoes and Herbs, 34
New American Beef Stew, 137
Salade Niçoise, 171
Green Lentil and Swiss Chard Soup, 210
Green Peppers Stuffed with Rice, Beans, and Feta, 132
Greens. *See also individual greens*
buying, 48
Mixed Greens with Blueberries and Feta, 50
for salads, 47–48, 164
Steamed Greens with Ginger and Water Chestnuts, 30
storing, 48
washing, 48
Grilled Fresh Vegetables with Dijon-Herb Sauce, 44
Grilled Fruit Kebabs, 260
Grilled Ginger Tuna, 92

Grilled Portobello Mushrooms with Garlic and Herbs, 25
Grilling, 262–63
Gumbo, Mushroom-Pepper, 146

Heirloom Whole Wheat Bread, 228
Herbs. *See also individual herbs*
  by ethnic cuisine, 282
  fresh vs. dried, 49, 267, 282
  herbes de Provence, 42, 284
  Herb-Garlic Marinade, 121
  listing of, 283–85
  phytochemicals in, 282
  storing, 282
  substitutions for, 267
  Whole Wheat Bread with Herbs, 226
Hoisin Vinaigrette, 121
Honeydew melons, 278
Honey-Roasted Parsnips with Sweet Potatoes and Apples, 33
Hotlines, 291
Hummus, Roasted Red Pepper, 200

Indoles, 290
Isoflavones, 290

Jambalaya, Portobello Mushroom, with Chicken, 128
Jicama, 62, 273
  Bean, Corn, and Pepper Salad with Chicken, 169
  Jicama and Orange Salad with Mint, 62

Kaempferol, 290
Kale, 29, 273
  Curried Sweet Potato and Apple Pilaf, 71
  Kale with Sweet Corn, 29
  New American Beef Stew, 137
Kasha, 67, 74, 163, 280
  Kasha Pilaf with Squash and Chicken, 163
  Quick Kasha Pilaf, 74
Kebabs, Grilled Fruit, 260
Kidney beans, 282
  Spicy Chili with Ground Beef over Spaghetti, 183
  Three-Bean Salad with Cilantro-Chile Dressing, 61

Vegetable Chili, 185
Kiwi, 277
  Fruit and Nut Salad with Pork, 165
Kneading, 227
Kohlrabi, 26, 273
  Braised Kohlrabi, 26

Lamb
  Couscous and Lamb Pilaf with Dried Fruits and Nuts, 159
  Greek-Style Potato and Green Bean Casserole with Lamb, 134
  Spiced Braised Lamb with Apricots and Carrots, 105
Lasagna, Spinach, with Red Pepper Sauce, 135
Layered Black Bean and Spinach Salad, 175
Leeks, 274
  Apple and Leek Frittata, 180
  Asian-Style Salmon with Sautéed Carrots and Leeks, 90
  cleaning, 274
  Mushrooms with Apple-Herb Stuffing, 23
  New American Beef Stew, 137
Lemons, 277
  Lemon Barley, 73
Lentils, 281
  Bean and Split Pea Chowder with Chicken, 218
  Green Lentil and Swiss Chard Soup, 210
  Lentil and Potato Stew with Veal and Rosemary, 143
Lettuce
  Arugula Salad with Radicchio and Blue Cheese, 52
  iceberg, 47–48
  Papaya, Red Pepper, and Pecan Salad with Chicken, 166
  Pear Salad with Ricotta Cheese and Toasted Pistachios, 65
  Salade Niçoise, 171
  Spinach, Romaine, and Strawberries with Balsamic Vinaigrette, 52
Lignans, 236, 290
Limes, 122, 277
  Lime and Ginger Pork Loin, 102

Lime-Peanut Dressing, 122
Limonene, 120, 122, 283, 284, 285, 290
Lutein, 37, 200, 289
Luteolin, 121, 284, 285
Lycopene, 2, 3, 114, 127, 289

Mace, 284
Magazines, 291
Mangoes, 114, 277–78
  Pineapple, Corn, and Mango Salsa, 114
Maple-Fig Bars, 259
Marinades
  advantages of, 86, 90, 92, 107
  Herb-Garlic Marinade, 121
  Papaya-Lime Marinade, 118
  Rosemary-Orange Marinade and Sauce, 120
  Yogurt Marinade with Ginger and Coriander, 120
Marjoram, 284
Meat. *See also* Beef; Lamb; Pork
  cancer risk and, 3, 289
  cooking methods for, 86–87
  freezing, 269
  Lentil and Potato Stew with Veal and Rosemary, 143
  marinating, 86
  overconsumption of, 1, 86
  popularity of, 86
  portion size for, 1, 3, 9, 86
  refrigerating, 270
MEDLINEplus, 292
Melons, 278
  Chilled Cantaloupe Soup with Mint, 223
Meringue Tartlets with Strawberries and Shaved Chocolate, 254
Microwaving, 263
Millet, 67, 280
  Millet with Sautéed Mushrooms and Pumpkin Seeds, 78
  Mixed Grains with Garlic and Scallions, 73
Mint, 284
Mirin, 155
Mixed Grains with Garlic and Scallions, 73
Mixed Greens with Blueberries and Feta, 50

Monoterpenes, 283, 285
Muffins
    Banana-Orange Bran Muffins with
        Pecans, 234
    defrosting, 270
    Flaxseed-Raisin Muffins, 232
    freezing, 269
    preparing, 224
    store-bought, 224
    types of, 224–25
    Walnut-Date Muffins with Rye, 232
    Whole Corn and Green Chile
        Muffins, 231
Mushrooms, 23, 274
    Broccoli and Straw Mushroom Stir-
        Fry with Shrimp, 148
    Chunky Tomato-Vegetable Sauce,
        109
    cleaning, 274
    Greek-Style Scallops, 97
    Grilled Fresh Vegetables with
        Dijon-Herb Sauce, 44
    Grilled Portobello Mushrooms with
        Garlic and Herbs, 25
    Millet with Sautéed Mushrooms
        and Pumpkin Seeds, 78
    Mushroom and Barley Soup, 215
    Mushroom-Pepper Gumbo, 146
    Mushroom Sauce, 108
    Mushrooms with Apple-Herb
        Stuffing, 23
    Orange and Sesame Stir-Fry with
        Bow Tie Pasta, 152
    Portobello Mushroom Jambalaya
        with Chicken, 128
    Potato, Pepper, and Cherry Tomato
        Frittata, 177
    Spinach-Stuffed Mushrooms with
        Feta, 199
    Whole Wheat Pasta with Zucchini,
        Mushrooms, and Basil, 83
    Zucchini and Portobello Stir-Fry
        with Chicken, 156
Mustard, 284
    Chinese-style, 90
    greens, 274
    Tarragon-Mustard Sauce, 111

National Agricultural Library, 292
Nectarines, 278

Grilled Fruit Kebabs, 260
    Nectarine and Raspberry Cobbler, 250
New American Beef Stew, 137
New American Plate Pie Crust, 243
New England–Style Chowder, 219
Newsletters, 291
Noodles. See Pasta
Nutmeg, 284
Nutritional analysis, 292
Nutrition.gov, 292
Nutrition information, sources of,
    290–92
Nuts. See also individual nuts
    Couscous and Lamb Pilaf with
        Dried Fruits and Nuts, 159
    Date-Nut Drops, 258
    Fruit and Nut Salad with Pork, 165
    nutritional value of, 198
    standard serving size for, 9, 198

Oats, 280
    Banana-Oatmeal Cookies, 257
    Carrot-Raisin Bread, 239
    Scottish Crackers, 240
Obesity
    cancer risk and, 287, 288, 289
    prevalence of, 7
    preventing, 2
Oils
    ratio of vinegar to, in dressings, 49
    types of, 48
Okra, 274
Olives
    blanching, 262
    Salade Niçoise, 171
Omega-3 fatty acids, 84, 86, 127, 235,
    248
One-pot meals. See also Casseroles;
    Chilis; Entrée salads; Frittatas;
    Pilafs; Stews; Stir-fries
    advantages of, 5–6, 125
    types of, 125
Onions, 274
    Black Bean Soup with Onion and
        Cilantro, 217
    Whole Wheat Bread with Onions,
        227
Oranges, 278
    Banana-Orange Bran Muffins with
        Pecans, 234

Cornish Hens with Orange Sauce,
    100
Cranberry Chutney, 118
Jicama and Orange Salad with
    Mint, 62
Orange and Sesame Stir-Fry with
    Bow Tie Pasta, 152
Orange-Honey Vinaigrette, 122
Orange Rice Pilaf with Dried Fruit, 72
Rosemary-Orange Marinade and
    Sauce, 120
Spinach and Orange Salad with
    Shrimp, 172
Strawberry-Almond Chutney, 116
Whole Wheat Fettuccine with
    Citrus Sauce, 82
Oregano, 284

Papayas, 278
    Papaya-Lime Marinade, 118
    Papaya, Red Pepper, and Pecan
        Salad with Chicken, 166
Paprika, 284
Parboiling, 261
Parsley, 284
Parsnips, 274
    Grilled Fresh Vegetables with
        Dijon-Herb Sauce, 44
    Honey-Roasted Parsnips with
        Sweet Potatoes and Apples, 33
Pasta. See also Couscous
    Angel Hair Pasta with Sesame-
        Peanut Sauce, 79
    Citrus-Braised Tofu with
        Vegetables, 151
    Fettuccine with Figs and Chiles, 80
    Orange and Sesame Stir-Fry with
        Bow Tie Pasta, 152
    Penne with Eggplant, Tomatoes,
        and Tuna, 127
    refrigerating, 270
    reheating, 270
    Spicy Chili with Ground Beef over
        Spaghetti, 183
    Spinach Lasagna with Red Pepper
        Sauce, 135
    standard serving size for, 9
    whole-grain vs. refined, 66, 79, 280
    Whole Wheat Fettuccine with
        Citrus Sauce, 82

Whole Wheat Pasta with Zucchini, Mushrooms, and Basil, 83
Peaches, 278
  Fruit and Nut Salad with Pork, 165
  Grilled Fruit Kebabs, 260
Peanuts and peanut butter
  Asian-Style Peanut Sauce, 110
  Cabbage and Carrot Slaw with Roasted Peanuts, 57
  Lime-Peanut Dressing, 122
  Sweet Potato Chili with Peanuts, 186
Pears, 278
  Grilled Fruit Kebabs, 260
  Pear Crisp, 248
  Pear Salad with Ricotta Cheese and Toasted Pistachios, 65
  Pear Sauce, 110
  Rice Pudding with Pears and Apples, 256
  Sweet Potato and Pear Stir-Fry with Chicken and Chile Sauce, 155
Peas, 281, 282. See also Snow peas and sugar snap peas
  Bean and Split Pea Chowder with Chicken, 218
  Bruschetta with Green Pea and Roasted Garlic Spread, 195
  Couscous and Lamb Pilaf with Dried Fruits and Nuts, 159
  Curried Cauliflower with Chickpeas and Green Peas, 26
  nutritional value of, 280
  Petite Peas with Garlic and Pimientos, 33
  Quinoa Pilaf with Peas and Sage, 77
  Red Pepper, Tomato, and Chicken Pilaf, 160
  Spiced Braised Lamb with Apricots and Carrots, 105
Pecans
  Banana-Orange Bran Muffins with Pecans, 234
  Papaya, Red Pepper, and Pecan Salad with Chicken, 166
  Quinoa with Dried Cranberries, Apricots, and Pecans, 77
Pectin, 235
Penne with Eggplant, Tomatoes, and Tuna, 127
Pepper (spice), 285

Peppers. See Bell peppers; Chiles
Perillyl alcohol, 249, 290
Petite Peas with Garlic and Pimientos, 33
Phenolic acids, 290
Phytochemicals. See also individual phytochemicals
  importance of, 2–3, 66, 287, 289
  interaction among, 3, 135
  maximizing number of, 14, 289
  sources of, 2–3, 86, 289–90
  types of, 114, 289–90
Phytoestrogens, 232, 290
Pies
  Apple Pie with Granola Topping, 247
  Cranberry-Apple Lattice Pie, 244
  freezing, 269
  New American Plate Pie Crust, 243
  Pumpkin Pie, 246
Pilafs
  Bulgur Pilaf with Red Peppers and Herbs, 74
  Couscous and Lamb Pilaf with Dried Fruits and Nuts, 159
  Curried Sweet Potato and Apple Pilaf, 71
  grains for, 158
  Kasha Pilaf with Squash and Chicken, 163
  Orange Rice Pilaf with Dried Fruit, 72
  Quick Kasha Pilaf, 74
  Quinoa Pilaf with Peas and Sage, 77
  Red Pepper, Tomato, and Chicken Pilaf, 160
  Snow Pea and Carrot Pilaf, 68
  traditional, 158
Pimientos, Petite Peas with Garlic and, 33
Pineapples
  Carrot-Raisin Bread, 239
  Fruit and Nut Salad with Pork, 165
  Grilled Fruit Kebabs, 260
  Pineapple and Pork Stew, 142
  Pineapple, Corn, and Mango Salsa, 114
  Sweet and Sour Mixed Vegetables with Pork, 157
  Three-Pepper Tofu Stir-Fry, 153
Pinto beans, 281

Green Peppers Stuffed with Rice, Beans, and Feta, 132
Pinto Bean Soup, 217
Three-Bean Salad with Cilantro-Chile Dressing, 61
Plums, 278
  Fresh Plum Tart, 242
  Grilled Fruit Kebabs, 260
Poaching, 263–64
Polyphenols, 290
Pork
  Fourteen-Vegetable Stew with Pork, 145
  Fruit and Nut Salad with Pork, 165
  Lime and Ginger Pork Loin, 102
  Pineapple and Pork Stew, 142
  Sweet and Sour Mixed Vegetables with Pork, 157
Portion sizes
  reducing, 8–9
  typical oversized, 1, 7, 8
  USDA standard servings vs., 8–10
Portobello Mushroom Jambalaya with Chicken, 128
Potatoes, 275. See also Sweet Potatoes
  baking, 261
  Broccoli and Potato Soup with Parmesan, 212
  Greek-Style Potato and Green Bean Casserole with Lamb, 134
  Lentil and Potato Stew with Veal and Rosemary, 143
  microwaving, 263
  New American Beef Stew, 137
  Potato and Watercress Soup with Shrimp, 212
  Potato, Pepper, and Cherry Tomato Frittata, 177
  Salade Niçoise, 171
  Two-Potato Salad with Spinach and Fresh Herb Dressing, 57
Pot Roast, Spicy Tomato-Pepper, 106
Poultry. See also Chicken; Turkey
  cooking methods for, 86–87
  cooking temperatures for, 268
  Cornish Hens with Orange Sauce, 100
  freezing, 269
  portion size for, 1, 3, 9, 86
  refrigerating, 270

Pressure cooking, 264
Procyanidins, 118
Protease inhibitors, 290
Prudhomme, Paul and Enola, 146
Pudding, Rice, with Pears and Apples, 256
Pumpkin
  Cranberry-Pumpkin Bread with Flaxseed, 236
  Pumpkin Pie, 246
  Sweet Potato and Pumpkin Purée, 43
Puréeing, 16
Purées
  Broccoli, White Bean, and Roasted Garlic Purée, 20
  Sweet Potato and Pumpkin Purée, 43

Quercetin, 3, 121, 235, 283, 284, 290
Quick Kasha Pilaf, 74
Quinoa, 67, 77, 280
  Corn and Quinoa Salad with Chicken, 170
  Mixed Grains with Garlic and Scallions, 73
  Quinoa Pilaf with Peas and Sage, 77
  Quinoa with Dried Cranberries, Apricots, and Pecans, 77

Radicchio, 275
  Arugula Salad with Radicchio and Blue Cheese, 52
Radishes, 275
Raisins
  Banana-Oatmeal Cookies, 257
  Carrot-Raisin Bread, 239
  Cinnamon and Raisin Couscous with Chicken, 139
  Couscous and Lamb Pilaf with Dried Fruits and Nuts, 159
  Cranberry-Apple Lattice Pie, 244
  Curried Sweet Potato and Apple Pilaf, 71
  Date-Nut Drops, 258
  Flaxseed-Raisin Muffins, 232
  Gingered Carrots with Golden Raisins and Lemon, 25
  Orange Rice Pilaf with Dried Fruit, 72
  Pear Crisp, 248
  Raisin Brown Bread, 238
  Strawberry-Almond Chutney, 116

Sweet and Spicy Carrot Salad with Pine Nuts, 54
  Sweet Curried Tomato Chutney, 117
Raspberries, 278–79
  Chocolate Angel Food Cake with Raspberries, 249
  Nectarine and Raspberry Cobbler, 250
Ratatouille, Classic, 46
Red Cabbage with Apples, 22
Red Pepper, Tomato, and Chicken Pilaf, 160
Refrigerator storage guidelines, 270
Resveratrol, 238, 290
Rice
  Bean, Corn, and Pepper Salad with Chicken, 169
  Brazilian-Style Seafood Stew, 140
  Broccoli and Straw Mushroom Stir-Fry with Shrimp, 148
  Brown Rice with Scallions and Fresh Herbs, 72
  Curried Sweet Potato and Apple Pilaf, 71
  Falafel-Style Chickpea Patties, 191
  Green Peppers Stuffed with Rice, Beans, and Feta, 132
  Mixed Grains with Garlic and Scallions, 73
  Mushroom-Pepper Gumbo, 146
  Orange Rice Pilaf with Dried Fruit, 72
  Pineapple and Pork Stew, 142
  Portobello Mushroom Jambalaya with Chicken, 128
  refrigerating, 270
  reheating, 270
  Rice Pudding with Pears and Apples, 256
  Snow Pea and Carrot Pilaf, 68
  standard serving size for, 9
  Sweet and Sour Mixed Vegetables with Pork, 157
  Sweet Potato and Pear Stir-Fry with Chicken and Chile Sauce, 155
  Three-Bean Chili with Corn and Turkey, 184
  Three-Pepper Tofu Stir-Fry, 153
  varieties of, 67, 279
  Vegetable and Rice Soup, 209

Zucchini and Portobello Stir-Fry with Chicken, 156
Roasted Asparagus with Garlic, 19
Roasted Beets with Dill Dressing, 19
Roasted Chestnut Soup, 211
Roasted Eggplant Spread, 199
Roasted Garlic and Shallot Sauce, 113
Roasted Red Pepper and Corn Soup, 206
Roasted Red Pepper Hummus, 200
Roasted Red Pepper Sauce, 108
Roasting, 261, 264
Rosemary, 285
  Rosemary-Orange Marinade and Sauce, 120
Rutabagas, 275
Rutin, 285
Rye flour, 232

Safety issues, 267–70, 292
Saffron, 285
Sage, 285
Salad dressings
  amount of, 49
  Apple Vinaigrette with Fresh Herbs, 123
  Asian-Style Dressing with Scallions, 123
  Dijon-Herb Dressing, 122
  Hoisin Vinaigrette, 121
  Lime-Peanut Dressing, 122
  oil-to-vinegar ratio in, 49
  Orange-Honey Vinaigrette, 122
  preparing, 48–49
  Rosemary-Orange Marinade and Sauce, 120
  store-bought, 48, 107
  storing, 270
Salads. See also Salad dressings
  Arugula Salad with Radicchio and Blue Cheese, 52
  Bean, Corn, and Pepper Salad with Chicken, 169
  Black-Eyed Pea, Corn, and Spinach Salad, 60
  Broccoli, Cherry Tomato, and Watercress Salad, 54
  Brussels Sprouts Salad with Garlic-Lemon Dressing, 50
  Cabbage and Carrot Slaw with

Roasted Peanuts, 57
choosing greens for, 47–48, 164
Corn and Quinoa Salad with
  Chicken, 170
entrée, 164
Fruit and Nut Salad with Pork, 165
garnishing, 48
Jicama and Orange Salad with
  Mint, 62
Layered Black Bean and Spinach
  Salad, 175
Mixed Greens with Blueberries and
  Feta, 50
Papaya, Red Pepper, and Pecan
  Salad with Chicken, 166
Pear Salad with Ricotta Cheese and
  Toasted Pistachios, 65
Salade Niçoise, 171
Shrimp with Grapefruit and Black
  Bean Salsa, 53
side, 47
Southwestern Black Bean Salad
  with Barley, 58
Spinach and Orange Salad with
  Shrimp, 172
Spinach, Romaine, and
  Strawberries with Balsamic
  Vinaigrette, 52
Sweet and Spicy Carrot Salad with
  Pine Nuts, 54
Three-Bean Salad with Cilantro-
  Chile Dressing, 61
Two-Potato Salad with Spinach and
  Fresh Herb Dressing, 57
White Bean and Tomato Salad with
  Parsley, 60
Salmon, Asian-Style, with Sautéed
  Carrots and Leeks, 90
Salsas
  Black Bean Salsa, 53
  Five-Pepper Salsa, 114
  Pineapple, Corn, and Mango Salsa,
    114
  store-bought, 107
Sandwiches
  Chili Burgers, 102
  Falafel-Style Chickpea Patties, 191
Saponins, 3, 170, 290
Sauces. See also Salsas
  Asian-Style Peanut Sauce, 110

Chunky Tomato-Vegetable Sauce,
  109
Cilantro Sauce, 113
Cucumber-Yogurt Sauce with Dill,
  109
Curried Fruit Sauce, 111
Dijon-Herb Sauce, 44
Mushroom Sauce, 108
Pear Sauce, 110
Roasted Garlic and Shallot Sauce, 113
Roasted Red Pepper Sauce, 108
Rosemary-Orange Marinade and
  Sauce, 120
Sesame Sauce, 196
Tarragon-Mustard Sauce, 111
Yogurt Marinade with Ginger and
  Coriander, 120
Sautéing, 264
Savory, 285
Scallions, 275
  Asian-Style Dressing with
    Scallions, 123
  Broccoli with Scallion Dressing and
    Hazelnuts, 20
  Brown Rice with Scallions and
    Fresh Herbs, 72
  Mixed Grains with Garlic and
    Scallions, 73
Scallops, Greek-Style, 97
Scientific research, 2–3, 286–89
Scottish Crackers, 240
Serving sizes, standard, 9. See also
  Portion sizes
Sesame and Garlic Spinach, 37
Sesame-Ginger Frittata with Broccoli
  and Shrimp, 178
Sesame Sauce, 196
Shallots, 30, 275
  Braised Collard Greens with Garlic
    and Shallots, 30
  Roasted Garlic and Shallot Sauce,
    113
Shrimp
  Brazilian-Style Seafood Stew, 140
  Broccoli and Straw Mushroom Stir-
    Fry with Shrimp, 148
  Potato and Watercress Soup with
    Shrimp, 212
  Sesame-Ginger Frittata with
    Broccoli and Shrimp, 178

Shrimp Curry with Asparagus and
  Snap Peas, 94
Shrimp with Grapefruit and Black
  Bean Salsa, 53
Spinach and Orange Salad with
  Shrimp, 172
Silymarin, 290
Simmering, 264
Slaw, Cabbage and Carrot, with
  Roasted Peanuts, 57
Snow peas and sugar snap peas
  Asian-Style Stir-Fried Vegetables, 17
  Shrimp Curry with Asparagus and
    Snap Peas, 94
  Snow Pea and Carrot Pilaf, 68
  Snow Peas with Cashews, 34
Soups
  Bean and Split Pea Chowder with
    Chicken, 218
  benefits of, 202
  Black Bean Soup with Onion and
    Cilantro, 217
  Broccoli and Potato Soup with
    Parmesan, 212
  Butternut Squash, Tomato, and
    Watercress Soup, 214
  canned, 202
  Carrot and Apple Soup, 209
  Chilled Cantaloupe Soup with
    Mint, 223
  Chilled Strawberry Soup, 223
  Easy Gazpacho, 220
  freezing, 269
  Fresh Corn Bisque, 205
  Green Lentil and Swiss Chard Soup,
    210
  Mushroom and Barley Soup, 215
  New England–Style Chowder, 219
  Pinto Bean Soup, 217
  Potato and Watercress Soup with
    Shrimp, 212
  preparing, 202
  refrigerating, 270
  Roasted Chestnut Soup, 211
  Roasted Red Pepper and Corn Soup,
    206
  Summer Squash Soup, 215
  Vegetable and Rice Soup, 209
Southwestern Black Bean Salad with
  Barley, 58

Southwestern Red Pepper Dip, 202
Southwestern Vegetable Frittata with
    Avocado and Salsa, 181
Soybeans, 282
Spaghetti, Spicy Chili with Ground
    Beef over, 183
Spaghetti Squash with Marinara
    Sauce, 38
Spiced Braised Lamb with Apricots
    and Carrots, 105
Spices. *See also individual spices*
    listing of, 283–85
    phytochemicals in, 282
    storing, 282
    substitutions for, 267
Spicy Chili with Ground Beef over
    Spaghetti, 183
Spicy Toasted Almonds, 198
Spicy Tomato-Pepper Pot Roast, 106
Spinach, 37, 275
    Baked Fish with Tomatoes,
        Spinach, and Olives, 88
    Black-Eyed Pea, Corn, and Spinach
        Salad, 60
    Curried Spinach Dip, 202
    Layered Black Bean and Spinach
        Salad, 175
    New England–Style Chowder, 219
    Sesame and Garlic Spinach, 37
    Spinach and Feta Dip, 200
    Spinach and Orange Salad with
        Shrimp, 172
    Spinach Lasagna with Red Pepper
        Sauce, 135
    Spinach, Romaine, and
        Strawberries with Balsamic
        Vinaigrette, 52
    Spinach-Stuffed Mushrooms with
        Feta, 199
    Steamed Greens with Ginger and
        Water Chestnuts, 30
    Sweet Potato and Pear Stir-Fry with
        Chicken and Chile Sauce, 155
    Two-Potato Salad with Spinach and
        Fresh Herb Dressing, 57
Spreads
    Broccoli, White Bean, and Roasted
        Garlic Purée, 20
    Green Pea and Roasted Garlic
        Spread, 195

Roasted Eggplant Spread, 199
Southwestern Red Pepper Dip, 202
White Bean and Sun-Dried Tomato
    Dip, 201
Squash, summer, 275
    Cinnamon and Raisin Couscous
        with Chicken, 139
    Classic Ratatouille, 46
    Grilled Fresh Vegetables with
        Dijon-Herb Sauce, 44
    Kasha Pilaf with Squash and
        Chicken, 163
    Summer Squash Soup, 215
    Whole Wheat Pasta with Zucchini,
        Mushrooms, and Basil, 83
    Zucchini and Portobello Stir-Fry
        with Chicken, 156
    Zucchini and Yellow Squash with
        Herbes de Provence, 42
Squash, winter, 275–76
    Acorn Squash Stuffed with
        Apricots and Cornbread, 41
    Butternut Squash and Barley
        Casserole with Turkey, 131
    Butternut Squash, Tomato, and
        Watercress Soup, 214
    New England–Style Chowder, 219
    Spaghetti Squash with Marinara
        Sauce, 38
Steamed Fish with Black Bean and
    Garlic Sauce, 89
Steamed Greens with Ginger and
    Water Chestnuts, 30
Steaming, 265
Sterols, 290
Stewing, 265
Stews
    Brazilian-Style Seafood Stew, 140
    Cinnamon and Raisin Couscous
        with Chicken, 139
    Classic Ratatouille, 46
    Fourteen-Vegetable Stew with Pork,
        145
    freezing, 269
    history of, 136
    Lentil and Potato Stew with Veal
        and Rosemary, 143
    Mushroom-Pepper Gumbo, 146
    New American Beef Stew, 137
    Pineapple and Pork Stew, 142

preparing, 136
refrigerating, 270
Sweet Potato and Apple Stew with
    Turkey and Cranberries, 138
Stir-fries
    Asian-Style Stir-Fried Vegetables, 17
    Broccoli and Straw Mushroom Stir-
        Fry with Shrimp, 148
    Citrus-Braised Tofu with
        Vegetables, 151
    Orange and Sesame Stir-Fry with
        Bow Tie Pasta, 152
    Sweet and Sour Mixed Vegetables
        with Pork, 157
    Sweet Potato and Pear Stir-Fry with
        Chicken and Chile Sauce, 155
    Three-Pepper Tofu Stir-Fry, 153
    tips for, 17, 147, 265
    Zucchini and Portobello Stir-Fry
        with Chicken, 156
Storage tips, 267–70
Strawberries, 116, 279
    Chilled Strawberry Soup, 223
    Fruit and Nut Salad with Pork, 165
    Meringue Tartlets with
        Strawberries and Shaved
        Chocolate, 254
    Spinach, Romaine, and
        Strawberries with Balsamic
        Vinaigrette, 52
    Strawberry-Almond Chutney, 116
Stuffing
    Chestnut and Dried Fruit Stuffing, 85
    cooking temperature for, 268
    Whole Wheat Stuffing with
        Cranberries and Walnuts, 84
Substitutions, 266–67
Sulforaphane, 54, 212, 290
Summer Squash Soup, 215
Sweet and Sour Mixed Vegetables
    with Pork, 157
Sweet and Spicy Carrot Salad with
    Pine Nuts, 54
Sweet Curried Tomato Chutney, 117
Sweet potatoes, 42, 276. *See also*
    Potatoes
    Cider-Glazed Sweet Potatoes with
        Cranberries, 42
    Curried Sweet Potato and Apple
        Pilaf, 71

Grilled Fresh Vegetables with Dijon-Herb Sauce, 44
Honey-Roasted Parsnips with Sweet Potatoes and Apples, 33
Sweet Potato and Apple Stew with Turkey and Cranberries, 138
Sweet Potato and Pear Stir-Fry with Chicken and Chile Sauce, 155
Sweet Potato and Pumpkin Purée, 43
Sweet Potato Chili with Peanuts, 186
Two-Potato Salad with Spinach and Fresh Herb Dressing, 57
Swiss chard, 276
    Green Lentil and Swiss Chard Soup, 210
    Steamed Greens with Ginger and Water Chestnuts, 30
Syringic acid, 200

Tabbouleh-Filled Cherry Tomatoes, 192
Tahini, 200
Tangeretin, 290
Tarragon, 101, 285
    Tarragon-Mustard Sauce, 111
    Tarragon Turkey Breast, 101
Tartar, cream of, 254
Tarts
    Fresh Plum Tart, 242
    Meringue Tartlets with Strawberries and Shaved Chocolate, 254
Telephone hotlines, 291
Terpenes, 290
Three-Bean Chili with Corn and Turkey, 184
Three-Bean Salad with Cilantro-Chile Dressing, 61
Three-Pepper Tofu Stir-Fry, 153
Thyme, 285
Tilapia
    Baked Fish with Tomatoes, Spinach, and Olives, 88
    Tilapia with Sweet Peppers, 93
Tobacco, 289
Tofu, 151
    Citrus-Braised Tofu with Vegetables, 151
    Three-Pepper Tofu Stir-Fry, 153

Tomatoes, 276
    Baked Fish with Tomatoes, Spinach, and Olives, 88
    blanching, 261
    Brazilian-Style Seafood Stew, 140
    Broccoli, Cherry Tomato, and Watercress Salad, 54
    Butternut Squash, Tomato, and Watercress Soup, 214
    Chicken with Tomatoes, Honey, and Cinnamon, 100
    Chunky Tomato-Vegetable Sauce, 109
    Classic Ratatouille, 46
    Corn and Quinoa Salad with Chicken, 170
    Easy Gazpacho, 220
    Greek-Style Potato and Green Bean Casserole with Lamb, 134
    Greek-Style Scallops, 97
    Green Beans with Tomatoes and Herbs, 34
    Layered Black Bean and Spinach Salad, 175
    New American Beef Stew, 137
    peeling, 261
    Penne with Eggplant, Tomatoes, and Tuna, 127
    Pineapple, Corn, and Mango Salsa, 114
    Pinto Bean Soup, 217
    Portobello Mushroom Jambalaya with Chicken, 128
    Potato, Pepper, and Cherry Tomato Frittata, 177
    Red Pepper, Tomato, and Chicken Pilaf, 160
    Roasted Red Pepper and Corn Soup, 206
    Salade Niçoise, 171
    seeding, 276
    Shrimp with Grapefruit and Black Bean Salsa, 53
    Southwestern Black Bean Salad with Barley, 58
    Southwestern Red Pepper Dip, 202
    Spaghetti Squash with Marinara Sauce, 38
    Spiced Braised Lamb with Apricots and Carrots, 105

Spicy Chili with Ground Beef over Spaghetti, 183
Spicy Tomato-Pepper Pot Roast, 106
Spinach Lasagna with Red Pepper Sauce, 135
Sweet Curried Tomato Chutney, 117
Sweet Potato Chili with Peanuts, 186
Tabbouleh-Filled Cherry Tomatoes, 192
Three-Bean Chili with Corn and Turkey, 184
Tilapia with Sweet Peppers, 93
Vegetable and Rice Soup, 209
Vegetable Chili, 185
White Bean and Sun-Dried Tomato Dip, 201
White Bean and Tomato Salad with Parsley, 60
Zucchini and Yellow Squash with Herbes de Provence, 42
Trans fats, 240, 243
Tricolored Peppers with Fresh Herbs, 37
Tufts University
    Health & Nutrition Letter, 291
    Nutrition Navigator, 292
Tuna, 127
    Grilled Ginger Tuna, 92
    Penne with Eggplant, Tomatoes, and Tuna, 127
    Salade Niçoise, 171
Turkey
    Butternut Squash and Barley Casserole with Turkey, 131
    cooking temperature for, 268
    Orange and Sesame Stir-Fry with Bow Tie Pasta, 152
    refrigerating, 270
    Sweet Potato and Apple Stew with Turkey and Cranberries, 138
    Tarragon Turkey Breast, 101
    Three-Bean Chili with Corn and Turkey, 184
Turmeric, 285
Turnips, 276
Two-Potato Salad with Spinach and Fresh Herb Dressing, 57

Umami, 117, 125
U.S. Department of Agriculture, 7, 8–9, 291

Veal, Lentil and Potato Stew with Rosemary and, 143

Vegetables. *See also individual vegetables*
Asian-Style Stir-Fried Vegetables, 17
blanching, 261
choosing, 14
Chunky Tomato-Vegetable Sauce, 109
Citrus-Braised Tofu with Vegetables, 151
Classic Ratatouille, 46
cooking techniques for, 14–15
cruciferous, 14, 21
Easy Gazpacho, 220
enhancing, 15–16, 107
Fourteen-Vegetable Stew with Pork, 145
freezing, 269
Grilled Fresh Vegetables with Dijon-Herb Sauce, 44
grilling, 263
health benefits of, 2–3, 14, 288, 289
introducing new, 15
listing of, 271–76
microwaving, 263
puréeing, 16
refrigerating, 270
roasting, 15, 264
root, 15
Southwestern Vegetable Frittata with Avocado and Salsa, 181
standard serving size for, 9
steaming, 265
Sweet and Sour Mixed Vegetables with Pork, 157
Vegetable and Rice Soup, 209
Vegetable Chili, 185

Vinaigrettes
Apple Vinaigrette with Fresh Herbs, 123

Hoisin Vinaigrette, 121
Orange-Honey Vinaigrette, 122

Vinegars
ratio of oil to, in dressings, 49
types of, 48

Walnuts
Date-Walnut Bars, 260
Walnut-Date Muffins with Rye, 232
Whole Wheat Stuffing with Cranberries and Walnuts, 84

Water chestnuts
Asian-Style Stir-Fried Vegetables, 17
Steamed Greens with Ginger and Water Chestnuts, 30
Sweet Potato and Pear Stir-Fry with Chicken and Chile Sauce, 155

Watercress, 54, 212, 276
Broccoli, Cherry Tomato, and Watercress Salad, 54
Butternut Squash, Tomato, and Watercress Soup, 214
Potato and Watercress Soup with Shrimp, 212

Watermelons, 278

WCRF. *See* World Cancer Research Fund

Web sites, 291, 292

Weight management, 2, 7–8, 287, 288, 289

White beans, 60, 281
Bean and Split Pea Chowder with Chicken, 218
Broccoli, White Bean, and Roasted Garlic Purée, 20
Vegetable Chili, 185
White Bean and Sun-Dried Tomato Dip, 201
White Bean and Tomato Salad with Parsley, 60

Whole Corn and Green Chile Muffins, 231
Whole Wheat Bread with Herbs, 226
Whole Wheat Bread with Onions, 227
Whole Wheat Fettuccine with Citrus Sauce, 82
Whole Wheat Pasta with Zucchini, Mushrooms, and Basil, 83
Whole Wheat Stuffing with Cranberries and Walnuts, 84
World Cancer Research Fund (WCRF), 287–89

Yams. *See* Sweet potatoes

Yogurt
Cucumber-Yogurt Sauce with Dill, 109
Greek-Style Potato and Green Bean Casserole with Lamb, 134
Yogurt Marinade with Ginger and Coriander, 120

Zeaxanthin, 289

Zingerone, 284

Zucchini, 275
Cinnamon and Raisin Couscous with Chicken, 139
Classic Ratatouille, 46
Grilled Fresh Vegetables with Dijon-Herb Sauce, 44
Kasha Pilaf with Squash and Chicken, 163
Whole Wheat Pasta with Zucchini, Mushrooms, and Basil, 83
Zucchini and Portobello Stir-Fry with Chicken, 156
Zucchini and Yellow Squash with Herbes de Provence, 42